Fourteenth Colony

ALSO BY MIKE BUNN

The Assault on Fort Blakeley:
"The Thunder and Lightning of Battle"

Early Alabama:
An Illustrated Guide to the Formative Years, 1798–1826

Alabama from Territory to Statehood:
An Alabama Heritage Bicentennial Collection [co-author]

Well Worth Stopping to See:
Antebellum Columbus, Georgia, Through the Eyes of Travelers

Civil War Eufaula

Battle for the Southern Frontier:
The Creek War and the War of 1812

Images of America:
The Lower Chattahoochee River

FOURTEENTH COLONY

The Forgotten Story of the Gulf South During America's Revolutionary Era

MIKE BUNN

NewSouth Books

Montgomery

NewSouth Books
105 S. Court Street
Montgomery, AL 36104

Library of Congress Cataloging-in-Publication Data

Names: Bunn, Mike, author.
Title: Fourteenth colony : the forgotten story of the Gulf South during America's
Revolutionary era / Mike Bunn.
Other titles: Forgotten story of the Gulf South during America's Revolutionary era
Description : NewSouth Books, [2020] | Includes bibliographical references and index.
Identifiers: LCCN 2020018838 (print) | LCCN 2020018839 (ebook) | ISBN
9781588384133 (Trade Cloth) | ISBN 9781588384140 (epub)
Subjects: LCSH: West Florida—History—18th century. | West
Florida—History, Military—18th century. | Florida—History—English
colony, 1763-1784. | Florida—History—Revolution, 1775-1783. | American
loyalists—Florida.
Classification: LCC F301 .B86 2020 (print) | LCC F301 (ebook) | DDC
975.9/02--dc23
LC record available at https://lccn.loc.gov/2020018838
LC ebook record available at https://lccn.loc.gov/2020018839

Design by Randall Williams
Printed in the United States of America by Sheridan

The Black Belt, defined by its dark, rich soil, stretches across central Alabama. It was the heart of the cotton belt. It was and is a place of great beauty, of extreme wealth and grinding poverty, of pain and joy. Here we take our stand, listening to the past, looking to the future.

To Zoey, my light and inspiration

Contents

Preface

The Revolutionary Era is one of the most storied and studied time periods in America's compelling national saga. Conjuring visions of righteous colonial protests in Boston Harbor, sober state-making in the chambers of Independence Hall in Philadelphia, and martial determination on the frigid meadows at Valley Forge, the 1760s and 1770s are venerated by Americans for having witnessed the formation of the United States from the cooperative efforts of thirteen former British colonies. It is an era studded with iconic moments and rich with legendary figures that are a part of our shared national canon. It is sadly ironic that this grand pageant is a heritage from which Gulf Coast residents have long felt detached owing in large part to geography, for an important but little known chapter in America's colonial and Revolutionary drama played out along their sunny shores.

British West Florida, stretching from the mighty Mississippi to the shallow bends of the Apalachicola and incorporating large portions of what are now the states of Louisiana, Mississippi, Alabama, and Florida, is the forgotten fourteenth colony in America's founding era. The colony and its sister province, East Florida, were erected by the British at the conclusion of the Seven Years' War in 1763 on the ruins of the vast but rather vaguely defined territory formerly claimed by French and Spanish colonials. Headquartered in Pensacola originally, with scarcely a European settlement west of Mobile Bay, the province grew exceedingly slowly and only began to come of age as the Revolutionary War flared up along the Atlantic seaboard. Eventually the colony featured clusters of European settlements at such places as Pensacola, Campbelltown, Mobile, Baton Rouge, Manchac, and Natchez, and it assumed a position as a dynamic and promising part of Britain's

North American holdings. But despite the grand visions of its leaders and the best efforts of its residents, the colony struggled economically and its representative government never quite became the force in provincial life that similar institutions in the east coast colonies did. In fact, West Florida is so obscure to us today at least in part owing to its relatively small population and its pressing daily concerns; the latter occupied residents and precluded their becoming a vital part of intercolonial discussions during a period of political unrest. As it remained officially loyal to the crown throughout the Revolution, West Florida is usually regarded as an afterthought where little of consequence occurred.

YET THE REVOLUTION DID find the colony, and the story of the ways it did so colorfully and substantively shapes the history of the region. First came politely declined invitations by the Continental Congress to join its sister provinces to the east in working towards the establishment of a new, independent American nation. Next came a wave of immigration after being declared a safe asylum for besieged loyalists elsewhere. In 1778 came a daring raid by a ragtag American force along the Mississippi which exposed the province's inadequate defenses and caused a great deal of unrest even if never seriously threatening its takeover by a Continental army. Finally came an audacious, prolonged, offensive spearheaded by the ambitious and capable governor of neighboring Spanish Louisiana, Bernardo de Galvez, which would ultimately bring about the end of West Florida's days as a part of the British Empire. Spain never formally allied itself with the nascent United States in its war for independence, but it recognized an opportunity to take advantage of a distracted colonial rival. Spain's stunning campaign to wrest control of West Florida from the British featured intense and spirited fighting from the fall of 1779 to the spring of 1781. This war within a war helped divert vital resources from other Revolutionary War campaigns by the British and culminated in the martial conquest of the colony by the Spaniards.

But despite all this, somewhat few people know the colony existed at all. A forgotten Gulf Coast entity which graced regional maps for less than two decades, the province goes virtually unmentioned in most histories of the

American Revolutionary Era and is all but unknown to the great majority of those living within its former borders today. The situation is understandable to some degree, as precious few historical sites commemorate the people, places, and events of the region's years as part of the British Empire, and almost no extant structures date to its mid-eighteenth century heyday. Its name alone can confuse some, to boot, as "West Florida" naturally connotes to the modern ear a certain geographical specificity that takes some explaining to communicate the true physical footprint of the colony. Save for the findings of some archaeological investigations and a few scattered historic markers (and one magnificent memorial statue in Pensacola), the British period in Gulf Coast history can only be imagined through the pages of the rather limited historiography on the subject. While that historical literature is solid and features the work of some eminent colonial historians, candidly it is not exactly brimming with best-sellers likely to be familiar to the casual historian. But the fact that the seminal events in America's founding drama—the political unrest and legendary war between the immortal thirteen rebellious colonies and Great Britain which witnessed the birth of the United States as an independent nation—occurred far away from the Gulf has probably been most responsible for rendering West Florida's story so overlooked, understudied, and poorly understood. Scores of textbooks and narrative histories chronicling the era do not so much as mention British West Florida, much less discuss its place in the Empire. It is not uncommon to find within these books maps depicting Britain's North American colonies during the Revolution as existing only along the eastern seaboard, with the amorphous southwestern frontier behind them labeled as simply "Indian land" or "Spanish territory." In short, Americans, both scholars and lay historians, often so associate our nation's founding era with the thirteen rebellious colonies that we have collectively forgotten that there even was an America farther west than the Atlantic coast in 1776.

WHAT FOLLOWS IS MY attempt to put West Florida back on the map of our historical consciousness. I tell the story of British West Florida, tracing the province from its humble beginnings and through the ravaging battles on land and water which led to its eventual transfer into Spanish hands.

The book is a narrative overview of this dramatic interlude in Gulf South history, designed to be an introduction to the broad arc of the life of the colony from the viewpoint of those who worked so diligently to establish it. It is a monograph and no comparative study by any stretch of the term. Further, while it contains information on how West Floridians lived and I hope helps readers understand their dreams and aspirations for the colony they labored to develop, it makes no attempt to be a definitive source on the rich native cultural traditions that thrived within its borders. Native societies inherently figure into the narrative, but I leave to other writers the relatively better-trod historical ground of indigenous views and reactions to West Florida's development.

I must point out that the title of this book employs a phrase rather well used in literature on the time period of America's founding. There are technically multiple competitors for the title of Britain's fourteenth American colony, ranging from neighboring East Florida to several concurrent holdings in Canada. It is a label I, as well as a few other authors of shorter works of fiction and nonfiction, similarly use in one fashion or another, not to communicate a literal sequential order of establishment, but rather as a pointed address of a general perception that the colony is somehow extraneous in our memory of America's founding epoch. I hope this book will help change that perception and will help the Gulf Coast reclaim its Revolutionary Era heritage, for West Florida's story is well worth telling and remembering.

ACKNOWLEDGMENTS

Writing a book of history is always something of a team effort. While the author may spend hundreds of hours alone sorting through research, drafting text, and carefully editing, such undertakings are only made possible by the work of numerous other individuals who assist in varying ways in finding crucial information, reviewing and polishing the manuscript, and making it available to the public. As is always the case, many more people should be thanked for their assistance and encouragement on this particular project than space, and my forgetfulness, will allow me to name.

Especially helpful in this undertaking were the staffs at Daphne Public Library, none more so than Reference and Adult Services Librarian Anne

Morris, who assisted me with a litany of requests for crucial interlibrary loans. The staffs at several other regional libraries were likewise accommodating, including the University Archives and West Florida History Center at the Pace Library, University of West Florida; the Marx Library, University of South Alabama; Draughon Library, Auburn University; Mobile Public Library; Alabama Department of Archives and History; Mississippi Department of Archives and History; and Historic New Orleans Collection. I appreciate the work of Felix Garcia Rodriguez at the Institute of Military History and Culture in Spain for helping me obtain some of the rare depictions of the fighting at Mobile and Pensacola featured in the book. I am in debt to the numerous individuals who read, edited, and critiqued all or parts of the manuscript at various stages of its production and helped me improve it along the way. I am honored that NewSouth Books has arranged for this book's publication, and I am grateful to Suzanne La Rosa in particular for taking such an interest in the project when it was little more than a concept. The whole team at NewSouth has been a pleasure to work with.

Finally, I owe a significant debt of gratitude to all those scholars of this topic who have come before me and whose work forms the book's foundation. The historiography of British West Florida may be relatively limited compared with some other topics in Gulf Coast history, but it is blessed with the excellent work of several eminent and pioneering historians. It is impossible to study this topic without some knowledge of the writings of Cecil Johnson, J. Barton Starr, Robert R. Rea, and Robin Fabel, among others. To them, some still living but many having passed on, my sincerest thanks and profound respect.

Fourteenth Colony

The British Takeover of the Gulf Coast

'The Scorching Lands of Florida'

British West Florida traces its origins to conquest in wars fought far from its borders. While the Seven Years' War, known in North America as the French and Indian War, raged from 1754–1763 across five continents and involved every major European power, it barely touched the Gulf Coast. The contest between French and British colonial forces and their Indian allies nevertheless profoundly shaped the region. The 1763 Treaty of Paris ending the war authorized one of the largest land transfers in history. By its terms the victorious British acquired, among other spoils, all colonial holdings in North America from the defeated French and Florida from the Spanish.[1]

The French had claimed the entirety of the Mississippi Valley since La Salle's expedition to find the venerable river's mouth in 1682 and began serious colonization efforts in the region in 1699. Using the claim to the Mississippi as a pretext for expanding their influence in the area but at first finding no suitable location for a colonial settlement along the swampy lower reaches of the river, they established their first Gulf Coast outpost at what is now Biloxi, Mississippi, after realizing the Spanish had beat them to Pensacola Bay. Fort Maurepas, as it was known, served as the first capital of the French colony of Louisiana, the enormous swath of North America which, on paper at least, stretched from the Gulf of Mexico to the upper Mississippi Valley. Dissatisfied with the location, the French colonists in 1702 founded an outpost further east at Mobile—first sited on a riverside bluff more than twenty miles north of its namesake bay before moving to its current location in 1711. For more than six decades the French worked diligently to develop the colony. Mobile had served as its capital for a brief time before the founding of New Orleans, the new capital. Throughout, Mobile remained one of the French colony's most vital population, economic, political, and military centers.[2]

But Louisiana never thrived as the French had hoped, and besides a few scattered villages—more often than not built around military outposts and a smattering of farms in the adjacent hinterlands—French presence in the region, if not influence, proved relatively slight. Still, the crafty French colonials had forged strong relationships with native groups such as the Choctaws, Mobilians, and Tomes. By virtue of these friendships, the French had managed to keep South Carolina and Georgia's more numerous and better-equipped British traders from gaining a foothold in the area. The sudden transfer of the land to the British without a shot being fired therefore shocked the local French as much as it did their Indian allies. By the proverbial stroke of a pen, decades of work by the French along the Gulf Coast unraveled and the size of the British empire in North America increased substantially.[3]

In technical terms, the Treaty of Paris specified that all French claims in North America except the Isle of Orleans (New Orleans) and certain islands in the St. Lawrence River and the Caribbean be ceded to Great Britain. But in the earlier secret Treaty of Fontainebleau, signed between the French and their Spanish allies once the scale of France's defeat in the war had become clear, the French ceded all their territory west of the Mississippi. The portions of the northern Gulf Coast not claimed by the French also came into British hands when ceded by the Spanish in exchange for the return of Cuba, which the British had captured during the war.[4]

To the east of what had been Louisiana's eastern border lay the Spanish territory affected by the Treaty of Paris. Stretching eastward from an ill-defined border with the French province—generally agreed to be at or near the Perdido River, and encompassing the small settlement at Pensacola—was Spanish Florida, a province which Spain had claimed for the better part of two and a half centuries by the time of the Seven Years' War. While the colony's primary settlements were located on the east coast of the rather sparsely inhabited peninsula, centered around St. Augustine and environs,

Pensacola had been a strategic site for Spanish colonial
interests since the late 1600s.
Precious little development
beyond the rudiments of a
military outpost had taken
place in the vicinity of the
town during the interven-
ing six decades, though, and
despite the ongoing work of
the Christian missionaries at
the scattered establishments
in the region, the area's Native Americans exhibited
no strong attachment to the
Spaniards. The transfer of
authority there promised to
be even less troublesome than
in the French lands.[5]

King George III (Library of Congress)

BRITISH AUTHORITIES MOVED QUICKLY to organize their newly won
North American territory. In the extreme northeastern reaches of the continent, they assumed administration of the former French province of Quebec,
while in its southernmost stretches they erected the brand new colonies of
West and East Florida from the wide expanse of Gulf Coast lands formerly
claimed by the Spanish and French. The British Board of Trade had at once
recognized that the area was too large for practical administration as a single
colony and set the Apalachicola River as the dividing line between the two
provinces. Stretching to the Atlantic and down the Florida peninsula to the
Keys lay East Florida; its capital would be at the relatively established city
of St. Augustine. To the west of the Apalachicola, stretching to the Mississippi, lay the colony of West Florida. Pensacola would serve as its capital.[6]

British officials viewed the creation of colonies in this subtropical region
as strategically advantageous even if not especially lucrative, as they facilitated

control of a number of major interior river systems and potentially important Gulf and Atlantic ports. They also provided an important new outlet for expansion. In a royal proclamation issued October 7, 1763, King George III officially prohibited settlement of much of the interior of North America which lay west of the Appalachians, south of the colony of Quebec, and north of the 31st parallel. He planned to reassert the British authority in a region where the contentious authority of multiple colonial governments had emerged and to keep the peace with several powerful native groups as well as limit potentiality for any clash with Spain in North America. In short, the British government hoped the move would forestall another war similar to the one it had just fought and won at high cost. The king hoped that future orderly acquisition of territory in this Indian reserve might take place as needed, its negotiation handled exclusively by the crown. These measures would sow the seeds of discontent in the established seaboard colonies by calling into question as never before their relationship with the mother country and set an unintended precedent of appearing to assert British respect of Native American sovereignty over the wishes of colonists. But all that lay in the future as officials organized a portion of their newly won territory into functioning parts of the British Empire, a process they were confident of accomplishing owing to more than a century and a half of North American colonial administration.[7]

West Florida, then the only British colony in North America technically west of the Appalachians, lay on the periphery of the Empire. The colony's southern border followed the seacoast from the mouth of the Apalachicola westward to Lake Borgne, where it met the border of Spanish Louisiana. It continued west through the Rigolets into Lake Pontchartrain, thence along Pass Manchac into Lake Maurepas, and finally along the Iberville River to its junction with the Mississippi. By the proclamation creating the colony, its northern border had been set at the 31st parallel, presumably to demonstrate a limit to intrusion into the continental interior which might quiet fears of local Indians as much as any strategic plan of allowing enough room for the province's settlements to expand from the coast.[8]

A year after the colony's founding, officials moved its border northward for several reasons. While the French, who had claimed the area prior to

A General Map of the Southern British Colonies, in America,
published by Sayer and Bennett, 1776 (David Rumsey Map Collection)

Great Britain's possession, had not attempted to develop cities very far
north of the sandy coastal beaches, they did establish outposts such as Fort
Toulouse and Fort Tombecbe well north of the 31st parallel, in what is now
central Alabama. Noticing this and that scattered settlements on the Mississippi and within the Mobile-Tensaw Delta already existed north of that
arbitrary line, West Florida's first governor, George Johnstone, recommended
moving the border of the colony to the 34th parallel, or roughly between
where Birmingham and Huntsville lie today. In the spring of 1764, however,
colonial authorities set West Florida's northern boundary along a line drawn
east of the confluence of the Mississippi and Yazoo rivers, or the parallel at
32 degrees, 28 minutes. That location carried with it the benefits of having a
natural landmark, incorporating the strategically defensible site of a former
French fort (Fort St. Pierre, a forerunner of modern Vicksburg, Mississippi),
and being far enough north to include virtually all of the scattered riverside

Map of West Florida by Bernard Romans (Library of Congress)

European-owned farmsteads and plantations in the region. As a result, the Chattahoochee River, which joins with the Flint near the modern Florida border to form the Apalachicola, became the eastern border of a colony 375 miles wide and roughly 150 miles north to south. Through generous land-granting policies, the British hoped to encourage relocations to this far-flung new province which seemed to enjoy few natural advantages and lay on the fringes of civilization, as the continent's North American colonists knew it at the time.[9]

Authorities sent Colonel Augustine Prévost, commander of the 60th Regiment, to Pensacola to administer the colony with a few hundred troops. Prévost was to take over the fort there and the surrounding territory claimed by the Spanish. He arrived in early August of 1763, the first British official in West Florida. A thirty-year-old Swiss-born soldier fresh off of the capture of Martinique and Havana in the campaigns of the Seven Years'

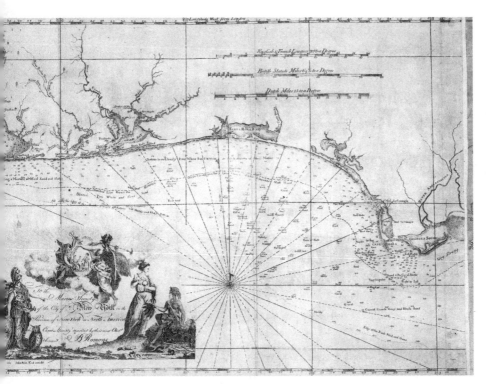

War, Prévost was to serve as interim military governor of the new British colony until the appointed governor arrived. He accepted the surrender of Pensacola from Spanish Governor Don Diego Ortiz Parrilla shortly after entering the town, and he held orders to allow the Spaniards time to settle their affairs and leave or swear allegiance to Great Britain and remain. The Spanish crown had already made provisions for the relocation of the town's citizens, though, and in September of 1763 eight ships carrying more than 600 troops, civilians, and Christian Indians—virtually the population of Pensacola—left for Vera Cruz in New Spain. Prévost immediately placed a small fortification on the end of Santa Rosa Island, guarding entrance to Pensacola Bay, and went about his assigned task in what initially amounted to more of an armed military camp than a town.[10]

A host of officers assisted Prévost in transforming the place into the best-defended British position along the Gulf Coast. Colonel Henry Bouquet had been appointed as brigadier general for the district, but he died days after arriving at Pensacola. He was succeeded by Colonel William Tayler, who served until March of 1767, when Frederick Haldimand, one of the most experienced military officials to serve in West Florida and also one of its most candid critics, arrived on the scene. Haldimand began his career as a Swiss mercenary and rose in rank as part of the British army after joining the force in 1755 and becoming among the most respected military commanders in North America. During the years he was stationed in Pensacola, Haldimand effectively improved the defenses of the town and bay, making it the most heavily fortified position in the colony. But Haldimand had at first professed shock at seeing how much work lay in store for him to make the almost abandoned and poorly supplied town both defensible and habitable. Its slapdash architecture exuded nothing so much as impermanence. He wrote in near despair of his surprise to see "the misery people lived in, being pent with high rotten palisados built for Spanish convicts; deprived of air and particularly of the sea breeze, the only comfort nature seems to intend for this place." Even the food was wretched, as troops survived on an unappetizing diet of tepid water, old bread, and insect-ridden salted meat. The fort allegedly defending the little waterfront clearing in which Pensacola lay consisted of an ill-planned and crumbling stockade so wanting that rather than attempt to improve it, engineers chose a complete rebuild. The circumstances were so bleak that Governor Johnstone had reported in his first months in office, "It is difficult to conceive any thing under that name (fortification) being more despicable." He went on to charge that the fort was little more than "a parcel of rotten stockades." The fortification, much like the city, would be built almost from scratch by the British during their occupation.[11]

AN ENTIRELY DIFFERENT SITUATION prevailed in Mobile. Moved in 1711 to its current location, the town had languished for a half century as more of a frontier military and diplomatic post for treating with local tribes than as a metropolitan community. Still, along two or three roughly north-south streets stretching parallel to the river, and a similar number running a mere three or so blocks away, were clustered a dozen or so businesses and an assortment of low-slung, sometimes haphazardly constructed, homes. At its transfer to British control the town claimed a population of about

350 people, a large portion of them slaves. Several dozen French families lived in the surrounding countryside on farms of varying sizes, largely clustered on the shores of the bay and area waterways stretching from Mon Louis Island, where the mainland met what is now termed the Mississippi Sound, up into the Mobile-Tensaw Delta. Unlike Pensacola's, most of Mobile's residents would stay through the British takeover.[12]

Major Robert Farmar (Alabama Department of Archives and History)

The British sent forty-six-year-old Robert Farmar to accept the transfer of Mobile into their hands. Farmar came to the gulf post with an unusual wealth of military experience and a greater familiarity with life in colonial America than many of his officer peers. He had grown up in the colony of New Jersey, where his father had helped found New Brunswick. The younger Farmar joined the American militia in the colorfully named War of Jenkins' Ear (1739–1748) fought between Great Britain and Spain over colonial trading rights. In such far-flung locales as Jamaica, Colombia, and Panama, Farmar got his first taste of military action. He also fought in the regular British army in Europe during the War of Austrian Succession, an international contest over the legitimacy of the holder of the Austrian throne into which the British were drawn by diplomatic alliances. Farmar remained in Europe after that war, serving at various peacetime posts in the British army until participating in some of the closing campaigns of the Seven Years' War. In the summer of 1763, while en route home from action in Cuba, his fleet was overtaken by a sloop carrying orders for the 34th regiment, which he commanded, along with the 22nd regiment, to proceed to the Gulf Coast and help organize British administration of the new colony of West Florida. Farmar would command at Mobile until the arrival of the colony's appointed Governor George Johnstone a year later.[13]

Farmar landed in Pensacola in September of 1763, where Colonel Prévost had taken charge of the town. He then moved on to Mobile, arriving on Thursday, October 20, where he soon encountered numerous unexpected and maddening delays in carrying out his charge. While Mobile is located along its relatively deep namesake river, approaching the city through the shallow upper reaches of Mobile Bay prior to the dredging of a regular shipping channel could be challenging for even modest-sized ocean-going ships of the day; vessels of deep draft required complex and lengthy circumnavigation of nearby waterways. The captain of Farmar's vessel was inexperienced in the waters around Mobile. The ship ignominiously stranded on a sand bar in the bay within sight of the city. The new commandant therefore had to be rowed from his ship to the wharf off Fort Conde. Instead of rolling out the red carpet, local French officials promptly asked Farmar to delay the unloading of his men and supplies from his ships and the ensuing formal changing of command in the city until they finished meeting with a large group of Indians which had begun arriving in the city for a previously scheduled meeting. As a final straw, Farmar found that "no lodgings or billets were assign'd" by the French, leaving him and his men little option than to stay aboard their cramped, stuffy ships.[14]

The delay threatened to disrupt an orderly transfer of power before it even got started. Farmar, whose men had been aboard ship for three months, demanded to land at once. He at length persuaded local French commander Pierre-Annibal de Ville to evacuate Fort Conde, and Farmar's men soon raised a British flag—taken from a mast of one of the troop transports—over the fort. Meanwhile the laborious landing of all the British guns, stores, and troops began; everything had to be removed from ships anchored several miles down the bay and transported to the site by smaller boats. Farmar soon discovered that the outgoing French governor, Louis Billouart, Chevalier de Kerlérec, had issued detailed instructions for the fort's transfer before handing over control of Louisiana to new leader Jean-Jacques Blaise d'Abbadie; the latter was to see through the actual transfer. Farmar and Abbadie's relationship would not always be smooth, but the two began converting a frontier region infused with French ways and customs into a part of the British Empire.[15]

At the heart of Mobile stood the military centerpiece in the region, the venerable Fort Condé, a massive brick fortification some ninety yards square. The post dominated the town and served as a visible reminder of its original purpose to help the French establish a colonial foothold on the volatile Gulf frontier. The fort was decades old and had undergone numerous repairs and alterations. By the time Farmar first laid eyes on what he would rechristen as Fort Charlotte, in honor of the queen of England, it was well past its prime and needed significant repair if not a complete rebuild to be a legitimate defensive post. Farmar described its condition in correspondence to be "ruinous," and found to his astonishment some of the cannons removed and those left in place "with their trunnions knock'd off, and render'd entirely useless" and barracks "tumbling down . . . the stockades all old and rotten." The fort's crumbling brick, weed-covered ramparts, rotten palisades, dilapidated barracks, and insufficient interior facilities were anything but inviting to the freshly arrived troops and far from promising for its planned role as an entrepôt for the new colony. Within weeks, British troops were set to work bringing Fort Charlotte up to standards.[16]

THE REGION'S OTHER EXISTING military posts, also in various states of disrepair, likewise demanded attention. British officials attempted to garrison most of them with at least a token force, but each effort proved a separate project that revealed both the frontier nature of the new colony and the shortage of resources which hamstrung its military administration. What to do with Fort Tombecbe, an irregularly shaped quadrilateral perched on a prominent bluff overlooking the Tombigbee River some 200 river miles north of Mobile, became a pressing concern. The French had established the post in the 1730s to serve as a base of supply in their campaigns against the Chickasaw. It had since become more valuable diplomatically than militarily, serving as a strategic meeting center in French negotiations with the powerful Choctaws. As the tribe was the most populous in the immediate area now coming under British control and the fort lay deep in their territory, it seemed logical to continue to garrison it for a similar purpose.

In November of 1763, Farmar sent a detachment of about thirty men of the 34th Infantry Regiment to take control of the fortification, which they rechristened Fort York. But Fort York proved far from a powerful frontier bastion and, given its condition and location, it would take much work—and precious financial resources—to transform it into one. The British high command therefore questioned its value to the new colony from the beginning. Farmar took the hint and soon abandoned the effort for more pressing projects elsewhere, leaving a lone trader named Jeremiah Terry to use it as a base of operations. Elias Legardere, named Commissary to the Choctaws, moved to the site two years later.[17]

In the spring of 1766, however, as skirmishing flared among factions of the Choctaws and Creeks and a consuming intertribal conflict threatened to engulf West Florida's northern frontier, British officials reconsidered the advantages of Fort York. In May about twenty men from the 21st Regiment, under the command of Lieutenant John Ritchy, were sent to garrison the outpost. A troubled journey upriver from Mobile delayed their arrival until fall, after which the men languished amid outbreaks of sickness and shortages of supplies. Dissension riddled the thinning ranks, and Lieutenant Ritchy and Commissary Legardere found themselves at odds over everything from consequential issues such as the extent of each's authority to trivial ones such as the appropriate housing for Legardere's dogs. The forlorn command soldiered on for another year despite ominous threats from the disgruntled Choctaw and miserable conditions, until officials decided to cut their losses and ordered the final withdrawal of the post's garrison. Fort York would not be reoccupied during British control of West Florida.[18]

Only months prior to the Fort York evacuation had a British detachment at last occupied Natchez, situated on a towering bluff overlooking the Mississippi River. Natchez was a strategic location for any power attempting to control the region and had long been important in French efforts to maintain their influence. But at the time of the British takeover Natchez stood as a tiny village with a checkered history and no fortification worthy of the name. Part of this had to do with setbacks suffered by the French due to their thinly stretched resources. But the situation also had connection to a legendary 1720s uprising that had become a cautionary tale in attempts at colonial hegemony in the Gulf South. In a devastating surprise attack, local Indians had massacred the garrison of the first French post there, Fort Rosalie. The first British detachment of troops sent there, from the 21st Regiment Scots Fusiliers, found the mouldering remains of French military endeavors to be more of a historical landmark than a functioning military post. In 1766 the troops built a new fort on the bluff where Rosalie had stood. The new fortification came to be known as Fort Panmure, though in official documents it was usually referred to simply as "Fort Natchez." Initially an isolated backwater, the post would become a vital part of British administration in the region in the next decade as the Mississippi Valley came to assume a prominent role in the development of West Florida.[19]

The British chose not to occupy another former French outpost deep in the backcountry although it had been even more pivotal in the French relations with regional tribes. Fort Toulouse, first built in 1717 at the confluence of the Coosa and Tallapoosa rivers in what is now central Alabama, served the French for decades as a vital focal point of diplomacy with the Creeks and a bulwark in defending Louisiana's frontier from British encroachment. Uncertain of its usefulness now that the British claimed dominion over much of the territory once served by the fort, authorities left it in the hands of trader James Germany, who was given permission to live there if he would report on Creek activities. The British would not garrison the post during their administration of the region.[20]

WHILE MANNING THOSE POSTS that authorities did garrison was usually a straightforward if grueling process, the experience of a contingent of the 22nd Regiment of Foot demonstrated the volatility of the region. The 22nd was sent to occupy Fort Chartres, which pro-French tribes had to that point prevented British troops from occupying. Major Arthur Loftus commanded the expedition. He led his troops out of Mobile in January of 1764 and, after a brief stop in New Orleans, proceeded up the Mississippi. Near a rocky bluff known to the French as Roche a Davion (now Fort Adams, Mississippi, but long known as Loftus Heights), a party of as many as two hundred Choctaw, Tunica, Avoyelles, and other warriors, lying in wait in the cover of thick brush, ambushed his flotilla of canoes with a hail of gunfire. A few of the British troops were killed instantly and many more were wounded before the oarsmen could get out of range of their attackers. Uncertain of who or what size force he faced, Loftus ordered his boats back downriver, eventually retreating back to Mobile. Shaken by the surprise attack, Loftus proved reluctant to return to the area even after being ordered to do so. Eventually Major Farmar relieved him of duty and himself piloted troops to their post, with the aid of some Chickasaws, this time without incident. The affair demonstrated just how quickly events could spiral into violence in the turbulent region, and how much the British had to learn about its peoples and their views of European colonial authority. It also convinced British authorities, had they any doubt remaining, of the pressing need to secure their new colony's western boundary.[21]

An age-old problem vexed colonial officials in their attempts to remedy the problems of defending the borders of their expansive new colony: too much to do and not enough resources with which to do it. Troops would be in relative short supply throughout British administration of West Florida, and money was chronically scarce. True, in 1763 the British army based four of its twenty American regiments in West and East Florida, but these men were a fraction of those required to accomplish all of the goals laid out for them. Plus, as will be seen below, sheer numbers tell only a portion of the story, for the condition—both physically and as it regarded morale—of the troops in West Florida proved to be a constant and debilitating problem. "A great many of our effectives are very old and infirm and ought to be discharged," complained Robert Farmar in a letter to Commander-in-Chief General Thomas Gage. Several of the others, he lamented, "are not worth detaining . . . take them altogether we have scarce a compleat company who can be looked upon as soldiers fit for duty."[22]

It all made some British officials question the value of the colony from the beginning. General Gage, charged with overseeing the disposition of crown troops throughout colonial North America, thought it an overreach to attempt to secure West Florida's remote frontier borders in a way which violated a basic tenet of sound military strategy as he viewed it—never try to take more territory than you can actually hold. He was not alone in viewing the new Gulf Coast colony with a jaded eye as it regarded its military preparedness. In addition, few observers seemed excited about its economic potential, and some openly questioned the wisdom of even attempting its administration. The region was not ideally situated for most agriculture as then practiced, and the few small, struggling former French and Spanish towns in the area were anything but prosperous. No less a figure than John Dickinson, author of the famed *Letters from a Farmer in Pennsylvania*, sarcastically observed at West Florida's establishment that "the British colonies are to be drained of the rewards of their labour to cherish the scorching lands of Florida . . . which will never return to us one farthing that we send them." General Frederick Haldimand was just as pessimistic after observing the situation firsthand. "What advantages either ourselves or the Spaniards can reap from West Florida or Louisiana is more than I can foresee."[23]

WITH THIS CYNICAL ASSESSMENT heavy in the air, officers sent to oversee the creation of the new Gulf Coast colony set about their daunting tasks. Among the first duties of civilian administration of the new colony of West Florida was how or whether to incorporate existing non-native populations into the British Empire. The great bulk of these individuals resided in and around Mobile, as Pensacola had essentially been abandoned by the Spanish. Mobile, as thoroughly a French town as could then be found anywhere south of Montreal, presented a unique situation. With France having been eliminated from the continent as a colonial power and few Mobile residents intrigued with the idea of moving to a Spanish-held New Orleans despite an open invitation from authorities there, most of its inhabitants had few clear options. How many would be allowed to stay, and under what conditions, became an issue under the purview of military commandant Robert Farmar. While still en route to Mobile in the late summer of 1763, Farmar had prepared a proclamation explaining how the change of government would affect the local populace. He had the missive drawn up in French and distributed to the residents of the city once he stepped ashore. The document explained the change of dominion of the territory, set out that the English language and British law would henceforth be official within the colony, and gave the local population a timetable for choosing whether to remain. Residents were offered three months to decide whether to take an oath of

PAR MONSIEUR
ROBERT FARMAR,

Majeur du 34me Regiment, & Commandant des
Troupes de sa MAJESTE' BRITANIQUE, dans la
Louisiane, &c. &c. &c.

Comme, par le Traité definitif de Paix signé le 10.me de Fevrier,
& Ratifié le 10.me de Mars 1763. Cette Partie de la Louisiane située à main gauche, ou du Côté Oriental de la Riviere
de Mississipi, depuis sa Source jusqu'à la Riviere d'Iberville,
& à travers des Lacs de Maurepas & de Pontchartain, jusqu'à
la Mer, est cedée en pleine possession à sa MAJESTE' BRITANIQUE.

P AR ces presentes il est ordonné, & requis de touttes Personnes dans le Maniment de
l'administration du droit Civil, de cesser touttes procedures en procès commencées, & de-
fendu de poursuivre dorèsnavant en procès, ou playdoiries, dans la forme & pratique des
Loix de France, les habitants presents etant devenus sujets aux Loix d'Angleterre, par
lesquelles ils seront paisiblement protegés dans leurs droits & propretés, & à fin que le Cours de
la Justice ne puisse souffrir aucun delay ou retardement, touttes causes, procès, & sujets de plainte
seront presentés, par ecrit au Commandant à Moibille, & touttes disputes triviales à l'Officier
Commandant des Postes circonvoisins aux parties offensées.

Les Habitants par ces presentes peuvent être assurés d'être protegés dans leurs droits, & propretés, & de n'être point, sans sujet, en aucune façon molestés ou incommodés par les Troupes,
& on s'attend que, de leur part, ils en agiront de même envers les Troupes, leur fournissant les
choses dont ils auront besoin, & que le païs produit, pour lesquelles on leur päyera en Argent
comptant.

Pour prevenir, autant qu'il sera possible, touttes fraudes, & disputes, par rapport aux achats, ou
ventes de terres, & propretés reelles, tous les biens en terres seront registrés dans l'espace d'un
An après la publication de ces presentes, & il ne sera point permis de disposer d'aucunes terres, ou
autres biens reels, jusqu'à ce que les titres & teneurs des dits biens puissent être verifiés par leur
enregistrements, & approuvés par l'Officier Commandant.

Ceux d'entre les habitants François qui seront choix de rester dans leurs diverses habitations,
& de vivre sous les Loix d'Angleterre, & sous le gouvernement de sa MAJESTE' BRITANIQUE, de-
veront, aussitôt qu'il sera possible, se rendre à Moibille, pour y prêter serment de fidelité. Ceux
qui ne voudront point s'y conformer dans l'espace de trois mois après la date de ces presentes,
seront depossedés, & obligés de quitter cette partie du pais cedée à la Nation Angloise. Ceux qui
s'y conformeront seront protegés dans leur propretés, & droits religieux, comme il est stipulé par
le traité de paix, iceux se comportant paisiblement, sans tramer aucun projet au prejudice des autres
sujets de sa MAJESTE' BRITANIQUE, ou de son gouvernement : Mais touttes les fois qu'on decou-
vrira qu'ils auront tâché de donner aux Indiens de mauvais prejugés desavantageux aux Anglois,
ou agiront en aucune façon, ou prejudice, ou faisant des attentats pour renverser le gouvernement
Anglois, on procedera contre eux comme revoltés.

Ceux d'entre les habitants qui seront portés d'inclination à quitter leurs presentes habitations,
& se retirer de cette partie du pais, auront un sûr & sauf transport de leurs effets, comme limité
dans le traité de paix.

Ces presentes seront lües dans l'Eglise de chaque paroisse par le Curé ; ou quiconque officiera
pour lui, quatre Dimanches successifs, & seront affichées aux portes des Eglises, & dans touttes les
places publiques, àfinque personne n'en pretende ignorance.

DONNEÉS à Moibille le present siege du Gouvernement Anglois dans la Louisiane.
ce   jour de   1763.

*Proclamation announcing British rule in Mobile prepared by Major
Robert Farmar (University Archives and West Florida History
Center, Pace Library, University of West Florida)*

allegiance to Great Britain; those choosing to do so could continue to reside in West Florida, those preferring not to would have to leave its boundaries but would be given eighteen months to sell their lands and other property that could not be removed.[24]

Most proved more eager to stay in the region than to take the required oath of loyalty to the British king, as many were concerned about freedom of religion. As with other British colonies in North America, the Anglican Church would be recognized as the official church of the state even though no such house of worship existed in Mobile at the time of the establishment of West Florida. But in a practical expediency in a land where the majority of the non-native population described itself as Catholic even if most did not regularly attend a church, the British policy of genuine religious toleration smoothed the way for the mostly French residents to become British citizens. Oath-taking proceeded slowly in the first few months, but by the spring of 1764, a substantial portion of locals had pledged their allegiance to King George III. Upon petition to the governor and council a year later, Mobile's French Catholics were even granted permission to build a new chapel, while plans for an Anglican church languished. A Capuchin priest, Ferdinand, who had been working in Mobile at the time of the establishment of West Florida, continued to serve the community's Catholic population for nearly another decade. Testing the limits of this ecclesiastical leniency, in 1772 emboldened Catholics in Mobile petitioned the colonial government (unsuccessfully) to provide an appropriation for the support of Catholic clergy. Other aspects of the legal integration of the local population into the new British colony were equally as vexing as those centering on religion. Regulations required residents to submit the titles to their land for registry and verification, for example, but so few could provide such proof of ownership that authorities eventually permitted mere demonstration of residence and cultivation of land as de facto title. Even the relatively few claims legally recorded by French officials were a source of confusion in their descriptions and authority and took years to sort out.[25]

HOW TO BEST CURRY the favor of the region's non-European inhabitants proved far more complicated, and in some measures urgent, than convincing colonists to swear allegiance to the British crown. For starters, Native Americans outnumbered the small, widely scattered, colonial population enclaves several times over. The Chickasaw, Choctaw, and Creek population who claimed the backcountry stood around 30,000 people at the time of West Florida's founding, whereas the entirety of the colony's citizenry numbered less than 2,000 individuals. A graphic reminder of this disparity occurred concurrent with Robert Farmar's assumption of command at Mobile in October of 1763, when large groups of Choctaws and Creeks began trickling in for a previously scheduled meeting with French officials. Within weeks some 3,000 Native Americans were encamped all around the town and daily making appearances along its streets.[26]

To the dismay of the newly arrived and scarcely supplied British, the natives came expecting the food and presents they had grown accustomed to during the tenure of the French. Farmar was dumbfounded, at a loss to know how he could obtain the goods necessary to entertain these uninvited guests and despairing of sanctioning this "most disagreeable custom which the French have introduced amongst the Indians . . . of constantly giving them victuals and drink." Yet he saw no way to avoid doing just that, at least at the moment. He was also likely aware that elsewhere in North America French-allied tribes led by Chief Pontiac had attacked British troops attempting to occupy former French outposts. As a consequence of this uncomfortable truth and communications with Governor Kerlérec preparatory to the transfer of the region, he begrudgingly accepted the Frenchman's advice that British administration of their new colony would be best served by demonstrating to the Gulf South's native population a peaceful transition of European authority featuring a degree of continuity. This meant, however, that the resource-strapped British on occasion had to play host to parties of tribesmen several times the size of their own military contingent.[27]

Farmar did have some able assistance in parlaying with the visitors in the unexpected first Indian congress in British Mobile, which witnessed as many as 500 Native Americans visiting the town daily. The new director-general of the French colony of Louisiana (soon to be handed over to the Spanish), Jean-Jacques Blaise d'Abbadie, came to Mobile for the occasion and jointly presided over proceedings with Farmar. Over the course of a hectic several weeks of meetings—small gatherings in private quarters and outdoor assemblies attended by hundreds—these two men explained to their guests that the French were leaving and the British would be moving in and assured their listeners of their friendly intentions. Except for an isolated riverside quarrel between Creek and Choctaw warriors which proved more spectacle than genuine threat to the security of the town but nonetheless petrified British officials, the congress proved a successful enough start to what would become a central component of international relations for West Florida's government. Plus, at the end of the seemingly endless rounds of the lavish dispensing of food, gifts, praise, and promises, a precedent had indeed been set; the British would honor longstanding custom as practiced by Gulf Coast colonial authorities and attempt to maintain tribal allegiance with what amounted to bribes.[28]

While the small group of military officials which comprised West Florida's government in the fall of 1763 delighted that relations with local native groups had gotten off to a good start, it labored under no illusions regarding its ability to keep the peace going forward. Leaders therefore accepted any assistance they could get with enthusiasm, even when it came in the unlikely form of a former French military officer who chose to stay in the region when the British arrived. The Chevalier Montault de Montberaut, who had resided in French Louisiana for a quarter century and in recent years had served at Fort Toulouse, believed he could create a lucrative new career for himself by offering his services to British authorities seeking to understand the political dynamics of working with the region's native groups. Not only did he have a familiarity with native societies, but he was one of the few people living in the area who possessed a facility with multiple Indian languages. The third son of a French nobleman, he had come to North America in search of fortune. He obtained a grant of land along the Fowl River south of Mobile on which he developed a plantation he called Lisloy. According to some accounts, he grazed as many as 500 cattle on the expansive estate, and he operated a second smaller farm north of town along the Tombigbee River.[29]

When local officials suggested hiring Montberaut to assist in their diplomatic efforts among area tribes, General Thomas Gage at first rebuffed the idea on the grounds he was a foreign Catholic. Solicitations from West Florida's governor once he finally arrived in the colony in 1764 and from Superintendent of Indian Affairs John Stuart ultimately won Montberaut a provisional commission as a diplomatic envoy. The British provided him with a generous salary, a house in Mobile, and a budget with which to purchase gifts to be used in his politicking with tribesmen. The British aimed to capitalize on Montberaut's status as a familiar figure among the Creeks and Choctaws and that he seemed to enjoy their esteem and trust.[30]

The first chance the Frenchman had to demonstrate his fidelity came in the spring of 1765. A large delegation of Choctaws began to assemble in Mobile to discuss concerns and get a better understanding of British aims. The Choctaws were understandably confused about how and why their longtime allies, the French, had left the region and were wary about the newcomers' designs on their lands. They had, after all, been told for so long by French emissaries that France was a mighty world power and that the British were a mortal enemy to the nation and its allies. Drawing on his substantial knowledge of indigenous languages and grasp of native rhetoric, Montberaut attempted to convince the visitors that their and British aims aligned and that it behooved them to work with the newcomers as they were now the sole colonial power with claims in the region they regarded as their ancestral homeland. Montberaut hosted two dozen individuals at a time in his quarters on multiple occasions, lavishing his guests with hospitality to grease the wheels of diplomacy. He must have been convincing, for by the end of April of 1765, many Choctaw leaders had come forward to exchange the medals of peace and friendship they had received from the French for British ones. Soon after, Montberault proved successful in getting the influential Creek chieftain known as The Mortar to meet at Pensacola and agree to a treaty specifying the formal cession of certain lands along the Gulf Coast for use by the British as well as adjusting the prices of selected trade goods.[31]

Although he did not yet know it, the meeting would be the pinnacle of Montberaut's short-lived tenure as a British diplomatic agent. Owing in part to questions about how he administered government funds, suspicions about the exact messages he was relaying to natives, jealousy of his success, and likely several other factors which we may never know in their entirety, the governor of the colony soon had Montberaut suspended from government service. He would end his days in his native France, leaving behind in West Florida one of the more unique legacies of colonial service in Gulf Coast history. The Frenchman had helped West Florida's fledgling administration through an inauspicious start to establishing control of the region. Creating a functioning government for the colony would take considerably more personnel and resources than a lone trader, however. It was to that task that officials were already turning their attention as Montberault left the scene.[32]

2

The Government of West Florida

'So Necessary for the Establishment of an Infant Colony'

A s a brand new colony, British West Florida had to be built from scratch in short order. Government officials had to be appointed and sent to the region, offices and institutions created, and policies and procedures enacted and overseen. It proved a pell-mell rush into state-building, at least in comparison to the more gradual process of evolution and assimilation into the Empire of peer colonies along the Atlantic seaboard.

The royal proclamation establishing West Florida functioned as a sort of constitution for the province. In some seventy-nine articles, it enumerated the general structure of its government and outlined much of how it should function. The proclamation specified that West Florida, similar to other royal provinces in North America, would be administered locally by an appointed governor, assisted by a lieutenant governor and an appointed advisory council. The council would form the upper house of a representative legislative assembly. Members of the House of Commons, the lower house of this lawmaking body, would be elected representatives. The chief justice, attorney general, and provincial secretary were to be appointed by Parliament, but the governor could appoint justices of peace, masters in chancery, and other minor officers.[1]

By design, West Florida's government operated almost exclusively on funding granted by Parliament, which oversaw a yearly appropriation for the colony's administration. Then as now, government funding never seemed adequate to the recipients. Between 1768 and 1781, yearly support of the local government ranged from a low of £3,900 and a high of £6,100, the bulk of which directly paid the salaries of its relatively few officials. In 1768 alone, for example, the salaries of West Florida government employees—including the governor, attorney general, judges, secretaries, surveyors, and provost marshal, some of which were full-time positions and others which received funds to offset certain expenses only—totalled about £4,400. By the early 1770s, average salary allotments had risen only to about £5,000, and by the end of the decade approached £6,000.[2]

To ensure this vital financial lifeline remained open, the colony was allowed to appoint a London-based agent to represent it before parliamentary leaders. Merchant Samuel Hannay filled the post during almost the entirety of the colony's existence, being appointed in 1767 and serving until the late 1770s. Hannay in essence served as the province's lobbyist, keeping its needs before the Empire's governing body and remaining in regular communication with colonial officials; without doubt he was the best-informed person in the mother country on West Florida's situation. That local officials valued his work is attested by both the fact that they encouraged him to remain in office through the tenures of several governors as well as that the council appropriated funds at one point to present him with a handsome "piece of plate" worth some £50 sterling for his effectual work.[3]

West Florida had

Seal of British West Florida (Mississippi Department of Archives and History)

another important contact in London in fiscal agent John Ellis. A politi-
cally well-connected and prominent scientist, Ellis corresponded with noted
naturalist Bernard Romans and, among others, internationally acclaimed
scientist Carolus Linnaeus. Ellis was a respected professional who had sought
the West Florida position in large part to advance his career. He hoped to
reap the rewards of botanical discoveries in West Florida's uncharted but
lush subtropical landscape; these might make their way into new medicines
and other marketable products. In return for a modest fee, Ellis, as "King's
Agent to West Florida," operating from his office at No. 5 Coney Court in
Gray's Inn in London, oversaw the distribution of much of the colony's al-
located funds. He in essence served as a comptroller for the province. While
he seems to have done his job as well as expected, his scheme of capitalizing
on the colony's potential botanical wealth never panned out. A number of
individuals sent him packets of biota, including sketches, seeds, and cuttings,
which he in turn sometimes shared with other scientist contacts in Europe.
But a great many of the specimens sent him were damaged, mislabeled, or
of little consequence. At least one large cache of specimens was lost at sea.
Ellis occupied his post from 1764 until his death in 1776. Little is known
about his successor, Christopher Nesham, who served as agent during the
tumultuous years of the American Revolution until the colony's transfer
to Spain.[4]

THE GENERAL ASSEMBLY, COMPRISING a fourteen-member House of
Commons and a twelve-member Council, served, on paper at least, as West
Florida's representative government. Qualified voters, based on a freehold
system, from each of several specified districts within the colony, could
elect delegates to the House as apportioned by area. As freeholders were
defined as property owners paying a certain amount of taxes, relatively few
met the requirements. Therefore officials determined to allow each house-
holder a vote as well. At first, regulations called for the House to contain six
representatives from Pensacola, six from Mobile, and two from Campbell
Town. These allocations changed over time reflecting the colony's population distribution. As the short-lived immigrant community at Campbell
Town dissipated, its representation was suspended after the fourth session

of the assembly, in 1771. Later, as settlement on the Mississippi began to outpace that in the east, representation in the lawmaking body was altered to include five districts, two in the burgeoning west; the town and district of Pensacola, Mobile, Manchac, and Natchez.[5]

The Assembly never played an important role in colonial affairs, partly due to its limited autonomy. It could only meet upon being summoned by the governor at his discretion, and any acts it passed would only become laws upon the governor's approval. Further, it could pass no laws on matters over which the king had exclusive authority, such as shipping. If its early journals are any indication, it suffered from a lack of respect in certain quarters as well; in 1768 the House of Commons introduced a bill imposing penalties on "any person or persons that shall publish and declare that the Acts of the General Assembly of the Province of West Florida are not of force." Relegated to a minor position in the infrastructure of West Florida's government, the Assembly met inconsistently and for the most part proved

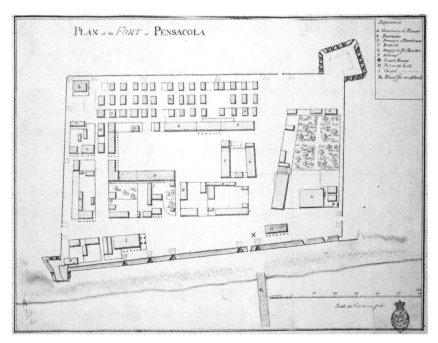

Plan of the Fort at Pensacola (Norman B. Leventhal Map and Education Center at the Boston Public Library)

ineffectual in its efforts to pass legislation. Reflecting its limited influence, the Commons House never even had a dedicated public building in the colonial capital. Instead, it gathered at first in private homes and later at a converted building within Fort George in Pensacola. For a while it met at a leased facility known as the "government house," which authorities also pressed into service as a church, courthouse, and one-time home of the provincial governor. The body did itself no favors in garnering esteem, as attendance at meetings was a chronic problem, and petty jealousies and perceived slights manifested themselves with regularity and determined the pace and substance of an unfortunate amount of its activity.[6]

The General Assembly held its first session in Pensacola from November 1766 to June 1767. Unbeknownst to attendees, it turned out to be the most productive in West Florida's history, as the body passed some fourteen acts signed into law by the governor relating to practical matters such as the establishment of government offices, regulating the institution of slavery, and promoting immigration. Despite the grand statements made by members at the opening of that first session affirming citizens' rights such as freedom of speech, the right of access to the governor, and the importance of elected officials in democratic government, the Assembly would never again be as prominent in colonial life as at that moment. The legislature met only a few more times while the colony remained under British control—December 1767 to January 1768; August to October of 1768; January to February of 1769; May to June of 1770; June to July of 1771; and October to November of 1778. Less than half the 103 total bills introduced within the legislature during the entirety of its meetings, ranging from regulation of the sale of liquor to procedures for branding cattle, were enacted as law. The Assembly did attempt to ask the home government for help constructing the fortifications, naval facilities, churches, and jails the colony lacked and sorely needed, and at one point, in a display of unity with its disadvantaged citizenry, allowed the salaries of its members to be used for relief of the poor in Pensacola and Mobile. But the irregularity and infrequency of Assembly meetings prevented it from becoming a real voice of the people in government affairs, much less a beloved champion.[7]

THE COUNCIL, APPOINTED BY the governor and serving as his advisory cabinet, played a much more substantive role in the colony's functioning. Owing to its composition and regular, more easily called meetings, West Florida essentially would be governed by its chief executive assisted by this body. The overwhelming majority of its meetings were held in the capital of Pensacola, but a handful were convened in Mobile. Whereas the entire Assembly met on the limited occasions outlined above, the Council met on average more than twenty times a year throughout the 1760s. In later years, the council would meet less frequently but still occupy an important and influential role in the colony's administration that far exceeded the input of the combined Assembly.[8]

But this did not mean that the Council operated outside the pervasive fractious political environment which plagued all levels of West Florida's government. The Council and the House squabbled routinely and evidenced a debilitating lack of communication, and rather than demonstrating the potential for collective action for the public good the Council could on occasion become involved in the petty bickering which made the government at best dysfunctional and at worst incompetent. When the Council sponsored a bill to address rampant horse and cattle theft, the House, for some reason miffed at the proposal, vetoed it on the grounds the punishments proposed were too severe; there was no alternative suggestion. On another occasion, when the Council recommended contracting with a Mr. Gaine of New York to print all laws passed in the first session of the Assembly, the House balked on the grounds that it had independently engaged a printer from Philadelphia. The fact that no general outcry against such unproductive quibbling and self-righteous shenanigans arose among the general populace had far less to do with acquiescence than awareness. Few residents had means of familiarizing themselves with the goings-on of legislative meetings given that there were no newspapers published in the colony. Plus, the relatively small population living on the Gulf Coast frontier, where the local government played a minimal role in their daily lives and seemed distant if not impossible to access, had no inclination to be concerned with what they often regarded as peripheral events. Nor would they have likely been highly critical of officials who, like them in most cases, could be understood as merely doing the best they could to establish law and order in an out-of-the-way, impoverished, and seemingly forgotten colony on the far fringes of the British Empire.[9]

THE REAL POWER IN West Florida's government throughout its existence as a British colony lay in the office of governor. The first appointed governor, George Johnstone, arrived in West Florida in October of 1764, a full year after the founding of the province, after multiple delays both personal and logistical. The transfer from military to civilian government at once began under his authority. A career naval officer in his mid-thirties, Johnstone had distinguished himself in action during the War of Austrian Succession and possessed a respectable service record. But he won appointment to his post in West Florida less on his resume than on the influence of powerful, well-connected friends whom he convinced to award him the position and on whom he would call often for support during what would be remembered as a divisive term of office. Johnstone is believed to have anonymously authored a prospectus, "Thoughts Concerning Florida," which appeared shortly before his arrival, outlining a master plan for the colony's development. Of course, the document recommended a naval officer like Johnstone himself as best suited to carry out the plan, but it did demonstrate a familiarity with the region's needs. While it is true Johnstone angled to get the post for personal advancement, he did give serious consideration to developing it into a flourishing province and genuinely thought his solutions would do the trick.[10]

However, Johnstone proved himself to be a vain and self-righteous man and is often remembered by historians for his proverbial thin skin and inability to work well with others. In fairness, it must be remembered that he came to his role as the holder of West Florida's highest office tasked with essentially creating a colony from scratch and possessed of a definite vision for success. When obstacles, detours, and doubts manifested themselves along the way, and they were many, Johnstone grew angry and bitter. From the beginning the governor asserted the colony must have an adequate system of defense, lucrative trading opportunities, and a stable government if it was to survive, much less reach its full potential. Few could argue with such an assessment, but adequate public funds, able-bodied troops, and supplies were always in short supply in West Florida, leaving the first of the colony's three-legged foundation on shaky ground from the start. Creative policies from a supportive home government and inspiring local administration, in Johnstone's eyes, could nonetheless shore up the other two. In these hopes, he would in the end be met with continual frustration and disappointment.[11]

Johnstone had grand dreams of the commercial opportunities lying within the colony's grasp at the opening of his tenure, and maintained

Commodore George Johnstone, by John Bogle (National Galleries of Scotland)

what one historian has termed a "buoyant optimism" about its future despite what ultimately became a series of setbacks. Over his years at the helm of West Florida's government, he entertained a number of schemes both practical and chimeric aimed at sparking a thriving colonial economy. Some involved recruiting immigrants with special skills to help kick-start local production of lucrative agricultural products, such as those with knowledge of grape cultivation and wine production or experienced divers to harvest pearls from the colony's waters. At one point, Johnstone even tried to get the Royal Navy to help him import camels on the premise they might be well suited as an effective mode of transportation along the sandy stretches of West Florida's coastal regions. Johnstone advocated for lenient immigration policies so that the colony might build up a population capable of producing surpluses of agricultural products large enough to serve as the foundation of a ready market for a variety of imported items. He hoped to wield generous land-granting policies outlined by the British government and an unusual tolerance regarding religion in a territory with a substantial Catholic population as key parts of a strategy encouraging a wave of immigration. In these hopes Johnstone, as well as his successors, would be disappointed, for immigration into West Florida lagged during its early years due to factors even free land and religious toleration could not overcome.[12]

For any of these designs to help drive economic development, though, Johnstone believed it paramount that, contrary to existing mercantile laws on imperial trade, West Florida be allowed legal economic exchange with the Spanish colonies in the greater Gulf basin. These were logical and ready commercial partners, in the governor's estimation, being neighbors with much more vibrant economies than the fledgling British province and having a potential trade surplus of goods. He bandied about ideas for how it all might work, suggesting deals be worked for the colony to export shipping industry items which the Spanish were eager to acquire, such as masts, bowsprits, pitch, tar, and turpentine. He also laid out plans for transshipping through West Florida's ports British textiles for dyewood and silver, and he requested from his home government a relaxation of the enforcement of the protectionist Navigation Acts—a series of trade laws regulating international commerce with British colonies. He even lobbied for a special sailing ship for the colony to help jump-start trade. Parliament proved unyielding, effectively shutting the door on the governor's proposed path to prosperity. Trade with the Spanish did take place, but primarily in the form of smuggling that was free of customs duties and thus of no direct benefit to the state.[13]

It would be Johnstone's attempt to form an effective and smooth-functioning local government, however, that not only punctuated the failure of his plan but led to his own ouster. The governor did in truth do a lot to build West Florida's governmental infrastructure: he established courts, assigned justices of the peace, and appointed the advisory Council which handled much of the legislative business done in the colony. But at times he proved anything but collegial with those with whom he had to work during his administration. Johnstone was by all accounts a cantankerous man, prone to confrontation and squabbling, who seemingly quarreled at one time or another with virtually everyone with whom he had extended dealings. Owing to his natural disposition and perhaps his experience in the navy, where strict obedience to authority was customary, Johnstone could come across as difficult and haughty. His personality and inflexibility colored his interactions with subordinates and played a key limiting role in the overall success of his administration.[14]

Almost immediately after arriving in Pensacola, Johnstone became in embroiled in a long-running dispute with military officials over the extent of his authority. The division between civilian and military authority had not been clearly defined in the colony's original charter, but Johnstone refused to broach any argument to his aggressive assertion of complete autonomy. As the top-ranking civil officer in West Florida, he believed he needed this authority to complete the tasks assigned to him on a raw, undeveloped frontier. He argued that "where ever the executive force is taken away, separated from the supreme judicative, that confusion must follow," and thus professed to seek power for the sake of order. Questions voiced by colonial military officers led to arguments and threats of courts-martial for insubordination that were at times both philosophical and farcical. He brought charges against one lieutenant colonel for, among other things, firing the guns at Pensacola in honor of St. Patrick's Day without orders, and he got into a fight with another for taking up residence in a house Johnstone had eyed as a meeting place for his Council. One dispute over the extent of Johnstone's control of the fort at Pensacola ended with troops locking him out of his quarters within the post. The governor found himself ignominiously reduced to climbing the wall to gain entry, only to be greeted by the bayonets of his own men. "At that time," wrote an official who witnessed the spectacle, "it was easy to know the opinion the people have of Gov. Johnstone's administration."[15]

Johnstone's running feud with the ranking military commander at Mobile, Robert Farmar, would likewise have been comical had it not threatened to compromise the colony's defensive preparedness. The supercilious Johnstone and the proud Farmar immediately became inveterate enemies, their disagreements and distrust of one another reaching such a nadir that they, though they occupied vitally strategic positions in the colony's governance, could only agree to meet in the presence of witnesses. Johnstone attempted to bring Farmar to trial for supposed irregularities, charging him with

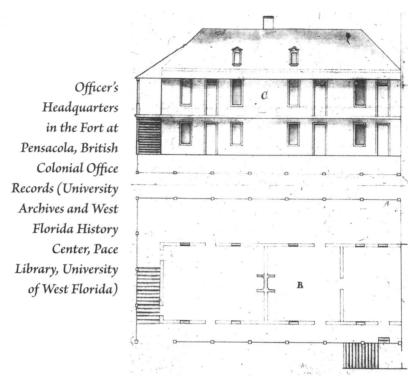

Officer's Headquarters in the Fort at Pensacola, British Colonial Office Records (University Archives and West Florida History Center, Pace Library, University of West Florida)

embezzlement, illegal trading, and inefficiency in carrying out his duties. At length Farmar was acquitted of most of the charges and judgment was suspended in the others, but irreparable damage to the relationship between the colony's civilian government and military establishment had been done in the very public argument between the two men.[16]

Johnstone did not confine his bickering to military officials. He had a number of disputes with members of his own administration which transformed sincere disagreement into raging controversy. He accused his lieutenant governor, Montfort Browne, of gross misconduct and initiated another unseemly quarrel which featured both men trying to undermine the other. He arbitrarily suspended the young attorney general of the province, Edmund Rush Wegg, who he seemed to distrust reflexively because of his age, on a charge of "Incapacity and Negligence" attributed to the "childish behavior of this youth." This prompted Wegg and his supporters to send a complaint to London accusing Johnstone of being nothing less than a tyrant. The governor's handling of the General Assembly provided further evidence for those accusing him of being an overbearing despot. As governor, Johnstone had the prerogative to call for meetings of the Assembly when he deemed necessary. This inherently led to problems during his and subsequent administrations, as Johnstone and future governors seemed to think the Assembly was not often necessary. Petitions asking for Johnstone to call the body to order were circulated as early as February of 1766, but it was not until August of that year that elections were authorized. Meetings at last began in November of 1766, but in January of 1767 Johnstone prorogued the gathering. In summoning this first abbreviated legislature, which met in Pensacola, he had promised it would next meet in Mobile. No effort was made to do this, however, frustrating officials there.[17]

Letters of complaint of Johnstone's handling of matters soon landed on the desks of high-ranking colonial officials including William Petty, Earl of Shelburne, who had been appointed as Secretary of State for the Southern Department in 1766. Shelburne's guiding philosophy in colonial administration was one of avoiding disruption, as he believed that given a peaceful and prosperous environment, British provinces would thrive. In-fighting, rivalry, and intrigue—exactly what he now got strong evidence of in West Florida—would lead to disaster in short order. Complainants accusing Johnstone of malfeasance characterized him as a virtual madman, despairing that "his thirst of power and command has, to the great detriment and imminent danger of this province, created innumerable disputes between him and the military." By early 1766 the anti-Johnstone uproar had led to circulation of plans by a handful of disgruntled individuals for an alleged rebellion against the colonial government and his displacement. Nothing came of the rumored conspiracy, but the whispers were strong evidence that the governor's intractability had made him a lightning rod for the type of debilitating controversy that worried authorities in London. Johnstone of course responded to the complaints as "without foundation, and can only be from the lowest class, stirred up by a wicked judge, a crazy colonel, a cheating merchant, and a foolish suspended attorney general."[18]

The fervor against Johnstone crescendoed in the fall of 1766, just as the governor committed a strategic blunder which proved the proverbial last straw with weary authorities in London. Relations with the Creeks had steadily deteriorated under Johnstone's administration, as incidents of cattle theft, fugitive slave harboring, and violence against British settlers rose. Most of the discord had roots in the inability of colonial officials to effectively police traders who took advantage of Native Americans, and it drove Johnstone to distraction. His was a black and white world in which one was a trusted friend or a bitter enemy—"an extreme man" in the words of his biographer—and he had no time for the vagaries of international diplomacy or the confusing array of individual ranks and actions that were a vital part of tribal politics. The governor demanded retribution for the British settlers who had been killed at the hands of the Creeks in recent years—there had been had least five murders in the past year and Johnstone claimed many more had occurred over the vast southeastern backcountry in the past decades. Johnstone belligerently threatened war with the entire Creek Nation should satisfaction not be forthcoming. "If you are for peace, say so, we wish to continue, if for war, say so, and we are prepared," he bellowed in a blind rage even as his superiors in the British government counseled caution. Nobody in London believed a costly and dangerous war with the Creeks, which by Johnstone's own estimation would necessitate over 2,500 British troops and Indian allies and require an enormous financial commitment, would yield positive results or improve the health of the colony. Rather, they feared such a conflict might actually destroy it. It all proved a convenient excuse for the governor's dismissal.[19]

Secretary Shelburne, finally having had enough of Johnstone's antics, recalled him in February of 1767, citing the king's disapproval of "every measure which can tend towards rashly rekindling the war between the Indians and his subjects in North America" and decrying "that Spirit of Disunion" which had arisen within the colony. Ironically, the governor had just departed the province on a leave of absence and when the order arrived in West Florida Johnstone was long gone. He never returned. The rocky tenure of West Florida's first governor had ended and a new era begun.[20]

JOHNSTONE'S DEPARTURE TEMPORARILY ELEVATED Lieutenant Governor Montfort Browne. In his instructions to the new acting governor, Lord Shelburne had made it clear he wanted restoration of a sense of the "harmony so necessary for the establishment of an infant colony," and he manifested high hopes for a smooth and progressive administration. Browne, however, could scarcely have been less prepared to take the reins in West Florida. While the native Irishman and experienced military veteran had served for several years as the colony's second in command, he in truth knew relatively little about the operations of the government of West Florida due to Johnstone's purposefully having kept him at arm's length. He lived in Mobile and was apparently seldom seen and little known among the colony's high-ranking officers in the capital at Pensacola. He would need quite a learning curve in short order to be effective, as well as to overcome the handicap of being an interim executive whose authority detractors knew would be fleeting. Plus, in the bitterly factionalized politics of the colony, Browne himself had been charged with financial irregularities; the possibility of an investigation into his affairs loomed even as he took office. By all accounts, Browne at least had ambition and energy on his side, and he needed all of both as he began his work.[21]

Browne set to his task with purpose, doing his best to restore order and civility in the colony's government and initiating negotiations with the disgruntled Creeks. After mere days in his new office, he called for the General Assembly to meet. When he learned of plans by General Thomas Gage, commander-in-chief of British military operations in North America, to reduce the number of troops stationed in the frontier colony and the abandonment of West Florida's Mississippi River outposts, he quickly and effectively urged a reconsideration of the measure and thus kept the defense of West Florida on the radar of colonial authorities. Browne even found time to make a formal tour of the developing western part of the province in the spring of 1768, becoming the first high-ranking government official in the colony to evaluate firsthand the fertile Mississippi River region to which a large percentage of immigrants to the colony were already flocking. Still, Browne had his detractors. He stood accused by some individuals of a host of irregularities from administering arbitrary justice to impropriety in the calling and disbanding of the General Assembly. Some, albeit with much less evidence, carped Browne became as much a tyrant as Johnstone, .[22]

His relationship with the General Assembly is revealing of the undercurrent of tension which characterized his administration. Browne prorogued the body in 1767 in its first gathering after Johnstone's departure, prompting a huffy seven-part resolution from the legislature outlining what it believed to be irregularities in Browne's handling of its branch of government and accusing him of undermining its authority with certain individuals in the Council. The relationship soured from there, devolving into debates on respect for the legislature by the governor and Browne in turn accusing members collecting their small salaries as evidence of greed and lack of public spirit. While the discord never rose to level that reigned during Johnstone's tenure, it restricted potential advancement in meeting the challenges of the developing colony while Browne occupied the governor's chair.[23]

JOHN ELIOT, WHO HAD been appointed to replace Johnstone as the colony's governor in early 1767, finally arrived in April of 1769 and relieved interim governor Browne of his duties. The twenty-five year old Eliot hailed from a wealthy and influential British family but had earned his way into military leadership through distinguished service in the Royal Navy. He had joined the service at the tender age of ten, and by seventeen had risen to the command of a twelve-gun sloop. Ironically, at one point during the Seven Years' War he served for a brief time under Johnstone aboard a British warship. Eliot arrived in Pensacola knowing he would be expected to investigate the alleged misappropriation of funds by interim governor Browne, and he put that simmering controversy to rest at last. He also well knew the unsettled state of affairs in the colony's administration and understood that a top priority during his tenure would be to calm the colony's turbid political waters and get officials working together more effectively.[24]

In some of his first actions, Eliot appointed a new Council, authorized elections for the General Assembly, and investigated the previous administration's handling of public funds, distribution of land grants, and other allegations of misconduct. Possessed of an amiable disposition and clearly talented, Eliot in short order ingratiated himself with many of those with whom he would have to work to make the new colony's government run effectively. By all appearances, his tenure as governor looked to be off to a promising start. It all came to a tragic and most unexpected end. On the evening of Monday, May 1, 1769, Eliot dined with Montfort Browne and several others at his home in Pensacola. No accounts of the dinner, or anything during the weeks leading up to it, indicate anyone had any idea that Eliot was a troubled man. But the next morning, he was found dead in his study, having hung himself during the night. The sudden death of the popular leader cast a pall over the colonial government and threatened to usher in renewed confusion and upheaval.[25]

Montfort Browne immediately resumed the post of acting governor while authorities began the search for a long-term replacement. In an interesting twist which provided a unique commentary on the state of West Florida's local administration, proceedings investigating Browne's financial activities, just begun under Eliot, were temporarily postponed. In one of his first acts once assuming the role of governor for a second time, Browne sent the new lieutenant governor, Elias Durnford, to England to answer the ongoing charges of financial irregularity as he attempted to keep order in West Florida. But the investigation into Browne's affairs was just one of his problems. Almost as soon as he resumed office, a petition appeared, signed by some fifty-seven inhabitants, which protested his appointment. At the same time, a letter of support signed by sixty-three citizens arrived at his office. To say the colony was of a divided mind concerning its leadership would be an understatement. Had he been aware of the developing factions at this point, King George III would only have been more frustrated. Weary of the dispiriting situation and constant reports of in-fighting, the monarch decided to make Browne's second tenure in office a short one indeed. When Durnford returned to West Florida in December of 1769, he carried with him official orders that he replace Browne as acting governor.[26]

Browne's rocky stay in West Florida would only get more interesting before he left the province early the next year. He became involved in a controversial duel in Pensacola with a man named Evan Jones. In the affray, Jones's pistol misfired but Browne's shot struck home, leaving Jones with a dangerous wound from which some doubted he would recover. But at length he regained his health, and the spectacle of a former governor already under suspicion for financial irregularities facing criminal charges for homicide was avoided. Browne then sailed to England out of West Florida's story in

Elias Durnford and Rebecca Walker Durnford
(from Colonial Mobile, *by Peter Hamilton)*

February of 1770. In his wake, however, he left a frothing sea of political dissension and controversy as citizens searched for stability and order.[27]

ELIAS DURNFORD SERVED AS West Florida's acting governor until August of 1770, when appointed governor Peter Chester arrived. Described by one historian as one of West Florida's most "useful and devoted" figures, and genuinely committed to trying to advance the colony by quelling inner turmoil, Durnford had arrived in Pensacola shortly after the establishment of the colony. He had seen extensive action in multiple theaters of the Seven Years' War, including in the Cuban campaign of 1762, and as a result had gained some familiarity with both the Gulf region and military engineering. A surveyor by trade, he had been appointed as West Florida's Surveyor General in 1763 through connections made in the war, where his talents had been recognized by his superiors. One of his first tasks had been to lay out the colonial capital city, setting a plat which to some degree would later be copied in other colonial cities. Since that time he had been very busy on numerous other projects and had become recognized as the colony's leading engineer.[28]

Nothing took more of his time than his role in the administration of the granting of land within West Florida, as the legal processing of every tract involved his drawings, entries into the colony's records, and tracking all of the requirements for the deeding of land by the government to individuals. In fact Durnford came to be in such demand for his services that some of the colony's leading officials, including the governor and lieutenant governor, at different times attempted to lay first claim to his contested time for important projects as a figurative line formed outside of office. His skills enabled him to earn a handsome living by West Florida standards, and by the time he assumed the office of acting governor he owned tracts of land along the Mississippi and Perdido rivers as well as a 5,000-acre plantation, Belle Fontaine, on the eastern shore of Mobile Bay. When he returned from England in the late fall of 1769, he brought a new wife, Rebecca Walker, to share his fortune.[29]

Durnford proved to be well liked by most of the people with whom he had to work to govern the colony, and during his brief tenure its government functioned as smoothly as it had at any point since its founding despite a number of vexing problems that increasingly had come to define local politics. Every leader of the province would struggle with how to manage and protect a colony whose primary settlements were so scattered, especially as the neighboring Spanish colony to the west grew in population and influence and the Native American groups with whom they shared the region demanded what to the British seemed a high price for their friendship. While Durnford proved unable to solve these problems in his nine months in the governor's chair, he did calm the colony's faction-ridden political waters as it entered a critical era of development. Durnford would remain active in colonial affairs after stepping down from the post, keeping busy with his surveying duties, scheming of ways to build a port on the eastern shore of Mobile Bay, dabbling in art, and, later, when the Revolutionary War broke out, taking an important role in the defense of Mobile.[30]

THE KING TAPPED PETER Chester as West Florida's governor in 1770. To the degree the colony's government ever found stability, it would be during Chester's more than a decade-long term of office, as he would lead the province for the remainder of its time as a part of the British Empire. Chester came to the job with twenty years of experience in the British military and a confidence in the possibilities for development of the province. He set to work repairing the colony's perpetually troublesome fortifications, worked diligently to encourage economic activity and immigration, and strove to be a voice of authority and reason in the local political scene. Chester did not succeed in everything, and his time in office proved anything but peaceful. Try as he might to remain above the fray, he, like the governors before him, ran afoul of several influential citizens. Various individuals and factions accused him at different times of such diverse failings as playing favorites in government appointments, irregularities in the granting of land, inaction in foreign relations when swift decision-making was required, not regularly calling the Assembly, and of diversion of public funds into his own pockets. In 1779 a vocal group of about 125 citizens even circulated a petition to have Chester removed from office. The king evaluated the petition along with Chester's lengthy rebuttal, but took no action and continued the governor in office.[31]

Chester had particular problems dealing with the General Assembly. He first fell out with the body in 1771 when he chose not to call the legislature back into fall session after a spring meeting, in part owing to his determination that the customary way of issuing writs of election violated orders from the crown. Representatives had become accustomed to operating on the premise that winning election for a convention of the Assembly equated to a year-long term of office, but Chester read the king's instruction to the colonial executive as giving him prerogative in determining tenure. When he issued the call for elections in 1772 with no terms of office specified, a small-scale rebellion broke out. With no quorum, the Assembly could not meet legally and Chester had it dissolved. He would not call it again until 1778, amidst the chaos of a true crisis sparked by war with Spain during the American Revolution.[32]

DURING THE ENTIRETY OF its existence, West Florida's governmental infrastructure was plagued with in-fighting, rivalry, and factionalism which it had to overcome to function effectively. At various times, it could not, and hence did not. But the issues it faced in the bayside villages of Pensacola and

Mobile were for the most part familiar problems, common by-products of politics as then practiced which might temporarily hamstring the government's efficiency but could usually be worked out. Other problems were more complicated. None were more important or vexing than how to maintain orderly trade and good diplomatic relations with the large and powerful native groups who actually owned the majority of the land within West Florida's borders and whose populations far exceeded that of the fledgling colony. It was to that issue that the colony's leaders devoted a considerable portion of their time and energy.

3

The Role of the Indian Trade

'The Original Great Tye Between the Indians and
Europeans Was Mutual Conveniency'

undamental components of British West Florida foreign policy
lay bound up in a regulated system of exchange with area native
groups. Cornerstones of both economic activity and diplomacy, the
trade formed the basis for building and maintaining relationships with area
tribes. The "soft tinkle of harness bells on pack horses, moving across miles
of wilderness," observed one historian of the era, spoke "louder than guns
or intrigue or any other force."[1]

This situation prevailed, in part, because native groups far outnumbered
most colonial settlements. At a time in which the entire population of West
Florida numbered less than 3,000, that of the Creeks, who resided in about
sixty villages to the north and east of the new colony's largest cities, along
the Coosa, Tallapoosa, Alabama, Chattahoochee, and Flint rivers and their
tributaries, is estimated to have been about 15,000. The Choctaw, concentrated in what is now central and southeastern Mississippi to the north and
west of the new province's initial settlements, numbered about the same.
Farther north, in what is now northern Mississippi and southwestern Tennessee, the Chickasaws claimed about 2,300 but exerted influence out of all
proportion to their relatively small numbers. In perhaps more immediate
terms to British colonial officials, all these demographics translated to as
many as 3,500 Creek warriors, 2,000 among the Choctaws, and several hundred among the Chickasaws; easily enough to overwhelm the small, isolated
garrisons whose job it was to defend the colony should relations with native
groups sour. And these were just the largest of the native groups occupying

the inland regions from which the new Gulf Coast colony had been carved. So it was that trade, the "great tye" of "mutual conveniency," in the words of British Superintendent of Indian Affairs John Stuart, would become a great source of diplomacy to the British in their administration of West Florida.[2]

By the mid-eighteenth century, the deerskin trade had become the life-blood of economic activity in a vast region stretching from the Atlantic to the Mississippi. This exchange introduced a wide array of desired goods into Native American societies, which collectively made life easier but ushered in fundamental changes in their culture. It brought cloth, duffel, stroud, and calico which could be made into blankets and clothing; ready-to-wear items such as hats, belts, shirts, and coats; accessories and decorative items such as ribbons, beads, mirrors, and handkerchiefs; housewares such as pots, pans, and kettles; and a variety of tools and items from knives, axes, hatchets, hoes, and kettles to guns, powder, and bullets. Traders also dealt in numerous other mass-produced utilitarian, decorative, and even sometimes ceremonial items. And, in what would become the bane of the trade for its debilitating effects among a portion of Indian society and its notorious role in lubricating certain trade deals, the traders brought alcohol—rum especially—by the barrel.[3]

Over time these items, however obtained, transformed Native American society. The introduction of metal tools and cooking wares wrought a slow but steady abandonment of the manufacture of traditional hand-crafted pottery and other items; European textiles replaced traditional clothing; guns superseded bows and arrows, and so on. Plus, differences in wealth as gauged by the ownership of private property such as peddled trading goods gradually introduced new concepts of status among peoples whose culture had revolved around more communal ownership. These sea changes within Native American life both inside and beyond West Florida's borders did not occur evenly or at once, but by the colony's formation they had been underway for nearly three-quarters of a century and were accelerating.[4]

In what became West Florida, the roots of the organized, regular system of exchange with European colonists by which these items were obtained dated back to the previous century and represented the first serious foray into the region by the English. In the 1680s English traders operating out

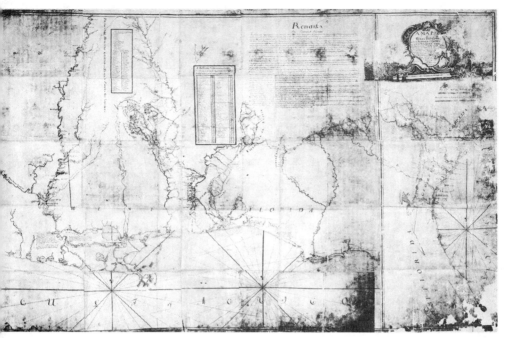

Map of southeast in the 1760s showing West Florida, portions of East Florida and Georgia, and the trading routes through Creek, Choctaw, and Chickasaw territory. (University of Michigan Library Digital Collections, William L. Clements Library Image Bank)

of Charlestown first established contact with the Creeks living along the Chattahoochee in what is now southeastern Alabama. A daring Henry Woodward had ventured to the area, far beyond the reach of his contemporaries operating out of the South Carolina and Georgia backcountry, seeking a new and profitable outlet for trade in which he and his compatriots might enjoy at least a temporary monopoly. Convivial and engaging, Woodward befriended the Creeks and attempted to seal a trade deal in classic style by promising them access to a wealth of desired goods at affordable prices. However, his arrival in the region provoked the Spanish in nearby Florida to attempt to oust him by force and alerted them that the English were aggressively seeking to expand their presence in the region. Twice they sent armies from Florida to track down Woodward and block the inroads their colonial rivals were making among the Creeks. In the end the Spanish only damaged the Creeks themselves and inadvertently accelerated the process the English had begun. Creeks, enchanted by the opportunities presented by their English courtiers, pursued their own course. They hid Woodward and his cohorts from the vengeful Spanish forces that burned native towns in frustration when he could not be found. Later, the Creeks would move eastward in large numbers to be closer to the English and out of the easy reach of the jealous Spaniards. Still, Creeks resisted entering into any binding trade alliance, and their allegiance to any European power would always be expedient and subject to change. The entire episode is a microcosm of the origins of the trade that had come to define the economy of many of the larger native groups of the Southeast with whom West Florida officials would later negotiate.[5]

THE OUSTER OF THE French and Spanish along the Gulf Coast in 1763 upset the delicate balance with European powers which West Florida's native groups had forged over the course of some seventy-five years of diplomacy and trade. Suddenly the Creeks, in the eastern portion of the province, were left to deal almost exclusively with British traders. The Choctaws, residing primarily in its western half, had easy access to the new possessors of Louisiana, although the trade they could provide paled to that of the British they now could access as well. Creeks and Choctaws had long been traditional enemies, and it was unknown how this newfound entrée to better and more plentiful British goods for the Choctaw, including weapons and ammunition, might play out. The Choctaws were equally alarmed at the loss of a longtime ally in the French, however, and unsure exactly how the less-familiar British planned to fill the void left in the region's power structure. Both tribes were wary that the other might gain an advantage in obtaining arms through trade with the British, and both were eager to have traders visit or reside in their villages. Recognizing how their takeover had unsettled regional dynamics, and desiring to start off on the right foot, British officials soon called diplomatic conferences with the Creeks and Choctaws in Mobile and Pensacola. In these meetings the British promised bountiful trade and friendship, while the Indians made it clear they expected to see promises lived up to. Choctaw leader Tomatly Mingo expressed the position of all concerned in a single, powerful, sentence couched in traditional symbolic language: "If I am become their Son, they must Act the Part of a Father in Supplying my Wants by proper Presents and also by furnishing a plentyfull Trade."[6]

Beneficial trade relationships require that both sides bring something of value to the table. In exchange for the diverse array of merchandise traders offered for sale, they customarily sought a much narrower but lucrative list of items from the Indians. Deerskins from the start served as the essential and often the only product the traders accepted as payment for their goods. The process of obtaining this trade staple transformed Creek society, as it turned a traditional practice sustaining families and households into a business that consumed much of the time and labor of the entire community. Male Creeks killed the animals in extended hunts ranging across enormous distances into the wilderness. This was no solitary

Creek hunters, ca. 1730s, by Phillip Georg Friedrich Von Reck
(Royal Library of Denmark)

stalking with handmade bows and arrows: armed with rifles and hunting in groups, they worked together in methodical fashion to fell as many deer as possible, sometimes burning swaths of land to drive deer into areas where they could be harvested more efficiently. Once the deer had been dressed, Creek women then spent hours preparing the skins both in temporary camps and within permanent villages, the work gradually becoming the focal point of domestic labor to the exclusion of many other traditional activities. The work was tedious and just the beginning of a remarkable multi-step process in which the harvests of the southeastern woods would end up on store shelves in European cities. Native women first scraped the fat and tissue away by hand, dried the skin in the sun, then soaked it in a solution which allowed the hair to be more easily scraped away. Then the skins were pounded to the desired softness, stretched, and smoked so that they could be stored for trade. Once bartered to traders, they were transported to ports where they were shipped across the Atlantic to be manufactured into leather for gloves, hats, pants, bookbindings, and other items. Beaver, martin, elk, mountain lion, otter, and fox skins were bartered as well, but up to ninety percent of the fur trade from southeastern ports prior to the Revolutionary War came from whitetail deer.[7]

But the deerskin trade was inherently unsustainable, an inconvenient reality which would manifest itself fully in the next generation but become clear during West Florida's heyday. A good Choctaw or Creek hunter could kill, individually, as many as 100 deer per year. As early as 1699, some 45,000 deerskins harvested in the southeastern backcountry were shipped out of Charlestown, the first primary port for the trade. With only brief interruptions, average exports from Carolina alone thenceforward hovered around fifty to sixty thousand skins annually from about 1720 until the 1760s, when the colony of West Florida was organized and the city of Mobile assumed a larger role in the regional trade. Of course, there were other points of export, and it must be remembered that the French, who until 1763 claimed an enormous territory that would come under British dominion, also exported considerable numbers of deerskins. The pace of deer harvesting which supported this trade was greater than the environment could maintain. It is estimated that by the time of the organization of West

Florida, as many as 400,000 deer were being killed annually in the south-east, their processed skins ultimately yielding between one and two million pounds of leather. The pace of this slaughter continued almost unabated until after the Revolutionary War, devastating the deer population and ef-fectively destroying the resource which made the trade possible. Coupled with the increased availability of manufactured textiles and a decline in the demand for deerskin products, this new economic reality would hit native groups in the southeast particularly hard in the years immediately after the British left the region.[8]

As the leading scholar on the trade has observed, all this economic ac-tivity caused "ancient Indian footpaths" to be transformed into "the most extensive system of trading paths found in English North America." Trails connecting eastern South Carolina and Georgia with what became central Alabama sprang up as economic lifelines linking coastal colonial business enterprises and eager Native American consumers came into their own. During the years of West Florida's existence as a colony, British traders op-erating out of Pensacola and Mobile began to make inroads into the routes long controlled by the trade hubs of Charlestown, Savannah, and Augusta. At any given time in the West Florida backcountry, caravans of traders from South Carolina, Georgia, and the new Gulf Coast province could be found crisscrossing these wilderness roads in search of the best deal. Indians them-selves supplied a great portion of the labor to transport goods from colonial ports to the interior initially, but horses eventually became more common. Tough, diminutive, Indian-bred packhorses provided the locomotive power that sustained the trade in its heyday. Traversing hundreds of miles of wil-derness trails in a single-file line carrying bundles of goods—commonly arranged in three, approximately fifty-pound packs—on their backs, these horses became an essential element in regional trade and a common sight at Native American villages across the region.[9]

Naturalist and author William Bartram accompanied a group of pack-horsemen on a portion of his journey through West Florida in 1777. His description of time among the traders reads as high frontier drama, and even though it took place near the end of the era of the cross-country cara-vans, it provides readers with a sense of how trade operated throughout the

Mico-chlucco, or "Long Warrior"
(*From* Travels *by William Bartram*)

eighteenth century on the southern frontier. Bartram joined a packhorse caravan in November of 1777 for a journey through Creek country. He reported the group contained about two dozen horses, guided by two Indians and a few traders. With a "shriek" which rang "through the forests and plain," the guides trekked single file along narrow wilderness trails in a noisy procession. Each horse wore bells for easier tracking should it become separated from the group, and each guide carried a whip he wielded to keep the animals moving at the right speed. Bartram found the result to be a "constant ringing and clattering of the bells, snaking of the whips, whooping and too frequent cursing these miserable quadrupeds." When they arrived at river crossings, they built rafts of logs or canes tied together with wild grape vines to float across, and when they encountered smaller creeks they often traversed felled saplings spanning the waterway and swam the horses across. The group greeted passing Indians along the trail with shouts of friendship, and as they approached a village one from the caravan would go ahead to give notice of their arrival. Within the villages they encountered not only residents, but many other traders. In a poignant revelation of just how thoroughly interactions with backcountry traders had transformed Native American communities in a generation, Bartram recorded conversing with an elderly chief. The man told how in his youth "they had no iron hatchets, pots, hoes, knives, razors or guns, but that they then made use of their own stone axes, clay pots, flint knives, bows

William Bartram
(Library of Congress)

and arrows," and he boasted of being the first man from his town to bring in such goods from the English in Charlestown.[10]

A DARKER SIDE TO the Indian trade emerged during the years of British hegemony along the Gulf Coast at the same time demand for manufactured goods among native groups spiked. Prior to the arrival of European traders in the Southeast, Native American societies practiced a form of slavery far different from that of the American agricultural communities of the nineteenth century. Broadly speaking, captives taken in intertribal warfare were often dealt with in one of two ways: warriors might be tortured and killed, or women or children might be enslaved and forced into domestic servitude. These enslaved individuals could often expect to find themselves integrated into the society of their captors over time, never on equal social footing but not as permanent bondspersons the term "slave" would later imply. These are of course generalizations, and a variety of specific circumstances came into play, but they roughly describe slavery as originally practiced by native societies such as the Creek, Choctaw, and Chickasaw. However, captives taken in war became marketable commodities in trade with Europeans as demand for labor in colonial settlements on the Atlantic coast, especially South Carolina, grew in the early 1700s. Large slave-taking raids into the Gulf Coast region, in which powerful tribes preyed on their weaker neighbors, took place frequently in the first half of the century. By the establishment of British West Florida, unprecedented numbers of African slaves were in the region, and the practice of Indian slavery was on the decline. But the nature of the institution had been forever changed among indigenous societies, and some Native Americans bought and sold black slaves just as their European trading partners did. Some slaves—it is impossible to know how many—labored as part of the deerskin trade, while others were put to work in agricultural pursuits.[11]

British colonial authorities attempted to regulate the Indian trade to ensure its smooth functioning. All traders were to be licensed by the government to operate only in specified villages and to observe strict limits on the extension of credit. They were also to be restricted in the trading of rum and prohibited from trading in certain kinds of weapons. Further, regulations called for set prices on certain goods as a way to ensure fair and consistent trade. Enforcing all of this taxed the British. The only reason they could have any hope of seeing these and other regulations observed lay in the fact that authorities had in 1755 created the Office of the Superintendent of Indian Affairs. The office initially oversaw northern and southern districts in North America, the dividing line being the Ohio River. Edmund Atkin served as the first director of the southern district. John Stuart, its second, took over in 1762 and from his office in Charlestown administered official Indian policy in West Florida until his death in 1779. Stuart was a native of Scotland who had worked as a merchant. His brother, Charles, served as deputy superintendent of the department during his tenure and resided in Mobile during much of his administration. From John Stuart's death until the colony's demise, Alexander Cameron, another veteran of the Seven Years' War and a longtime agent among the Cherokee in Georgia, North Carolina, and what is now Tennessee, served as superintendent for the Southwest.[12]

Stuart had confronted a difficult situation in 1762. The Choctaws were unhappy about not having been consulted before the transfer of authority in the region from the French, with whom they were on friendly terms, to the British. A few smaller tribes, what the French called "petites nations," had left the region when the French were forced out. Even though they were more familiar with each other, nor did the Creeks celebrate the arrival of the British on the Gulf Coast. They were concerned about having one less European power to bargain with, worried about the consequences of their traditional enemies, the Choctaw, having easy access to better tools and weapons, and suspicious of the intentions of the avaricious British as regarded their lands. Plus, the native groups made it clear they expected the British to continue the French diplomacy tradition of lavish gift-giving. Squaring British aims with native concerns, fears, and jealousies while policing the traders actually in Indian villages proved to be a difficult task indeed.[13]

THE FACT THAT IN some respects London transferred more authority for the conduct of the Indian trade to officials in North America during West Florida's colonial years helped give the superintendent's office a fighting chance to accomplish its mission. Local regulations, driven by an understanding of local conditions, stood much better odds at proving effective than sweeping continent-wide standards. British colonies in North America therefore began to adopt their own regulations as soon as allowed. West Florida became one of several colonies to do so in the form of a series of rules on the Indian trade within its borders based on Stuart's recommendations, based on the codes enacted in other southern colonies. The code developed under Stuart's direction, informally referred to as the "Plan of 1764," was never officially adopted but nonetheless formed the basis of Indian policy pursued by authorities. As originally composed, Stuart's code consisted of nineteen specific regulations which can be grouped into seven categories of provisions broadly aimed at development of good relations between native groups and colonial settlers: 1) the maintenance of peace between the British settlers and native groups in the colony, 2) agreement that tribesmen would become British subjects, 3) the providing of law and order in the maintenance of trade, 4) a promise to seek justice through the courts for aggrieved parties in the case of murder, 5) assurance that settlers would not encroach on Indian lands, 6) a commitment to ensuring rights of Indians and settlers were observed throughout the region, and 7) the setting of specific prices for several categories of common trade goods. These policies would undergo much modification but served as enduring, guiding principles in what was, for the majority of its existence, West Florida's paramount foreign relations concern.[14]

Local officials eagerly complied with measures meant to make trade function with minimal incident out of self-serving practicality if nothing else. Robert Farmar's instructions to his men at the onset of British administration embodied the spirit of equanimity authorities tried to encourage so as to avoid conflict: "Suffer no men under your command to abuse, ill treat, or

take any thing from . . . the Native Indians, but oblige them to pay a reason-
able price for what they want . . . You are to use your utmost endeavours to
cultivate, and preserve a good understanding with the Indians."[15]

The rules promulgated by colonial officials were agreed to in large congresses. In such conferences with the Choctaws, Chickasaws, and Creeks,
held in Mobile and Pensacola during West Florida's ownership by the British,
treaties of friendship were drafted which outlined the rules of exchange. During the deliberations, pledges of friendship were reaffirmed over luxuriant
feasts and gifts of goods, and Native Americans via interpreters were given
a chance to air grievances over such issues as trade terms and European
settlement. These elaborate productions, full of pomp and ceremony, could
last for weeks and might be attended by thousands. They were spectacles
to behold, especially for those citizens of the Empire new to the colonial
southeast who viewed the manners and customs of the area's indigenous
peoples as exotic. Warm welcomes and generous displays of hospitality were
not only common but expected, and the symbolic smoking of a calumet of
peace between native and European leaders was a highlight of the gatherings. "The dance of the Calumet, the peace Song, the brushing with Eagles
Tails, are the finest ceremonys I ever saw," wrote one of the few captivated
British military officers who recorded his observations of Native American
behavior at these gatherings. "I believe I have got more improvement by
keeping company with the Indians, than by any Company I have kept for
a great while."[16]

Negotiations could last for several days up to a few weeks, over the course
of which concerns of both parties might be broached gently after introduc-
tory jeremiads providing the context of the issue and assuring peaceful
intent. "Friendship between us," waxed a British speaker at a congress in
Pensacola in 1771, was "Like new fallen snow which had hardly whitened
the ground, that were united like the new Planted Vines, whose tendrils
had just Interwoven . . . if no accident happened, the Snow of Friendship
would be deep and cover all the Black Spots and the Interwoven Tendrils
would grow Strong Like Iron." However long they might dally in getting to
the point, in the end weighty issues were discussed and both sides made it
clear what they wanted in fair prices for trade and respect for the boundaries

between European communities and native hunting lands. The British often couched their words in condescending language attempting to mimic native oratorical style, assuring tribesmen that their king, the "great father," wanted the best for all of his "red" and "white" children alike and promising all their suggested measures were for the betterment of both peoples. Natives were unfooled by such imagery, but often played along by illustrating the points they wished to make within the paradigm set out by the European negotiators. Tomatly Mingo, for instance, a prominent Choctaw chief, is recorded as asserting at a congress that "it is true I am a poor red man who came into the world naked, and since my rising manhood have acquired no necessary arts to supply those wants; yet I am going to deliver my sentiments to my Father boldly as a man who does not regard trifling inconvenience."[17]

Elaborate demonstrations of changing international alliances manifested during these conferences in the form of the designation of "medal chiefs" among the Creek and Choctaw. These chiefs were recognized by the British as important contacts with whom issues concerning their respective tribes might be discussed. Any who had received such designation by the French, who began the practice among the native groups of the Gulf Coast, were asked to surrender the medals given prior in exchange for new ones bestowed by the British as demonstration of friendship and honor. The designation of medal chiefs provided the British a ready-made category of leaders in native societies with whom they could negotiate and in effect interposed a new hierarchy of critical contacts within each tribe. The system's effects on intratribal government is beyond our scope here, but the fact that the recognition of medal chiefs sometimes had more to do with expediency than actual rank only muddied the international waters in which the British attempted to establish their new colony.[18]

In return for British regulation of trade and pledges of friendship and aid, tribesmen usually agreed to live in peace with the colonists, to return any runaway slaves or deserting soldiers that might find their way into their villages, and offer up for punishment any Indian who might kill a white man. They also made certain cessions of land along the Gulf Coast for colonial settlement which proved critical to the success of the province. Indians generally understood these land agreements a little differently than their

European neighbors, viewing these first compacts in the vein of granting permission to use land rather than a formal transfer of communally owned property. In practical terms, it made little difference. During British administration of West Florida the Creeks yielded a swath of land along the eastern bank of the Alabama River north of Mobile, abandoned their claims to the islands in the Mobile-Tensaw Delta, and relinquished a strip of land fifteen miles wide surrounding Pensacola. The Choctaws ceded to the British those portions of their lands south of the 31st parallel as well as territory north and west of the junction of the Alabama and Tombigbee rivers.[19]

Not coincidentally, the territory granted the British happened to be on the fringes of Creek and Choctaw domain, in areas claimed by ancestral right as hunting grounds but not heavily populated and with no permanent villages. The Indians agreed to the cessions at least in part due to a sort of practicality: having Europeans who controlled access to prized trade goods beholden on some level was in their self-interest, especially if the ceded land was not, from the viewpoint of the tribe, especially valuable. The trouble was the British never seemed satisfied with what was given. Governor Chester in the 1770s, for example, complained to Superintendent Stuart that the Creeks had "given us nothing but Sands," and needed to be told that if they wished to continue to "come here frequently in great numbers, and expect to be supplied with Provisions and other Presents" then they "should furnish us with some proper Lands to grow them upon." The tribes would be pressed for more and more land in the region during British administration of West Florida, which they sometimes deflected by delay or complication in establishing who had the right to convey it, but rarely provocative refusal. But the British at this point were targeted in requests for territory, and the era of pressing native societies for wholesale divestiture of tribal lands in the Gulf South would not occur for another generation.[20]

THE BRITISH FOUND THAT no matter how thorough and well-meaning their regulations, they could not enforce law and order across the backcountry. Part of the problem lay in geography, as the traders operated in Indian villages far from the observation of British officials. There was an element of truth in the perception that traders operated outside the bounds of law and order due to their extended sojourns in the unregulated hinterlands; that played a key part in the categorization by some of traders as brigands. But the inability to police traders uniformly also had to do with the simple fact that they could be a rough and near-ungovernable set. While upstanding, educated men and a growing number of mixed-blood capitalists, who married into tribal communities or were the product of such unions and had a foot in both the native and the European colonial worlds, could be found among their numbers, the nature of the profession made it an attractive pursuit for the avaricious and unprincipled. A 1764 report by the British Board of Trade described traders then in the field as in general "the very worst and most abandoned set of men," and even one of their own contemporaries indicted his colleagues as "a monstrous Sett of Rogues for the major Part of whom the Gallows groans." Part of this unsavory reputation had to do with observations of their behavior in colonial towns, when, much like a prover-bial sailor on shore leave after an extended tour of duty, they appeared for a short time and, in the words of one historian, "celebrated with a bottle in one hand and a gun in the other." Fiercely independent and prideful, noisy and rowdy, and perpetually in pursuit of a profit, many came to be regarded as virtual transient outlaws.[21]

Even more damaging to the trade than their comportment in colonial towns, and by extension British attempts at maintaining order in the region, was their unscrupulous behavior towards the Indians with whom they dealt. As traders began to pour into the West Florida's extensive backcountry in the late 1760s and early 1770s, the inability of British authorities to enforce all the rules on licensing and pricing became obvious. Traders used false weights, peddled damaged or inferior merchandise at full price, watered down the rum and tafia they used to get their customers drunk to lubricate deals, used abusive language, and committed outrages such as plundering graves, attacking villagers, killing game, or seducing Indian men's wives. Government officials worried this litany of abuses might, in and of itself, lead to armed conflict.[22]

No aspect of the trade caused quite as much unrest within native so-cieties as the unregulated introduction of copious amounts of rum into their villages. Liquors had been a small part of Indian backcountry trade

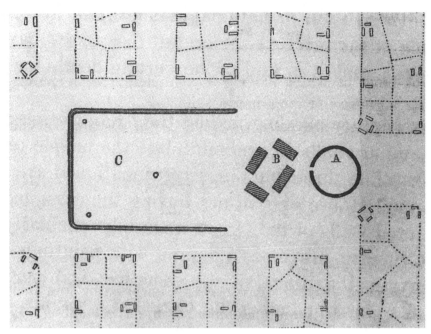

Depiction of the layout of a Creek town, by Ephraim G. Squier
(From "Observations on the Creek and Cherokee Indians,
1789," by William Bartram)

in years of French rule, but rum trafficking grew exponentially under the British. By 1770, Deputy Superintendent for Indian Affairs Charles Stuart estimated an astonishing eighty percent of trader purchases of deerskins in the southeastern backcountry were made with rum as a part of the deal. Alcohol seemingly brought out the worst in everyone involved in the trade, as traders found it easy to cheat intoxicated customers who in their haste to have a good time might exchange the work of weeks or months for a few days of frolic. A Choctaw chief summed up the situation in a complaint to British authorities pointedly blaming alcohol for a host of evils: "I am now to tell you the Cause of the disorder and Quarreling between us and our white men. It is rum. It pours in upon our nation Like a great Sea from Mobile and from all the Plantations and Settlements round about." Illustrating the massive quantity of alcohol traders introduced into Native American villages, one historian found that during a single ninety-day period, trading houses at Pensacola, second to Mobile as a distribution point for spirits, dispensed an astounding 30,000 gallons of rum.[23]

How to regulate renegade traders operating as veritable rum peddlers, who lived and worked far out of easy reach of colonial authorities and were a primary source of contention with native populations, proved an impossible task fraught with consequences for the security of the colony. The job drove every governor of the colony to distraction and led some officials to throw up their hands in exasperation at their tasks on occasion. The Deputy Superintendent for Indian Affairs, corresponding with the governor's office in the 1770s, penned his frustration with a system in which his department was inadequately staffed and funded to police individual traders, which put into words the sentiment: "it is by no means to be wondered at if anarchy prevails."[24]

JEALOUSIES AMONG TRIBES IN part exacerbated by access to trade and competing alliances with Europeans were another unfortunate by-product of the business. The era of British West Florida was as unsettled as any in Southeastern Indian country, and featured near-constant, small-scale fighting among the Creeks, Choctaws, and Chickasaws which often had little to do with their European neighbors. But the extensive system of international trade in some ways turned these traditional rivalries into arms races and wrought disorder which colonial authorities clumsily tried to manipulate. The history of intertribal diplomacy in the Southeast is another complex story in the region's history beyond our scope here, save to say that the attempts by the British to use allied native groups as shields against their own interests sometimes backfired. In the longstanding feud between the Creeks and the Choctaws, a relatively ancient animosity among neighboring tribes which occasionally broke out into violence and raged with particular ferocity in the 1760s and 1770s, the British attempted not so much to stop the fighting as to ensure that neither side grew strong enough to threaten them directly. British authorities were deeply concerned that the Spanish might make inroads among the native populations and somehow incite them to violence against West Florida. It gave a special urgency to the diplomatic efforts of British authorities as it regarded relations with Native Americans.

Governor Chester pointed out bluntly that the British must meet the needs of the Choctaws, Creeks, and Chickasaws "lest our neighbors should take the advantage of our neglect, and draw them over to their Interests."[25]

West Florida made efforts at befriending both, only to have the Creeks grow weary of their half-hearted friendship as many tribesmen came to believe the British were inciting the Choctaws to war on them in an effort to keep both tribes preoccupied and weakened. Scattered attacks on British citizens resulted, which of course soured the relationship between natives and colonial authorities and at times threatened to escalate into open warfare. Occasionally traders were slain when pent-up frustration at abuses coupled with weariness over intrusion into native lands bubbled to the surface. At other times settlers' isolated farms were destroyed and their inhabitants killed in unpredictable waves of violence that disrupted life in the colony out of all proportion to their scale. In the early 1770s in particular, several scattered instances of violence occurred in the West Florida backcountry in which Indians raided farms around Mobile Bay, Pensacola Bay, and the Pascagoula River. Native groups never made any organized, large-scale, attack on British interests, and there is no evidence they ever seriously planned to do so. But assaults of any size shook Europeans to the core, exposing deeply held fears about the dangers of attempting to live in a frontier region.[26]

In the end West Florida's development proceeded despite this Damoclesian sword of native unrest hanging over it, real or imagined. Few of the new colony's immigrants had illusions they were moving to anything but a borderland when they sought grants of arable acreage in its interior in the first place. Most likely would have regarded the continual, uneasy diplomacy with native groups as simply part and parcel of life in outposts of British North America such as West Florida. The colony might have been relatively unestablished, and it may have been on the very fringes of civilization as British colonists would have defined it, dependent to an alarming degree on the good deportment of willful traders operating out of sight, but the place still had an unmistakable allure.

4

Settlement

*'The soil appeared to me to be remarkably good, the
situation of the place delightful, the ease of transportation
of produce to market very apparent.'*

West Florida held great promise as a place where an agricultural society might thrive, there seemingly being something to recommend virtually every corner of the new colony. Pensacola claimed an excellent harbor and protected bay, viewed by many as the finest anchorage on the gulf. Mobile occupied a strategic position at the mouth of one of the largest systems of navigable rivers on the continent. The well-watered interior of the colony featured areas of fertile soil, forests chock-full of prime timber, and thousands of acres of ideal pasturage, all teeming with stupendous herds and flocks of game animals and abundant fish. Anyone willing to make the effort, it seemed, could scarcely find a location more conducive to living off the land.

British authorities encouraged settlement of the new colony through the granting of tracts of this promising land. With the exception of a relatively small amount of town lots set aside for development of planned urban communities, a trifling amount of acres reserved by the king for military installations, and, in the off chance valuable materials were discovered in the territory, a few mineral reserves, officials threw practically the entirety of West Florida open to settlers by dangling the lure of free land with minimal fees or entanglements. With the sanction of the king, the governor and council (and even on occasion the king himself) distributed hundreds of thousands of acres in West Florida to prospective settlers—overwhelmingly white Protestant farmers—on generous terms. Local grants could be obtained on the promise to settle and improve within ten years of the transaction on the basis of what was known as a headright system. In basic terms, the "family right" provisions of the plan stipulated that every head of household requesting to settle in the colony qualified for receiving up to 100 acres; each dependent actually brought into the province—male or female, slave or free—warranted an additional fifty acres. If a family could demonstrate their ability to cultivate it, even more land might be obtained

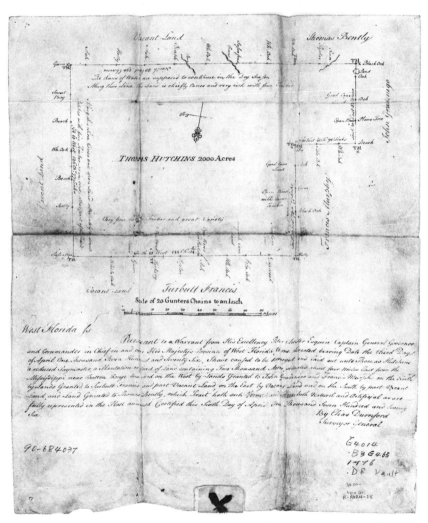

Land grant issued to Thomas Hutchins (Library of Congress)

through a "purchase right" by paying a modest additional fee for every fifty acres so obtained. Veterans of the French and Indian War were eligible for certain numbers of acres according to their rank; officers up to 5,000 acres, and so on, with privates qualifying for fifty-acre tracts on the strength of their service. Grants were to contain profitable and unprofitable lands in proportion, and restrictions on river frontage were outlined. Land deemed barren could be granted on the condition it served as grazing grounds for cattle. With the exception of a brief halt in distribution of grants per authorities in London in 1773, sparked by government efforts to get better control of colonial affairs in America, the grant system as originally devised persisted as the primary vehicle for development of the province throughout British tenure.[1]

Obtaining a grant, though, could be a lengthy process involving a mountain of paperwork and an assortment of small fees. Applicants began by making a request and a demonstration of their eligibility for review by the council. The process could take months to work its way through the cumbersome colonial administrative system, the epicenter being the office of the provincial secretary in Pensacola. Once a grant had been given, the governor issued a warrant to show approval of the petition and had dockets placed in the offices of the registrar and auditor to show the tract had been claimed. New grants were supposed to be surveyed within six months of allocation and a patent registered, which involved a small fee. The processing of all the required paperwork was complicated by the persistent shortage of patent officers, leading to frustrating delays and backlogs of applications.[2]

By the 1770s securing a typical medium-sized land grant in West Florida might involve some seventeen fees payable to various government offices. Most grants required payment of a modest quit-rent (at first of two shillings per 100 acres but later changed to a half penny per acre to offset administrative costs), due within a number of years of the grant. This was not a rent of the type we are familiar with today, but rather a commutation of several recurring fees into a single, simple payment for services rendered by the government for orchestrating the distribution and recording of land. Most landholders were required to begin payments of these quit-rents within two years of acceptance of the property, but military veterans who had distinguished themselves in war enjoyed the privilege of postponing payments for up to a decade. Mandamus grants, or those issued at the discretion of the Privy Council, were exempted from quit-rents for a period of five years. All these exemptions and delayed payments effectively meant that the government of West Florida by design collected little if anything in quit-rents on the land it disbursed. In his study of the inner workings of the colony, a leading historian of the era could find no proof these quit-rents were regularly paid, and forfeiture was extraordinarily rare. With hundreds of thousands of acres at their disposal and a sparsely populated province to develop, British authorities proved generous in utilizing the one resource they had in plenty—land—to promote the settlement of West Florida.[3]

Government officials intended the land-grant system to create a class of small farmers and merchants which would underpin the building up of a self-sufficient colonial society. Out of practicality, not philosophy, then, did they discourage the establishment of large plantations in which thousands of acres might be concentrated in the hands of the wealthy. Large absentee owners holding their lands for purely speculative purposes would do nothing to promote economic growth. Still, authorities did look the other way as some expansive swaths of land, with only a fraction of their acreage developed, were conveyed outside the official rules, for obvious personal gain to influential individuals. Between 1764 and 1777, in an overt bypass of customary petitions procedures, some forty-five orders in council were issued for land in West Florida totaling more than 350,000 acres. The smallest deeded a handsome 2,000-acre spread while the largest bequeathed a princely 25,000-acre estate.[4]

Distributing land did not necessarily correspond to rapid settlement. By informed estimates, as few as one in six proprietors of land in the colony made a serious attempt to settle and cultivate their grants during British administration. While some of this slow pace of settlement can be chalked up to immigrants' difficulties in making a major cross-country move, a certain amount seems due to the under-the-table land dealings with wealthy speculators. In a notable example of how the system could be manipulated, the wives of the governor, lieutenant governor, and four councilors each were awarded 1,000 acres, separate from the larger grants given their husbands.

In fairness, the king did make extraordinarily large grants of 10,000 or 20,000 acres on rare occasions, which accounted for a portion of the land conveyed to wealthy but usually absentee owners. The Earl of Eglinton and Samuel Hannay (colonial agent in London) received tracts of twenty thousand and five thousand acres respectively along the Mississippi directly from the crown, and Lord Ellibank and Count Bentinck each were handed title to tracts of more than 10,000 acres near Pensacola. But most of the insider trading took place under local administration. Montfort Browne, for example, at one point attempted to transfer to his brother title to the entirety of Dauphin Island, to which he laid contested claim as an alleged site for settlement of immigrants.[5]

These were the exceptions, however, and by far most grants were of more modest size and obtained by family groups. Records of grants distributed in the colony's registers reveal the conveyance of numerous grants of 500 and 1,000 acres and many of 400, 250, 100, and even a few for as little as fifty acres throughout British tenure. It would be on these plots that the hearty souls who settled the province would begin their lives in West Florida.[6]

THE BRITISH PROMOTED SETTLEMENT by touting the new colony in newspapers, magazines, pamphlets, and books as a wonderland of fertile soil, mild climate, and abundant rivers. In one of the first such glowing descriptions, written by none other than Governor George Johnstone shortly after his arrival in the province, the potential for a flourishing economy in a region blessed with a healthful climate was a clear theme. "The soil is rich," Johnstone promised, "capable of producing wine, oil, silk, indigo, tobacco, rice, and all the fruits of southern climates, together with those of more northern latitudes, even on the sea coast." It had bountiful stands of timber, "live oaks, cedar, pines of the best kind cover the banks of every river and bay," which he portrayed as all "full of the best and most delicious kinds of fish . . . groupers, snappers, brim, and cod." Others seconded this assessment of the bounty. "The sea fish . . . are in such innumerable quantities as exceed even imagination," wrote Governor Chester. The colony, in Johnstone's estimation, enjoyed a "peculiar situation . . . its numerous bays and very commodious harbours, shut out from every wind, will facilitate that commerce which its advantageous situation seems naturally to form for it in a degree superior to any other of our colonies."[7]

Such extolling of the virtues of West Florida's geographical setting by colonial officials would become a familiar refrain. In one of the most widely circulated and officially sanctioned descriptions of the region, for example, Captain Philip Pittman's *The Present State of the European Settlements on the Mississippi* (1770), the area was characterized as ideal for immigration and a sort of agricultural utopia. Promotional tracts such as these were often all potential immigrants had to go on about the land and its possibilities, short of venturing there to evaluate it in person. Some degree of truth lay in all of these embellished descriptions, but they failed to mention that the region also experienced long periods of extreme heat and humidity, lay subject to ravaging hurricanes and tornadoes, could be plagued by hordes of insects, and that among its strips of arable land were long stretches of sandy barrens and swamps. Plus, while West Florida did enjoy a long growing season, frigid temperatures in its customarily cool and wet winters could kill fruit trees and crops even along coastal areas. Even stoic Lieutenant General Frederick Haldimand, who had seen service across the globe before he arrived in Pensacola, warned the climate might be too much to bear. He described sweltering summer conditions which made him "yearn for the ice of Canada." In a classic understatement which belied his frustration, he wrote in private correspondence that Pensacola's charm "has been exaggerated like all the other advantages of this province."[8]

The majority of immigrants to West Florida who were drawn by these real or imagined lures were enterprising people of modest means looking for a new start in this far-flung addition to the British Empire. Most made their living from the soil and found their way to the Gulf Coast province while fleeing economic hardship elsewhere, drawn by its abundance of inexpensive agricultural land. "West Florida," in the words of one of the leading historians of colonial America, "attracted American settlers used to frontier hardships." A majority hailed from other British colonies along the Atlantic seaboard. These migrants ordinarily made their way to the Gulf Coast overland or by following one of the many rivers which drained into the Gulf, but some arrived via ship sailing into the Gulf of Mexico, usually at Pensacola or Mobile.

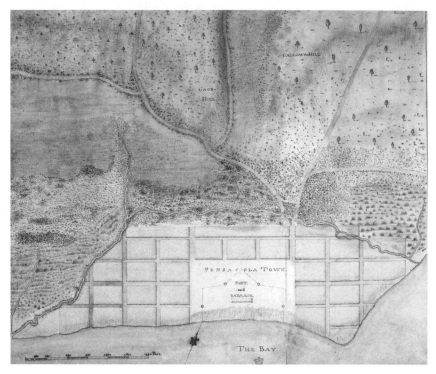

*Map of Pensacola, 1774 (Norman B. Leventhal Map
and Education Center at the Boston Public Library)*

A sizable minority came directly from the British Isles, especially Scotland, where deteriorating economic conditions and lack of opportunities drove many to consider a risky transatlantic migration to a region about which they had little knowledge. In smaller numbers, immigrants from Caribbean colonies such as Jamaica, the Bahamas, St. Vincent, Antigua, and other islands arrived at the Gulf ports of Pensacola and Mobile in perhaps less desperate straits but likewise seeking a chance to make their fortunes. Even a few Germans were in the mix, primarily wealthier individuals from the thriving "German Coast" along the Mississippi who had some experience in the operation of large plantations and were looking to expand their holdings. Governor Johnstone had also lobbied to recruit disenchanted Norwegian, Dutch, and New Englander populations, which he believed to have their own particular set of frustrations in their current homes.[9]

Some Irish and French indentured servants hoped to flee grinding poverty in their homelands by exchanging several years of hard labor for the chance for a new start. Others, such as the French Huguenots who settled Campbell Town, the government-subsidized community near Pensacola, came to escape religious persecution. At least a few Jewish merchants and traders are documented to have been living in the colony by the late 1760s, as well. All were welcomed by the colonial government to further the "speedy settling and peopling of this Province" so long as they swore allegiance to the British crown. With this diverse mixture of people seeking opportunity—the desperate and the oppressed, the poor and the disadvantaged, the financially stable but restless, and a smattering of the relatively wealthy—West Florida entered life as one of Britain's North American colonies.[10]

IRONICALLY, THE FIRST MASS movement of people within the new colony had been an exodus. Some of the smaller tribes in the region, especially the "petites nations" the French had so relied upon in their administration of the Mobile area, migrated west into Spanish Louisiana. The Apalache, for example, who had relocated to the Mobile Bay area shortly after the founding of the French colony and had been their staunch allies for decades, moved across the Mississippi and settled along the Red River rather than become subject to British authority. A few other groups followed, including bands of Choctaw, Alabama, Taensas, Biloxis, and Pascagoulas. But in general, the larger native groups which controlled the bulk of the territory within and adjacent to the boundaries of the new British province, the Creeks and the Choctaws, stayed in place and watched with apprehension as officials attempted to lure settlers into portions of their ancestral lands.[11]

While we might recognize them as pioneers today, West Florida officials could sometimes describe the first wave of immigrants to their colony in less than flattering terms. In a report on the potential of the colony Elias Durnford warned of the "ungovernable spirit of these new settlers . . . without education, without religion or principles fit for the bond of society." Governor George Johnstone, if anything, gave an even less generous description to the newcomers which were to build the new colony into a thriving part of the Empire, derisively categorizing many of the immigrants as "the refuse

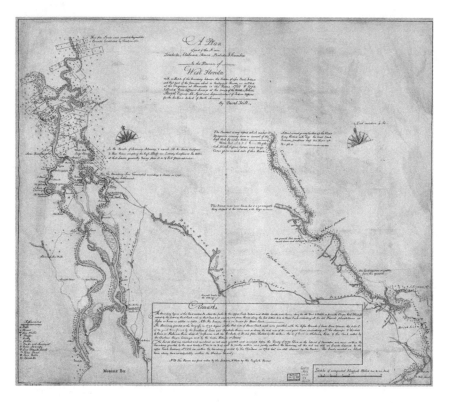

**A Plan of Part of the River Tombecbe, Alabama, Tensa, Perdido &
Scambia *by David Taitt, 1771, showing the location of settlements*
(*Library of Congress*)**

of the Jails of great Citys (sic) and the overflowing Scum of the Empire."
Although they were reluctant to acknowledge the fact, there was some
truth to the rumors that female convicts and prostitutes had been shipped
to the new colony and represented a larger portion of the population than
in some other places.[12]

The first immigrants arriving after the establishment of the colony
tended to settle in or near Pensacola and Mobile. These somewhat small
but established towns were the colony's original administrative centers and
their location along its two finest Gulf ports made them obvious choices for
the farmers and traders moving to the unfamiliar area and hoping to find
an economic environment conducive to success. In the environs of Mobile

Bay—stretching from its namesake city up to the junction of the Alabama and Tombigbee rivers—settlers formed several small communities along and within the Mobile-Tensaw Delta. A few French farms had been scattered along the lower reaches of the Delta prior to it falling under the purview of the British, but by the terms of a 1765 agreement the Choctaws and the Creeks gave permission for settlers to move into the area which had been a peripheral border region of the tribes' respective domains. Soon a cluster of farms were in operation along the rivers north of Mobile, most run by families of modest means. Among them a few true plantations operated in similar fashion if not scale to those at the height of the later antebellum era. Settlement also occurred below Mobile and along the Eastern Shore, as during the British period homesteads popped up along the Dog River and Mon Louis Island and small settlements were established in what are today Montrose, Daphne, and Spanish Fort.[13]

The largest number of land grants in terms of sheer volume if not acreage were made in the vicinity of Pensacola, which early on experienced the fastest growth of all West Florida communities. As the lands around the town tended to be less fertile than those in the Mobile area and the rivers of the region smaller and less alluring for trade, settlement there became much more concentrated in the city itself. Prior to 1770, few other regions of European settlement more developed than an occasional isolated trading house existed in West Florida. Along what is today the Mississippi Gulf Coast stood a few scattered homesteads, the bulk of which were concentrated along the Pascagoula River and traced their roots to the days of the administration of the French. To the west, running along the length of the colony's western border of the Mississippi River, could likewise be found a few isolated riverside farmsteads. Small clusters of rude log cabin homes dotted the rural landscape at lengthy intervals at such places as Walnut Hills, and aside the Big Black River, Bayou Pierre, as well as at Grand Gulf and Petit Gulf.[14]

By the early 1770s, the colony's population distribution began a dramatic change as settlers en masse discovered the rich lands along the Mississippi. Compared to the region's unproductive sandy coast, trackless briar-choked thickets, endless expanses of longleaf plains, and copious

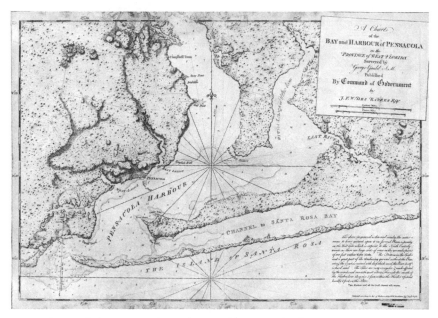

A Chart of the Bay and Harbour of Pensacola, by J. F .W. Des Barres,
1780, by George Gauld (Library of Congress)

swampy bottomlands, the rich lands of the lower Mississippi Valley rang
with a lustrous siren call. Fertile, temperate, and adjacent to an enormous
waterway draining half the continent, West Florida's western extremity
began to transition from a rough and tumble military outpost into the type
of province authorities had envisioned.[15]

Local officials touted the Mississippi Valley as a cure to lagging interest
in settlement of the colony. On an exploratory visit in 1768, Lieutenant
Governor Montfort Browne extolled its rich black soil, beautiful rolling
hills, easy river access, and abundant wildlife, praising it as possessing "the
most charming prospect in the world" and declaring he would "be happy to
spend the remainder of my days in this most delightful country." Browne had
his reasons for such effusive praise. He genuinely believed in the prospects
for the region but might have also hoped to wield the area's desirability into
a future new colony. He published in 1772 a four-page pamphlet entitled
"Reasons for the Immediate Establishment of a Civil Government in the
British Dominions Adjoining to the River Mississippi in North America."

Whatever his motivations, he put his money where his mouth was and along with several other West Florida officials sought some of the largest grants of land along the Mississippi. Others were equally smitten. "The climate on the banks of the Mississippi is healthy, the lands exceeding fertile, and produce great quantities of timber fit for ship building, and making of different kinds of lumber," gushed Governor Peter Chester. "No soil is more proper for the cultivation of rice, indigo, hemp and corn. The navigation for vessels is very easy and practicable down the Mississippi, so that the produce of the country may with great facility be exported to Great Britain by which the inhabitants would be enabled to take in return the manufactures of the Mother country to supply their own consumption and the Indian trade." Another observer exulted that "the land here is vastly rich and if cultivated with Industry wou'd produce every Thing desirable."[16]

While many at first believed the area just north of Mobile, in the rolling hills and lush valleys drained by the broad lower reaches of the Alabama and Tombigbee, held great promise as a potential breadbasket for the colony, it would be the land farther westward which stirred British souls. Then-Lieutenant Governor Elias Durnford in 1774 wrote "A Description of West Florida" for the Earl of Dartmouth, Secretary of State for American Affairs, describing in the western section of the colony abundant herds and flocks of wild animals including bear, deer, turkey, geese, ducks, and land suitable for growing indigo, tobacco, rice, cotton, hemp, flax, pulse, oranges, figs, peaches, pomegranates, mulberry, pears, and apples, as well as the keeping of cattle, sheep, and hogs. Governor Chester likewise bragged to authorities in London of that region's copious wildlife: "Bear, Deer and wild Fowl are plenty . . . fine Fish of various kinds . . ." Durnford's findings paralleled those of early immigrants, who were enchanted with the teeming animal life in the colony with its "sky swarming with Flocks of Wild Geese and other Water Fowl." Some of these accounts describe species of fauna which are long vanished or nearly so from the region, such as buffalo, wolves, mountain lions, and Carolina parakeets. One observer on the Mississippi, for example, commented on how the noisy flocks of "perroquets are in great abundance, and they feed upon the Shumach Berries." A veritable land of plenty, the west became the only region of

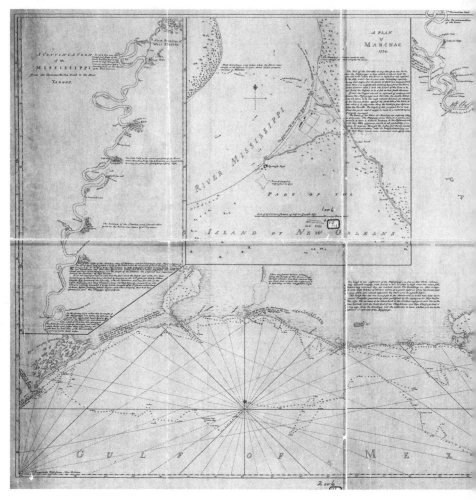

A Plan of the Coast of Part of West Florida & Louisiana as surveyed
by George Gauld, 1778 (*Library of Congress*)

the colony to experience a true immigrant influx during its years under
British dominion.[17]

RELATIVE WAVES OF SETTLERS, at least compared to the sluggish growth
in other sections of the colony, soon began arriving. They in large measure
verified Browne's exuberance and then some, delighting in the beauty and
bounty of the country. One early settler described the colony's western lands

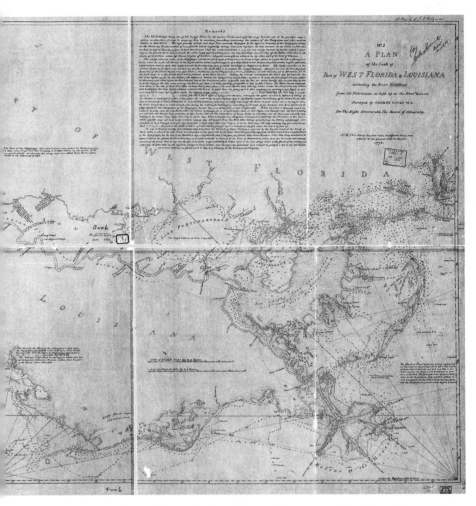

as "the most fertile, beautiful, healthy and variegated lands in this province, or perhaps in the whole continent of America." Between August 1770 and November 1773 alone, more than ninety percent of the nearly one million acres of land grants the West Florida colonial government recorded lay along the Mississippi or its tributaries. By 1774, the colonial government saw the necessity for appointing justices of the peace in the growing area and restructured the representation in the General Assembly to recognize the area's rise. This land rush did not necessarily correspond to the population boom officials hoped, however. During one of the busiest three-year periods of West Florida's Mississippi Valley settlement, 1773–1775, it is estimated just over 400 families settled along the colony's western border. The Natchez District became the centerpiece of this western migration. A triangular-shaped tract of territory bordered on the west by the Mississippi and stretching diagonally from a narrow strip at the "Walnut Hills"—modern Vicksburg—southward to a forty-mile-wide swath along the border with Spanish Louisiana, the district by the mid-1770s contained several small European settlements in addition to its namesake community of Natchez.[18]

West Florida's emigrants often arrived in family and community groups, as they banded together for protection and camaraderie on the long journey to new lives on an undeveloped frontier. The undertaking could be quite hazardous, especially if an overland trek was attempted through the uncharted wilderness where the only things approximating roads were traders' paths. Unbridged streams and rivers had to be crossed, a host of sometimes dangerous wild animals roamed, disease and sickness daily stalked, and potentially aggressive Indians lurked in a wilderness where travelers were "warn'd of the approach of Day by the Hooping of Owls." Cross-country travel could be uncomfortable with privations and difficulties as immigrants slept in the elements and frequently endured meager monotonous diets along the route and well into the first year of settlement before initial crops matured. An observer of the westward immigrants wrote with disillusion in 1770 how he witnessed new arrivals "subsist chiefly on venison, buffalo and game which they kill . . . they are with their wives and children destitute of almost every thing." Groups of families made the trip to West Florida from not only Georgia and the Carolinas but as far away as Virginia, New Jersey, Pennsylvania, and Connecticut. The grand adventure of moving to this new land was an experience none would ever forget and likely was retold around dinner tables for generations. As few would make such a perilous cross-country trip again, immigrations were landmark events that represented a complete separation from all the settlers had known and a bold new start in a new world.[19]

Family and neighborhood groups were often preceded by an individual or small party of close friends or family members who sought out and scouted grants of settlement land before returning home to help organize the venture for the rest. The Truly and Holt families, comprised of the widow

Sarah Holt Truly and six of her children along with her two brothers and their families, for example, moved from Tidewater Virginia to Natchez in the early 1770s. The Holt brothers made two scouting trips to the region before finding the right spot and returning with the rest of the family. They loaded up all their belongings and set out with their few slaves overland across Virginia to the Cumberland Gap and then down the Ohio River to the Mississippi, where they journeyed southward to Natchez and began new lives in West Florida. Such caravans of settlers could be quite large. Daniel Huay of Connecticut, for example, guided nearly a hundred people from Pennsylvania to the Natchez region in the 1770s, and Congregational Church minister Samuel Swayze helped lead an equally large group from New Jersey to a 25,000-acre tract in the Natchez District in 1773. The land Swayze sought out, like so many tracts settled in the district, originally had been granted to French and Indian War veteran Amos Ogden. He sold most of his land to brothers Samuel and Richard Swayze. After arrival, the settlers formed an agricultural community which became known locally as the "Jersey Settlement," one of several clusters of farmsteads which lent the region a rare degree of cohesiveness in an otherwise sparsely settled frontier.[20]

Also in the Natchez area, in an example of another migration pattern, Anthony Hutchins helped families from Virginia and North Carolina obtain then settle on a grant of thousands of acres. Hutchins himself had arrived in the territory in the company of a small caravan traveling overland from the Carolinas in 1773, and his story is in some ways a microcosm of the West Florida immigrant experience. "Having the prospect of a large family with but a slender support," he remembered later, he like so many others had "determined to try his fortune in a new country." He first journeyed to the region the year prior to seek out a piece of land to purchase, which he located with the assistance of a local Indian. He returned with his entire family and slaves soon thereafter, their possessions packed into wagons pulled by his horses while his cattle walked behind. Neighboring families joined them on the trek, a grueling three-month slog through the southeastern backcountry during which they made nightly camps and in large part subsisted on provisions brought with them such as beans, corn, and barreled pork. The only fresh food they might have obtained would have come through hunting and fishing or perhaps the slaughter of some of the cattle that made the journey with them.[21]

No shining city greeted them on arrival at Natchez to mark the end of their wilderness trek, as what would soon become a thriving town was still a slapdash village surrounded by "a wilderness ... where the buffalo, the bear, the panther and the wolf had their hiding places ..." Bread and butter, among the basics of life back east, were luxuries on this frontier. Instead, during their first year along the Mississippi as they attempted to grow their initial crops they survived, according to Hutchins, on "Indian potatoes which after being boiled were mashed and minced in about equal parts with dried and pounded venison and baked on a board ... sometimes a little bear oil was mixed with it." There were few markets where necessities such as clothing could be purchased, and precious little money to make the transaction even had they presented themselves. So Hutchins's group made their own clothes with cotton they grew themselves. They hunted, fished, gathered wild fruits, and would have even looked to the woods for herbal medicines. As if these struggles and inconveniences were not enough, they had to guard against the occasional raid on their crops and livestock by sometimes equally desperate area Indians. The settlers' was a precarious life of both privation and determination, but it was typical of the experiences of West Florida's immigrants.[22]

PERHAPS NO GROUP IMMIGRATION scheme to West Florida involved more land, people, and greater distance than that spearheaded by Phineas Lyman of Connecticut. A veteran of the French and Indian War who along with hundreds of Connecticut troops had participated in the siege of Havana, Lyman lobbied British officials to grant him and his compatriots an enormous tract of land—a veritable colony unto itself—as a reward for their service. In furtherance of this goal, he organized the "Company of Military Adventurers," comprised of colonial military veterans from New England like himself, as a lobbying organization. The group elected Lyman as president along with other officers. The scheme involved dozens of families, none more prominent than that of Israel Putnam, who had already seen service in both the French and Indian War and in campaigning during Pontiac's

Rebellion; he would become a celebrated national hero for his actions at the Battle of Bunker Hill a few years later. Lyman's group pushed hard for land in the new colony of West Florida and showed particular interest in the lush Mississippi River region to which so many other settlers were then flocking. He first requested some 150,000 acres and at length secured more than 20,000 acres in the western extremity of the colony in the vicinity of where Bayou Pierre met the waters of the Big Black River. Converting that promise in official terms into something for the group and determining its location and actually settling it proved much more complex than anyone originally thought.[23]

The Adventurers got to work in short order. In late 1772, the group sent a party to the Mississippi Valley to scout the region. Upon landing in Pensacola in 1773 to meet with local colonial officials, the scouts were notified the council did not have clear authority to convey the lands believed given to Lyman. However, desirous of receiving settlers such as the New England group into the struggling colony, the council persuaded Governor Peter Chester to allow the party to explore the area on which they hoped to settle and report back in hopes some clarity on the situation might be gained in the interim. Satisfied with this course of action, the scouting party ventured westward and explored a stretch of the colony's western border. They found the region around the Big Black River and the Walnut Hills especially intriguing, but were alarmed to discover numerous squatter homesteads scattered throughout the area on some of the choicest tracts of land. They also were disillusioned by the disposition of the local Choctaws, who expressed their great surprise at the purported purpose of the group. Returning to Pensacola, the party discovered no official word from London had yet clarified the terms of their grant. Local officials nonetheless agreed to temporarily reserve thousands of legally unclaimed acres along the Mississippi, while waiting on notification from the British government on how to proceed. Meanwhile, the frustrated but patient company scouts returned to Connecticut to await official word from West Florida's government.[24]

The scheme never materialized as planned, as a crown-sanctioned grant never arrived, and many members of the group lost interest over time. A few hundred settlers did trickle in to the region and settle on the lands originally granted Lyman, some who later abandoned the colonization effort after remaining in limbo for an extended period. Lyman and members of his extended family did attempt settling the area, bringing his wife, children, and several slaves from his Suffield, Connecticut home to the banks of the Mississippi above Natchez. There Lyman would die in 1775, preceded to the grave by a son and followed shortly after by his widow as she attempted a forlorn journey back home. The sad, drawn-out saga illustrates the sometimes cumbersome bureaucracy that attempted to administer land distribution in the vast hinterlands of the colony and how it stood about as far removed from the cognizance of London officials in heart and mind as perhaps any place in the Empire. It also alludes to the tragedy and failure of the long move west for many.[25]

The tragic experience of a member of one of Lyman's Military Adventurers, Mathew Phelps, illustrates this last point in dramatic fashion. Phelps had determined to move west from his native Connecticut after hearing "much talk about the goodness of the country near the Mississippi." In 1773 he journeyed by ship down the east coast and into the Gulf as part of the company's scouting group to inspect the land for himself with an eye towards a spot for his family to settle. Immediately after exploring the land around the Big Black River, which empties into the Mississippi between the modern Vicksburg and Natchez, he became sure of his "determination to remove thither . . . The soil appeared to me to be remarkably good, the situation of the place delightful, the ease of transportation of produce to market very apparent." Having befriended a local resident during his explorations in the area, Phelps paid him a small sum to secure title to a tract of land and hold it until he could return with his family. Phelps soon became well acquainted with the colony's reputation for unhealthiness, being laid low for four days during his travel back downriver to New Orleans on the first leg of his return voyage.[26]

In late summer 1774 he returned with his wife and children in the company of two other families, just as, in his words, "the quarrel between Great Britain and the American colonies began to approach a serious crisis." No sooner had they entered West Florida than several members of the group, including Phelps, his wife, daughter, and youngest son, became very sick with an "exceedingly severe" fever. They made camp and suspended travel. His daughter, Abigail, promptly died from the illness, leaving the grieving father "to inter her remains the next day, with my own hands, as decently as I could." Only a week later his son also died, and Phelps had to bury him alongside his sister. The grief-stricken caravan, after consoling one another, pressed on aboard small boats despite being "worn to a skeleton by sickness and uncommon fatigue." By November the group had reached Petit Gulf but could go no further as illness continued to stalk them. The other family continued on while Phelps stopped to nurse his wife, who was far too ill to continue the grueling journey. Phelps recorded touchingly that "the dear companion of my early joys, the partner of my choice, and gentle soother of my anxious care, was now apparently approaching swiftly to her disso-lution." She died days later near the plantation of a Mr. Alston, where she was buried.[27]

Dispirited but with no real home to return to, Phelps pressed on to-wards the tract of land he had eyed the year previous with his two surviv-ing children, a ten-year-old girl and a six-year-old boy. Along the journey upriver they were joined by another traveler heading the same direction. The group had the misfortune to encounter one of the Mississippi's infamous whirlpools. Their boat upturned and while the adults swam for the shore, the children became hopelessly trapped in the swirling torrent. Phelps at-tempted a daring rescue by clinging to a riverside sapling, but it collapsed into the river under his weight and he was forced to watch helplessly as his "lovely babes sank both together to the shades of death." Devastated and inconsolable, Phelps recorded in the memoir he composed later that "the whole appeared to me like a most horrid terrifying dream." When he finally arrived at the Big Black River, stunned and careworn, he found title to the land he had entrusted the settler to secure had been forfeited and another family occupied it. It seemed a fitting end to his tribulations. A Mr. John Storrs living nearby, however, perhaps taking pity on the weary man, gave him a small bit of acreage along with a few cattle, hogs, a horse, and farming implements to help him get a start in this new land. Phelps would stay in the area for several years but returned to his native Connecticut after the takeover of the region by the Spanish at the end of Revolutionary War. He eventually remarried and started a new family, but he likely wrestled with the demons of his West Florida experience the rest of his life. Not everyone faced the trials that Phelps did in attempting to settle in the colony, but his story is a poignant reminder that immigration was much more complicated than a simple change of address.[28]

FOR FEW COULD THE journey to a new home in West Florida have been more traumatic than the many slaves forced along the journey by owners or sold into service in the colony from other regions. Land distribution policy at the time incentivized slave importation, as the more bondsmen one could claim, the more land the grantee qualified for under government regulations. While few planters in the Revolutionary era claimed as many bondsmen as the large-scale slave drivers would in the antebellum era, a large number of immigrant groups were accompanied by small groups of enslaved individuals about which we know almost nothing. They would have shared in the trials of the journey and then some, as they commonly would have been expected to help maintain wagons, provide forage for horses, and help drive cattle. We can only imagine their thoughts at the prospect of being brought to an unimproved section of wilderness where grueling labor in clearing a farm and establishing a home awaited; many had surely heard rumors of the unhealthiness of this western land or had watched as members of the white families they labored for, or some among their own number, sank in sickness in the unforgiving climate. An unknown but perhaps equal number of slaves were transported to the colony from points west under the auspices of dealers operating illicitly from their bases in Spanish Louisiana. These served as one of the best and easiest markets for slaves in the new colony. Other enslaved persons arrived in West Florida at the ports of Mobile and Pensacola or along the banks of the Mississippi aboard merchant ships from other British colonies or the Caribbean; they were sold as any other commodity. It is unknown exactly how many slaves arrived in West Florida directly from Africa, but it is believed to have been a distinct minority. Throughout West Florida's time as a part of the British Empire, enslaved people comprised about a third of its population.[29]

Even with all the migratory activity described above, the population of

West Florida remained relatively small and scattered throughout the tenure of the British. At the time of its formation, the colony contained as few as 2,000 non-Indian residents, a large percentage of them military personnel and government officials and an assortment of various contractors. Due to the overall slow pace of immigration, and a steady trickle of departures, by the late 1760s its population had barely grown. By the end of the decade, perhaps only 3,000 or so British subjects called it home. While estimates are impossible to verify, by the mid-1770s, after the first substantial wave of immigration, officials believed there were nearly 5,000 residents in the province. The population peaked during the years of the American Revolution, when a number of loyalists found their way to the Gulf Coast seeking asylum from persecution elsewhere. In 1779 West Florida claimed a population of perhaps 6,000. A little more than half of West Florida's residents lived in the Natchez region by 1780, with the remainder scattered throughout the rest of the vast expanse of the colony. Whether they lived along the dirt streets of the colony's small towns, in cabins perched along riverside bluffs, or in isolated homesteads hidden deep in the murky half-light of the region's subtropical forests, West Floridians were linked by the common bond of a shared struggle to earn a living in their provincial home.[30]

5

Daily Life

'The most disagreeable and unhealthy place in America'

"**N**o country, perhaps, on the face of the earth," touted one early glowing description of West Florida published in a London magazine, "possesses so pure, serene, and temperate sky, visited with the agreeable vicissitudes of seasons, but none of them extreme." Emigrants to the new colony, however, often found that West Florida's subtropical climate could be far from as mild as they might have been led to believe by such literature. While the settlers found the sanguine autumns, featuring an extended period of pleasant weather, and the quick arrival of spring, providing a long growing season, to be serene qualities, they were less enamored with the long summers. Brutally hot and humid for interminable weeks, it could seem as if West Florida was, in the words of one resident, nothing less than a "great oven." Naturalist Bernard Romans, who visited the area in the 1760s and wrote about his experiences in the landmark publication, *A Concise Natural History of East and West Florida*, was astounded by the sheer heat of the Gulf Coast summer and included comments about its deleterious effects on the human body. He described with incredulity temperatures "so burning hot, that undoubtedly very sudden rarefactions of the humours are often experienced . . ." Romans reasoned that the "abundant perspiration" which resulted from the heat to be the blame for resulting health issues, noting that "water, as soon as drank, penetrates the open pores, so that the human skin seems to be comparable to a wet spunge when squeezed." One did not tolerate the heat so much as survive it.[1]

But other aspects of the natural environment must be taken into consideration to have any real understanding of daily life in the colony. The place was plagued by mosquitoes and all other manner of worrisome biting and stinging insects for most of the year, and drenching rains and sudden severe storms could pour through makeshift roofs and make town streets and wilderness roads all but impassable. The threat of hurricanes, then as now, was a yearly concern, but with no advanced warning system such as exists today, even smaller storms could be surprising and devastating. Winters were rarely severe, but there could be frigid spells that shocked the system of even those from colder climes. But physical discomfort was only part of the challenge of living in the new province, for it could be a sickly, even deadly, place.[2]

Dangerous communicable diseases plagued the new colonists, making life at times miserable for many and sending—owing to the then-primitive state of medical knowledge—an alarming portion of the population to an early grave. West Florida had a protracted "sickly season" from late spring to early fall when fevers and a variety of other maladies spread easily. With what were described as "bilious, putrid, nervous, and malignant fevers" stalking residents and a panoply of other unpleasant sicknesses such as dysentery, scurvy, dropsy, typhoid, typhus, consumption, asthma, malaria, pneumonia, smallpox, venereal diseases, and yellow fever carrying off lives with startling regularity, West Florida acquired a reputation as "a grave-yard for Britons." The place was decried as "good for nothing but destroying Englishmen" declared one despairing observer, while another termed it simply "the most disagreeable and unhealthy place in America."[3]

Records of the time reveal residents at a loss to even name some of the terrible illnesses that claimed lives with brutal efficiency, describing the cause of death sometimes in more descriptive than clinical fashion: "fits," "nervous fever," "worm fever," and "decay." A register of births and burials in 1770 gives as the cause of certain deaths "flux," "consumption," "black scurvy," and "excessive drinking." That women survived pregnancy and childbirth at all given the crude state of medical practice and the frontier conditions—even the wife of the lieutenant governor reputedly gave birth on the dirt floor of a hut—seems in hindsight a marvel. There were, in addition, a host of other dangers typical of frontier regions regardless of climate, such as drownings, snakebites and other animal attacks, accidents, and murders. Even one of

the first accounts of the maintenance of a jail in the colonial capital references individuals being held on suspicion of having killed a fellow citizen
or Indian. It all combined to give the colony a well-earned reputation as an
especially dangerous place which belied the rosy picture officials painted
to entice settlers. It took special fortitude to survive, much less thrive, in
British West Florida.[4]

Yet for all of its dangers, observers such as Bernard Romans found that if
the new residents could endure long enough to acclimate to the subtropical
environment, they just might flourish. He noted that during his travels in
Mobile he met a few longtime residents of French extraction in their 90s
and mentioned at least one person reputed to be over 100. He met one man
who gave his age as 83 and recorded that he saw the man's mother making
bread. "Many more of this kind might be mentioned," Romans asserted as
a curious counterbalance to prevailing notions of the unhealthiness of the
colony. Few other observers noted incidents of such heartiness, though, and
even if accurate such accounts must be regarded as intriguing but incongruent outliers of the possibilities for adaptation—and some exceptionally
good genes.[5]

THE REGION'S UNFAMILIAR AND unforgiving climate decimated in particular the ranks of the first troops stationed there. Fevers, diarrhea, and a
host of other maladies greeted soldiers garrisoned in close quarters at Pensacola and Mobile. The majority of troops experienced some illness; even
the doctors were debilitated at one time or another. Within six months of
arriving at Mobile and Pensacola in 1765, for example, well over 100 men of
the 21st and 23rd infantry regiments lay incapacitated, stricken with communicable illnesses which ravaged those unaccustomed to the hot, humid
conditions. So deadly did the post at Pensacola become that a quarter of the
men of the 34th regiment were dead within a month of its arrival shortly
after the establishment of the colony. Troops were described as suffering
from "putrid bilious fever succeeded by an epidemic of flux" which spread
quickly to affect virtually the entire garrison. At other times "fever and
ague" or the "dry bellyache" ravaged the men. Chronic infirmity, Frederick
Haldimand reported to superiors in 1768, made it impossible to keep as

little as three of ten companies from a regiment on active duty at any given time. Indeed, disease and illness would be the constant adversary of British troops in West Florida; at one point during the Revolutionary War siege of Pensacola in 1781 only a little over half of the troops at the post were listed as fit for duty. The situation became so dire that local officials requested new troops be sent to the colony only in the winter—regarded as the healthiest of seasons on the Gulf Coast—when they had a better chance of surviving the gradually rising temperatures of the spring and summer. But in truth the redcoat troops found the damp, cold winters on the coast could be almost as debilitating as the midsummer heat. A disheartened Haldimand wrote General Gage during a particularly vicious cold spell in Pensacola that he simply did not know how "a European constitution can stand" the piercing cold which chilled him as much or more than the snow-filled scenes he had experienced in Canada.[6]

The danger of the unfamiliar, debilitating, contagions troops encountered was compounded by miserable living conditions and inadequate medical facilities. The makeshift barracks were commonly crowded, stifling hot in summer and insufferably cold in winter, and plagued at all times by mosquitoes and vermin. Unclean and as a rule unsanitary, they served as incubators for disease among troops weakened by the climate and suffering from bad food and polluted water. Troops lived on rations of tough, sometimes wormy, salt meat and other barreled provisions. They supplemented their diets with fish when they could. Fresh vegetables were a luxury. The men battled illness with what they had available, which, owing to a severe shortage of medicines and commonly subpar medical care even for the day, in large part amounted to little more than copious amounts of rum, Madeira, or other spirits when available. Believing spruce beer would help fight scurvy, General Haldimand ordered several kettles sent to the post at Pensacola for his men to brew the concoction themselves as a sort of cure-all he pronounced as "much more wholesome for the men than hot rum new from the still." In fact he, along with other officers, decried rum as leading to disorder and drunkenness in the camps but continued to distribute it as necessary for shoring up constitutions weakened by the sweltering heat of a West Florida summer. Plus, making a bad situation worse, officials at first balked at the exorbitant expenses of creating and supplying makeshift hospitals at the colonial outposts. Thanks to Haldimand's insistence, one was finally established in Pensacola by 1767 and proved its worth in short order.[7]

The work of Dr. James Lorimer accomplished more for the health of His Majesty's troops than any single pest house, ration of spirits, or other homespun remedy. Already an experienced and respected professional at the time of his arrival in Mobile in the summer of 1765, Lorimer would labor in West Florida for nearly fifteen years. During that time he would achieve a measure of fame for his writings on botanical discoveries in the province in the pages of the American Philosophical Society's publications. But his work improving the living conditions for troops became his lasting legacy. Upon landing on the colony's shores, Lorimer recognized at a glance some of the problems perpetuating chronic illness among enlisted men. He went to work immediately in recommending better housing and hygiene, access to clean water, fresher food and a more balanced diet, and the digging of proper latrines at encampments to slow down the spread of disease. He even suggested a redesign of the fort at Pensacola to allow for better air circulation. He worked tirelessly to overcome the chronic shortages of medicines and medical supplies which hamstrung the efforts of medical professionals. Through Lorimer's efforts, large quantities of the chemicals, exotic roots, and extracts used in compounding medicines of the day were imported into the colony, such as camphor, cortex cinnamon, paregoric, chamomile, gentian, Peruvian bark, and tartar emetic. Perhaps most important, Lorimer exerted his influence to develop and improve the effectiveness of the colony's military hospitals.[8]

Lorimer encouraged officials to post troops stationed at Mobile on the higher ground along Mobile Bay's eastern shore during the deadly summer season. He believed the shady, breezy, bluffs of what is now Baldwin County to be the perfect refuge from the swampy pestilence prevailing among the closely quartered troops in the city of Mobile. Locating a pristine spot along the "red cliffs" near the modern community of Montrose, which he described as "sufficiently high, and there are . . . some springs and small rivulets of the finest water I have seen in this country," he determined to establish a hospital. In 1770, he prevailed upon Governor Durnford to authorize construction

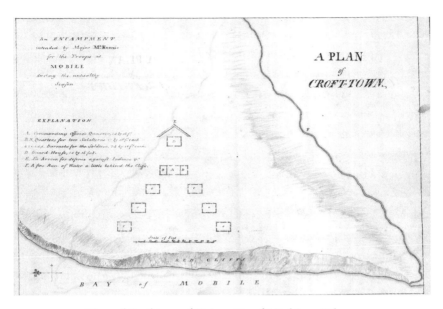

Plan of Crofttown (University of Michigan Library
Digital Collections, William L. Clements Library Image Bank)

of the facility at a spot along Rock Creek a short distance from the governor's own plantation home. When completed in the spring of 1771 by the men of Captain Crofton's 31st infantry, "Fort Crofton," or "Crofttown," as it would become known, looked more like an armed encampment than a medical institution. It featured a stout wooden stockade for a battery with a blockhouse and powder magazine surrounded by a series of pine huts that would house sick men. The place soon proved so healthful and such a respite from prevailing conditions across the bay that there was talk of moving the entire post there. It offered easy communication with Pensacola and relatively deep water just offshore as well as potentially serving as a first line of defense for the growing number of plantations and farms in the vicinity. At least one local official questioned its worth, though, citing in a 1772 letter to General Gage that in the frequent transporting of sick men back and forth across the bay between Mobile and the new post, a half a dozen troops had been lost to drowning. "Fort Crofton" remained a vital health facility for Mobile's beleaguered garrison for the remainder of Britain's tenure in West Florida. It was a monument to the effect better conditions could have on the overall health of the troops serving in the sultry Gulf Coast climate.[9]

As might be expected, desertion became a problem among underpaid, lonely, and bored troops living in such conditions. While never involving large numbers of troops, desertion was most pronounced on the western outposts, where escape down the Mississippi to New Orleans or simply across the river into Spanish Louisiana for some proved too inviting a temptation to resist. Even the first expeditions into the region, such as those conducted by Major Loftus in 1764 and Major Farmar in 1766, witnessed the desertion of dozens of men. Authorities did what they could to deter the practice, enforcing stricter discipline and, on occasion, publicly whipping those attempting to desert as a discouragement to their colleagues, but small numbers of disgruntled troops continued to sneak off from time to time, usually by themselves or in pairs. By 1768, officials estimated nearly 150 British deserters were then living in New Orleans. That year General Haldimand, with permission of Governor Ulloa of Louisiana, published news of a pardon for deserting soldiers in the Spanish capital in hopes of luring them back and then shipping them off to the island of Grenada where the untrustworthy troops could remain in British service but be considerably less able to abandon their posts. A few trickled back into British ranks, but the offer did not solve the problem. Throughout West Florida's time as a British colony, up to the final military campaigns waged for its possession during the Revolutionary War, small numbers of desperate troops would demonstrate their dissatisfaction by deserting for an unknown fate elsewhere.[10]

Life for civilians in West Florida had its own challenges and proved anything but easy. The new colony's two primary cities, Mobile and Pensacola, were still little more than undeveloped villages when the British took over the region. Consisting of clusters of haphazardly arranged and constructed homes with a smattering of businesses and nearby military fortifications in varying states of disrepair, both communities made a poor first impression on British officials familiar with the relatively ancient establishments of Europe and the more prosperous New World colonies elsewhere. Upon first laying eyes on Mobile in 1764, an underwhelmed Robert Farmar recorded with no little sarcasm how the city "at present carries the appearance of a little hamlet formed of Negro Huts, rather than a well populated town in Canada." Livestock roamed the town's muddy streets, which were flanked by an assemblage of low-slung, mostly wooden structures some observers thought to mimic Indian housing in construction. This architectural hodge-podge, though "not ill built" and giving the appearance of a quaint "country village," in the generous words of the colony's first governor, nonetheless seemed entirely inadequate to host its existing populace, much less the influx of troops and government officials on the way. Further, its setting amidst a low-lying, marshy plain along the slow-flowing and broad Mobile River, where the streams of the Delta enter Mobile Bay, produced mixed opinions both as to beauty and practicality. Some decried the setting as desultory, describing its swamps and sluggish waterways as a depressing, literal backwater. Others, such as Captain Philip Pittman, complained of the site for a far more immediate and practical reason—observing that as the place lay subject to tidal fluctuations, when the waters receded they left

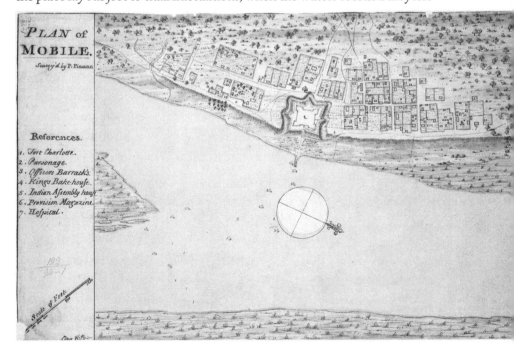

Map of Mobile, by Phillip Pitman, 1763 (Norman B. Leventhal Map and Education Center at the Boston Public Library)

an abundance of small fish stranded in the marshes near the town which "in the heat of the sun in summer kills the fish; and the stench of them, of the stagnated water in the neighbouring swamps, and the slimy mud, render the air putrid." From a military standpoint, the difficulty in defending the place and its relatively unproductive surrounding lands made it a problematic possession, to say the least.[11]

Still, Mobile had possibilities that even the most jaded could recognize. There could be little doubt that it held the potential to become one of North America's most important ports. Mobile stood on a Gulf Coast bay at the mouth of a major river system draining an enormous expanse of land covering a large portion of the territory between Georgia and the Mississippi River. Its equivalent on the Gulf could only be found in Spanish Louisiana, at New Orleans, and that port stood some 100 miles from the open ocean. But visions of a grand future escaped most of its first British immigrants, in part owing to the logistics of simply getting there. "The Barr of Mobile is one of the most dangerous parts on the whole coast," noted one observer, as "the Channell is a Narrow Passage of fifteen feet of water between two great reefs of Breakers . . ." This identified a very real problem, one that Mobile deals with today through the constant dredging of a shipping channel the inhabitants of West Florida could scarcely have envisioned as possible. At the time of the colony's founding, many large, deep-draft, ocean-going vessels could only deliver or receive cargo at the port by offloading freight onto light-draft vessels for transport through the upper bay—a laborious, time-consuming endeavor that did little to endear the port with mariners. Mobile would grow under British administration, but slowly, as its population by the time of the Revolutionary War numbered only 800 or so people—an inordinately large percentage of them bachelors—a doubling of its initial population but far from the boom which officials had hoped.[12]

Initial impressions of Pensacola proved equally discouraging to the British. In fairness, it must be remembered that since the former Spanish town had been abandoned at the transition of authority, the community had to be virtually created anew. Its underwhelming appearance in 1764 made the prospect especially daunting. The town at the onset of British administration consisted of little more than a cluster of dwellings fronting the bay, the developing fort its dominant feature. A few dozen small plaster or bark-sided and palmetto thatch-roofed wooden houses "through which the firmament appeared"—what Governor Johnstone referred to as "an assemblage of poor despicable huts"—comprised the entirety of its domestic accommodations. Everything seemed ramshackle, and the fact that the town sat in a sandy, unproductive stretch of land made some despair of its future. One dismayed arrival in the fall of 1764 wrote of how all aboard the ship which brought him into Pensacola Bay were "shocked to see so dismal a place . . . the soil is a fine white sand . . . which can produce no one thing on earth." So little of the area was under cultivation or could even be made into productive farmland that it appeared the new colonial capital must for the foreseeable future be dependent on the Mobile area for provisions. In fact, during the colony's first decade military officials at Pensacola would supply the troops in large part with meat and vegetables from Mobile. Troops survived at times on rations of flour and salted beef as much as three years old, while attempting, with mediocre results, to work small garden plots in Pensacola's sandy soil. Of course officers enjoyed finer fare on rare occasions, such as when, in what amounted to a true luxurious indulgence, General Haldimand received from General Gage and his wife "2 barrels of New Town pippins, two pieces of beef, and two bottles of gravy." Haldimand's celebrated box of goodies aside, prevailing circumstances made for a rocky beginning to Pensacola's planned role as a colonial administrative center.[13]

BUT LIKE MOBILE, PENSACOLA had some advantages that could not be overlooked. For all the health dangers Pensacola Bay posed, the British still viewed it as more wholesome than Mobile, as it sat on a slight elevation directly on a bay instead of on a lowland plain surrounded by a swampy river delta. Its harbor, on a deep and protected anchorage which had been recognized as an excellent moorage for ocean-going ships as far back as the sixteenth century when Spanish explorers first encountered it, made it strategic no matter the size of its town or the richness or sterility of its soil. "Nature seems to have intended to place the seat of commerce on this bay," gushed Governor George Johnstone, who believed the town was destined to become not only the political but the economic capital of the new colony.

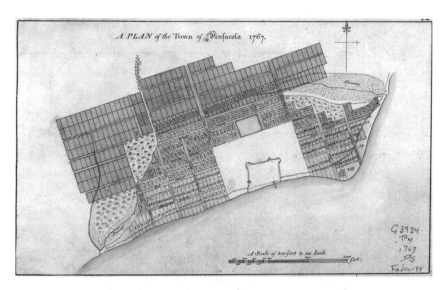

Plan of Pensacola, 1767 (Library of Congress)

Mariners regarded Pensacola Bay as without question the best on the Gulf of Mexico not only for its deep water and sheltered location, but because it had no troublesome bar such as Mobile's to hinder navigation. By 1764 the Royal Navy had sounded and charted the bay and begun to take steps toward the establishment of a significant naval station there while its land fortifications were strengthened. The port at Pensacola would remain the primary one for the colony, both commercially and militarily, throughout its years as a British possession.[14]

The city itself would be developed almost from scratch by the British. A new street plan devised by Elias Durnford, featuring two main thoroughfares arranged at right angles (George and Charlotte, now Palafox and Alcaniz) and a number of smaller side streets and a few public squares, gave order to its arrangement. Durnford's neat grid included hundreds of lots, carefully measured off at 80 by 160 feet, which were soon distributed by lottery and assigned to grantees. By 1768 as many as 200 new homes of varying quality had been erected along the community's sandy streets. But shabby, slapdash architecture seemed to define the place for observers throughout the British period. Descriptions of the capital conjure images of a built environment with few public structures save for the fort and streets lined with a variety of hastily constructed homes of questionable sturdiness, built with whatever timber, thatch, or ballast stone happened to be at hand. Leaky roofs in the rainy subtropical environment were common, and glass window panes were a luxury few could afford even if they had the access.[15]

Governor Chester, dismayed upon his arrival by the "ruinous and uninhabitable" condition of the house set aside for the governor, did work hard to bring about construction of an impressive governor's house, referred to at the time as a "Palace" and which would have surely become a landmark in both the town and colony, but cost and delays prevented it from ever being finished. By the time of the Revolutionary War, its hulking shell would be converted into a warehouse and barracks. The city would eventually acquire some marks of sophistication by the 1770s, however. During his brief visit to the city in 1775 William Bartram noted the "spacious, neat building" in which the secretary of the colony by then resided and observed that there were by that time "several merchants and gentlemen of other professions, who have respectable and convenient buildings in the town." Entering the capital city, Bartram remembered being passed by the governor in his "chariot," returning to town from a visit to his nearby plantation. While Pensacola may have not become a metropolis by European standards, it nevertheless became a somewhat refined and busy place of business by the late 1770s.[16]

The danger of fire in the closely packed town, as in every community of any size in the colony, was omnipresent, and roaring blazes consumed parts of the city on more than one occasion. To prevent such infernos, laws were enacted to prevent the carrying of open fire in the streets. The town did have a public market, and, at length, a jail, but the latter's unguarded windows reputedly served as easy points of entry for contraband or exit for inmates. The above anecdote speaks to the reality of governmental administration and its overwhelming focus on Pensacola as a military installation and political administrative complex rather than a true urban center. During the majority of the town's years under British control, its government can be said to have been much more reactive in attempting to keep order than proactive in town-building. A great deal more time was spent regulating the firing of muskets in the streets, licensing taverns, policing public drunkenness, making sure no cattle were driven or horses ridden in the streets "faster than a walk," or ensuring the burning of grass was regulated and hunters did not leave deer carcasses near plantations than on the development of services and infrastructure. This might be attributed at least in part to the fact that both Pensacola and Mobile would remain primarily male inhabitations during their years at part of the British Empire, filled with troops, officers, and a few soldiers and officer's wives, giving the communities a feel more in line with a military encampment than a cosmopolitan city.[17]

WEST FLORIDA'S TWO OTHER early significant towns were planned and developed entirely under the auspices of the colonial government. Lieutenant Governor Montfort Browne organized Campbell Town a short distance northeast of Pensacola near the banks of Escambia Bay as part of an immigration scheme bringing French Protestants to West Florida's shores. Persecuted in their homeland for their religious conviction, a group petitioned for land and free passage to the new colony shortly after learning of its establishment. Browne seized on the opportunity, seeing in it a chance to encourage foreign immigration which would both boost the colony's population and further its economic development. He also would personally recoup a small amount of money per person he brought to the province from the Board of Trade. He arranged to have West Florida's fledgling government underwrite expenses to bring dozens of French Protestants to the Gulf Coast in a gamble that the group could found a thriving agricultural community to help diversify the colony's exports. The immigrants were to be provided transportation across the Atlantic and a 20,000-acre township on which to settle, along with tools, several months of provisions, and even a pastor. In exchange, the French agreed to cultivate grapes and silkworms, potentially lucrative crops with which few in the colony had any experience. The community became known as Campbell Town, presumably named in honor of a person of that name but exactly who that might be is unclear in the historical record. About four dozen settlers arrived in 1765, and Campbell Town quickly assumed a position on maps of the new colony and even enjoyed representation in the West Florida General Assembly despite the fact it was little more than a highly experimental cluster of family homes.[18]

The town never flourished. Many settlers regarded its location as unhealthy and exposed from the beginning and looked for a more inviting locale. A fort to help protect the town was discussed but never built. Plus, it soon became apparent that clearing the area's forests in an effort to earn a living through the laborious work of viticulture—at best a questionable proposition in the subtropical climate—and attempting the slow and risky work of managing a silkworm colony in a hurricane zone were tasks too daunting even for the desperate. Some of the settlers left the site within six months of their arrival for other opportunities, and by 1768 the place stood practically abandoned.[19]

The planning of the town of Manchac in the colony's western reaches represented a different dream but yielded the same results, only at even greater expense to the crown. The community, never more than a small cluster of rough log homes, a trading house, and a dilapidated military outpost, sat astride a shallow stream called Bayou Manchac, often referred to at the time as the Iberville River, approximately 100 river miles northwest of New Orleans. It seemed on paper destined to rise to fame and fortune owing to its vitally strategic location, for the Iberville flowed between the Mississippi and the Amite rivers and in theory allowed the bypassing of New Orleans in transcontinental shipping. It could only do so through a cumbersome route involving navigation of the Iberville into the Amite, eastward into Lake Maurepas, through Pass Manchac into Lake Pontchartrain, thence through Lake Borgne and into the Gulf. If it all sounds complicated, it was, due in no small part to the fact that the Iberville, the key navigational stretch, could only be traversed by vessels of very shallow draft during brief periods of high water. For as many as nine months a year, the Iberville presented itself as less a river than a muddy ditch. Yet the possibility of opening the Mississippi River to West Florida ports without going through Spanish-held New Orleans proved too intoxicating a vision to colonial leadership to view the situation in a practical manner.[20]

As early as 1764, officials sent troops and slaves under the command of Lieutenant James Campbell to the area to begin the Herculean task of manually widening and deepening the channel of the Iberville. These men were charged with what amounted to the creation of an eighteen-mile long canal some six feet deep through the swampy bayous of the lower Mississippi

Valley using only shovel and spade. They could see they were on an expensive and labor-intensive fool's errand, but leadership back in Pensacola persisted in pressing the work. On it went, with predictable results and under several gubernatorial administrations in fits and starts, for nearly a decade. When at one point during a period of high water in 1769 a small schooner managed to make its way from Lake Pontchartrain through the ad hoc waterway to the Mississippi, a jubilant celebration ensued. But the success proved fleeting, for days later came the sobering news that the Iberville was again dry and unnavigable. By 1770 General Thomas Gage, grown weary of the wasted effort and expense of what he viewed a hopeless task, suspended the work. Although interest in the project rekindled among undaunted local officials from time to time—as late as 1779 schemes for obtaining the men and materials for the big dig were still under discussion—the Iberville never became a serviceable waterway.[21]

As went the experiment in navigational channel improvement on the Iberville, so went attempts to establish a trading town along its marshy banks. When officials envisioned the creation of a navigable bypass of the Mississippi, they could not help but think of the associated trading community that would naturally spring up at the junction of the waterways. Realizing the strategic economic importance of the location, they also viewed a military outpost as necessary. In 1766, they erected Fort Bute—named for John Stuart, Earl of Bute, an important friend of Governor Johnstone—at the confluence of the Mississippi and the Iberville to protect the crucial planned navigational route. Around this small stockade they then waited for a trading town to arise which would surely serve as an entrepôt for immigration from Louisiana. They assumed that disgruntled Spanish subjects, especially the recent Swiss and German immigrants living along the great river's western shores, would logically choose to cross the Mississippi and settle in a thriving and prosperous West Florida once they saw the success of the new waterway. A planned community, officially named Harwich but known locally as Manchac, was laid out near the fort, but the response to the sale of its lots proved lackluster and, in similar fashion to Campbell Town, the community existed only on paper. It was nonetheless at one point offered representation in the colonial assembly. Later, Dartmouth, a second town, would be planned at the junction of the Iberville and the Amite rivers, in hope of an increasing interest in the Mississippi Valley by immigrants to the colony. But neither town ever developed into anything more than a few isolated homesteads. Wealthy speculators snapped up the majority of lots in the planned towns hoping to cash in on a quick resell of their property should development occur. It never did, the paramount reason being the glaring failure of the experiment on the Iberville.[22]

WHILE NO OTHER LARGE cities existed in West Florida, several communities which would soon find places on regional maps could trace their origins to this period. Opposite Mobile on the Eastern Shore stood a cluster of farmsteads and a few "straggling houses," in the words of one observer, known as The Village. The hamlet featured a landing on the bay and lay connected by road to Pensacola. The first settlers of the community had located there during the days of French rule, but during its time as a part of a British province it began a steady development that witnessed a substantial concentration of homes. Similar clusters of settlements began to grow up all along the shores of Mobile Bay from Crofttown to Fish River along its eastern shore. On its western boundary, from the vicinity of Dog River below Mobile as well as north along the southern reaches of the Alabama and Tombigbee rivers, the antecedents of a number of other small communities were being formed. To the west along what is now the Mississippi coast, a similar pattern of development was occurring, albeit on a smaller scale. Between the Pascagoula and the Pearl rivers, in places that would later be known as Pascagoula and Biloxi, were an estimated 500 inhabitants, primarily of French extraction, living on scattered farms. Further west, a grouping of homesteads along a stretch of the Mississippi River north of New Orleans, claiming a population of perhaps 100 people, was taking the first steps toward consolidation into what would become Baton Rouge.[23]

In the 1760s, northward along the mighty river, in the community which gave its name to the lush Natchez District, sat a small grouping of ten to twenty log homes perched on a bluff. This village and the surrounding countryside began a remarkable period of growth as immigrants flocked to the region in the 1770s, but by the mid-1770s Natchez proper still amounted to

View of a Cottage on the Island Massacre near the Mobille, W. Florida,
October 1764 (*Norman B. Leventhal Map and Education
Center at the Boston Public Library*)

little more than an unorganized assemblage of homes. Authorities authorized
the laying out of the town in 1776, but no formal survey for a grid of streets
or sale of lots would be completed until the time of Spanish dominion following the Revolutionary War. Within a decade after the conclusion of the
war, Natchez, as the leading trading and administrative center of Spanish
West Florida, would surpass both Mobile and Pensacola in population,
wealth, and influence. Upstream of Natchez lay several smaller collections
of homesteads, several of which would become small towns in their own
right during the ensuing Spanish era but could claim their days as part of the
British Empire as their founding era: Petit Gulf, Grand Gulf, Port Gibson
and Walnut Hills—the future city of Vicksburg—among them.[24]

The famed journey of naturalist William Bartram through sections of
West Florida in 1775 provides us with one of the most detailed accounts
of the natural environment of the colony and also the people, both native
and of European heritage, who called the area home. His sojourn across the
colony took him through its rich forests, into some of the most prominent
Native American villages of the day, along its majestic waterways, and onto

the streets of its largest colonial cities. His remarkable narrative describing the places and the people he saw, which he completed in the 1780s but did not appear in print until the 1791 publication of his book, *Travels*, is regarded as a classic work in American literature and is a landmark in the natural and cultural history of the Gulf Coast. Let us follow him along portions of his journey to see the area through his discerning eyes and learn more of the environment of West Florida and the people who lived there.[25]

Bartram entered West Florida traveling west from Georgia upon crossing the Chattahoochee near Uchee Creek, in the northeastern reaches of the colony in what is now Russell County, Alabama, in July of 1775. Creek Indians ferried him and his companions, a group of traders bound for Mobile, across the waterway with what he remembered as "cheerful and liberal assistance." Bartram would go on to write much about the culture and society of the welcoming natives, but it was the beauty, fertility, and diversity of the natural environment that first engrossed him. In some of the most colorful language in his narrative, he expressed his rapture and wonderment upon passing "expansive savannas, groves, Cane swamps and open Pine forests, watered by innumerable rivulets and brooks . . ." He marveled at "the Canes and Cypress trees of an astonishing magnitude" and was enthralled by "the stately columns of the Magnolia grandiflora." "What a sylvan scene is here!" he exclaimed in exaltation at the natural spectacle he beheld during his explorations of the Mobile-Tensaw Delta area. He recorded the display he witnessed during the journey by sketching richly detailed images of many species of plants and animals and by collecting samples of flowers and leaves, etc . . . Exactly what the area Indians who observed this curious visitor thought of his utter fascination with the land can only be guessed, but he apparently did acquire the nickname of "pug puggy"—or "flower hunter" in the Muskogee language—for his unusual preoccupation with the natural world.[26]

Bartram proved to be a little less enraptured with the people he encountered, but he nonetheless observed them closely. In the process he left us with one of the more poignant accounts of native society within West Florida. Bartram traveled through several Creek towns along his route through what is now southern Alabama, recording detailed descriptions of not only their physical appearance but informed examinations of their culture, lifestyles, and worldview. His writing sparkles with compelling snapshots of these complex, close-knit societies. Bartram related seeing the clusters of wooden-framed, plastered, houses with roofs of cypress bark which formed the core of these communities, their numbers in some cases dwarfing those of any European enclave in the region and their sophistication equal to or exceeding them. He commented on the fashion in which the Creeks practiced agriculture, each family tending a section of communal fields on which an array of fruits and vegetables were grown, and admired the skill with which Creek women produced and decorated an infinite variety of pottery. He quickly discerned and carefully related the spiritual and practical importance of the Creek tradition of having "white" or "peace" towns and "red" or "war" towns. This organizational feature involved much more than a simple division of governmental authority, he explained; it was indicative of a way of connecting human spheres of influence and physical space.[27]

As an honored guest, Bartram was afforded incredible opportunities to observe native culture and tradition while being treated to lavish hospitality. He described witnessing "a grand entertainment at the public square, with music and dancing" and feasting; the elaborate rituals associated with rank for seating in the town square when leaders gathered to conduct business; the drinking of the traditional "black drink" and the generous sharing of tobacco from pouches made from the skins of various animals. Throughout his travels, he noted he was "every where treated by the inhabitants with marks of friendship, even as though I had been their countryman and relation." Other travelers would likewise comment on Indian hospitality, one venturing through Creek country describing a meal at a village in 1770 as featuring "spread bear skins for us to sit upon and soon after brought large jars of homony which tho' unseasoned even with salt I then thought delicious eating."[28]

Bartram found aspects of Creek culture to both praise and condemn. He believed many of them to be "proud, haughty, and arrogant," yet in the same breath lauded their warriors as "brave and valiant in war, ambitious of conquest, restless and perpetually exercising their arms, yet magnanimous and merciful to a vanquished enemy . . ." He stood deeply impressed with the way they seemed to delineate themselves from the aggressive European intruders already living and trading among them. "We did not know before they came amongst us," he recorded as having heard at one gathering, "that mankind could become so base, and fall so below the dignity of their nature." Bartram described the Creeks as seeking to protect themselves from the ever-strengthening and pervasive influence of their European neighbors. In a microcosm of the multi-faceted ways this complex collision of cultures was playing out in individual families, he recorded that during a stay with the leader of one village he found that the father desired to send his children to Savannah or Charlestown for an education but his wife did not agree with the plan. The Creeks Bartram encountered were truly inhabiting a rapidly changing frontier where lifestyles, economies, and political authority of old and new worlds were coming into unavoidable contact and forming something new. No one could know exactly what the future held for either, but change seemed certain.[29]

It took a sophisticated observer such as Bartram to appreciate the pace and scale of the disruption introduced into regional native society by European colonists, for in West Florida itself it would have been easy for a casual observer to draw the conclusion that colonialism had been a failed enterprise. Bartram recorded seeing the abandoned high-water mark of French influence in what is now central Alabama, for example, during a tour of the site of Fort Toulouse. Calling the spot at the confluence of the Tallapoosa and Coosa rivers "one of the most eligible situations for a city in the world," he found its only occupants to be "yet lying, half buried in the earth, a few pieces of ordnance," and "two or three very large apple trees, planted here by the French." He described the largest British city in the central section of the colony, Mobile, as a languishing community "now chiefly in ruins, many houses vacant and mouldering to earth." Traveling up the Tensaw River north of the city, he noted passing by "ruins of ancient French plantations." In contrast to the activity and vibrance he described in Indian towns, the European inhabitations he mentioned presented the appearance of profound, unpromising distress. Yet the pressures being exerted on the Indians by the struggle playing out among the colonial powers in the Southeast proved consequential indeed. Regionally, if not locally, the power and leverage of the newcomers was proving ascendant in a struggle for autonomy that increasingly seemed stacked against the Indians. Not only had trade begun to transform the native economy and culture, but the European desire for more and more land already seemed unending.[30]

IRONICALLY, IN COMPARISON TO the astute observations of native society by Bartram, we have much fewer accounts of contemporary British society in West Florida. Fellow naturalist Bernard Romans did leave some of the few accounts of West Floridian's daily routines which survive, noting, for instance, the disarmingly casual everyday dress of colonial citizens. "They are very plain, their dress consists of a slight waistcoat of cotton, a pair of trousers of the same and often no coat the women also dress light and are not very expensive; happy frugality!" But few literate onlookers found much in West Florida society to comment upon, leaving us to assume a great deal of continuity in lifestyle among West Florida's colonial subjects and those in the British colonies elsewhere in North America. In general terms the colony was probably too small, too poor, and too short-lived for any unique culture to develop. The shared bond of its citizens appears to have been a common struggle for economic stability on what might they might have easily imagined to be a forgotten frontier.[31]

Transportation in this expansive region could be slow and difficult. Overland travel was hampered by the fact that so few improved roads of any significant distance existed in the colony. A road of varying quality connecting Pensacola and the Mobile area did exist by 1770, complete with a regular ferry operation for crossing the Perdido River. But should a person wish to travel from one of West Florida's major communities beyond the farmsteads on its periphery they would almost always have to take the narrow Indian or trader paths which cut through the dense forest. These paths were just wide enough to permit single-file foot or horseback traffic in most cases, making vehicular traffic, such as wagons or carriages, impractical. The ferries at the Perdido and connecting Mobile with the "Village opposite the Town of Mobile" aside, the crossing of most other rivers required either swimming or the construction of an ad hoc raft. There were no wayside inns.[32]

Most communities looked towards the rivers and bays on which they were located for contact with the wider world, as residents deemed the uncharted hinterland behind them virtually inaccessible. As a consequence, a wide variety of craft large and small plied West Florida's waters and served as the primary means of transportation of both people and goods into, out of, and within the colony. These ranged from ocean-going brigs and sloops to innumerable smaller rowboats and canoes and all manner of vessels in between. On average, in any given year perhaps a few dozen ships might dock in the harbors of the colony's two major ports of Pensacola and Mobile, bringing trade goods and news of goings-on in the wider world. Still, communication between the widely separated communities of the province proved anything but regular and reliable. It could take weeks to get mail or goods between Pensacola and the Natchez District, for example, the route requiring travel through the Gulf, into Lakes Maurepas and Pontchartrain, and along the shallow and often unnavigable Iberville and Amite river system into the Mississippi and thence a hard journey upriver featuring tiresome rowing, winding, or warping by the crew. Many vessels did enter the Mississippi at its Gulf outlet and travel through Spanish territory and by the city of New Orleans with permission of the Spanish, but that route was subject to not only the interference of Louisiana's authorities but required an even longer, arduous journey against the mighty river's current. Receiving communications with the outside world proved as painfully slow as internal shipping; at a time when it took some six weeks for mail to reach New York from London, it could take twice that time for correspondence to be brought from the eastern seaboard to the primary towns of West Florida. Within a few years after the colony's founding a packet system linking Britain's North American colonial holdings and including Florida ports along the route was in operation, but service could be very irregular and at times was suspended for long intervals. One must also not forget that mariners sailing to or from West Florida ports had to deal with all the dangers that have confronted those attempting to navigate the open seas from time immemorial, ranging from storms and stranding to mechanical failure and piracy, and the loss of ships and their entire crews and cargo was not infrequent during West Florida's time as a British colony.[33]

Despite the colony having the Church of England designated as the official faith of the province, organized religion played a small role in the life of West Floridians. With all the difficulties of establishing the colony and encouraging its settlement, officials never got around to constructing an Anglican church. A Protestant minister did serve as chaplain to the troops at Fort Charlotte, and shortly after the creation of the colony the Bishop of London did send two clergymen to the region—Samuel Hart to Mobile and William Dawson to Pensacola. Others would follow, including a Dr. Wilkinson in Mobile and Nathaniel Cotton in Pensacola, but while Mobile seems to have had a pastor working on some level in the town throughout its British period, Pensacola did not replace its last one, Cotton, following his death in 1771. These Anglican ministers conducted services attended by modest numbers in homes or other available buildings and never enjoyed substantial financial support. For a time worshipers met at a public house that doubled as a courthouse in Pensacola, but one observer thought it in "such a dangerous situation that I shall be almost afraid of venturing to attend Divine Service there." In fact the only actual church standing in all of West Florida in the 1760s was the Catholic one in Mobile. West Florida's council requested the Board of Trade to assist it in building houses of worship in the colony, along with proper court buildings and a place of assembly for its legislature, but to no avail. The Board did authorize a modest appropriation for the functioning of churches if they could be built and to regulate the creation of parishes, but local resources and priorities never allowed for their construction while the colony was part of the British Empire. "We have not even any place of worship for asking the blessing of Providence on our endeavours, neither any place for holding courts of justice, nor even the meeting of the Assembly, except such changeable apartments, as are hired on the occasions from the scanty contingencies of the Province," read one 1766 petition which describes in miserable detail the backwardness of facilities in the colony.[34]

West Florida proved somewhat unusual among the North American colonies for the degree to which its authorities manifested tolerance regarding religion. This is owed more to practicality than conviction, since the region had been a Catholic domain throughout its colonial history and the British desired to both keep some of the current residents and entice new ones. Dissuading the practice of the Catholic faith could in many instances be tantamount to banishing the population from West Florida's borders, and officials were simply not prepared for such an event. In few British colonies would less prohibitions be placed on the free exercise of religion or play less of a role in participation in political life as a consequence.[35]

THERE WERE NO PUBLIC schools in West Florida. A schoolmaster for the colony had been appointed in 1765, but no schools were ever built. Considering the citizenry's limited resources and time, plus their location on the periphery of what most considered the civilized world, formal education for the bulk of citizens' children proved impractical. The wealthy could of course hire private tutors or send their children elsewhere for education, but a small percentage of West Floridians enjoyed such privilege. Governor Johnstone dreamed of a college where Indians and European settlers could be taught at public expense, but that vision proved to be as far as any leaders could go towards creating any sort of educational institutions in the colony.[36]

Despite all these factors working against educational pursuits in the colony, a small number of widely respected intellectuals did rise to prominence. None was more accomplished than Scottish-born William Dunbar, who emigrated to America in search of fortune in 1771. Arriving first in Philadelphia, he would by 1773 find his way to the Mississippi Valley where he would become a prosperous West Florida planter by the time of the Revolutionary War. But he would go on to become one of the most accomplished scientists in early America, in addition to being a businessman working as an inventor, surveyor, botanist, zoologist, astronomer, and mathematician. Dunbar would become a member of the American Philosophical Society and rank men such as Thomas Jefferson among his personal friends.[37]

Bernard Romans, another noted intellectual to spend time in West Florida, left us with some of the most detailed descriptions of the Gulf Coast region during the time period. A Dutch-born British citizen, Romans began his career in colonial America as a surveyor in the 1760s. He produced charts of coastal East Florida prior to receiving a large grant of land near Pensacola and a contract to survey the portions of West Florida claimed by the Choctaw and Chickasaw. Working from September of 1771 to January of 1772, he traversed the colony and created one of the most detailed maps of the region produced during the era. Romans hunted, fished, and even traded in slaves to make ends meet while working as a surveyor, but his interest in botany—both as a scientific and economic endeavor—became his passion. Romans sought to identify native plants which could be used for medicines or dyes and to determine which food crops might yield the greatest return through cultivation in West Florida's specific environment. He made valuable discoveries that cemented his reputation as a botanist, such as his finding a variety of the prized cathartic Jalap plant in the colony. He even lobbied government authorities for the creation of a provincial botanical garden where he could cultivate and study various species of plants, and in 1774 he was named official botanist for the colony. Romans left West Florida for New England in 1773, though, where he would serve in a Connecticut militia unit during the Revolutionary War.[38]

Two minor literary figures are associated with the colony. Archibald Campbell, who one historian has referred to as the origin of "belles-lettres" in West Florida, was the son of a professor at St. Andrews University in Scotland. He came to West Florida during the administration of Governor Johnstone to take a position as a purser in the colonial government. The governor shared Campbell's fondness for poetry, and the two are said to have spent long hours on the lonely coastal frontier's muggy evenings in deep conversation about classic literature. Campbell composed a manuscript of commentary on the poems of Ossian and other subjects, which he managed to have published on his return to London in 1767. Entitled *Lexiphanes and the Sale of Authors*, the book enjoyed a measure of acclaim and went through multiple reprintings. For a brief nine months, James Macpherson, a literary figure of some note in England, lived in Pensacola while working a stint as secretary to Governor Johnstone. He would later serve in Parliament but become best known for his books of poetry and history, such as *Fingal, an Ancient Epic Poem in Six Books*, *The Works of Ossian*, and *Original Papers, Containing the Secret History of Great Britain from the Restoration to the Accession of the House of Hanover*.

While his writing is linked specifically to the neighboring colony of East Florida, the dramatic account of survival after being shipwrecked near St.

Marks penned by Pierre Viaud merits mention among the literature associated with the colony. Viaud survived a harrowing weeks-long ordeal after the ship he was a passenger on ran aground at Dog Island in 1766 just east of the mouth of the Apalachicola River. Starving, sick, and scared to death of the wild animals they encountered, he and a small number of other passengers endured in the elements long enough to be rescued by some troops from a nearby British post who happened to notice them after more than eighty desperate days. The book's embellished account of the episode, which includes an infamous description of cannibalism, became an international bestseller after its initial publication in 1768. English translations of the original French text appeared as early as 1771. What effect this widely circulated but rather unsavory account of the Florida shores might have had on those considering migrating to the region can only be speculated, but it likely could have only solidified in readers' minds the dangers posed to life in the undeveloped province.[39]

In the end the realities of life in the raw, rugged Gulf Coast borderland of the mid-eighteenth century afforded precious few opportunities for such niceties as educational discovery and enjoyment of the arts. Daily existence—which as Viaud's narrative demonstrated in graphic fashion could be a trial for the unprepared—for most was defined by the pressing need to harness the physical and financial resources necessary for existence. So it was that in West Florida, much as in every place and time before and since, most people's day-to-day lives revolved around earning a living.

6

Earning a Living

'We remain here, instead of improving, in much the same situation we were in some years ago.'

Alarge portion of West Florida's citizens drew their living from the land, and their world revolved around it and the products they could gather from its cultivation. On small family farms and larger slave-operated plantations scattered across the colony, colonists cleared forest tracts and labored in the Gulf Coast heat and humidity to produce vegetables, grains, and fruits for sustenance and local trade; cultivated plants such as tobacco and indigo or harvested timber in search of a lucrative cash crop; and herded livestock in the effort to both become self-sufficient and achieve economic stability. The struggles endured in those elusive goals are an integral part of the colony's story.[1]

Corn proved the ubiquitous foodstuff for West Floridians, and rows of the staple were grown on almost every farm large or small. Other vegetables which found their way onto settlers' tables and to urban markets were peas, beans, pumpkins, potatoes, carrots, onions, artichokes, radishes, turnips, and cabbage. With varying success, West Floridians worked hard to cultivate fruit trees. Figs, peaches, pears, plums, and pomegranates were abundant, while oranges were limited to coastal areas. Watermelons seem to have been grown with ease. Preserved among General Haldimand's correspondence is a note that he sent the seeds from a locally produced variety which he claimed to be the best he had ever eaten to General Gage for his own cultivation. Apples proved difficult to grow consistently in the region's subtropical climate, while persimmons, found throughout the interior of the colony's forests, and native nut trees such as hickory were harvested on occasion. Wild blackberries, muscadines, and strawberries and other ber-ries were gathered when available and in some instances were cultivated. Attempts were made at growing imported grapes, but never with enough success to make it a viable enterprise. Farmers kept bees for their honey and wax. Colonists tried to produce rice in conducive lowland areas, but as the crop proved extraordinarily labor-intensive and required specialized skills and conditions, it was cost-effective to simply purchase it from elsewhere. Owing to the unsuitability of the climate, some other common foodstuffs had to be imported as well, such as the wheat flour used to make bread. Not surprisingly for a coastal colony with plentiful seafood resources, a few indi-viduals earned a living as commercial fishermen, to a large degree in oysters.[2]

Despite extensive trial and no little tribulation, the residents of West Florida never hit on a reliable cash crop for developing a prosperous economy. Many believed tobacco, already a staple elsewhere in the southern colonies and in world demand, might fit the bill. Farmers throughout West Florida attempted to master the multi-step, labor-intensive process of growing and curing the plant to tap into its lucrative markets. They prepared planting beds in the winter, covered the sprouts and transplanted them in the spring, carefully mounded hills of earth around the base of the plants when about five inches tall, minded them intensively throughout the growing season, harvested the leaves in the fall, hung them to dry in tobacco houses, removed the center rib and rolled them into carrots when cured, packed them into barrels, and then transported them to ports for shipment to transcontinental or international markets. Neither the quantity nor the quality of tobacco produced in West Florida secured a foothold in a competitive trade domi-nated by Caribbean and Chesapeake producers.[3]

West Florida planters grew more substantial quantities of indigo for processing. Blue indigo dye was in high demand in European markets for use in the production of clothing and other textiles, and indigo cultivation offered even more promise than that of tobacco. Planters across the colony tried their hand at its production, a long and, like tobacco, multi-step process demanding patience and skill. Indigo required first laboring for months to protect the fragile plant from pests. Next came a series of technical pro-cedures, any one of which could ruin the effort, to transform the harvest

1. Negre qui ejambe le tabac.
2. Negre qui torque le tabac.
3. Negre qui le met en rolle.
4. Tabac a la pente.

Depiction of tobacco processing (Library of Congress)

into raw material suitable for export. Growers steeped the plants in vats of water to begin fermentation, carefully draining the liquid before placing the plants in another vat of water known as a "beater." The mixture would then be agitated for an extended length of time before draining off the liquid and placing the residual matter in a third vat to settle and solidify. The resulting dark blue mud could then be scooped into bags and hung up to dry. Once dry, it could at last be cut into cakes and prepared for shipping. Despite the hurdles involved in its manufacture, production of indigo in West Florida increased dramatically from the 1760s to the 1770s. In 1768 less than 500 pounds were exported, but more than 15,000 pounds were shipped from Mobile and Pensacola alone in 1772, easily making indigo one of the more widespread and successful agricultural endeavors in the colony. The output paled in comparison to the more than one million pounds exported from the neighboring colony of East Florida between 1768 and 1784, however. Still other, even more productive, areas of indigo cultivation crowded the highly competitive international market. The difficulty in its production and the several available sources combined to prevent indigo from ever becoming the agricultural panacea of which many in West Florida dreamed. While some planters did find a measure of success with it, few flourished.[4]

WEST FLORIDIANS ATTEMPTED TO cash in on other agricultural enterprises both conventional and speculative. In one of the more unique undertakings, some residents tried to produce a marketable red dye and food coloring known as cochineal, derived from the insect of the same name. The prized dye, which could be produced in shades of scarlet and crimson, was highly valued in Europe for use in textiles and paints. Mexican growers dominated world supply, as the cochineal bug was not only native to the region but had been harvested and processed there since the time of the Aztecs. That colonies of the bugs, normally gathered on cactus plants growing naturally in much more arid regions, might have been introduced to the British Gulf Coast shows to some degree both the agricultural experimentation in the province and the desperation with which residents pursued an economic niche. Cochineal production was never widespread and the experiment

Depiction of indigo processing (Library of Congress)

proved short-lived since there was no ready market sufficient to reward the risky trial. Some West Florida planters tried manufacturing lye and potash from the region's abundant timber resources, the latter a form of potassium carbonate used as a fertilizer and in bleaching textiles and the manufacture of glass, soap, and other products. Like other efforts, these required a multi-step, labor-intensive technique, with the end product competing for space in an oversupplied market. Few could pin their economic futures on such a proposition.[5]

It comes as a surprise to some that cotton, ubiquitous to the region a generation later, played a minor role in the colony's agriculture. This can be attributed to the fact that processing the fiber proved so labor intensive that most farmers maintained only small patches for domestic use. The patenting and mass production of a capable cotton gin would not come until the turn of the century, and without it few West Floridians were willing to bet their financial future on a crop with no clear path to financial success. Nevertheless a few pioneering individuals, such as Pascagoula-area plantation owner Hugo Ernestus Krebs, were already working hard on the development of machinery which would make large-scale cotton cultivation feasible. Krebs is reputed to have experimented during the 1770s with some of the earliest known cotton gins to be made in the Gulf South. At least one observer, Bernard Romans, thought cotton held a bright future regardless of the difficulty in processing it. Terming cotton a "very useful" commodity, he thought the North American colonies would "do well to manufacture all our necessary clothing in Florida from this staple" and hoped a way might be found to effect its "universal propagation."[6]

To the degree West Florida agriculturalists gained traction towards establishing staple crops, they found it in lumber and livestock herding. The colony's timber resources were legendary. "In timber no country on earth can surpass it, either in quantity, quality, or variety," exulted Romans. Lumber figured in the building of a great majority of the structures in West Florida and in other ports into which its ships sailed. Lumber was indispensable in an endless variety of other manufacturing enterprises during this era prior to synthetic materials. Enduring and insect-resistant cypress and cedar—prized in construction in the damp Gulf Coast environment and

Much of the interior of West Florida contained endless tracts of pine forests, source of the raw material for the colony's lumber and naval stores industries (Library of Congress)

beyond—could be found in its lowlands; live oaks, whose tough, gnarled trunks provided stout ship keels and ribs, could be found in a belt stretching across the width of the colony; any number of other hardwood species, which provided material for decking and interior ship construction as well as the raw material for gunstocks, tool handles, wheels, furniture, barrel staves, and hundreds of other items, were readily available across the region. However, the sturdy, tall, straight, and abundant native longleaf pine, at the time found in endless tracts across much of the colony, provided the quickest and easiest return on investment. This was because the tree proved so versatile in the manufacturing of a variety of products associated with both domestic construction and naval pursuits. Durable longleaf pines proved perfect for the fashioning of sturdy masts able to hold sails to the strong winds of the open ocean, and the tar and pitch which could be harvested from living trees was an essential and unduplicated resource for sealing the tiny gaps between wooden planks to make ships seaworthy. But pine resin could also be harvested and developed into turpentine for a number of other domestic, industrial, and even medicinal uses.[7]

Livestock herding became perhaps the most consistently profitable agricultural pursuit of the era, as large quantities of cattle and hogs were raised throughout the colony's settlements to supply not only the needs of area farms and plantations, but the residents of its primary population centers, both European and Native American. Most small West Florida farms contained herds to supply immediate needs of meat, milk, and butter, while the excess could be sold for profit. Larger planters commonly kept several hundred cattle and hogs; in some rare cases more than a thousand animals grazed free-range on the rich forage in the sparsely inhabited backcountry. In huge swaths of West Florida's acreage, herding in fact represented the sole economic activity. Even Dauphin Island became one big cattle pen, with so many animals that despite the constant depredations of Indians who killed

Scenes such as this depiction of cattle herding would have been common near West Florida's communities (Library of Congress)

and barbecued a few without permission from time to time, the herd only grew larger. According to one tally, less than five years after West Florida's establishment there were already an estimated 7,000 cattle in the province, a figure that likely significantly undercounted the true number. That number grew exponentially as the colony developed, but it is difficult to estimate the true numbers of the herds roaming West Florida's pine savannahs and natural pastures owing to the paucity of records. Anecdotes tell the story in perhaps more straightforward reality. During his visit to the colony in the early 1770s, Bernard Romans estimated there to be more than 10,000 cattle and horses between the Perdido and the Tensaw rivers alone. Another observer traveling through the Mississippi Valley region a short time later recorded that several planters had as many as 1,000 cattle each, along with many horses and flocks of chickens. By far, herding involved among the largest concentrations of capital in West Florida.[8]

COLONISTS ENGAGED IN STILL other trades, but with varying degrees of success and smaller numbers of beneficiaries. Traders annually shipped large amounts of skins obtained from Indians—overwhelmingly those of deer but including on occasion smaller numbers of beaver, otter, fox, and other animals—out of Mobile and Pensacola as an important part of the colony's economy. It is estimated that more than 100,000 pounds of skins were exported from the colony per year in the 1770s. Officials made halting steps to encourage the development of West Florida's feeble industrial scene by drawing on its natural resources. There were a few brick kilns and saw mills near important population centers, and some attempts at shipbuilding in major ports. Governor Johnstone at one point offered a cash reward for anyone who could develop a viable saltpeter manufacturing facility in the colony. A persistent shortage of skilled artisans, such as stonecutters, bricklayers, and carpenters, hampered development along these lines as much as the lack of capital and access to reliably lucrative markets. While all these endeavors were but a small part of the colony's lagging economy, they illustrate the variety of ways West Floridians aggressively pursued financial stability and fought for a space in the international marketplace.[9]

Activity in the ports provides a concise snapshot of West Florida's place

View of Pensacola, in West Florida, by George Gauld, 1770s
(Library of Congress)

in world markets of the day. Pensacola served as the primary entrepôt for international trade, generally carrying on about five times as much shipping activity as Mobile. The scale never reached impressive numbers, but nearly 150 vessels are documented to have docked in the two harbors between 1768 and 1772, one of West Florida's busiest periods of financial activity. A majority of these ships hailed from other North American colonies with some arriving from the West Indies, Great Britain, and Ireland. These ships brought cargoes of fruit, tobacco, paper, housewares, furniture, gin, wine and rum. When they left, they carried lumber, skins, and other products produced in the colony in relatively modest amounts. About a third made for the West Indies upon departure.[10]

West Florida subsisted on what has been described by one historian as a "marginal economy" throughout its existence as a British colony. While an initial spurt of economic activity in its major ports augured financial potential, trade in the province never reached expectations. With no staple crop, a small, decentralized population, and a frontier location, trade proved anything but predictable or profitable for most. Merchants often labored under a chronic shortage of goods, currency, and customers, their enterprise dependent upon an elementary system of credit that was neither standardized nor well-regulated. The upshot ended up being a financial scene that appeared stagnant for long stretches with intermittent periods of high activity. Governor Chester summed up the long pattern of miniscule growth by writing resignedly well into his tenure in the 1770s that "we remain here, instead of improving, in much the same situation we were in some years ago."[11]

The travails of Charles Strachan of Mobile illustrate the challenges individual immigrants faced as they pursued success in business. Strachan migrated to Mobile from Scotland in 1764, an agent of a trading firm which saw in the fledgling colony a potential economic opportunity. He bought a four-room house upon his arrival and immediately entered into business as a merchant. He quickly discovered just how slow trade could be. There were few active traders in town, and owing to the fact that area Indians had recently spent more time attending congresses than hunting, the supply of skins lay low as well. Strachan endured months with virtually no financial transactions, and the scarcity of food and money left him wondering if he might starve to death. An extended period of sickness, common among new arrivals in the port city, made that grim ending a real threat. With so much free time on his hands, Strachan had plentiful opportunity to ponder the economic situation of the struggling colony. He, like many others, believed the most consistent and promising possibilities for trade lay in doing business with the neighboring Spanish and could only be frustrated when local military officials discouraged such intercourse per British mercantile policies. In his diary Strachan expressed exasperation at colonial officials when they seized a Spanish vessel laden with prized silver and gold at Pensacola, wondering to himself why authorities would seek to "discourage a trade that consumes such a quantity of our manufactures and brings us cash in return." Rather, he observed West Florida endure such shortages of grain that even the chickens many residents kept in their yards were dying while goods rotted on the shelves of stores. Strachan was rescued from his plight in 1769 when he received notice of having been named beneficiary of his grandfather's estate in Scotland. For most of Strachan's contemporaries, of course, no such windfall awaited.[12]

About the time Strachan made a hasty exit from the colony, merchant John Fitzpatrick entered for the possibility of trade with the Spanish at the border town of Manchac. A veteran of the French and Indian War,

Fitzpatrick had set up shop in New Orleans after his service but was forced to leave the city in 1769 when Governor Alejandro O'Reilly, attempting to enforce trade rules, made all English merchants exit the Spanish colonial capital. Fitzpatrick determined to stay in the region, though. He went to Mobile to obtain supplies for the opening of a store at Manchac and arranged to have future deliveries from a schooner operating out of Pensacola. The settlement he would call home for the next decade had already failed in dredging the Iberville River as a man-made bypass to the Mississippi. But it occupied a strategic spot for a businessman desiring to tap into the upper Mississippi Valley fur trade via the Amite River or conduct clandestine transactions with the citizens of Spanish Louisiana. Fitzpatrick did a brisk business at times in both, but those spurts of activity were separated by longer periods of idleness and uncertainty. Yet Fitzpatrick stayed, married a French woman from New Orleans, and managed a farm with a few slaves until the invasion of the territory by Spanish forces during the Revolutionary War. Afterwards, like his neighbors, he moved across the river to Spanish territory and continued to farm and trade.[13]

Fitzpatrick had company in conducting illicit trade with West Florida's neighboring Spanish colony. In truth a considerable portion of West Florida's trade came through such covert smuggling. It is inherently difficult to assess the role of clandestine illegal transactions in the regional economy, but authorities in both West Florida and Louisiana were aware it was a chronic problem they were poorly equipped to monitor. West Florida merchants traded for Spanish indigo, cochineal, tobacco, and Mexican logwood as well as manufactured goods such as textiles and clothing, shoes, hats, and cutlery. They also tapped into the stream of deerskins and other peltry from the upper Mississippi Valley. Perhaps the most lucrative items traded were slaves. This officially unsanctioned trade resulted in Spanish silver coins becoming virtually legal currency in West Florida by the mid-1760s. Officials in Louisiana and Mexico enabled illicit trade by facilitating its conduct and reaping its rewards. Spanish authorities gave the British free right of navigation on the Mississippi, including the right to warp or tie up their vessels on either side of the waterway. Many West Florida traders had supply bases in New Orleans prior to the onset of tensions between Spanish and British authorities during the Revolutionary War. Louisiana Lieutenant Governor Francisco Bouligny reported as late as 1776 that of the roughly $600,000 in annual trade in his colony, he believed only $15,000 was accounted for legally and the remainder attributed to activity with the British. Clandestine traders were especially active in the Manchac area on the porous Mississippi border. Jacob Blackwell, collector of customs at Mobile, even suggested that two customs houses be located near Manchac, one on the Iberville and the other at Lake Pontchartrain, to generate revenues from the plentiful flow of illicit goods being transported in that corridor.[14]

Residents and local officials appealed repeatedly to authorities in London to allow some legal exchange with Louisiana and Mexico, citing their unique situation, geography, and the benefits that might accrue to both locals and the expanding British Empire, as well as the impracticality of attempting to halt it. In the 1770s, former governor Montfort Browne developed a "Plan of Mexican Commerce" with a military officer in Mexico which suggested Dauphin Island become a base for international trade. West Florida never became a free port during its years of British administration, despite the concerted efforts of several of its leaders and the fervent wishes of no few of its citizens; a great part of its economic life therefore occurred unofficially and off the books.[15]

NOT ALL OF WEST Florida's agriculturalists conducted their business in secret. While they were always in the minority, a distinct class of planters rose to wealth and no little prominence. Dozens of substantial plantations could be found in the colony during its years as a British holding. Some of West Florida's plantations were large indeed, comparing in size if not opulence with the grander estates of the region's famed antebellum era. As a case in point, the holdings of Patrick Strachan along the northern reaches of the Tensaw River stretched over 2,000 acres (he held a total of some 11,000 in the colony) on which he raised crops and managed herds of more than 600 cattle and nearly 100 horses. Others such as Elias Durnford claimed 5,000 or more acres. However, the houses of West Florida's planter class, being rather unpretentious single-story dwellings of locally hewn timber, as often as not covered with weatherboard siding and featuring plastered interior walls, wood-shingled roofs, multiple fireplaces, and a surrounding gallery, would have appeared modest by the standards of later planters. The plantation of Philip Livingston along the Amite River in the western reaches of the colony, part of holdings which included an astounding 40,000 acres in the colony, gave a deceptively simple appearance. An unassuming log home with clapboard sides, it nonetheless contained a cellar in which could be found dozens of varieties of liquors, barrels of pork and beef, and luxuries such as sugar, cheese, vinegar, and spices. The plantation of Arthur Neil, near Pensacola, stood as one of the more ornate in the region, being a massive two-story edifice filled with imported furniture, carpets, curtains, and wallpaper.[16]

Claims filed by loyalists for reparation of damages sustained during the Revolutionary War give further tantalizing clues regarding the scale and scope of plantations operated by the colony's elite planter class. While some planters sought compensation for the loss of modest holdings, such as John

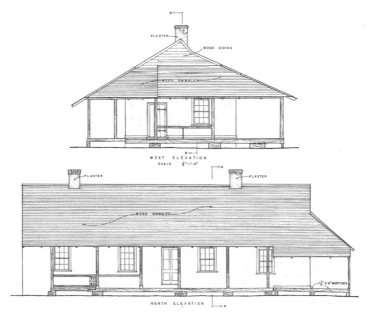

Elevation of the Krebs House in Pascagoula created by the Historic American Buildings Survey in the 1930s. The house, still standing, is believed to have been built in the 1770s. (Library of Congress)

Firby's small house and 200-acre property near Pensacola, or William Jackson's 350 acres along the Tombigbee which included a peach orchard and a 30-ton boat, a few claimed the loss of thousands of acres of land operated by as many as three dozen slaves. In the western reaches of the colony one planter claimed to have lost 30,000 acres, including large herds of livestock, numerous outbuildings, and of course many slaves. John Blommart of the Natchez area claimed the loss of a house and sawmill and also indicated his home contained a library of fifteen books along with several sheets of music, maps, and charts.[17]

One of the most refined and best-documented West Florida plantations belonged to Robert Farmar. Located on the banks of the Tensaw River northeast of Mobile on land purchased from French settlers, his estate encompassed well over 1,000 acres, of which about 100 were cultivated by some sixty slaves under the direction of overseers. A number of tenant families also lived on portions of his land. The plantation's massive central house stood on the bluff overlooking the river; called "Farm Hall," it served as Farmar's residence from about 1771 until his death in 1778. Owing to his famed hospitality and exceptional resources, the home became a meeting place for traders traveling through the area and visitors to the region, including William Bartram. Its furnishings demonstrated Farmar's unusual wealth. On display in the home were a large library, a mark of both money and refinement, and a collection of expensive furniture including a feather bed with rose-colored sheets on a mahogany frame, several ornate tables, at least three mirrors, and an elaborate set of china of more than fifty pieces. White curtains hung over the windows, and the walls were decorated with military mementos from Farmar's career, such as a gold medal, silver gorget, and a dress sword.[18]

SLAVE LABOR POWERED THE agricultural production of these plantations. Most of the larger farms were worked by at least a few bondsmen, with the largest slaveholders laying claim to as many as three dozen individuals. Throughout the 1760s and into the 1770s, the number of slaves in the colony steadily grew. By the mid-1770s an estimated 1,500 enslaved people resided in West Florida, the lion's share laboring in the plantations along the

Mississippi. The colony's attorney general, Edmund Rush Wegg, employed nearly two dozen slaves on his plantation near Mobile. Perhaps the largest slaveowner in the colony was Richard Ellis, who in 1776 claimed eighty-one bondsmen. When one considers that a prime hand might fetch $300 to $500 depending on physical ability, special skills, and age, during the era of British administration, the wealth required for such an investment becomes obvious. Hence, only the richest of the relatively poor colony's citizens could purchase slaves in considerable numbers. The average planter held fewer than eight slaves, and a minority owned none. Many slaveowners moved to the region with their human property in tow, as the colony's land distribution system provided grants to immigrants based on the number of individuals who would be occupying the acreage, thus encouraging the institution of slavery. But many immigrants purchased slaves on arrival through traders operating out of Spanish Louisiana or from traders doing business in port cities.[19]

Slaves in West Florida lived severely proscribed lives of constant toil in difficult conditions. Hard labor and long hours in clearing fields, tending crops, processing harvests, cutting lumber, managing livestock, and other duties were their lot. Exposure to long, brutally hot summers and wet, sometimes surprisingly frigid winters was compounded by the fact that most slaves subsisted on simple, monotonous food and slept in primitive cabins featuring dirt floors and little if any furniture. Slave clothing consisted of only the barest of necessities, with replenishment infrequent. In an era of primitive medical care, in which the cause and spread of many common diseases was unknown and malnutrition and communicable disease were rampant, the enslaved suffered maladies in incredible rates.[20]

But health and working conditions were only the beginning of slaves' woes, as they were subject to the same restrictions, punishments, and indignities as bondsmen from the later antebellum era about which we are collectively more familiar. Some of the first acts passed by the colony's General Assembly outlined regulations on the administration and treatment of slaves. These were added to in the ensuing years so that by the 1770s a lengthy and elaborate code of laws governed slavery. The long lists of specific prohibitions and punishments found in these acts—some of the most verbose passed by the Assembly during West Florida's existence—defined the place of slaves in colonial society. The government established as a bedrock principle that the children of all slaves residing in the colony after passage of the first of these acts in 1767 "shall be and are hereby declared to be and remain for ever slaves and shall follow the condition of the mother." As chattel, slaves were subject to severe punishments for infractions deemed as promoting disorder. The striking of a white man by a slave could legally result in the offender's death in certain circumstances, and a slave committing any felony such as being in possession of stolen goods, or committing arson or poisoning, could be executed. As was the case throughout the era, whipping became the preferred mode of punishment for failure to obey commands or perform as desired, and owners or their overseers wielded the lash frequently as both a corrective and example to others. Slaves were monitored closely in their limited sanctioned travel in the colony and prohibited from gathering in unauthorized groups for any reason. While some were allowed to tend small garden plots to supplement food supplies, they could not legally own the land, its products, any herds of animals, or gamble or buy liquor. Conducting any business on their own behalf was strictly prohibited. In a telling commentary on their status in colonial society, it was determined by the general assembly that the "wanton killing of a slave" by a white man could be treated as a felony, but only in the case of the second such offense would the transgression meet with capital punishment.[21]

Complete control of masters over the bodies of their chattel was as absolute in the colonial era as in later years. At least a few bondsmen were branded like cattle to demonstrate ownership. While the numbers and percentages are unknown, it is clear that some masters raped their female slaves. In fact one of the highest documented prices paid for a slave in the British period—the 1772 purchase of a "mulatto" girl named Tonette by one William Ogelvie for $500 milled Spanish dollars—is suspected as being evidence of this type of relationship. "It is possible," wrote one authority on British West Florida, "that Tonette's ability to perform manual labor was not her only recommendation."[22]

West Florida's legal code bore evidence of slaveowners' constant fear of insurrection and their efforts to maintain strict control of their bondsmen.

Severe punishments awaited those who harbored runaways while those who captured escaped slaves reaped substantial rewards. Those who neglected to regulate their slaves according to the code could be punished. In an effort to maintain good order among the enslaved population, owners were obligated to give sufficient clothing and "wholesome food" to slaves. Not all these regulations were strictly enforced at all times. We have little evidence of how the assembly's suggestion that slaveowners not beat or disable slaves "without sufficient provocation" played out in reality, or how effectively laws specifying that if a white person "willingly, wantonly, or bloody-mindedly kill a Negro or slave" upon the first offense pay a fine of £100 sterling deterred that crime. While owners could emancipate their bondsmen, they could only do so provided they supplied a security of £100 sterling ensuring the slave would not become a burden to the province. Interestingly, in a response to a presumed attempt, the assembly ruled that slaves could not be freed merely "by virtue of becoming a Christian."[23]

Not surprisingly, slaves sometimes ran away despite the threat of severe punishment if apprehended. Runaways were common on the colonial frontier, but unlike later generations of bondsmen who might look north to a region where they might have the possibility of freedom, the destination of those taking flight in West Florida could be much less certain. Slavery was legal throughout colonial America during the years of West Florida's time as a British possession, and there were no large free black communities that escapees could easily disappear into, nor could they rely on any network of safe havens operated by sympathizers. Some runaways sought refuge among the area's Native American villages in locations where they had enough familiarity with Indians to be confident they might find asylum. The phenomena had become common enough by the second year of British dominion in West Florida that Governor Johnstone informed Choctaws and Chickasaws assembled for a conference in Mobile that he expected them to return anyway runaway slaves they might be harboring in an exchange for a reward. Other runaways, especially those from the western reaches of the colony along the Mississippi, might have fled to one of the nascent "maroon" (escaped slave) communities in the swamps where those seeking freedom reputedly gathered and tried to live in hiding. Still others took their chances on finding better situations in Spanish Louisiana even though slavery was practiced there as well. But slaves in Louisiana sometimes attempted to do the same thing by crossing the Mississippi in the opposite direction, with the result that West Florida's trackless backcountry contained at any given point an unknown number of refugee bondsmen legally belonging to both Spanish and British masters. As early as 1766, the governors of the two colonies communicated about the "reciprocal advantage" they would enjoy by agreeing "mutually to surrender the slaves that may desert." Surviving records indicate that on a case by case basis, if not by formal standing, such reciprocity did occur, but it probably had more to do with the owner's position and influence than any general policy. In one 1768 instance, for example, the slave of a British military officer in Pensacola was caught in New Orleans and returned "in irons." Whether a small private farmer in the colony's backwoods could have affected the same result if his slaves crossed the Mississippi can only be speculated as so few examples of capture and return are cited in the records, but it seems doubtful. It must be remembered that none of the potential destinations of runaway slaves could be counted on as a secure long-term option. Each involved a daunting degree of risk and uncertainty and whatever tales of success might have been known within the slave community were more often than not tantalizing oral legend. Running away in the colonial era was truly an act of desperation, a physical demonstration that the slave preferred living—or dying—in any circumstances other than continued bondage.[24]

Still, even fleeting freedom proved a tremendously powerful allure for the enslaved. Even pioneering scientist William Dunbar, residing near Baton Rouge in the western extremity of the colony on a plantation worked by over two dozen enslaved individuals, seemed unable to comprehend why his slaves occasionally ran. Upon capturing two runaways who had repeatedly fled and had been given brutal punishments, he wrote of his confusion: "Poor ignorant devils, for what do they run away? They are well clothed, work easy and have all kinds of plantation produce at no allowance." To be sure, not everyone in West Florida thought like Dunbar. The colony came about during the height of the Enlightenment, a time in which many intellectuals in colonial America came to regard the institution of slavery as an archaic practice, incongruent with the fundamental values of their contemporary society which increasingly cherished such notions as liberty and opportunities for individual betterment. It is the uncomfortable truth, though, that the majority of white West Floridians believed black people were inferior to whites intellectually and thus were inherently suited to bondage and toil.[25]

While the great majority of West Floridians could be classified as either free whites or enslaved blacks, there did exist within the colony a small number of individuals who fit neither category. A few free blacks, perhaps as many as fifty at any one time, resided in the colony. These individuals, having either been manumitted by owners or having purchased their own freedom, were primarily clustered in the port towns of Mobile and Pensacola. At least in its early years, West Florida also contained a small number of indentured servants. This ancient custom, on its way out of practice by this time, often involved a wealthy landowner paying the passage and living costs for an immigrant in exchange for their labor for a number of years. During this time, the servant might learn a trade such as blacksmithing, coopering, or as a shipmate by which to earn their own living after their term of service. One or two of these workers, white European or Caribbean immigrants for the most part, usually labored for a single owner, in contrast to the gangs of slaves found on plantations. But their labor was regulated, and laws were on the books for corporal punishments should they run away and obligating their employers to fair treatment.[26]

FREE, ENSLAVED, OR INDENTURED, West Floridians lived in an inherently provincial and for the most part impoverished world. Travel and communication were difficult, and the day-to-day requirements of making a living, and in truth sheer survival, on an undeveloped borderland precluded most from having the time or opportunity to be attuned to political events elsewhere. Just as West Florida was coming into its own as a colony, though, a movement advocating the independence of the American colonies was taking shape to the northeast. Residents could scarcely have imagined it at the time, but it would in the end alter the course of the province's history and bring about the end of its days as a British possession.

The Coming of the Revolutionary War

'The inhabitants in general (are) self-interested and without public spirit, whose minds are only attached to gain and their private concerns.'

Of the more than two dozen British colonies in North America and the Caribbean in 1775, only thirteen rebelled and took part in the war which resulted in the independence of a new nation. West Florida did not participate for several reasons. For one, it took little notice of the separatist movement developing in the seaboard colonies owing to its remote location. The colony lay on the periphery of British authority and just learning about the growing rift between the other colonies and the mother country proved difficult. The closest major port of one of the thirteen colonies which took up arms against Great Britain was more than two weeks of difficult and unpredictable travel time from West Florida, and with no local newspapers to spread what little news did reach the colony's shores, a small portion of the population had a firm grasp on the situation. Plus, with West Florida's weak and infrequently meeting legislative body, there was no active representative government to serve as a forum for the issues which sparked unrest elsewhere or to advocate for or against the actions and responses of other colonies.[1]

When mentioned at all, West Florida is often labeled a "loyal" colony in histories of the Revolutionary War. While technically correct, the term connotes a stronger conviction than existed in the hearts and minds of its inhabitants. The rank and file of West Florida's population probably could be described more accurately as self-interested than overtly loyal. West Floridians not in the employ of the British government—and that was a smaller percentage of the population than in most of its sister American colonies—without doubt enjoyed the measure of protection being a part of the Empire brought them, liked the rather generous land distribution policies sanctioned by the home government, and had no qualms with the low level of taxation in the colony. Further, the most pressing concerns of residents on the Gulf frontier had more to do with economic opportunity and governmental stability than abstract political philosophy. In short, support of the British government, or at least taking no hostile action towards it, became both practical and expedient.[2]

A few diehard loyal idealists in the colony certainly looked askance at what they perceived to be the festering rebellion on the seaboard promulgated by malcontents prior to the outbreak of war, but they were a distinct minority. The majority of West Floridians can be best understood as more opposed to taking action that might upset the status quo than willing to give any material support to the government structure of which they were a part; a lukewarm and conditional loyalty, to say the least, but a circumstance that, given the situation, Great Britain was happy to have. During the height of the war which would soon find its way into the colony, an exasperated General John Campbell would decry the lack of patriotic spirit exhibited by West Floridians in what amounts to a concise summary of the prevailing attitude: "the inhabitants in general (are) self-interested and without public spirit, whose minds are only attached to gain and their private concerns. In short nothing can be had from them . . . but at an enormous extravagant price, and personal service on general principles of national defense is too generous and exalted for their conceptions." West Florida was no hotbed of rebellion, but neither was it a bastion of loyalist principle.[3]

Accordingly, West Floridians displayed little or no reaction to the passage of most of the acts which so animated rebellion in the North American seaboard colonies in the 1760s and 1770s. In part this can be credited to the aforementioned lack of awareness, but also in part to haphazard enforcement and inapplicability. The Sugar Act, for example, passed in 1764 to raise tax revenue through the collection of an unenforced existing levy on molasses, went almost unnoticed in West Florida but caused uproar in New England. The tax hit rum producers especially hard, but West Florida had just been established and was not producing rum or much of anything to which the tax applied. The Townshend Acts, proposed by Chancellor of the Exchequer Charles Townshend and passed in 1767 and 1768 by Parliament, in similar fashion proved to be a nonissue despite a circular letter being sent to Pensacola from Lord Hillsborough urging the people of West Florida to join the government in denouncing the rebellious actions elsewhere. The acts aimed at raising tax revenue and enforcing trade regulations, especially regarding smuggling, and are commonly cited as a major landmark on the road to revolution in the thirteen rebellious colonies. But the provisions of the acts applied to taxation of such things as glass, lead, and paint which were being brought in to the colony in exceedingly small quantities, and taxes or fees on them could easily be avoided. Further, with few public officials in a position to see that provisions against smuggling were carried out, the relatively small number of traders working on the Gulf Coast simply found clandestine ways to continue their business.[4]

The one parliamentary measure which sparked local conversation was the Stamp Act. The act, passed in 1765 to help offset the great cost of the French and Indian War, placed a direct new tax on Britain's North American colonies by requiring a wide range of paper to carry a revenue stamp. Suddenly the cost of almost all printed matter, from a variety of common legal documents to newspapers and playing cards, became for the first time the object of government taxation and thus a little more expensive. While no organized resistance occurred in West Florida, murmurs of discontent among the cash-strapped populace abounded. Governor Johnstone took notice but at first reported the frustration lay exclusively within "the lower class of people" in his colony, presumably because he thought these people had less understanding or appreciation of the need of government to raise revenue to perform its duties. Writing to the Board of Trade in 1766, though, the governor admitted the Stamp Act had become a somewhat controversial topic across all classes, as "circumstances respecting this law did certainly fall extremely hard on this province." He reported, "The Spirit of what is there (the seaboard colonies) called Liberty begun to infuse itself here, and many Arguments were handed about, to show why the Act should not take Place."[5]

Indeed, the Stamp Act seemed to spark in West Florida the closest thing to direct opposition to the authority of the British government at

A woodcut which appeared in a Pennsylvania newspaper disparaging the Stamp Act of 1765 Library of Congress)

any point in the Revolutionary era. Shipmasters reputedly referred to the obligatory taxed paperwork as "badges of slavery," and some inhabitants attempted to avoid the tax through a variety of means, all ending short of outright refusal. They complained they had not been properly informed of the measure by the governor and that it should not go into effect until a stamp distributor had been commissioned; failing in these tactics, they tried to delay the processing of paperwork for land grants and other official documents involving the payment of the tax. Governor Johnstone came to blame some of his unpopularity on the Stamp Act, and, while he had been never been universally popular in the colony, the claim may have had some merit. As if the act was the proverbial last straw regarding his administration of the colony, rumors circulated that a coup aimed at removing him from office was in the works. Hinting at the level of angst in the colony, Johnstone wrote, tongue in cheek, that he believed some of West Florida's inhabitants "would now as civilly put me to death for believing the legislature of Britain has some authority in West Florida." However, Mobile and Pensacola's quibbles with the Stamp Act appear to have been purely economic, and they never became the powder keg of idealistic discontent that, say, Boston or Philadelphia, became. Still, it is clear that local leaders worried the general populace's resistance to the British government's assertion of its autonomy within colonial affairs might lead to trouble, and they welcomed the Stamp Act's repeal in 1766.[6]

AMONG THE FEW VOCAL advocates in West Florida of some of the tenets of patriot thought was, ironically, its attorney general, Edmund Rush Wegg. He never openly agitated that the colony join the rebellion or, as far as is known, attempted to form or participate in any covert group working in support of American colonial independence such as the Sons of Liberty. However, he did question more vocally than most of his peers the extent of the British government's authority over its colonists and the autocratic nature of West Florida's government in terms that at times sounded in step with the patriots. Wegg questioned the validity of the Stamp Act on philosophical as much as economic terms. Later, when Governor Chester attempted to deprive Mobile County of representation in the general assembly, Wegg protested that "no man can be bound to any government, unless his own consent is conveyed either by himself or representative." While Wegg might have been a far cry from a rebel akin to Sam Adams or Patrick Henry, his words show that notions of liberty as envisioned by colonials elsewhere were bandied about by at least a portion of West Florida's residents.[7]

Such discussion would have been natural for most West Floridians, who came of age within an empire whose home government based itself on a vision of democratic representative government within a long tradition of liberty as defined by English history. While few of the colony's citizens may have been likely to identify with the republican ideals which the American Revolution ultimately inspired, most had a concept of government that included some degree of consent of the governed as requisite for its just establishment. That some of these people expected these principles to be carried out in West Florida is evidenced less in public acts than in private correspondence owing to the nature of colonial society and the lack of any type of regularly published periodical which might be used to track popular sentiment such as exists for other contemporary North American colonies.[8]

"These riotous Oliverians," wrote an exacerbated General Frederick Haldimand in one letter discussing conditions in the colony in the 1760s, for example, "will be the cause of my remaining upon this continent longer than I wish." Haldimand had seen a good deal of Britain's North American provinces by the time he washed up on West Florida's shores, and that he drew no clear distinction between the Gulf Coast colony and those elsewhere may be telling. In another case in point, in 1768 an observer living in Pensacola wrote in condescending fashion to a friend in South Carolina of how the members of West Florida's General Assembly claimed in grand fashion to be the "guardians of the people's liberties" but proved mostly ineffectual. Obviously both gentlemen believed that some colonial residents took to heart accepted ideals of liberty as it was coming to be defined in Britain's North American holdings. It is important to note, though, that while these occasional vague references to political sentiment may be tantalizing evidence of some connection with the spirit of patriotism around which other colonies were beginning to coalesce, they are rare and exceptional within the overall volume of surviving records of life in West Florida.[9]

Perhaps the best illustration of how marginal and undeveloped was this association with political thought being crafted within the seaboard colonies is the response to the only known formal invitations to join them West

Meeting of the first Continental Congress, 1774 (Library of Congress)

Florida received. When the first Continental Congress met in Philadelphia in the fall of 1774 in response to the passage of what later became known as the "Intolerable Acts," a series of acts aimed at enforcing parliamentary authority in the wake of the Boston Tea Party, West Florida was invited to send delegates. A three-member commission consisting of Thomas Cushing, Richard Henry Lee, and John Dickinson drew up the letter requesting West Florida elect representatives to the assembly, which delegates from twelve of the fifteen colonies in what is now the United States attended. Attorney General Wegg received the letter, which alleged that "so rapidly violent and unjust has been the late conduct of the British Administration against the colonies, that either a base and slavish submission, under the loss of their ancient, just, and constitutional liberty, must quickly take place, or an adequate opposition be formed." Wegg, despite his past record as one of the few officials in the colony to publicly support the conceptions of liberty espoused elsewhere on the continent, dutifully handed the appeal over to Governor Peter Chester, who tabled the potentially inflammatory request without a response. "I had great reason to apprehend from the spirit and temper of many of the inhabitants, that the calling of a House of Assembly would neither promote His Majesty's service, nor be productive of any advantage to the colony," Chester reported. If there was further effort to have the request considered, the evidence has not been found.[10]

Wegg followed the same plan of non-intercourse the next year when a second Continental Congress met in the spring of 1775 and determined to ban trade with West Florida and other loyal colonies. That congress became the political entity that would manage America's Revolutionary War and form its first functioning collective government. In the wake of the fighting between British troops and continentals in Massachusetts—which was the opening campaign of the war and rallied other colonies to join the rebellion—West Florida's official stance was steadfast loyalty. Writing to his superiors in London in the summer of 1775, Governor Chester claimed that "We are in a State of great Tranquility here, and I am happy to say that the Inhabitants of this Colony are well attached to the Constitution."[11]

Seeing the stark contrast between the rebellious seaboard colonies and the Gulf territories, on July 5, 1775, the Earl of Dartmouth declared West

The Earl of Dartmouth
(Library of Congress)

Florida to be a "secure asylum" for persecuted loyalists. He had notice given throughout the disaffected colonies that West Florida would serve as a haven for those elsewhere "too weak to resist the violence of the times and too loyal to concur in the measures of those who had avowed and supported the Rebellion." Those responding to the offer were to be given grants of land to ease their transition. The grants were exempt of quit-rents for a decade and allotted in quantities of 100 acres per head of household and fifty more for every other white or black man, woman, or child in a family group provided they could cultivate the acreage and they agreed to take an oath of loyalty to Great Britain. Soon petitions began flooding into government offices by people filling out the required affidavit stating they were seeking asylum in West Florida to "avoid the troubles then prevailing" in their home colony and that they were "well attached to His Majesty's government and disapprove of the present rebellion in the northern colonies."[12]

Some, such as Thomas Meaton of Maryland, claimed to have been "dayly pestered by their officers to take up arms in defense of America," and threatened by neighbors for not enlisting in the rebel cause in addition to losing a house, land, livestock, and slaves. Others claimed to be fleeing "anarchy and confusion" where one was "placed under necessity of forfeiting his allegiance to his majesty or losing his life and property with the lives of his family." William Weir sought to "settle himself here, in hopes of finding an asylum and retreat, from the disorder and confusion, which at this time unhappily prevails in the Northern Colonies." It is possible not all who migrated to West Florida to take advantage of this generous land distribution policy were in serious jeopardy of losing their lives or property. Others may have been less steadfastly loyal to the crown than fearful of the chaos of unpredictable partisan violence in the backcountry, for a substantial portion of very large grants were awarded to planters bringing large numbers of slaves, appearing more like speculation than necessary flight. All the petitioners seemed eager to take advantage of the British government's "favourable intentions toward the friends of Government that should emigrate." But neither the British government in London nor local authorities in Pensacola cared all that much about motivations. The former wanted to make a public effort to help distressed citizens and strengthen a bastion of perceived royal sentiment during a quickly escalating conflict, while the latter were delighted to at last benefit from a mass movement that promised more economic activity in the struggling province.[13]

The asylum measure sparked the largest migration into West Florida which the colony would witness during its time as a British possession. Between 1775 and 1779, West Florida received an estimated 2,500 settlers fleeing patriot strongholds elsewhere. The bulk of them opted for lands in

Loyalists desiring to flee the rebellious colonies and scenes such as that depicted in Raising the Liberty Pole, *by John C. Mcrae and Frederick Augustus Chapman, were offered asylum and generous grants of land in West Florida (Library of Congress)*

the western section of the territory or, in smaller numbers, the area around Mobile. The influx more than doubled the population of the fast-growing western section and brought to record heights the overall number of inhabitants of West Florida. Nearly half of the new arrivals hailed from Georgia and South Carolina, but individuals from every colony then in revolt, as well as the Caribbean colonies of St. Vincent, Jamaica, and Grenada, could be found among the immigrants.[14]

Most of the new arrivals believed they were leaving areas that had or were to become theaters in the growing war between Continental forces and Great Britain, but few were unaware that a different set of concerns lay in store in their place of refuge. During the course of the Revolutionary War, rebels in the southern colonies especially feared that Britain and loyalists would stir up Native Americans in the region against them. Though complicated alliances involving the Creek and Cherokee did figure into the scope and scale of the war in nearby Georgia and the Carolinas, West Florida seemed a world away from such internecine warfare. In fact officials there, where, in the words of one historian, "insecurity abounded on all sides," strove as much to maintain the neutrality of native groups as to secure their active assistance in open warfare. Both British West Florida officials and Spanish authorities in Louisiana did covertly woo the Creeks and the Choctaws to their side or at least try to keep these native groups from working actively against their interests. Official policy as determined in London was that Superintendent of Indian Affairs John Stuart would strive to use regional tribes as allies. Both Stuart, and, after his death, successor Thomas Brown, as well as other partisan operatives, complied as best they could.[15]

Creeks and Choctaws themselves were divided over how much support to give the British and in general were more concerned with keeping open channels of trade than taking a stand for or against continued British rule of its North American colonies. Many Native Americans just hoped to remain neutral. But this stance became complicated by the inconvenient reality that neutrality could mean fewer of the supplies to which they had grown accustomed. At least partially owing to these economic realities, Chickasaws and Choctaws were successfully recruited by British authorities in West Florida to help monitor the Mississippi River for rebel activity.

While Creeks, Chickasaws, and Choctaws did work in small numbers to help support British military interests in West Florida—most notably in the defense of Pensacola—no group clearly aligned itself militarily with either West Florida or Louisiana exclusively, and the potentially overwhelming number of native warriors in the region was never brought to bear for either Britain or Spain in the campaigns along the Gulf Coast.[16]

As the Revolutionary War evolved from a localized affair in New England into a major international conflict in 1776 and into 1777, West Floridians for the first time became uneasy about their safety from threats within and without their borders. Several ships en route to or from West Florida ports were captured in the Gulf by American privateers, and rumors began to circulate that the colony might become a target of the rebels. At various times nervous residents believed a rebel army might descend on the Gulf Coast from the north overland or via the Mississippi, or that a menacing continental naval expedition would suddenly appear off its shores. Late in 1776 word spread that an American army of some 7,000 men had assembled on the Ohio River, poised to make an offensive into the Gulf region. Although there were in fact some fleeting thoughts among the rebels for seizure of West Florida, most of the rumored plans were both untrue and unrealistic. But fear of attack did bring the colony's poor defensive preparations into sharp focus. The colony had no effective naval force, its small and scattered military installations were miserably prepared, and as late as 1777 only about 800 troops could be found in the entire province—the majority inadequately trained, haphazardly equipped, and often in poor health.[17]

Fears were only heightened by the fact that the colony had strained relations with neighboring Spanish Louisiana and that the border between the two provinces, the Mississippi River, might prove an easy avenue of invasion. Louisiana claimed a non-Indian population of somewhere between sixteen thousand and eighteen thousand people, much larger than that of West Florida, and might more easily than the distracted British tap into its vast colonial network for military aid should open warfare erupt. Americans had been suspected of visiting New Orleans to obtain aid for the rebel cause almost from the opening of the war, a situation which Governor Chester took so seriously that he at one point wrote Louisiana Governor Luis de Unzaga reminding him in no uncertain terms that the patriots were the enemy of Great Britain and that supplying them was a provocative act. One brazen patriot interloper into the region in August of 1776, believed to be Captain George Gibson, was even reported to have flown "Rebel colours" on his boat as he made his way down the Mississippi to New Orleans and upon arrival made menacing threats about Continental forces capturing Mobile and Pensacola while requesting material aid from the Spanish. Making matters worse to British eyes, this troublemaker's boat reputedly left New Orleans loaded down with powder and supplies. Governor Chester wrote to Lord George Germain in the aftermath that there was now "reason of apprehending that if the Rebellion should Continue another year the River Mississippi will be a Channel through which the Rebels will receive considerable Supplies of Ammunition unless we obtain Strict Orders from the Court of Spain to prevent their Subjects from furnishing these supplies."[18]

Unfortunately for the British, Gibson's visit proved to not be an isolated situation, as observers soon reported Americans regularly being allowed to obtain provisions in the Spanish capital. In April of 1777 British observers reported seeing a Spanish vessel at New Orleans flying "a flag in which was a snake and a hand grasping thirteen arrows and the field divided into thirteen stripes of different colors"; it was as clear a sign of Spanish sympathy with the patriot cause as could be given. To the frustration of local officials, no substantial military assistance from other quarters appeared to be planned for West Florida as the threat to its safety grew in 1776 and into 1777. The home government offered platitudes and counseled vigilance instead of moving to send the forces which might protect the distressed colony, warning an isolated and overwhelmed Governor Chester that "you cannot be too much on your guard."[19]

A key player in facilitating Spanish support of the patriot cause and fomenting heartburn in West Florida was New Orleans resident and native Irishman Oliver Pollock. He had migrated to North America in his twenties, shortly before the founding of West Florida, having fled his homeland in part due to its overbearing rule by the English. Pollock settled in Philadelphia and then worked with Spanish authorities as a trader in the West Indies before moving to New Orleans. Pursuing a career as a merchant and plantation owner, Pollock amassed a considerable fortune and became a close friend and confidant of Spanish Louisiana's leadership. Owing to his interest in the development of the Mississippi Valley, his attachment to the Spanish, and especially his pronounced personal disdain of the British, Pollock by the time of the Revolutionary War had come to so sympathize with the American cause that he would use his influence and wealth to support the rebels in substantial ways.[20]

By 1777 he had become an official commercial agent of the upstart United States with the full knowledge and blessing of Spanish authorities. During the war Pollock helped secure and ship enormous amounts of supplies from New Orleans to Continental forces. He made available an estimated more than £300,000 worth of supplies, easily worth millions of dollars in today's currency, for which he received irregular and incomplete reimbursement from the fledgling American government. In truth Pollock used so much of his personal fortune to support the patriots that by the end of the war he would be in significant debt himself and later need the help of another prominent patriot financier, Robert Morris, to put his affairs back in order. The actions of men such as Pollock were not only sanctioned but openly encouraged by Spanish authorities in New Orleans, who came to realize the opportunity presented to them by the Revolutionary War. With Great Britain distracted by the war with the Americans, the time seemed right to exact a measure of revenge for the territorial losses suffered by Spain during the Seven Years' War.[21]

BERNARDO DE GALVEZ, AN experienced military veteran from an influential family, assumed leadership of Spanish Louisiana at the age of thirty in January of 1777. Galvez's father, Matias, was a respected administrator who would occupy several important posts in the government of the Spanish colony of Guatemala, while his uncle Jose de Galvez had served as Spain's minister to the Indies prior to being appointed inspector general of New Spain. The younger Galvez of course enjoyed certain privileges through these connections, but he took full advantage of them by distinguishing himself in military action. As a teenager he had taken part in the Spanish invasion of Portugal, and while in his twenties he had earned distinction for bravery and ability in campaigns against the Apaches in New Spain. Prior to his arrival on the banks of the Mississippi, he had also served in the Royal Cantabria in France, during which time he learned the French language. Sent to Louisiana in 1776 to assume the governorship, he in short order became popular among his subjects, due in no small part to his marriage in November of 1777 to Felicite de St. Maxent d'Estrehan, the daughter of a prominent local French gentleman. But Galvez proved himself to be a competent, fair, and decisive administrator in addition to having social grace and political savvy, and he made it clear from the beginning of his leadership of the colony that he intended to assert Spanish sovereignty.[22]

Galvez moved in the first year of his administration to enforce trade regulations with West Florida which had long been observed loosely and at times ignored. For years prior to his arrival, British ships had traded in New Orleans under the pretext of exercising their right of navigation, with Spanish authorities complicit in this interpretation of their respective countries' regulations on foreign trade because it promised to be mutually beneficial. Some English traders even resided in New Orleans, conducting business in the open while leaders in both colonies looked the other way. In Galvez's estimation, trade with the neighboring British colony had proven anything but reciprocal, however, as Louisianans sold much less than they bought from West Floridians. The governor was also keenly aware of the benefit this provided the British in time of war. To continue business as normal would not only provide succor to the isolated British colony to his east, but would be an affront to the French, whom Spanish authorities were allied with and who were already providing aid to the Americans in their war for independence from Great Britain. When the captain of the British sloop *West Florida* seized three small Spanish boats on Lake Pontchartrain on the charge of cutting timber on British property, an outraged Galvez retaliated in swift and strong fashion. In a clear shot across the bow of his startled British neighbors, on April 17, 1777, the Spanish governor seized eleven British boats on the Mississippi on charges of illegal trading and the next day ordered all British traders working in New Orleans to declare their loyalty to Spain or leave Louisiana within two weeks.[23]

Galvez justified his crackdown on the grounds that the right of free navigation of the Mississippi as outlined in the 1763 Treaty of Paris did not carry with it the guarantee of expectation of free trade within Spanish territory, but the British had little doubt that a broader and darker agenda lay behind the action. They sent representatives to New Orleans to protest Galvez's high-handed actions and demand restitution. While Galvez refused to reconsider, he realized the provocative act could lead to a conflict for which he was not entirely prepared. He did eventually reverse his ban on British traders in New Orleans—likely in part because locals clamored for the slaves they were able to obtain from them—and allowed them to stay for a while on a promise to not disturb the peace. He even sent an olive branch of several casks of flour to Pensacola when he heard of a food shortage in the British capital. But Galvez refused to allow the British to take any military action on the Mississippi to discourage its navigation by rebel captains. When the British frigate *Atalanta*, sent to Louisiana to carry the news of the West Florida government's dissatisfaction with Galvez's actions, left the port to investigate claims of an American vessel at the river's mouth, Galvez warned the captain sternly that the river was neutral ground and any military aggression on its waters would be unacceptable to the Spanish king.[24]

While Galvez maintained public neutrality, behind the scenes he was working to prepare for an inevitable rupture with the British. He quietly planned to improve Louisiana's defenses and enlisted spies to gather information on the defenses of West Florida. Soon Galvez had in hand detailed descriptions of forts and troop dispositions, information on the status of the British relationships with Indians, and reconnaissance of the geography of West Florida. The British returned the favor to a degree, engaging in their own espionage aimed at learning the same things about Louisiana. But the first action of the war in the region would be ordered from neither Pensacola nor New Orleans, but by the American Continental Congress.[25]

8

Willing's Raid

'All was fish that came into their net.'

A s early as the summer of 1777, proposals for an attack on British interests along the Mississippi River and possibly even the capture of the port towns of Mobile and Pensacola had been bandied about by American political and military leaders and even in the sessions of the Continental Congress. Several influential men, such as prominent financier Robert Morris, had advocated opening a southwestern theater of the war as a first step toward clearing the Mississippi River for potentially lucrative trade with the crucial port of New Orleans and its pro-American Spanish leadership. Meanwhile, noted figures General Charles Lee and Sam Adams advocated that Florida should be an American province, and a scheme for an attack on the colony with the avowed purpose of forcibly adding West Florida to the American confederation had been promulgated by Colonel George Morgan and backed by none other than General Benedict Arnold. Even Virginia governor Patrick Henry corresponded with the Spanish about a potential offensive against West Florida which might benefit the patriot cause. Ultimately the various plans were disapproved by the congress on the grounds of impracticability. Congressman Henry Laurens of South Carolina became the foremost naysayer to what many dismissed as wild-eyed schemes for expanding the war, suggesting that if the new American government could spare the men and the funds necessary for such ambitious undertakings, it would perhaps be better served to devote those precious resources toward defending its cash-strapped southern colonies then actively resisting British rule.[1]

Still, intrigue associated with expanding the war into the Mississippi

Valley and the Floridas continued to swirl. In September of 1777, as the Continental Congress temporarily met in York, Pennsylvania, in the wake of the British occupation of the erstwhile United States capital of Philadelphia, James Willing brought yet another dubious scheme to the attention of political leaders. He was the son of a former mayor of Philadelphia and brother of Thomas Willing, congressional delegate and business partner of Robert Morris. James Willing proposed a raid on West Florida and its relatively unprotected British holdings via the Mississippi to obtain the neutrality of the region and secure a vital line of supply with New Orleans. Willing not only had the ear of influential insiders, he also had the credibility that came with having lived in Natchez for a brief time and hence purportedly knowing the lay of the land and the sentiments of the people. Willing certainly reported what many suspected—that West Florida's Mississippi frontier lay exposed and inadequately defended, and that British citizens in the area held little allegiance to either the British crown or the neighboring Spanish authorities across the river in Louisiana and were thus ripe for picking.[2]

In truth Willing had been an unsuccessful businessman in the Natchez region where he resided for only a few years and had recently returned to his home in Philadelphia deeply in debt. And while he did know many of the residents of the area well, he was not generally on the best of terms with them. William Dunbar, a planter who lived downriver from Natchez, remembered unflatteringly that Willing was "intimately acquainted with all the Gentlemen upon the river at whose houses he had been often entertained in the most hospitable manner and frequently indulged in his natural propensity of getting drunk." Further, his apparently outspoken support of the American cause at the onset of hostilities between the colonials and British troops had made him a bit of an outcast in what was in truth one of the relatively more loyal pockets of British settlement in the province.[3]

It remains unclear what exactly Willing's plan entailed and how much knowledge members of the congress had of the details of his scheme, in large part because Willing himself never divulged plans in their entirety or, more likely, changed his aim once the mission was underway. But a congressional committee on commerce approved his request on November 21, 1777, and commissioned him a naval captain. Ostensibly, he and a small force of subordinates would travel down the Mississippi to deliver dispatches to Spanish authorities and take delivery of supplies Galvez had stockpiled for Americans in New Orleans. Willing later claimed he had permission to capture British property as he saw fit in the course of his expedition, as well; it was an important caveat considering what actually occurred.[4]

WILLING CHOSE FORT PITT, a post originally built during the French and Indian War at the confluence of the Monongahela, Allegheny, and Ohio rivers (present-day Pittsburgh) as his point of embarkation. Styling himself as "Captain in the service of the United Independent States of America," by the end of 1777 he had recruited a small volunteer army of two dozen men and secured a boat—the inauspiciously named *Rattletrap*. Willing and his little band of raiders departed Fort Pitt on January 10, 1778. As they floated southward, they picked up additional recruits, probably lured by the promise of a share of the booty in what they clearly understood to be less a covert political mission and more an unvarnished raid on British property. By the time Willing and his little band reached the northern border of West Florida, he is believed to have had nearly fifty men. British observers on the river watched this nondescript American force as it made its descent but could only speculate as to its mission until it made landfall at Walnut Hills, site of modern Vicksburg, on February 15, 1778.[5]

Stepping ashore, Willing and his few dozen men surprised a small British guard and opened their campaign by plundering a nearby trader's house. After securing pledges of neutrality in the ongoing Revolutionary War from its incredulous occupants, who no doubt thought the conflict a world away, Willing continued downriver towards Natchez, surprising a few scattered settlers as he proceeded. The *Rattletrap* finally pulled up to Natchez on February 19, 1778. There Willing startled the residents of the small and virtually defenseless town, dramatically raising the American flag and demanding the surprised locals pledge their neutrality in the war. When a hastily assembled committee of community leaders approached him to see what all the fuss was about, Willing secured from them an agreement stipulating that the residents of Natchez would not "in any fashion take arms against the United States of America, or help to supply, or give any assistance to the

Willing's Marine Expedition, February, 1778, *by Charles H. Waterhouse*
(*The Marine Shop*)

enemies of said States." In return for not involving themselves in America's war for independence, Willing promised that their "persons, slaves, and other property of whatever description shall be left secure and without the least molestation." He then turned his attention to the surrounding countryside and moved downriver, grandiosely claiming that residents of the entire district were "prisoners on parole" and would be protected from harm so long as they complied with his demands.[6]

In the days that followed, Willing orchestrated what can only be termed a mission of unvarnished plunder, in the words of one historian "making a nuisance of himself and arousing the enmity of the population . . ." He and his band burned plantations and stores of goods, destroyed indigo processing facilities and other agricultural machinery, stole slaves and a variety of personal property, and killed livestock as they moved. From the selective way these raids were carried out in the Natchez area, it appears Willing might have been taking revenge on former enemies from his days as a resident of the region as much as doing anything to advance the American war effort. This supposition was shared by one witness to the mayhem, who suspected Willing had a sort of "black list, containing the names of persons to be destroyed," a theory with which some later historians have agreed. Also supporting the claim is that the property of planter Anthony Hutchins, whom Willing apparently held particularly enmity for, became among the first to be assailed even though the pledge of neutrality Willing had secured seemingly promised no harm to be done in the area. Willing's men killed Hutchins's cattle and hogs and then stole personal property and a number of slaves. The unfortunate Hutchins, in his sickbed at the time, was taken prisoner while Willing's raiders ransacked his home in their search for valuables.[7]

Willing's small force grew as it advanced southward. Several opportunistic volunteers, lured by the promise of the treasure to be obtained and sold in New Orleans, added to its numbers. These late-comers became a particular point of controversy as they were of uncertain official status as part of the expedition the Continental Congress tacitly approved, but they became an integral part of Willing's plans as his force gathered momentum. It is difficult to know exactly how many men Willing commanded at any given time and from where they came along the course of his chaotic journey below Natchez, but it is generally accepted that he had about 100 men in his charge by time he reached the Spanish capital. Local resident Matthew Phelps reported that Willing actively recruited men in the Natchez District for service in his American force, and that he even arrived in Natchez with blank commissions for volunteers. Phelps believed that since some along the river were "well disposed to the American cause . . . he enlisted about eighty hunters." But after a series of "eloquent harangues" in support of his "wild career" and the unrestrained plunder of the inhabitants he authorized, several of these men became disenchanted and returned to their homes. Nearer New Orleans Willing is alleged to have received additional aid. Regardless of how many men assisted him in his mission, he managed to wreak havoc out of all proportion to the number of raiders involved and to instill terror in West Florida's citizenry and government. In a meeting of the Council in Pensacola during the crisis, members taken aback by the reports of the appearance of the rebel band all along the western border wondered if rumors that Willing had some 2,000 men might be true.[8]

As Willing's small band of opportunistic volunteers made their way down the Mississippi, the theft and destruction only increased. The area between Natchez and Baton Rouge was hardest hit. "All was fish that came into their net" remembered a disillusioned William Dunbar, who had the misfortune of having his plantation along the path of raiders. Dunbar left a particularly lucid account of his encounter with Willing's men.

William Dunbar (Library of Congress)

He reported the raiders shot livestock, pilfered jewelry and other private possessions, looted wine cellars, and burned a few homes and outbuildings in his neighborhood. "The Houses were immediately rummaged and every thing of any value secured . . . twas not enough to pillage and plunder . . . his ruin must be completed by a piece of wanton cruelty." Dunbar reported that they robbed him personally "of every thing that could be carried away—all my wearing apparel, bed and table linen: not a shirt was left in the house—blankets, pieces of cloth, sugar, silver ware." They no doubt would have taken his slaves as well had he not been one of several plantation owners who had sufficient notice of Willing's arrival to send them across the river, into Spanish territory, for security.[9]

Many residents of West Florida in the Louisiana border region sought safety in Spanish territory in the wake of Willing's raid. So many clustered along the south bank of the Amite River, near its confluence with Bayou Manchac, that a new community arose which came to be known as Galveztown. The forming of the village as a sort of asylum for British refugees had been sanctioned by its namesake governor in response to the desperate pleas of those living in the area. Galvez's generosity could be traced in large part to his awareness that a depopulation of the British side of the border would be beneficial to Spanish interests. To the numbers of British refugees he soon added Canary Islander immigrants brought to Louisiana at Spanish expense in hopes of creating a border farming community which could double as an observation post. By 1779 several dozen British and Islander families resided in or around the settlement, and a town plan in traditional villa style had been drawn up by authorities. At its peak, Galveztown claimed a population of as many as 400 people and contributed a group of militia in support of the governor's military campaign designed to wrest control of West Florida from the British. British officials, alarmed at the growth of the upstart community, in 1779 made an effort to construct a new fortification, Fort Graham, on the banks of the Amite to keep better tabs on developments in the region. The post, however, was soon abandoned. In similar fashion, the community which sparked the outpost's establishment barely outlived the Revolutionary War, fading away as the threat of being caught in the crossfire of war subsided. By the early 1800s it was a ghost town.[10]

The raiders led by Willing did not confine their offensive to riverside homes, but also terrorized merchant boats navigating the Mississippi. Near Natchez the raiders, operating as adventurers "dressed in hunter's frocks" captured a number of small boats plying the river, and closer to New Orleans they absconded with a small packet, the *Rebecca*. After reaching the Spanish capital, the raiders seized cargoes of lumber, flour, and slaves aboard the *Neptune* and the *Dispatch* below the city. Willing's men also reputedly captured a British merchant ship, the *Chance*, in Mobile Bay and made away with its cargo.[11]

Legend holds that a detachment of Willing's force made its way as far east as Mobile seeking to recruit more volunteers and foment support for the American cause. The same reports have it that some of the raiders traveled into the Tensaw region north of town and distributed copies of the Declaration of Independence. Some published histories of the region even claim that one member of the expedition may have been jailed at Fort Charlotte. However unlikely it all may be, if indeed any of Willing's men did work their way through the Mobile area, it would appear they were unsuccessful in stirring up the populace to support their efforts. There is no evidence they

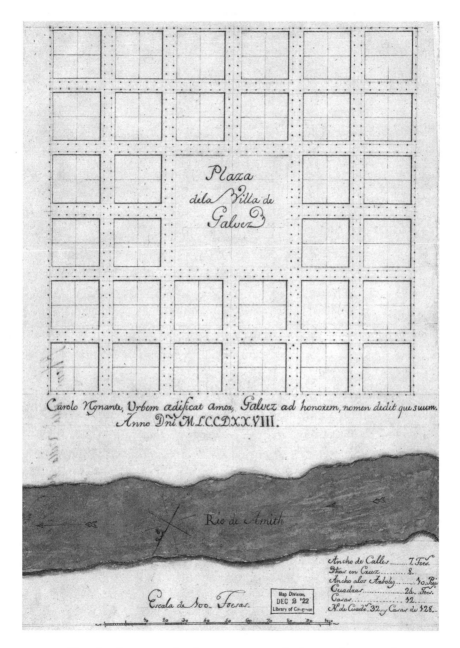

Plan for the town of Galveztown, 1778 (Library of Congress)

visited destruction on private parties such as took place along the banks of the Mississippi, and no indications they drew any support from the area while fomenting unrest between Natchez and New Orleans. Still, the perhaps far-fetched rumors of Willing's few dozen poorly organized raiders sweeping through the entire width of West Florida unrestrained are an important part of the story of the affair, for they reveal the level of panic and uncertainty it created and hint at the rumors the raiders apparently spread about their being just the advance of a larger force of invaders.[12]

Though caught completely off guard, the British scrambled to meet the threat. Officials at Pensacola organized an infantry force of perhaps two dozen men, headed by General Assembly Speaker of the House Adam Chrystie, to intercept the intruders and put a halt to their progress. A rare outspoken loyalist, Chrystie reputedly armed and outfitted some of his own slaves from his plantation on the Amite River for defense of the colony and helped raise other troops for regional defense. In early March of 1778, Chrystie's force left from Pensacola aboard the *Hillsborough* and the *Florida* and arrived at the colony's western border region a few days later. There Chrystie discovered his own plantation in ashes, courtesy of the American marauders. Hearing there were rebels at the small outpost at Manchac, Chrystie's men stealthily moved on the place on March 14. The next day they pounced on the handful of unsuspecting Americans lounging about the small fortification, first capturing an unwary sentinel and then rushing to attack the remainder of the force. In the brief melee of fighting—the only engagement on land between British and American forces during the Revolution in what would become the state of Louisiana—Chrystie's men killed at least one American and wounded a number of others while taking more than a dozen prisoner. The attackers suffered a single casualty. It was too little, too late to stop Willing's scattered force in its overall mission, but it was a first step towards restoring order.[13]

WHILE ALL THIS WAS going on the British navy also swung into action with the limited resources available in the region. Admiral Peter Parker, in response to the persistent appeals from local officials, had tried to maintain a "mosquito fleet" in the Gulf, but at the time of Willing's raid only the sloops *Hound, Stork, Sylph* and the *West Florida* were available for service. Campbell dispatched Captain John Ferguson of the *Sylph* and Captain Joseph Nunn of the *Hound* to New Orleans to protest Spanish complicity in the raid, demand restitution for the captured vessels and property, and prevent the raiders' escape into the Gulf. He stationed the *West Florida* in Lake Pontchartrain, to be assisted on land by a token infantry force, to secure the passes that could be used in reaching the Gulf. Nothing immediately substantive came of Ferguson's presence in the Crescent City. There was a near-farcical correspondence between him and Galvez in which the Spanish governor refused to satisfy British demands during debates over proper protocol regarding salutes to their respective flags and some quibbling over describing the Spaniards' guests as "rebels." Eventually, Galvez agreed to return some seized ships to their British owners.[14]

Despite the mounting show of force by the British, the raiders took their time evacuating the region, lingering along stretches of the river and randomly terrorizing the local populace. Frustrated locals attempted to organize a defense of their own once it became clear that Willing's "detestable banditti" had no intention of keeping their promise to refrain from harming private holdings after securing the pledge of neutrality from the residents of Natchez. A makeshift volunteer militia formed there and, under the command of a British officer who had not taken the oath of neutrality, determined to resist the invaders should they again appear. The militia first removed the flag of the upstart United States that Willing's men had arrogantly placed on Fort Panmure, an action one observer described in a flourish by noting "their colours were soon torn down and now ly dejected at our feet, and those of the Britannick Majesty most splendidly appear in triumph." They then hastily shored up the fort, and sent a few volunteers out to protect nearby settlements.[15]

The aggrieved Anthony Hutchins, who suffered so much at the hands of Willing's men when they first arrived, became involved in the effort once he made it back to Natchez after temporarily being held prisoner in New Orleans. Now harboring a personal vendetta against his captors, Hutchins advertised cash rewards for the capture of Willing and the American sympathizer Oliver Pollock in New Orleans. He also began planning to ambush the American raiders and rebel sympathizers should they show themselves near Natchez again. When a small group of Americans under Willing did arrive to discuss the terms of the neutrality city leaders had hastily agreed to a few weeks after their first entrance into the town, Hutchins's men were prepared. A small skirmish occurred on April 16 near Natchez in which four or five rebels aboard bateaux were killed and several others captured. One loyalist firing from onshore was wounded. Governor Chester would later commend the effort by having his council appoint Hutchins as an officer in the provincial militia, and the colonial legislature drafted a resolution of thanks for his "extraordinary zeal and indefatigable activity" in resisting the rebels.[16]

Infighting quickly destroyed the effectiveness of the ad-hoc garrison at Fort Panmure after the skirmish, however, and it transformed into more of a mob than a fighting force. According to one volunteer, "the most

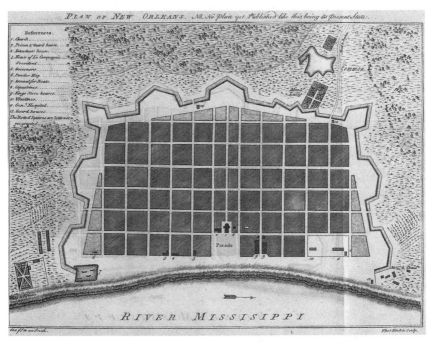

Plan of New Orleans, The Capital of Louisiana,
*by Richard Benning, 1770 (Norman B. Leventhal Map
and Education Center at the Boston Public Library)*

important concern of each party" became "to guard vigilantly against the subtlety and power of the other." Hutchins soon overreached his authority with the volunteers as he reputedly "allowed his private resentments too far to influence his publick conduct." Despite this devolution of the local militia into squabbling factions, its armed resistance restricted the raiders' activities in and around Natchez and helped instill a measure of confidence in the panic-stricken population.[17]

The majority of Willing's men at last reached New Orleans by mid-April of 1778. Governor Galvez, claiming neutrality in the war between Great Britain and its rebellious colonies, allowed the raiders safe quarter even as he simultaneously granted entry to a few of the refugees they had displaced. Willing arrived with documents making official Pollock's appointment as an agent for the United States Congress, and thus his complicity in the affair, and an unknown but sizable amount of plundered goods. According to some estimates, valuables and slaves worth at least $70,000—well over $2 million in today's currency—were put up for sale in the city with the permission of Spanish authorities. Galvez reputedly helped arrange for the return of some of the slaves to British owners but looked the other way as Willing's men disposed of the loot from their forays.[18]

BY MAY, WILLING SEEMED at a loss for what to do next, as gathering British forces prevented an easy escape back to the northeast. It did not take long for him and his band of marauders to wear out their welcome in New Orleans, either. His mere presence in the city during their unexpectedly extended sojourn became a growing source of frustration for Spanish authorities as spring turned into summer since it fostered increased British scrutiny of their activities and a litany of demands that Galvez do something about the situation. Further, Willing's delay in evacuating the city also postponed his taking supplies to American forces in the main theater of the war as planned and sparked a falling out with his erstwhile primary supporter, Oliver Pollock. Pollock had been a chief Willing ally and enabler until the early summer, when he began to grow frustrated with what he perceived to be Willing's dallying, lack of direction, and mounting expenses. "What his next pretence for tarrying here will be God knows, but . . . I am determined to stop all supplies in order to get him away," wrote an exasperated Pollock in August. Making a bad situation worse in the Spanish capital, Willing's men seemed quickly to lose whatever order they had during that sultry summer and generally made themselves a rowdy nuisance. Soon the little army began to shrink in both size and commitment as its future activities became less and less certain.[19]

In August, the majority of the remainder of Willing's men left after Galvez promised them safe passage north through Spanish territory to Kaskaskia in the Illinois country via a trek through what are now central Louisiana and Arkansas. Willing himself, accompanied by an entourage of about ten men, finally left town on November 15, 1778, on a private boat to attempt the perilous journey home. He was a wanted man, though, and the British navy doggedly pursued before overtaking the party at sea off the east coast and nabbing Willing as their prisoner. They clapped him in irons on Long Island, where they kept him for two years before he was released in a prisoner exchange. His capture ended, at long last, the only significant altercation between American and British forces in West Florida during the Revolutionary War.[20]

Spain's complicity in the affair definitively ended the possibility of continued friendly relations between Spanish Louisiana and British West Florida. Communication between Campbell and Galvez became more acrimonious in the wake of the American raid, and, as tensions mounted between patriot and tory sympathizers doing business in New Orleans, Galvez grew concerned with keeping the peace in his own capital. On April 16, 1778, he had fanned the flames of the brewing discord with his British neighbors by summarily ordering all English subjects in New Orleans to assemble at the government house and take an oath to not disturb the peace or leave. Those who remained, he was wary of still, knowing his actions could be observed with ease and reported to officials at Pensacola.[21]

The March of Galvez

*'The time is not very distant when our inveterate foes
will be entirely excluded from the continent.'*

Willing's raid accomplished precious little in tangible terms for the American cause it allegedly represented and in fact proved the catalyst for bringing the poor state of the defenses of West Florida into the sharp focus of British officials. The undisciplined escapade, in the estimation of Oliver Pollock, had merely "thrown the whole river into confusion and created a number of enemies and a heavy expense." Most residents of West Florida prior to Willing's arrival had regarded the Revolutionary War raging far from their borders as a foreign affair which they had no intention to participate in, but his behavior and the fact that the leadership of the neighboring colony of Spanish Louisiana had openly aided the forces of a nation with which Britain was at war awakened the leadership and citizenry alike to the danger they faced. "The entire province was thrown into great excitement and apprehension by this occurrence," remarked Governor Peter Chester, who saw the incident briefly spur a newfound patriotism, or at least an alarm with a rare display of partisanship, among many of the startled British subjects in the affected region. Meanwhile in Pensacola and Mobile, leaders suddenly grew concerned about potential enemies and enacted ordinances that "strangers," or new arrivals in the colony, be required to take an oath of allegiance to Britain and declare disapproval of the American rebellion.[1]

The raid spurred British authorities locally and across the Atlantic to reevaluate the colony's military preparedness. Officials in London were so dismayed that an "inconsiderable party of the rebels from Fort Pitt" could ravage a region that ostensibly lay under British protection that they at first questioned whether the money previously invested in the colony's sagging defenses was simply a grand waste of public funds. The correspondence from West Florida's distressed governor in the wake of the event could have hardly instilled confidence in the province's security. "The Calamitous and distressed Situation to which the Western parts of the Colony have been reduced by the unexpected Invasion of the Rebels . . . has created in me the most anxiety," Governor Chester admitted in a letter to superiors in Great Britain. "I most sincerely lament," he reported with dejection, "that the security of the other parts of the Province would not permit the sending of a greater force for the protection of our western settlements." With it clear that defenses had to be improved, British officials soon swung into action.[2]

The British army had only a few hundred troops thinly scattered across the entirety of West Florida at the time of Willing's appearance; most were haphazardly trained and equipped and serving at dilapidated, "weak and ruinous" posts spread across the colony's unusually long borders. Willing had highlighted the insufficiency of this arrangement, as well as the fact that under current conditions the Mississippi, and potentially other rivers draining the enormous area or even the Gulf itself, might serve as an open door for invasion of the territory by any aggressor possessed of even modest naval resources. Before Willing had even reached New Orleans, on March 21, 1778, Lord Germain, British secretary of state for the colonies, ordered General Henry Clinton to send 3,000 troops to the Floridas to bolster defenses, where they would be divided between bases at St. Augustine and Pensacola. More than 1,200 troops, mostly German mercenaries of the Third Waldeck Regiment, accompanied by a scattering of loyalist volunteers from Pennsylvania and Maryland, would be assigned to the defenses of West Florida. The reinforcements were delayed in their arrival until the fall, however, with their commander, Brigadier General John Campbell, not reaching Pensacola until January of 1779.[3]

Campbell was not impressed with what he found. He reported to General Clinton in February of 1779 that the fortifications in the province were "almost a scene of ruin and desolation" and noted some were improperly placed and new ones needed to be built in unprotected strategic locations, especially along the Mississippi. Doing so would require a Herculean effort owing to acute logistical challenges, according to Campbell, who despaired of his task as he was "without money or credit for contingent expenses; without vessels proper for the navigation, or even bateaux for the transporting of provisions adequate to the undertaking; without artificers wherewith to carry on works, whether by land or water; without any provision of materials to work upon, and without any prospect of their being procured by contract, or any otherwise but by the labor of the troops; without tools for accommodating the few artificers that could be found among the army; without engineers' stores; without even provisions . . . to justify sending many troops to the Mississippi." He further bemoaned that the soldiers he had to rely on for the colony's defense needs were, in his unflattering estimation, "composed chiefly of Germans, condemned criminals and other species of gaolbirds" whose loyalty he doubted.[4]

Campbell nevertheless dutifully went to work. He oversaw immediate improvements to existing fortifications, giving attention to their military strength as well as their livability for the troops, and ordered that a new post be built along the Iberville at Manchac. Despite his successes, Campbell thought of himself as in a trap on an undeveloped borderland, far from the scene of any real action, and pleaded with General Clinton to assign him to another post.[5]

If Campbell had doubts about his task in West Florida, the newly arrived troops with which he garrisoned his forts considered their posting a true hardship duty as well. They found the subtropical climate oppressive, complaining of the intense heat which forced laborers repairing the fort at Pensacola to work at night to avoid the searing temperatures. Others, unfamiliar with the Gulf Coast, figured themselves stranded on a wild and uninviting backwater. One of the German troops in British service, Phillipp Waldeck, described West Florida in despondent terms as "a desolate, uncultivated, waste, and here on the seacoast wholly unfruitful land. Wholly cut off from the world . . ." Perhaps disillusion with his assignment colored his estimation, for other men under his command marveled at the agricultural undertakings on display and the diversity of wildlife. They were intrigued with the numerous lemon, orange, peach, and fig trees they saw growing in area orchards and remarked on the novelty of seeing "buffalo or wild oxen" roaming in the woods. Others were shocked and terrified at the number of predatory wild animals which roamed the region, such as bears, large cats, alligators, and other "monsters." One soldier reported seeing a massive alligator dead and lying in the marsh near Pensacola. To his surprise and horror, within the beast's belly was discovered "completely unexpected, a negro of about 20 years of age." The situation in West Florida was far from inviting for those shipped in from elsewhere during a brutal summer, sparking one commander to sarcastically sum up the situation by noting that "if soldiers are satisfied in this place, they never will complain elsewhere." Most were of course not satisfied, and some demonstrated the fact by deserting when the opportunity arose. Whether these troops would be able and willing to defend the colony in the event of an emergency remained an open question as the long, hot summer of 1779 gradually gave way to fall.[6]

COUPLED WITH THE OBVIOUS malaise of the troops sent to their defense, the fact that the local government seemed patently inadequate to the task confronting it could not have helped the confidence of West Florida's nervous citizenry. So chaotic did the situation seem that the Council considered but ultimately did not press for a declaration of martial law. Whether that would have prepared the colony to face the coming storm can never be answered. What is clear is that with the means it had at its disposal, the colony's legislature appeared out of touch at best and incompetent at worst.[7]

The General Assembly called in the wake of Willing's exploits highlighted its ineffectiveness. Governor Chester had authorized elections for the assembly after several years without its meeting, in large part to discuss defense needs and, most assumed, to finally enact a coherent militia law. But he had attempted to reduce Mobile's representation in the process, a high-handed move which subverted any congenial spirit between the governor's office and the assembly which might have yielded a productive session. Chester had determined that Mobile and Charlotte County, in which it lay, would have a combined representation rather than the city and county each having designated representatives. Although Mobile claimed perhaps only a little more than 100 eligible voters, they were seemingly to a man outraged at Chester's attempt to diminish their political voice, especially since he proposed to continue to allow Pensacola to send its own city and district representatives to the Assembly. Mobile's delegates asserted that their city, "by far the most important of any in the province, for its antiquity, commerce and revenue to the Crown," deserved the same treatment as the capital city. Chester proved unyielding, pronouncing it his prerogative to call the assembly in a manner of his choosing by virtue of the king's instructions.[8]

A devastating hurricane which wrought immense damage to Pensacola inauspiciously delayed the gathering at the appointed time in October, as well, a fitting metaphor for the storm of controversy that would hamstring the government when it finally got down to business afterward. Despite the clear emergency, petty rivalries and festering jealousies got in the way of real business. A bill for regulating the militia, endorsed by the council, was read at least eight times with no action taken before the assembly was dissolved by Chester, who saw no progress towards that goal or of addressing other important matters regarding trade and diplomacy with native groups in the region. Chester decried the squabbling and inaction, scolding the assembly that "you still have matters of privileges more in view than His Majesty's interests and the internal economy and defense of the Colony." The Speaker of the House promised the governor the body had the interest of the colony in mind, offering that it, "you may be assured, will meet with every attention in our power . . . We will . . . endeavor to make every possible provision for those essential purposes that this Province can afford." Chester at last prorogued the contentious gathering in November after six weeks of acrimony with virtually no laws of substance having been passed. He stated he intended to call it into session again once the rebellion had ended, but West Florida's General Assembly would never meet again.[9]

The ineffectiveness of the legislative session stymied efforts to augment crown forces with local troops. Instead of having the benefit of a functioning militia, the government was reduced to asking for short-term volunteers which it would direct and incentivize. A few men did offer their services, including the aforementioned John Hutchins at Natchez and John McGillivray, an Indian trader living in Mobile, who offered to raise a combined force of settlers and Native Americans to clear the Natchez District of rebel sympathizers. But these would be the exceptions. There would be no rush to arms in defense of the colony by residents in West Florida. General Campbell found the situation so disheartening that he could not help but complain in private to superiors about the "backwardness" of the colony in seeing to its own defense. But in truth the civilian government did precious little to encourage loyalist sentiment or to raise the alarm among the populace at a pivotal moment for a call to arms. "Basking in a misplaced complacency," in the estimation of one of the colony's leading historians, the actions of Governor Chester and his council seemed to belie any sense of urgency.[10]

WHILE THE BRITISH DALLIED in West Florida, the Revolutionary War raged ever more closely to the colony's borders. After back and forth fighting primarily in the northern colonies for the first few years of the war—at Boston, Massachusetts; Princeton and Trenton, New Jersey; Saratoga, New York; and Brandywine Creek, Pennsylvania—the action in that theater ground to a stalemate in the summer of 1778. British forces were fortified in New York, too strong to attack directly but not themselves strong enough to initiate a new offensive. British officials then turned their attention to the

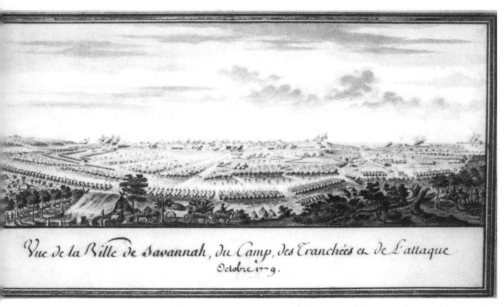

The Siege of Savannah (Library of Congress)

Depiction of the British surrender at Saratoga (Library of Congress)

southern colonies which had theretofore seen little large-scale fighting, in the belief that the suspected large number of loyalists there would flock to arms in defense of the crown and that the resulting victories would remove several colonies from the war and weaken rebel resistance elsewhere. Savannah, Charlestown, and other areas in North Carolina and Virginia for the first time became major targets of British military strategy. In neighboring East Florida, patriots in 1777 and 1778 attempted attacks on St. Augustine.[11]

Plus, even as the war raged closer and closer to home, a new, troubling international dimension opened in 1778 that some believed further imperiled West Florida. France, after prolonged debate and clandestine involvement in the American war effort, finally entered the Revolutionary War on the side of the United States with the signing of the Treaty of Alliance on February 6, 1778, on the heels of the stunning rebel victory at Saratoga in the fall of 1777. The French soon went to work to persuade their own ally, Spain, to join them. Spanish resources could be critical in securing a quick victory for the Americans and curtailing French exposure in what would soon become an almost global conflict. Outside observers including none other than George Washington recognized as much, expressing in private correspondence that the British navy could likely more than counter the efforts of the French and the Americans unless Spain tipped the balance. French diplomats began the long process of recruitment with vigor, although the concept of such an alliance had been floated for years prior and its potential had long been an open secret.[12]

Spanish leadership at last relented to French pressure with the Treaty of Aranjuez, signed on April 12, 1779, making the alliance official. The compact made France and Spain partners in the war effort with very specific terms advantageous to each. For Spain, one of the most lucrative opportunities was the possibility to regain control of Gibraltar, the rocky peninsula guarding the entrance to the Mediterranean which the British had long held, and the island of Minorca. Spain made it clear it was not officially allying itself with the upstart United States with the signing of the treaty even though everyone knew its aims—which included the repossession of territory in North America and the Caribbean lost to Great Britain in the Seven Years' War—would substantially benefit the American war effort. The declaration of war on the British came on June 21, 1779.[13]

Spain's belated entry into the war can be credited entirely to self-interest. Spain long resented British encroachment on colonial holdings in the Americas and seethed at the loss of territory during the Seven Years' War. But while many residents of Louisiana may have sympathized with the American cause, Spain's government did not. A European government attempting to administer a global colonial empire found little encouraging in the strength and vitality of the American independence movement, and the dangerous precedent its success might set was unsettling to some. Officials were aware, however, that Spain's participation in the conflict would clearly benefit the rebel cause; it was a price they were willing to pay for the dual aims of repossession of territory and the weakening of a hated rival.[14]

Having been armed with knowledge his home country intended to declare war well before the act occurred, Bernardo de Galvez had been making plans for his own preemptive strike on British interests. In the words of the foremost historian on the campaign about to commence, "procrastination was not in the nature of the governor of Louisiana." He reasoned a quick, surprise move on British posts before they could organize an offensive of their own would be the best way to defend his vulnerable capital and to realize the war aims of Spain in the region. Galvez did worry about the defenses of his own colony, however, especially that whatever plans he made would rely at least in part on the militia. Despite a bold front of aggressive confidence, he fretted that volunteers could not be counted on once the bullets started to fly. He began to organize them all the same, and took steps to marshal all the other military resources at his disposal as he mulled over the best course of action should the opportunity to strike West Florida arise. By the time official word of the declaration of war arrived, Galvez stood poised to take the offensive.[15]

IRONICALLY IT WOULD BE the rumors of a British move against New Orleans that nudged him to make the first move in the late summer of 1779. British Secretary of State George Germain, aware of the relatively weak defenses of New Orleans and its geographic position, virtually surrounded by multiple water approaches which naval forces might utilize to advantage in an attack, had recommended an expedition to capture the city in secret orders to General John Campbell on June 25, 1779. Germain believed a surprise attack on the Louisiana capital would neutralize the developing Spanish threat before it gained further momentum and allow West Florida to better prepare for aggression from any quarter. General Campbell, commanding British forces in West Florida, had deep misgivings about his ability to comply with the suggestion. His many recent reports on the military situation in his province had already demonstrated that he had neither the troops, ships, nor supplies to pull off such a bold mission. He had no illusions as to the relatively weak condition of his forces, either, and the colony's disaffected population was unlikely to provide reliable support to an effort which would need every locally available resource. Still, he planned as best he could for an assault as ordered and began assembling a small flotilla for the expedition in September of 1779. Campbell's first reaction to the news that Spain had already declared war on Great Britain was to notify only certain key military officers in the hope they could plan for the conflict before the general population panicked or the Spanish launched their own attack.[16]

Meanwhile, bits and pieces of information on potential British designs on New Orleans reached Galvez courtesy of his spy network. From his trusted agent Jacinto Panis, he had learned of the surprise and uproar the Americans had created as well as details of the strength of defenses and number of troops in the colony. Panis had been sent by Galvez to Pensacola by way of Mobile under pretext of looking for deserters, and he had been in West Florida when news of Willing's raid arrived. Galvez also knew from careful, secretive reconnaissance of the disposition of the scattered, lightly defended posts throughout West Florida and likely had some knowledge of the generally low morale in the sickly, isolated garrisons. He also learned of the reinforcement of the British post nearest New Orleans, at Manchac, and that authorities were attempting to embargo ships in the harbors at Pensacola and Mobile and were rounding up vessels that might serve as troop transports. Galvez regarded all these movements as ominous even if he understood the overall state of British military preparedness as more ripe for being attacked than going on the offensive. But the final straw provoking action proved to be an intercepted letter from British officials in London to General Campbell in Pensacola in which they ordered an attack on New Orleans should Spain enter the war between Great Britain and its American colonies. He immediately put long-developing plans in motion. Galvez's monumental decision to strike first would alter the course of Gulf South history.[17]

The Spanish commandant had assembled a formidable army. Throughout the summer of 1779, under the guise of improving the defenses of his colony, he had been busy collecting troops and supplies for use should military action against British forces became necessary. By August he had at his disposal at least 170 regular Spanish soldiers stationed in Louisiana, an additional 330 recruits from Mexico and the Canary Islands, about seventy-five local militia and volunteers, an estimated eighty free blacks, and a few American volunteers. When the secret plan for a major offensive became clear, even Oliver Pollock proved eager to participate, eventually going along as Galvez's aide-de-camp. Just as final preparations were being made, however, a deadly hurricane threatened to undo all of Galvez's careful planning. The sudden storm destroyed numerous houses in the Spanish capital, sunk ships at anchor in the Mississippi, drowned livestock, and decimated crops for miles. Undeterred in his mission, the determined governor, mistaking word of Spain's recent compact with France as an endorsement of the American rebellion, on August 20, 1779, had the independence of the United States proclaimed "by the beat of drum" and had Spain's declaration of war on Great Britain announced at a large public gathering called at the Cabildo, the government center in the heart of New Orleans. He cast his upcoming mission as defense of the colony owing to Britain's declaration of war on Spain for its recognition of American independence. Few present realized how far Galvez intended to go to defend the colony.[18]

With the echoes from the drumbeats of the gathering still echoing through the cobbled streets of the Spanish capital, Galvez's campaign against the British swung into motion. He put his men on the march on August 27, 1779, first advancing northward out of the city along the Mississippi, where he would be joined by an additional 600 men, including German settlers, Acadians, and more than 150 Indian warriors living along the Louisiana-West Florida border who had been persuaded by Galvez's rhetoric that to fight for Spain was to fight for their own best interests. The governor soon commanded more than 1,400 men. He revealed the true nature of their mission once they neared his first target—the small outpost of Fort Bute at Manchac, northwest of New Orleans in the far southwestern corner of West Florida.[19]

A relatively diminutive fortification situated on a swampy floodplain along the Iberville River, Bute consisted of a square wooden stockade and several interior huts serving as living quarters for its garrison. The British were under no illusions as to its strength and had a short time prior sent two galleys and a few additional troops to shore up the exposed post, but as Galvez approached it still needed substantial improvement to serve as an effective border defense. The commander of Fort Bute, Lieutenant Colonel Alexander Dickson, had already determined his position indefensible and chose simply to abandon the post for a stronger one upriver at Baton Rouge before Galvez approached. Dickson destroyed many of the provisions recently sent to prevent them falling into enemy hands, and he left only a token detachment of about twenty German mercenaries at the fort as a guard. The Spanish army arrived on the scene days after Dickson's evacuation and camped within short marching distance of the fort on September 6, 1779. Early on the morning of September 7 the Spanish opened the attack with a battalion of snappily dressed creole militia under Captain Gilberto Antoine de St. Maxent in the vanguard of the advancing column. A brief, one-sided firefight commenced in the gray morning light as the crackle of musketry rang out. The fort's defenders stepped up to fire a volley or two from their parapet, only to have the Spanish reply in exponential volume. It all ended as quickly as it began as the overwhelmed garrison surrendered within minutes. The defenders suffered a lone unlucky soldier killed in the brief skirmish while the remainder became prisoners; the Spaniards did not lose a man. Galvez planned for the fall of Bute to be just the first step in a blitz on British posts along the Mississippi, and he allowed his victorious army just a few days rest before moving on to Baton Rouge.[20]

AS THE ADVANCE BEGAN several other components in Galvez's strategy were falling into place. Captain Carlos de Grand-Pre was leading a small detachment of Spanish troops to Roche a Davion, a landmark bluff along the Mississippi between Baton Rouge and Natchez, to cut off communication along the waterway by the British and further isolate the their posts at those locations. Meanwhile another small Spanish force had been sent to monitor traffic on the Amite River and guard against information arriving along that waterway from the east. And along the peaceful shores of Lake Pontchartrain, one of the more unique occurrences of the war along the Gulf Coast began to unfold. The lake, immediately north of New Orleans and forming part of the watercourse borderline between West Florida and Louisiana just east of the Mississippi, at the time was an international waterway under the complete control of neither the Spanish nor the British. At the outbreak of war, Governor Galvez had given his blessing to a scheme proposed by Oliver Pollock to fit out a boat, which he had originally acquired to ferry supplies to the American army, for disrupting British communications on the lake. Pollock had commissioned the *Morris* (the captured *Rebecca*), under the command of Captain William Pickles, for the task. The boat essentially functioned as an American privateer with a mixed American and Spanish crew. On September 10, 1779, Pickles spotted a choice prize on the lake and moved to capture it. Flying a British flag to deceive his prey, he crept up alongside the Royal Navy patrol ship *West Florida* near the windswept northern shore. Lieutenant John Payne, commanding the *West Florida,* no doubt wondered about his unidentified approacher until Pickles hauled in his ensign and set gaudy American colors to the breeze. Suddenly a vicious close-quarters fight, which would become known as the Battle of Lake Pontchartrain, opened. Payne was mortally wounded and the *West Florida* was eventually boarded and its crew captured amid a cloud of sulphurous smoke from the discharge of guns both large and small. A short time later an emboldened Captain Pickles pulled his boat up to the north shore of Lake Pontchartrain, secured the allegiance of the startled residents along Bayou La Combe as "true and faithful subjects to the United Independent States of North America," and audaciously announced his claim to possession of the area.[21]

About the same time, Vicente Rilleux, a native of New Orleans with roots in the Pascagoula area, struck out against British interests in similar fashion on behalf of the Spanish. His target was a British transport in the confined waterways near Manchac loaded down with supplies and more than fifty troops. Utilizing an armed schooner, Rilleux took the unorthodox step of offloading the ship's small-caliber swivel guns along the banks of the pass with a portion of his crew while his boat lay in wait. He ordered his men to open fire with repeated broadsides as the British boat approached, to be accompanied by much uproarious yelling and cheering to create the impression the vessel was under attack by a much larger force. The crew of the British boat, mostly German mercenaries, at once sought shelter below deck. Rilleux's command pounced, boarding the vessel and closing the hatches on the Germans. It was an unceremonious affair for British arms but not the end of their setbacks on the waters of the West Florida-Louisiana border. At least three other small vessels would be captured by the Spanish in the area before the end of hostilities.[22]

Back in Pensacola, Governor Campbell of course had no information about what was happening until far too late to do anything about it. On September 14, 1779, a full week after the fall of Fort Bute, he finally learned of the Spanish advance. He immediately wrote to Lord Germain

dejectedly that the Spaniards "have got the start on us." Reporting he had
received intelligence that Galvez had authorized "the Independence of the
American States . . . publickly recognized by beat of drums," he expressed
his disappointment that he would at once have to shift from an offensive to
defensive plan even though he had no clear concept of Spanish intentions.
By the time he received more information from the western border which
clarified Spanish strategy, though, there would be precious little left in his
colony's western borderland for him to defend via land or water.[23]

Galvez's army arrived at Baton Rouge on September 13 in good spirits
but much diminished in overall numbers. Illness and fatigue reduced his
troops nearly by half in slogging through the trackless, mosquito-infested
lower Mississippi Valley terrain. The physical breakdown of a significant
portion of his army gave urgency to offensive operations, for Galvez knew
he could only keep his fighting force in the field for so long and needed
to make progress quickly. Considering the strength of the position they
encountered at Baton Rouge, he knew that would be a challenge. There,
at Fort New Richmond, which had but a short time previous been the
grounds of the Watts and Flowers plantations, approximately 400 British
troops and 150 settlers and slaves defended a stout post on a bluff of the
Mississippi with a commanding view of the river for several miles in each
direction. The fortification bristled with a dozen brooding cannon and lay
ringed by a ditch some eighteen feet wide and nine feet deep. Further, it
stood surrounded by well-made chevaux-de-frise and a substantial earthen
wall. Lieutenant Dickson, who had fled Fort Bute earlier, commanded. As
its size, solid construction, and menacing outer defenses precluded an immediate frontal assault, Galvez determined to lay siege and bombard the
place with the ten pieces of large-caliber artillery his men had lugged through
the swampy backcountry. He hoped the fort would either be destroyed or
its isolated garrison, cut off from resupply, would be forced to capitulate.[24]

Galvez employed a ruse in a gamble to bring about a quick decision.
Rather than undertake a traditional siege, in which he might attempt to
surround the fort and advance on it through regular approaches, he sent
a detachment of his men through the woods a few hundred yards to the
north with orders to create a noisy diversion and deceive the garrison into

thinking an assault might be coming from that direction. Meanwhile, he had the remainder of his men set up his cannon in a concealed position elsewhere. The trick worked to perfection. The British focused their attention on the detachment, firing wildly into the brush and turning most of their heavy guns in the direction of the phantom assault. When Galvez opened up with the artillery he had managed to position at relatively close range on the morning of September 21, 1779, the defenders of Fort New Richmond were taken by surprise. According to legend, one of the first shots in the bombardment came crashing through the wall of the building in which Lieutenant Dickson was having breakfast. Regardless of how thoroughly it disrupted the morning routine of the British garrison, by midday the devastatingly accurate Spanish artillery fire had caused immense damage to the fort and rendered continued resistance foolhardy. Around 3:30 p.m., Dickson had the white flag raised so that he could discuss surrender terms with his wily adversary.[25]

To Dickson's consternation, Galvez refused to accept his surrender unless the British post at Natchez, Fort Panmure, be included in the capitulation. It was an unconventional demand but one the British commander had little option to dispute given his situation, and after some quibbling he reluctantly agreed to the terms. The Battle of Baton Rouge had been a small affair in terms of casualties—one or two Spanish soldiers killed and perhaps four British—but it had yielded Galvez 350 more prisoners and, due to the bloodless taking of Natchez, effective control of the Mississippi from the northern border of West Florida at Nogales all the way to the river's gulf outlet.[26]

Galvez immediately sent a detachment of fifty troops upriver to take formal possession of Fort Panmure. The dumbstruck commander of the post, Isaac Johnston, could hardly believe what had happened but saw no option but to comply when presented with a copy of the arrangement agreed to by Dickson. He therefore handed over the fort without a shot being fired on October 5, 1779. The Spaniards gave the surprised locals a period of several months to decide to take an oath of loyalty to Spain or leave the area. The people of Natchez could scarcely believe their luck; only a year and a half ago their settlement had been ravaged mercilessly by a small band of American marauders from upriver and now it had been captured

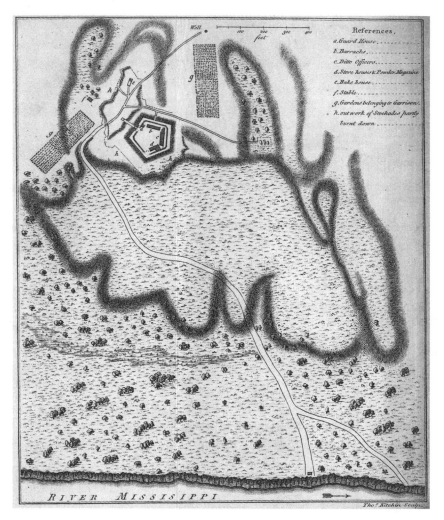

Fort Panmure (Library of Congress)

by an even smaller contingent of foreign troops after a battle downriver
they had known nothing about. In neither episode had any resistance by
British arms been manifested. In a letter sent to Lieutenant Dickson shortly
after the capitulation which had been signed by fifty-nine of "His Majesty's
dutiful and royal subjects" in Natchez, townspeople vented some of their
frustration by expressing sarcastically their desire to "beg leave to return
you our most sincere thanks for your generous and disinterested attention

to our welfare in the capitulation of Baton Rouge. From every circumstance we had not a right to expect such terms, and are fully impressed with the idea that we owe them to the unexampled bravery of you, the officers and men under your command." They closed with a final jab, communicating how they were consoled in their reversal of fortune that at least Dickson's garrison was now "in the hands of a brave and generous conqueror." It was an inglorious and humbling denouement to a campaign which caught the British on West Florida's western border totally flat-footed and augured poorly for the defense of the rest of the colony.[27]

FOR THE SPANISH, JUBILATION prevailed. In a matter of weeks Galvez had captured eight ships, three forts, more than 550 prisoners, numerous British flags, and secured operational control of a valuable territory at the cost of less than ten men killed and wounded. The governor won immediate promotion as Field Marshal for his exploits, and many that accompanied him, including Esteban Miro and Francisco Bouligny, whose names would figure prominently in the future Spanish administration of the region, would later assume posts of high rank in part owing to their participation in the stunningly successful action. The victories indicated the possibility of a surprisingly rapid decision in the war between Spain and Great Britain on the Gulf Coast that, when combined with the successes of the American movement for independence elsewhere, promised a wholesale change in the North American colonial infrastructure. From New Orleans, Oliver Pollock gloated in their aftermath that he now had "reason to hope that the time is not very distant when our inveterate foes will be entirely excluded from the continent." Mississippi River merchant and future politician Julien Poydras de Lalande celebrated the recent Spanish success with a poem entitled "The Capture of the Bluff of Baton Rouge by His Excellency de Galvez," which he published in the fall of 1779; a portion included these lines of plaudit:

> ... Nothing could shake the brave Besiegers
> Despite deadly missiles which menaced their lives ...
> ... Their bullets, striking, threw down his earthworks;
> Devastation and death marked his steps everywhere ...

> ... I wish in his honor to institute a Festival
> Which will consecrate forever his new Conquest ...[28]

British authorities in Pensacola were taken aback as the details of Galvez's campaign trickled into the capital over the fall. Stupefied at the scale of the loss in such a short time, General Campbell was left the unenviable task of trying to explain to an alarmed Lord Germain. Expressing his "grievous mortification" at having to inform him of the thoroughness of the Spanish offensive, Campbell forthrightly summarized the affair in December by concluding that "Spain had predetermined on a rupture with Great Britain ... had laid their plans ... and it would appear, had even fixed on the day ..." In this sober analysis he stood correct, but a firm grasp of his adversary's previous military strategy did nothing to help him prepare for the inevitable next move of the Spanish. Simply put, the British seemed at a loss for what to do. And in all honesty, in the disconcerting aftermath of the raid along the Mississippi, few locally or in London seemed to believe the British were up to the task of defending West Florida regardless of the Spaniards' avenue of approach. Campbell despaired that he was "environed on all sides by the Spaniards, and exposed to their attacks from the Havana, La Vera Cruz, or New Orleans ...," while Lord Germain expressed his concern that the recent "very unfortunate events in the King's affairs" would "be attended with very injurious consequences to the remainder of His Majesty's possessions in West Florida."[29]

Authorities soon snapped out of their daze and scrambled to defend what remained of the colony. In an effort to find help, Governor Chester issued a proclamation requiring all citizens to take an oath of allegiance and those eligible for militia service to come forward immediately. He had to have been heartened to learn of the flickers of loyalist determination within his province in the wake of the Spanish onslaught, even if based more on self-preservation than any principled stand for the British flag, such as came from the settlements in the Tensaw-Tombigbee region north of Mobile. In October of 1779 a group there requested permission to construct a fort for protection from the Spanish and offered to fight for the province where needed. The Council naturally granted its permission, though what progress was made towards the fort's construction, if any, is unclear. It is believed that some residents from the Tensaw-Tombigbee settlements did take part in the defense of Mobile the following spring. The British also attempted to bolster their few warships. Military leaders in West Florida had long been convinced that the only effective way to defend their far-flung colony was with a fleet of warships, but now that the hour of crisis had finally arrived, the small, worm-eaten force they had cobbled together appeared entirely inadequate. Most of the relatively diminutive vessels Admiral Parker had sent to the region the previous fall were already of diminished capacity. The *West Florida* had been ignominiously captured, and repairs were needed for others including the *Hound* and the *Port Royal*. Plus, in a bad omen amidst a veritable avalanche of setbacks, lightning had struck the mast of the *Hound*, shattering it to splinters and injuring several crew members.[30]

In the spring of 1780 the HMS *Mentor* augmented the British fleet. Its

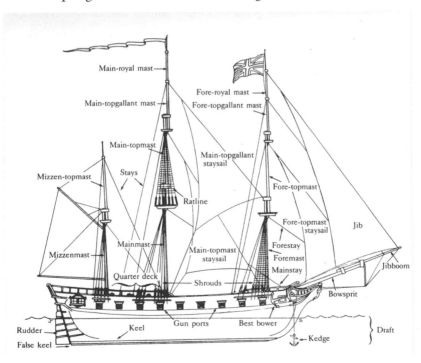

Sketch of the HMS Mentor, *from* The Log of the H.M.S. Mentor
(University Press of Florida)

role is the best-documented of the ships in the small naval force charged with defending West Florida, and is in some ways the story of this small contingent in microcosm. The 250-ton sloop had been constructed in Maryland as the *Who's Afraid* and equipped to carry some two dozen guns and a complement of 160 men. At least a quarter of the crew consisted of teenagers, and more than half of the remainder were in their twenties. The great majority hailed from England, with a few coming from Ireland, Scotland, and Wales, but the crew also contained a smattering of men from other British colonies including Jamaica and St. Kitts. The ship's captain, Robert Deans, had been in naval service in some capacity since his teenage years and had seen extensive service during the Seven Years' War and in multiple locations already during the Revolutionary War. This reasonably well-armed ship, equipped with copper plating to deter the worms which ravaged so many other boats in Gulf waters, appeared just the vessel needed to bolster West Florida's naval defenses. On its maiden voyage out of Pensacola, it captured a Spanish sloop bound for Mobile. But it was soon discovered that several time-consuming upgrades would be needed if the boat was to provide steady service on the open waters of the Gulf. These being made, the boat headed out on patrol again, eventually capturing another Spanish ship, the uniquely named *Jesus, Maria and Josef*, as well as other prizes. The *Mentor* alone could not deny the landing of Spanish forces in their later campaigns for Mobile and Pensacola, though, and the crew of the ship ended up providing perhaps its most effectual service in helping to build and man the fortifications around Pensacola. In similar fashion, most of the small fleet local colonial forces assembled provided little effective protection to remaining British waterside posts, and their crews were ultimately pressed into service as ground troops during the campaign for Pensacola. Much of that story lay in the future as a period of stunning reverses for British arms in West Florida drew to a close and another chapter in the war for control of the colony was set to open.[31]

The Capture of Mobile and
the Battle at The Village

*'With these small victories our men are gradually
gaining a certain feeling of superiority over the enemy,
which could be very useful from now on.'*

Bernardo de Galvez took precious little time to bask in the stunning initial victories of his first campaign against British West Florida. By January of 1780, he stood ready to take to the field again in his quest to forcibly wrest the colony from British control. He had chosen to target Mobile next. Not only was the city one of the colony's population centers and major ports, but it stood between him and Pensacola and served as a vital supply point for the British capital. Galvez knew much of Pensacola's provisions, especially meat, came from the Mobile area, and he also knew that Mobile played a critical role in British communication with the Chickasaws and Choctaws. Plus, he knew from his spy reports that Mobile's defenses were wanting and believed it could be taken in short order.[1]

Galvez had encountered some resistance to his approach from superiors in Cuba, however, and they had proven slow to send him the men and materials he believed necessary for the campaign. He proceeded with his plan nonetheless, convinced of its soundness and confident he could pull it off with the resources he himself could gather. A small force under Elias Durnford was stationed at Fort Charlotte, but its progress on repairing the crumbling masonry fort had proven exceedingly slow owing to several factors, not the least of which was that nearly a third of the men were sick at any given time. Galvez planned to overwhelm the outpost before it could be strengthened, thus leaving Pensacola alone standing between him and total control of the colony.[2]

The multi-national, multi-ethnic army with which Galvez would move on Mobile proved more than sufficient. Combined with forces sent from Cuba which would meet him en route, his army would eventually outnumber the defenders at least five to one. Galvez departed New Orleans on January 11 with some 750 troops: about 275 regulars in the Spanish colonial army, about 325 white militiamen, just over 100 free black militia volunteers, about twenty-five Americans, and two dozen carefully selected slave laborers who had experience with guns. The force was transported down the Mississippi and through the Gulf by a small fleet of about a dozen vessels. A sudden winter storm temporarily scattered the ships in the open waters of the Gulf, but by February 9, 1780, they had arrived at the mouth of Mobile Bay. The fleet had been joined at Ship Island by none other than Captain William Pickles, victor of the Battle of Lake Pontchartrain, aboard the repurposed West Florida.[3]

As Galvez's fleet pulled up to windswept Mobile Point to locate the narrow channel into the bay, they found to their surprise a British merchant ship run hard aground in the choppy shallow waters. The Spanish quickly captured the stranded vessel, the Brownhall, and its small crew, hoping to score some loot and deprive their adversary at the same time. As the convoy tried to enter the bay over the treacherous bar a short time later, several ships in the Spanish caravan likewise ran aground and had to be offloaded of their men and cargo to be refloated, forcing a frustrating delay in the Spanish advance. One boat, the Volante, remained hopelessly stuck despite laborious efforts to free it and the jettisoning of thousands of pounds of unessential items. As thunderstorms rolled in and conditions deteriorated on February 14, the Volante began taking on water. Eventually Galvez had no choice but to salvage what supplies and weapons from the ship he could and abandon it to its fate amidst the waves.[4]

Placing the Volante's guns ashore on the western tip of Mobile Point on February 17, Galvez ordered the construction of a small battery manned by about 100 soldiers and sailors to guard against any British naval relief force being sent against him during the upcoming expedition. It would be

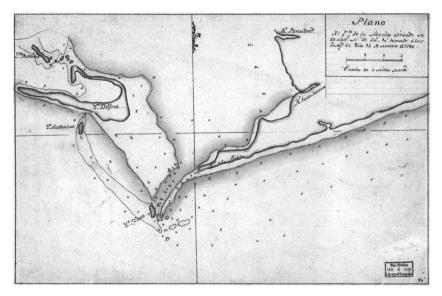

Mobile Point, 1780 (Library of Congress)

the first fortification of its kind on the spot which would figure prominently in defense for the region for the next century and a half. Galvez placed a trusted subordinate, Jose Antonio de Evia, captain of the ill-fated *Volante*, in charge of a similar hastily built fortification on Dauphin Island at the same time. Before finally moving up the bay towards Mobile, Galvez was joined at Mobile Point by five ships from Havana carrying approximately 1,400 troops and a copious amount of supplies for the expedition.[5]

With his army now swelled to more than 2,000 men and with a flotilla at his service, Galvez moved into Mobile Bay and headed north. He landed his force on the western shore approximately fifteen miles below the city of Mobile, at the mouth of a short, meandering stream known as Dog River. Here the Spanish unpacked their haversacks, hauled barrels and crates of foodstuffs from the dank holds of their ships, and established a base camp near a plantation owned by a Frenchman named de Mouy. Galvez needed to organize his army before proceeding cautiously towards the city. Not only must he be careful not to expose his men to any surprise attack by the British while on the march through unknown territory, but he could only move as fast as his men could push, pull, and drag the several heavy siege

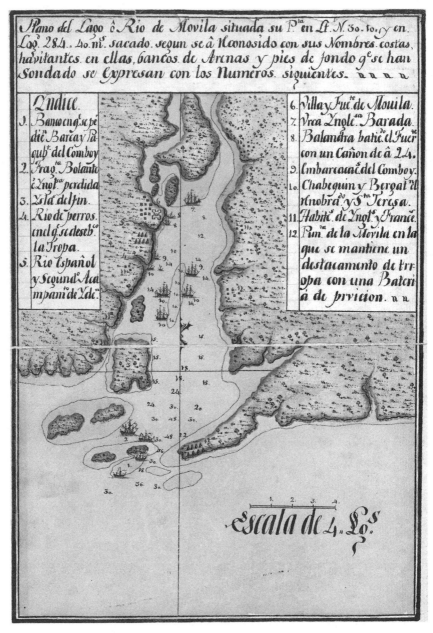

Plan of the Lake and River Mobile, *showing the progression of the Spanish advance on Mobile (University of Michigan Library Digital Collections, William L. Clements Library Image Bank)*

guns he brought along for the reduction of the centerpiece of the defenses of Mobile, Fort Charlotte. The Spanish troops heaved the massive artillery pieces, each weighing over two tons and featuring nine-foot barrels, northward at a snail's pace as they essentially opened a new road through the bayside forest. As the area was drained by numerous small creeks and rivulets, the troops had to construct several makeshift bridges as they moved the cumbersome weapons. By February 28, the plodding invaders had at last arrived at the outskirts of Mobile. The next day the British fired on a Spanish scouting party reconnoitering Fort Charlotte, while one of Galvez's ships, the *Valenzuala*, moved into the Mobile River and lobbed a few shells in the direction of the fort. The battle for Mobile had begun.[6]

Inside Fort Charlotte were approximately 300 troops, consisting of nearly 100 men of the 6th Royal Regiment along with a few dozen militiamen, about two dozen loyalist troops from Maryland, some sailors pressed into service as ground troops, a small number of local citizens, and several black men officially designated as servants or laborers but many of whom had been armed by the officer in charge, former West Florida governor Elias Durnford. The post's armament consisted of more than forty pieces of artillery. This somewhat unconventional force determined to defend the town to the best of their ability despite the odds against them and had taken some drastic measures to that effect prior to the arrival of Galvez's army. To create clear fields of fire for gunners and to eliminate as many covering positions as they could in case of enemy approach, the British had burned several houses and other buildings in the immediate vicinity of the stockade. The result was a fort facing the river and ringed by a wasteland of destruction that could only be captured after a difficult fight.[7]

GALVEZ CAREFULLY SURVEILLED THE situation upon arrival in front of Fort Charlotte and planned his course of action. His decisions were at least in part informed on the defensive preparations at Mobile by intelligence he obtained from his own men and a few townspeople. Reputedly an escaped slave from the fort turned up in the Spanish camp on Dog River with details on British troop strength, for example. Such information would have been valuable, but was easy enough to obtain otherwise, as Spanish surveillance had revealed all the general needed to know. On March 1 he sent Francisco Bouligny, lieutenant governor of Louisiana, under a flag of truce through the no man's land between the lines to demand the surrender of the bold little outpost. Bringing Durnford's attention to the fact that the Spanish army outnumbered those within the fort several times over, Bouligny warned him he should yield immediately or suffer devastating consequences. Durnford replied defiantly, acknowledging the disparity of forces but claiming the fighting ability of his troops to be "much beyond your Excellency's conception." He explained capitulation without a fight was out of the question, for "were I to give up this fort on your demand I should be regarded as a traitor to my king and country." He hedged his bets by ending with a genial tone of praise, observing that "the generosity of your excellency's men is well known to my brother officers and soldiers," and expressing his expectation to be treated fairly "should it be my misfortune to be added to their number." Extending an awkward professional courtesy, he asked if Bouligny would be so kind as to dine with him before returning to his army. The two enjoyed a sumptuous meal and drank glasses of wine to the healths of their respective kings and friends before an amicable parting.[8]

Durnford then gathered his men and read aloud Galvez's demand for surrender. When he then read to them his reply, they erupted into cheers. Seizing on the energy of the moment, Durnford at once offered any man in his confident command too afraid to stand with him a chance to leave at that moment with no consequences. As he had calculated, not a soul took him up on the offer. Relieved and heartened that this gesture "had the desired effect," Durnford reported in his account of the coming siege that his troops then "went to our necessary work like good men." But Durnford knew all too well the long odds his spirited garrison faced, and he had rallied his men in large part to buy time. Sometime during the advance of the Spanish army, which his scouts had easily detected, Durnford had sent a hurried request to Pensacola for reinforcements. A relief force of more than 500 men, including regulars, Waldeck troops, American loyalists, and a number of allied Indians, had hastily assembled and began the march west towards the imperiled city of Mobile. Neither they nor Durnford had any idea whether they would arrive in time.[9]

On March 2, 1780, the Spanish army moved into a camp a mere 2,000 yards from the western gates of Fort Charlotte and formally began the siege. They began by constructing batteries from which their large artillery pieces could be protected as they rained destruction on the British post. With an inspirational speech from Galvez ringing in their ears, they put shovels to the ground to begin work on what would soon be six earthen gun emplacements positioned a few hundred yards north and west of the fort. That same day a small group of British troops crept out of the fort to spy on the Spaniards' activity at close range but had to beat a hasty retreat when they were discovered and fired upon. In the confusion of this opening skirmish, a few men, including Deputy Indian Commissary Charles Stuart—for some reason involved in this vanguard reconnaissance—were captured. In Fort Charlotte, Durnford noted uneasily in a communication to military officials in Pensacola that he could see at least two warships within two miles of his position and was informed at least eight lay near the Dog River that very moment. Menaced front and back, by land and water, the British steeled themselves for the coming assault.[10]

As siege operations proceeded over the next few days, Galvez and Durnford opened a friendly exchange of gifts and conversation which formed a bizarre interlude in the campaign. On March 4, Durnford sent through the lines a letter concerning the treatment of prisoners along with several bottles of wine, a dozen chickens, loaves of bread, and a lamb for Galvez in addition to some provisions for the prisoners he had captured two days earlier. In return, the chivalrous Galvez sent the British commander a selection of some of the finest items in his commissary: a case of Bordeaux wine, a box of oranges, a box of tea biscuits and corn cakes, and some Havana cigars. The two then exchanged cordialities, with Galvez promising to treat well the captives he held or might capture, and both mutually agreeing that a house near the fort where sick and wounded men were being tended to would not be disturbed by the respective military forces. In the midst of this polite banter, though, Galvez reproached Durnford for burning swaths of the town he was charged to defend in order to create clear fields of fire for his guns. Admonishing Durnford that he was "commencing to destroy the town in favor of a fortress incapable of defense," Galvez offered not to

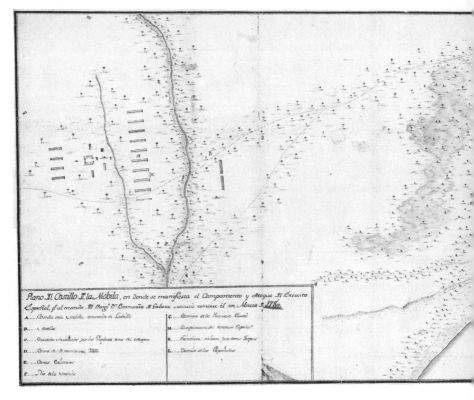

Map of the siege of Mobile (Instituto de Historia y Cultura Militar)

construct any batteries closer to the fort than the farthest residences of Mobile's citizens from the post (only a few blocks) if Durnford would cease his arson. The British commander replied he was only doing what was necessary and made no promises. A week into the standoff, the batteries the Spanish were feverishly working on were nearing completion, hurried on by word from their scouts that British reinforcements for the beleaguered post were en route from Pensacola. Galvez sent a small detachment across the bay to observe the reinforcements and prepared to open his assault on the fort at the earliest practicable moment.[11]

Under cover of darkness on the nights of March 8 through March 11, Spanish work parties put the finishing touches on battery positions for the eight eighteen-pounder guns and the single twenty-four pounder they had hauled to Mobile after landing below the city. It was slow, laborious manual

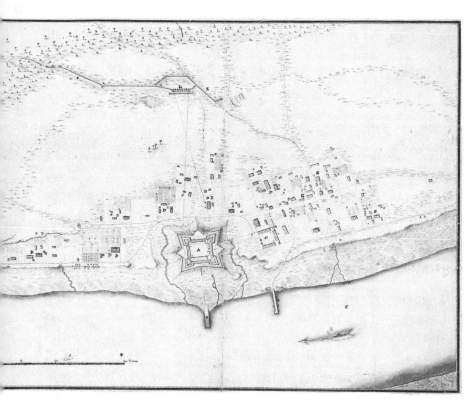

labor made all the more difficult by passing storms and the fact that Durnford did what he could to discourage their progress. Several times he had sent out small detachments of skirmishers to fire upon exposed workers. On one such sortie, one of the black workers in Galvez's army received severe wounds in a firefight that also claimed the life of a British soldier. As many as six more Spanish troops were killed in scattered fighting as construction on the earthworks continued. Not all the casualties were the direct result of the exchange of fire; one unlucky Spanish soldier lost his life when a tree he was cutting down fell on him.[12]

By the morning of March 12, Galvez had his guns in position just a few hundred yards from the fort for the final bombardment. At ten o'clock he opened on the fort with a thunderous barrage that rang out across the lower Mobile-Tensaw Delta. In short order, the deadly accurate fire of the Spanish artillerymen dismounted some of the guns at Fort Charlotte and inflicted heavy damage on its walls, opening gaps reportedly big enough for a man to walk through. Durnford replied to the steady cannonade as best he could with his more numerous but smaller caliber artillery pieces, and in the spirited exchange of fire his cannoneers put one Spanish gun out of action. As the fight wore on, it became increasingly one-sided as it became hazardous for the defenders to expose themselves on the parapet long enough to return fire. Surprisingly, the several hours of cacophonous shelling resulted in the death of only one of the troops inside Fort Charlotte. As the sun began its slow descent into the western horizon, Durnford's longsuffering little force found itself low on ammunition and their ragged and battered fort in danger of being rendered untenable.[13]

Meanwhile, on the bluffs along the Tensaw River northeast of Mobile, the British relief force from Pensacola had just arrived and could hear the battle raging. The men had embarked on their journey nearly a week before arriving on the easternmost waterway of the labyrinthine Delta river system, but wet weather and the high-water levels of several stream crossings had made their trek a grinding slog. The group experienced a "very trouble-some passage" of the rain-swollen Perdido just outside the colonial capital and reported the roads they traveled, through what is now central Baldwin County, Alabama, were merely "deep and miry" paths. Their plan had been to build rafts after arrival on the Tensaw and make their way to Mobile by floating across the Delta waters and into the Mobile River. Though they feared they were too late to render assistance, a contingent of the men nonetheless pressed on to surveil the city. The scene they beheld revealed the fate of the fort had already been decided.[14]

At dusk on March 12, 1780, Durnford raised a flag of truce over the ramparts of his battered fort and the guns of the contending armies at last fell silent. With the echoes of the cannonade resounding in their ears, representatives of the Spanish army stepped out between the lines and approached the fort. Durnford notified the Spanish emissaries that he requested a ceasefire until morning, at which time he proposed to make a formal surrender of Fort Charlotte to Galvez and have his men strike out for Pensacola. Galvez summarily rejected the offer, making clear his determination to continue the bombardment unless the entire British garrison agreed to lay down its arms and become his prisoners. He gave Durnford only four hours to make his decision. With no other option, Durnford accepted the terms. At ten a.m. on Tuesday, March 14, 1780, the British garrison marched out of their fort, colors flying and drums beating, and stacked arms. Moments later, the British colors were lowered and the Spanish flag was set to the breeze over Fort Charlotte.[15]

THE CAPTURE OF MOBILE was of enormous consequence in the war between the Spanish and the British despite its relatively small casualty figures—the British suffered only one man killed and eleven wounded in the fighting in front of Mobile, while the victory came at the cost of eight killed and about a dozen wounded for the Spanish. Not only had the British lost another strategically vital post controlling one of West Florida's most important harbors and interior river systems, but they had seen another of their armies captured and hauled off to prisons in Vera Cruz and Havana. Even the retrograde movement of Campbell's tardy relief column proved fraught with setbacks for the British, as Spanish forces captured a small detachment of Royal Foresters left behind to drive cattle back to Pensacola, and, in crossing some of the still rain-swollen streams between Mobile and the capital, a few more luckless British soldiers lost their lives. For the aggressive Galvez, his only regret was that his troops could not further press their adversary.[16]

The newly minted "Governor of Louisiana and Mobile" wanted to follow up on his success at Mobile by moving straightaway for Pensacola, but he needed more men and supplies and the cooperation of authorities in Havana to obtain either. He therefore determined to return to New Orleans to plan his next move and left his trusted subordinate, Colonel Jose de Ezpeleta y Galdeano, in charge at Mobile to solidify Spanish control of the city and surrounding region. A veteran soldier who had served in Spain's military since his teenage years and had seen action in the Caribbean and the Mediterranean prior to service on the Gulf Coast, the thirty-nine-year-old Ezpeleta had earned Galvez's trust as a man of action and vision. Ezpeleta immediately set his men to repairing Fort Charlotte—which the Spanish apparently did not take the trouble to rename but simply referred to as "Fuerta Carlota"—and moved to shore up other regional defenses. In this work he apparently enjoyed the services of not only the several hundred troops left in his charge by Galvez, but also of many slaves, including some obtained locally from British plantations as well as some secured from Spanish authorities in New Orleans.[17]

Ezpeleta also assumed political administration of the town in the spring of 1780. He oversaw the distribution of food and supplies to visiting Choctaws and Creeks in an effort to keep them from actively taking the side of the British, and he began the formal administration of the oath of allegiance to the mixed French and British citizenry desiring to stay in the area as demanded by the Spanish crown. Most citizens, especially those of French heritage, decided to take the oath instead of making a troublesome and uncertain move eastward into the shrunken remainder of West Florida. Ezpeleta discovered in his new role as commandant that the same illnesses stalked his men as had the former occupants, and throughout the summer into the fall a substantial portion of the men he needed to carry out his administration of the conquered city could be found in the hospital rather than on active duty.[18]

Nonetheless, Ezpeleta devoted most of his time in the spring, summer, and into the early fall of 1780 to military activities in the district he commanded. He had plenty to keep him busy. Galvez, before his departure, had authorized the construction of an observation post on the eastern shore of Mobile Bay near The Village (La Aldea to the Spanish), the small farming community which traced its origins to the earlier French occupation of the region. The post, now under Ezpeleta's purview, could guard against any approach by the British from Pensacola, help prevent desertions from Mobile's garrison, and assist in establishing a Spanish presence in the region where lay numerous colonial farms and plantations along the rivers and bay opposite Mobile. Records are unclear as to the size, construction, and even the specific location of this outpost, but it likely consisted of some form of lightly fortified wooden stockade along the shoreline at the head of the bay near the route of modern Interstate 10 between the present-day Alabama cities of Daphne and Spanish Fort, about eight miles east of the city of Mobile. Just under 200 men eventually garrisoned the place, consisting of an assortment of troops from regular colonial regiments along with a small number of men of the New Orleans Colored Militia and a detachment from the Royal Artillery Corps for the operation of its two cannon. For the British in Pensacola and their Indian allies, it would prove too inviting a target to pass up.[19]

SIGNS THAT THE BORDER region between Pensacola and Mobile had become a theater of action in the war abounded in the summer and early fall of 1780 as isolated skirmishes flared. This interlude in the war began in earnest in June, when a party of a few dozen Indians attacked a British military patrol twenty miles west of Pensacola. While there was no evidence they were associated with the Spanish, the incident was suspicious enough that British officials decided to strike the Spaniards utilizing their own allied Native Americans as soon as an opportunity presented itself. Before they could act, in July of 1780, the Spanish undertook a mission to scout British positions near the Perdido, inspect the road connecting The Village and Pensacola, and, they hoped, possibly encourage desertion of British troops. Throughout the ensuing

Statue of Galvez in Spanish Plaza, Mobile (Mike Bunn)

months small groups of forces ranged along the narrow paths serving as the primary land routes connecting the British capital and the Spanish beachhead on Mobile Bay, each attempting to surveil their adversary. At least twice in the fall of 1780, Indians under the influence of the British, likely Creeks, approached The Village under some vague agreement to attack the place. In the most organized of these rather unsophisticated efforts, a party of more than 130 Indians and a few Royal Foresters departed Pensacola in late October for the Eastern Shore on a mission to "dislodge 100 Spaniards who have taken post and fortified themselves there." Upon arriving near the Spanish position in early November a firefight broke out in which a few men on both sides were killed before the British-allied Indian force melted away in the face of the Spaniards' artillery. A few British plantations in the region, including one owned by Elias Durnford, apparently came under assault during this period as well. But the majority of the casualties in the desultory skirmishing were some unsuspecting French farmers residing along the eastern shore of Mobile Bay, who a party of Indian warriors fell upon through some misinterpretation of plans or because they presented targets of opportunity.[20]

Unbeknownst to Ezpeleta, these scattered, small-scale actions were just the beginning of formal British plans to regain lost territory and halt the Spanish army's progress in rolling up the defenses of West Florida. Lord Germain, buoyed by the recent news of the resounding victory against the Americans at Charlestown, South Carolina, and still somehow optimistic about the likelihood for success of an offensive against the Spanish at New Orleans, had ordered British warships to the Gulf Coast from Jamaica in the wake of the loss of Mobile to protect what remained of the imperiled colony. Locally, General John Campbell was confused why the Spanish had made no serious advance towards Pensacola after their capture of Mobile, but he decided to take advantage of the respite with an attack of his own. Gathering all the information he could about the disposition of Spanish forces occupying the Mobile Bay area, he planned a combined-forces assault on the outpost at The Village which might put his men in a position to retake Mobile. The plan called for a small naval squadron to be sent into the bay with orders to capture any enemy vessels they encountered and prevent reinforcement from Mobile while an infantry column advanced on the eastern shore to "drive the Spaniards from a fortification at that place and to destroy it."[21]

Campbell soon assembled an infantry force of more than 500 men. It included about 100 men of the 60th Regiment of Foot; a similar number of loyalist volunteers from Pennsylvania and Maryland who had recently been sent to Pensacola for service in West Florida; a few dozen soldiers of the veteran German mercenary Waldeck Regiment; about a dozen Royal Foresters; and more than 300 allied Creek Indians. Colonel Johann Ludwig Wilhelm Von Hanxleden, leader of the Waldeck troops, commanded. Though they were foreign troops hired by the British for assistance in the Revolutionary War, the Waldeckers, named in honor of Prince Friedrich Karl August of the Principality of Waldeck, were respected professional soldiers who had already proven their mettle in campaigning in the northeast. Their valor is at least partially demonstrated by the high casualty rates they sustained in British service—of the 1,225 Waldeck men sent to the war in North America, fewer than 500 returned home. The mixed British column, along with two four-pounder cannon they had to lug through the wilderness roads en route to their destination, departed Pensacola on January 3, 1781, intent on surprising and routing the Spaniards at The Village.[22]

Waldecker soldier (Prints, Drawings and Watercolors from the Anne S. K. Brown Military Collection, Brown University Digital Repository)

A few days later, on January 5, 1781, the HMS *Mentor*, HMS *Hound*, and the sloop *Baton Rouge* slipped into Mobile Bay flying the flag of Spain so as to deceive the small garrison stationed on Dauphin Island. When the unsuspecting Lieutenant Martin Galiano and thirteen of his men went out to meet the unexpected boats, they promptly were taken prisoner. The British at once sent a detachment of troops from the ships ashore in an effort to capture some of the cattle the Spanish kept on the island to replenish their supply of fresh meat as well as to neutralize the remainder of the garrison. They had not gotten very far when the first shots of the campaign aimed at the recapture of Mobile were fired. The Spanish soldiers remaining on the island, less than twenty in all, gathered themselves and let loose with several volleys of musketry at the thieves. In the confusion of the short firefight, the Spaniards had three men captured, but remarkably, no one on either side was killed. Realizing they were outnumbered and unaware what further reinforcements might be lying in wait aboard the ships just offshore, the Spanish troops determined discretion to be the better part of valor and retreated back towards Mobile to ring the alarm. British troops quickly moved in and set fire to their abandoned blockhouse and barracks, but, themselves unaware of what, if any, Spanish forces remained on the island and unnerved by the ferocity of the resistance they stumbled into, moved back to their ships as well. What had begun as a grand cattle raid netted them a mere three calves. Realizing that dallying at the mouth of the bay might endanger the security of the army they knew should be soon arriving in front of the outpost at The Village, the naval officers had their ships continue along their main mission by moving farther up into the bay where they could contest any reinforcements being sent by the Spanish from Mobile. Early on the morning of January 7 they heard firing and saw smoke rising to the northeast.[23]

Just before dawn that morning, a Sunday, the British force had arrived at The Village and, under cover of a thick fog, stealthily advanced on the Spanish garrison. Lieutenant Manuel de Cordoba, outside the fort's walls at the time, is believed to have been the first of the Spaniards to see the line of British troops moving through the dim gray morning light. At first he apparently mistook the approaching troops for his own men, which was easy enough to do since no one at the post suspected the British of having an army in the field so close to their position, and the snappily dressed red-coated regulars and blue-coated Waldeckers would have been indistinguishable in the predawn darkness. The split-second mistake proved fatal, for the attackers shot him down before he could raise the alarm. Before the other troops within and without the fort—some dozing and others leisurely beginning their morning routines—could discern the danger posed by the gunshots, the British column was upon them.[24]

Hanxleden had divided his men into two columns as they made their way to the Spanish entrenchments, ordering the Indians to surround the palisade while the other troops attacked head-on. His orderly plan broke down into a confusing free-for-all almost immediately, however, and in a matter of moments became a brutal, close-quarters contest featuring hand-to-hand combat and a flurry of shouting, gunshots, and bayonet thrusts. Some of the most eager British troops, led by his Waldeckers, nearly overran the Spanish in their outer works before they could even mount a defense, but, without adequate support in the vanguard of the attack, were forced back by desperate defenders. Several Spaniards were gunned down or bayoneted in their trenches during the opening moments of this first furious assault. Others, caught outside the palisade, fled for their lives ahead of the advancing Indian warriors covering the open ground between the fortification and the shoreline, running towards the water where a lone small boat lay moored. A number were cut down by pursuers who, according to witnesses, "followed them chin-deep in the water to get their scalps." As the shoreline became enveloped in smoke hanging heavy in the foggy atmosphere, the Spanish position appeared to be doomed.[25]

The Spanish had been caught completely off guard and pressed almost to the point of breaking. Their defense had been made all the more difficult by the fact that their artillerymen could not bring their big guns to bear owing to rains of the previous day having soaked the matches and cords they needed to fire rounds. At length the defenders, under the direction of Lieutenant Ramon de Castro, rallied and slowed down the attackers before they could breach the palisade's walls. "Our men . . . resolved to sell their lives dearly," later reported Colonel Ezpeleta, and poured volleys into the oncoming column. The biggest factor in Spanish resistance may have just been a lone casualty from one of those broadsides. Early in the chaos of the frenzied initial assault, the stalwart Colonel Hanxleden, whom even Ezpeleta acknowledged to be "the best officer of Pensacola," fell dead from a musket shot. With their leader's body laying at the foot of the palisade, the British attack began to lose coordination and devolve into isolated pockets of uncoordinated fighting. Command of the attacking force fell to Captain Philip B. Key (uncle of future composer of the American national anthem Francis Scott Key), the erstwhile leader of the corps of Pennsylvania and Maryland loyalists. Suddenly thrust into overall command of men he had little familiarity with, the majority speaking a foreign language, Key was hard pressed to manage the attack effectively much less keep up its original momentum.[26]

Many of the Indians that had marched with the British column—over half of their force—became the first to disengage. Their initial fervor seemed to lose steam once they no longer had stragglers outside the walls of the fort to chase down, and they appeared to have little enthusiasm for a more traditional advance on a fortified position. With a majority effectively out of the action after its first moments, the battle settled into a firefight between much more evenly matched forces. The contest raged with bitter ferocity for only a few more moments that must have seemed interminable to the combatants. Several more men fell as the firing crescendoed, including additional pivotal officers from the ranks of the attackers on whose leadership the direction of the assault hinged. When a Waldeck officer and one of the 60th Regiment fell dead in rapid succession, the entire offensive at last lost all cohesion. Small groups of troops and Indians continued to fire on the fort in uncoordinated fashion for a few more minutes until the result became obvious. William Augustus Bowles, a Maryland Tory and colorful character who would one day proclaim himself the leader of the entire Creek Nation, claimed to have fought in the battle dressed as an Indian. In his telling, he was among the last to break off the fight, firing into the palisade at short range from the cover of a nearby tree until it was rendered a pile of splinters by a well-placed artillery round. It is doubtful that Bowles actually participated in the affair, though he was later captured with the garrison at Pensacola at the end of the war, but his dramatic, embellished account seems an appropriate metaphor for the ending of the failed British assault. Their best-laid plans rendered a shattered dream, the attacking army had no option but to make an unceremonious retreat back to the colonial capital.[27]

The Spanish hastened the retrograde movement of the British force with the spirited fire of their artillery, at length becoming involved in the fight and taking deadly aim on the fort's assailants even as they disappeared into the tree line. Lacking the manpower with which to cut off the enemy's retreat, they could only watch as the British disappeared out of range. Noticing the British ships still in the bay the next morning, Ezpeleta was uncertain if another attack might be coming and hurried a messenger to New Orleans with an urgent request for reinforcements. The British frigates, soon realizing their army had been repulsed, in short order moved back down the bay to see if they might help cover the retreat. Finding themselves to be of no use to the beaten force and hearing a rumor that a Spanish fleet from Havana was en route to Mobile, they weighed anchor and returned to Pensacola. Meanwhile, the exhausted Spanish garrison at The Village began the grisly task of laying to rest their slain comrades and the British dead left on the field. They buried Colonel Hanxleden under the shade of a large tree, and according to one of his men "fired a rocket over his grave as tribute to his honor."[28]

The battle would be remembered as the bloodiest day of the Revolutionary War in what became Alabama. At least fifteen and perhaps as many as twenty members of the attacking army lay dead on the eastern shore's sandy soil once the smoke had cleared. Many more were wounded, with at least three casualties unable to retreat with the army and taken prisoner. An inordinately large portion of the British casualties occurred within its Waldecker regiments, which suffered the devastating loss of nearly all of their officers. For their part, the Spanish reported fourteen killed and twenty-three wounded in repulsing the attack. Spanish authorities were elated with the results despite the casualties and proved generous in handing out commendations to the victorious army. They recognized several individuals for their actions in the battle; Lieutenant Ramon de Castro was honored with a special annual pension for bravery displayed in repelling the British at close quarters, and he was promoted to the rank of captain. At least three other men—Lieutenants Rosella and de Guardamuro, and Sublieutenant Pedro—received promotions. Lieutenant Cordoba, the unfortunate officer who became the first Spaniard to fall in the fight, was honored with a posthumous promotion.[29]

Ezpeleta positively gloated in his army's triumph in the report on the battle he submitted to Galvez. "With the greatest satisfaction I can report to you that every one of the attacks thrown against us by the enemy has been repulsed," he exclaimed. "With these small victories, our men are gradually gaining a certain feeling of superiority over the enemy, which could be very useful from now on." Indeed, in turning back the attempt to recapture Mobile, the battle set the stage for the campaign against West Florida's capital city.[30]

The Siege of Pensacola

'So superior an army, fleet and artillery must at last carry their point.'

B ernardo de Galvez began planning an assault on Pensacola virtually as soon as he accepted the surrender of Fort Charlotte in Mobile. He endeavored throughout the spring and summer of 1780 to accumulate the men and supplies he needed for the mission, grudgingly postponing the opening of the campaign until fall as he did so. At length, after a visit to Spanish authorities in Havana, he secured several thousand men and at last planned to move on the British colonial capital. As it had prior to the launching of his first strike of the war, however, fate, in the form of another Gulf hurricane, intervened. A sudden ferocious storm in late October scattered the fleet being sent for his campaign, forcing another frustrating postponement. As Galvez renewed his request for support in early 1781, word of the attack at The Village lent his scheme a new urgency. The British clearly had designs on reversing recent gains by the Spanish and remained a formidable foe. Spanish officials again made troops, ships, and supplies available, this time in the form of a fleet carrying approximately 1,500 troops which departed Havana in late February. Galvez's strategy called for the multiple forces at his disposal to converge on Pensacola from Louisiana, Mobile, and Cuba beginning in March of 1781.[1]

Capturing Pensacola would be the most difficult undertaking Galvez had yet attempted in the war. It was easily the best-fortified position in all of West Florida, protected by a daunting ring of forts the British had spent considerable time and expense improving, all manned by well-equipped garrisons. It could only be approached through a narrow harbor entrance bristling with guns and monitored by a small but swift flotilla. Fort Pensacola, the largest fortification in the colony and the headquarters for troops stationed in its namesake town, stood in the heart of the city a few blocks from the glistening waters of Pensacola Bay. Overlooking the town from nearby Gage Hill, a half mile to the north, was Fort George, a frowning quadrangle-shaped fortification with a double stockade surrounded by a ditch. More than twenty guns within protected bastions providing sweeping fields of fire. A few hundred yards distant, on another bluff to the northwest, stood the smaller Queen's Redoubt with perhaps four guns and 100 men, with the similar Prince of Wales Redoubt, garrisoned by perhaps 75 men, protecting communication between the two. Elsewhere around the city were other defensive works of varying sophistication. Local townspeople had donated money and manpower towards the construction of two redoubts protecting eastern and western approaches to the city; records indicate the one on the east was completed but it is unclear how much work had been done on the one on the west side prior to the arrival of the Spanish. At least one local planter had fortified his plantation with a stockade and artillery so that it might serve as refuge in case of emergency.[2]

Before attempting to deal with any of these defensive positions, Galvez would have to get his ships into the bay, past the eleven mammoth thirty-two-pounder guns of the Royal Navy Redoubt guarding its entrance and a smaller blockhouse on Siguenza Point to its east. On that point, the western-most tip of Santa Rosa Island, stood a small unfinished battery. A makeshift flotilla, underwhelming in its overall firepower but having the potential to play a vital role in monitoring and reporting on enemy approach, was stationed within the bay. Its vessels included the *Hound*, the *Port Royal*, and the *Earl of Bathurst*. Before the coming siege was over, the crews of these ships, totaling more than 250 men, would render valuable service in the defense of the town not on the water but by serving as ground troops in some of the fortifications mentioned above.[3]

Major General John Campbell stood in overall command of the defense of the city, a town of perhaps 200 houses of "considerable curiosity and comfort" clustered along the waterfront. A veteran Scottish soldier who had seen action in the Seven Years' War and in the fighting around New York against General George Washington's forces earlier in the Revolutionary

War, Campbell had proven himself to be an able leader and well understood the task he faced. He had his doubts that some of the motley assemblage at his disposal were adequately motivated. Campbell commanded nearly 2,000 men at Pensacola, including regular British troops of the 16th and 60th regiments; a company of the 4th Battalion of Royal Artillery; some Waldecker troops; a small number of loyalist volunteers from Maryland and Pennsylvania; a few West Florida Royal Foresters; a troop of cavalry; and some armed sailors. As many as five hundred allied Indian warriors, whose numbers and commitment fluctuated over the campaign, were also nominally under Campbell's command. There is evidence a small number of slaves and/or free blacks served in the British ranks at Pensacola as well; nearly fifty black men would be mentioned by the Spanish in their reports of troops captured during the action.[4]

THE SPANISH FLEET HOVE into view on the tranquil blue horizon in the afternoon of Friday, March 9, 1781. Observers could see a veritable forest of masts and ominous dark hulls bearing down on Pensacola, nearly three dozen ships in all, visible in the distance and closing fast. The fleet contained "at least fifteen ships of the line, five heavy frigates, a twenty-gun ship, two King's snows, armed brigs, row-galleys" and other support ships. That evening the fleet pulled up to Santa Rosa Island several miles from its western end, where Galvez disembarked about 500 men under the command of Colonel Francisco Longoria with orders to capture the small British outpost at Point Siguenza. He then offloaded the rest of his infantry, nearly 1,500 men. Longoria's men arrived at the end of the point after a slog of some nine miles to discover the battery they were to secure abandoned. Before they could move to take advantage of the situation, though, they came under fire from the *Port Royal* and *Mentor*, on patrol in the area and having observed the landing. Having no ability to return fire from the distance at which the ships sat in the bay, the men retreated eastward, out of artillery range, and went into camp.[5]

There was even more give and take in this first clash of the opposing forces on the barrier island in front of Pensacola. The first Spanish troops ashore had surprised and captured a few British soldiers they found wandering on

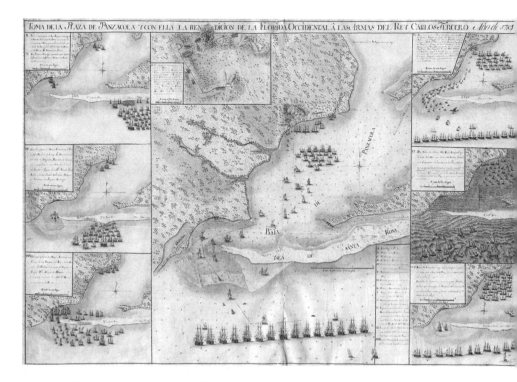

Map of the Siege of Pensacola (Instituto de Historia y Cultura Militar)

the island upon their arrival, as the incredulous troops had gone to tend some cattle being kept on the island but were somehow completely unaware of the Spanish presence. The Spaniards soon went to work on their own battery on the northern side of the island, concealed from easy view of the sailors on duty in the bay, and opened up on the unsuspecting *Mentor*, still lying offshore, in the predawn hours of March 12. They struck the boat over two dozen times before forcing it to withdraw. The British returned the favor in dramatic fashion the next night when, shortly after midnight, they hauled a captured small Spanish schooner, the *Santa Servanto*, into the bay right under the noses of the sleeping sailors onboard the fleet bobbing at anchor near the mouth of the bay. A few days prior a launch from the *Mentor* had been out on patrol when it spotted the schooner and captured its six-man crew and its cargo. To their great surprise and Galvez's embarrassment, they had happened upon the governor's personal baggage, including clothes, wines, personal goods, and a large amount of cash, silver, and other valuables. A lone Spanish brig which had been sent to sound the bar at the harbor entrance fired a ragged last-minute volley at the little launch as it passed in the distance, but it continued on into the harbor at Pensacola to the cheers of the sailors aboard the British boats.[6]

Galvez desired to get his fleet into Pensacola Bay as soon as possible, but doing so proved to be much easier said than done. While the bay is one of the best deep-water ports on the Gulf, gaining its entrance involved navigating narrow passes with which the Spanish captains were unfamiliar. On the first attempt to feel out their way into the bay early on the morning of March 12, one of the lead ships, the *San Ramon*, ran aground and had to be offloaded in an effort to be refloated as British gunboats hovered in the distance. After the incident Squadrón Commander Captain Jose Calvo de Irazabal and Galvez met to discuss their options. Calvo warned that forcing an entry under the circumstances might threaten the entire fleet with destruction, as it might become stranded in the shallow pass or run the risk of having adverse winds blow them aground, and cautioned Galvez that much more sounding work needed to be recorded before he would take his ships into the bay. He suggested that Galvez consider landing his infantry on the mainland and capturing the Royal Navy Redoubt first. The captain, backed by a few other officers, flatly maintained they would not attempt an entry into the bay under the current circumstances. Galvez, impatient to move on Pensacola, would brook no delay. He believed he had the clear authority to order the movements of the entire fleet based on communications with authorities in Havana prior to the opening of the campaign, and was taken aback and angered by Calvo's intransigence. Although the fleet lay at the very doorstep of the capital of West Florida and at long last a force sufficient for its reduction stood ready for action, a dispute over chain of command now threatened to jeopardize the entire operation.[7]

Galvez decided to take matters into his own hands. While there was in truth some debate over the extent of his authority over the fleet from Cuba, he had clear and total command of the handful of vessels from Louisiana— his flagship brig *Galveztown*, the sloop *Valenzuela*, and two smaller support ships. He therefore determined to enter the bay with them alone. It was a bold move and a daring gamble, for even if the risky maneuver proved successful, for him to stand any chance of capturing Pensacola the remainder of the fleet's chastened captains had to follow him in. Shortly after three in the afternoon on March 18, 1781, Galvez had his personal pennant raised aboard the *Galveztown* and ordered a traditional fifteen-gun salute fired to announce his presence. Weighing anchor a few minutes later, his small flotilla began its move towards the harbor entrance. The Spanish troops ashore on Santa Rosa Island broke out into riotous cheering as they observed the action, their enthusiasm doubling once the ships came under fire from the British batteries along the lower bay. As cries of "long live the king" rang out on Siguenza Point, Galvez moved into the pass and British shells began ripping through his ships' sails and rigging. They moved determinedly onward despite the resistance they encountered. By sunset, all four of the ships had moved safely into the bay and come to anchor under the protection of the guns of the Spanish battery recently erected on the island. Galvez ordered another fifteen-gun salute fired which announced to the stunned observers, Spanish and British, of his success.[8]

It was the stuff of legend, and would make Galvez an international hero. For the moment, his bold foray changed the dynamics of the campaign for Pensacola by instilling confidence in the Spanish soldiers and sailors and lending pride and energy to their efforts.[9]

Captain Calvo nearly squelched the momentum before it got started by refusing to have the rest of the fleet follow Galvez. Upstaged, he complained bitterly to all who would listen that the governor's display of bravado had in fact been rash and dangerous. He called his men on deck of his flagship to announce that he would bring the matter before the king at the first opportunity, and derided Galvez as a traitor whom he would like to see hanging from the yardarm of his ship. Galvez sent his aide over to meet with Calvo to attempt to apologize for the unintended slight to his honor and try to reduce the tension. Through a combination of the messenger's tact and diplomacy and a reassessment of the advantageous situation in which the fleet now sat, Calvo had a change of heart. The next day, March 19, 1781, he led the rest of the fleet into the bay as the British guns ineffectively boomed just out of range.[10]

AS THIS SCENE PLAYED out, reinforcements elsewhere were moving to unite with Galvez and increase the size of his army. His trusted subordinate, Colonel Ezpeleta, was marching east from Mobile with nearly a thousand more troops from the regiments of Principe, Espana, Navarra, and Havana, along with some volunteers from Catalonia. Ezpeleta's men had encountered some resistance from a small band of British troops as they approached a crossing of the Perdido where the British had a small observation post, but they had brushed them aside and pressed forward. They arrived at Tartar Point, just outside the city, on March 21. Another thousand men from Louisiana would join the growing army just days later. Even more Spanish and French troops would soon be on the way. The attacking army was of such size that the British defenders could only hope to hold it back with the greatest effort and no little luck. As the Spanish host gathered in front of the city in late March, General Campbell ordered all of his remaining troops to take position in their fortifications and prepare for action.[11]

Beginning in the last week of March and continuing throughout April, Galvez's army moved inexorably closer to the British fortifications in what would become the longest siege of the Revolutionary War. Galvez brought his ships as close as possible to the harbor and offloaded his troops at Sutton's Lagoon just west of the city. After establishing hospitals and fortified camps on the mainland, he began a steady movement towards the British lines. As at Mobile, the Spanish exerted Herculean effort over the course of several weeks as they pushed, pulled, and dragged their heavy artillery through the swamps, ravines, and dense wilderness bluffs surrounding Pensacola. Meanwhile, Galvez's infantry went to work on a network of trenches on the high ground northwest of the outer line of the city's defensive positions from which it could fire into the British lines. It was dangerous work, for the city's defenders did not stand by idly as the Spaniards advanced. They launched several small sorties from their works into the besiegers' lines. By early April the campaign had become a series of almost round-the-clock, small-scale fights along the opposing lines. In one of the largest of these skirmishes Galvez himself sustained wounds that quite nearly took his life. While observing the action near an advanced battery on April 12, 1781, the governor was struck by two bullets from a British volley. One hit a finger

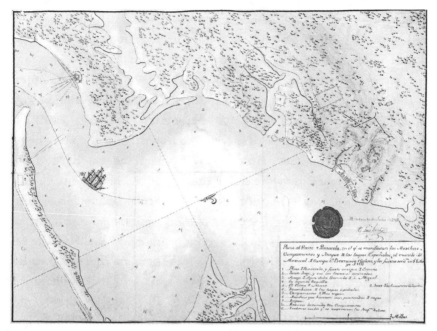

Plan of Pensacola showing its defenses along with Galvez's approach to the city and the location of his army's encampments (University of Michigan Library Digital Collections, William L. Clements Library Image Bank)

before lodging in his abdomen while the other ripped into his stomach. Had they been fired from a shorter distance, they might have killed him on the spot. As it was, the general shook off his serious but non-life threatening injuries after a few days of medical care and rejoined his army at the front.[12]

The city of Pensacola became caught in the crossfire between the combatants as the siege progressed. Galvez corresponded with Campbell as he maneuvered his army, urging him for the sake of humanity not to destroy private buildings in the town in a misguided effort to defend the community. Campbell complied with the request to the degree he could, stating he had no intention to destroy his own capital and that the city would remain a safe place for noncombatants and the sick and wounded despite the war raging around them. In late April, as the Spanish were completing their siege lines, Campbell sent Galvez a special request, asking that he refrain from having his gunboats in the harbor fire at the fort lest errant shots destroy nearby homes. Galvez agreed, but despite the efforts of both sides a few fires nevertheless broke out in the town during the bombardment, and there was some unintentional destruction of private property.[13]

For the civilians trapped in the city, the siege was a harrowing ordeal aside from any risks of having their dwellings destroyed by cannon balls or flames. James Bruce, the collector of customs of Pensacola, wrote letters—among few of the type to survive—to friends in London describing the deteriorating conditions. Bruce reported general suffering due to a lack of food and supplies, as by the end of the siege it had been many months since ships had arrived with trade goods in Pensacola's harbor. He wrote of miserable conditions as near-starving citizens were forced to endure the constant anxiety of war for weeks, observing in summary that "the distresses of the inhabitants are not to be described." Yet he remained hopeful and defiant until the end. On May 7, 1781, he wrote with pride that "we have still English collours flying on Fort George altho . . . the enemy is working hard night and day to get nearer our batterys." Without a "miraculous escape," however, he had no doubt but that "so superior an army, fleet and artillery must at last carry their point."[14]

Facing a desperate situation, General Campbell used every means of defense at his disposal. To augment his army's numbers and instill terror in the ranks of the besiegers, he employed allied Indians, bribed with presents and vague promises he knew he could not fill in their entirety, who conducted ranging, unconventional attacks on the Spanish forces. Elaborately painted, tattooed warriors menaced the Spanish lines and struck fear in the hearts of the besiegers. It was more than Galvez could take, for he both loathed and feared the unpredictability of Indian-style warfare and knew it would frighten and discourage his men. At the outset of the campaign he pledged to not use allied Indians if Campbell would not, so as to "shelter us from the horrible censure of inhumanity." In truth Galvez had few Native American warriors he could have called up, and he knew Campbell to have a substantial number of Creeks potentially at his service. While Galvez did disdain the natives' hit-and-run tactics and looked on their occasional scalping of victims as barbaric, his motivations in trying to minimize Native American involvement were at least as much practical as idealistic. At any rate, Campbell disregarded his appeals. Throughout late March and into mid-April, British-allied Indians kept the Spaniards off balance and probably checked some of their aggressiveness.[15]

In perhaps the largest of these isolated firefights, on the afternoon of March 28, several hundred warriors attacked the Spanish in waves of intense but inconclusive fighting. That affair was atypical, however, as most of the clashes between Galvez's men and British-allied warriors involved small groups of combatants and took the form of surprise attacks and ambushes occurring when the Spanish had their guard down. In one skirmish, for example, Indians fell upon an unsuspecting Spanish soldier away from the main line and after dispatching him took his head as a trophy. Even though the number of Spanish scalps taken during the siege was small and made no appreciable difference in the pace of the advance, the threat of a sudden gruesome death weighed heavily on the minds of the most advanced and exposed battalions. Although Galvez could not know it, Campbell struggled to keep more than a token number of Native Americans actively engaged in this work, though, and those he had he could rely on for only a short time. By mid-April, after several weeks of a siege they had little stomach for and perhaps sensing the lengthening odds faced by their British friends, the disenchanted allied warrior force began to melt away. A disheartened Campell dismissed their efforts as having been made with "more noise than advantage" and by the end of the month had settled in for a traditional siege between colonial armies.[16]

To Campbell's consternation, even some of his regular troops grew weary of the strain of duty and left as well. By early April he knew of at least eighteen men who had deserted and several more would by the end of the month. By some estimates, more than three dozen soldiers deserted British ranks during the siege, most of them trickling into Spanish lines and a few simply disappearing into the countryside. These numbers were not dramatic but were nonetheless a devastating blow to an outnumbered army that needed every man it could get, and they were a telling sign of problems with morale. As the campaign stretched into its sixth and seventh weeks, the fighting grew more intense and even more vigilance would be required from the beleaguered British garrison. By late April the Spanish army had in some locations approached to within 400 yards of the British lines, close enough for a quick dash to at last force the issue should it so desire. Campbell still had enough spirited men in his ranks to take the fight to the Spaniards, though, and he continued to attempt some isolated sorties to break up the relentless progress of the besiegers and make them hesitant in their work. On May 4, for example, a group of soldiers advanced under orders from the Queen's Redoubt, bayonets fixed, and temporarily seized portions of the Spanish lines and a haul of supplies while killing an estimated twenty of Galvez's men. The British also managed to set fire to some of the Spanish fascines, spike some of their guns, and capture several troops before making their way back into their own lines. Such successes proved temporary as the overwhelming numbers of the attacking force began to tell as the siege wore on.[17]

The plight of the defenders of Pensacola grew even grimmer on April 19, 1781, when more than a dozen ships carrying additional reinforcements from Havana appeared in the bay. Aboard were some 3,700 troops, among them about 700 French soldiers who had been a part of an allied fleet which happened to be in Cuba taking on provisions for a cruise aimed at breaking up the British blockade of a South American port when it was invited to take part in the reduction of Pensacola. The new arrivals swelled Galvez's force to more than 7,000 men and more than sixty ships, astounding numbers for a Gulf Coast military campaign which spelled certain doom for the West Florida capital. By the next week Galvez had almost a thousand men feverishly digging earthworks from which he could assault Fort George.[18]

By April 29 the besiegers had constructed nearly a mile of trenches winding their way through the low hills northwest of the British bastions. Two days later they completed batteries which could rain deadly short-range fire on the British position. The heaviest artillery bombardment of the campaign ensued as the Spanish army pounded the British fortifications day and night. Campbell's men returned fire but simply could not keep pace with the Spanish barrage. On May 3 alone, Spanish artillerists fired more than 500 solid shot and nearly 200 shells at their targets. Some of the fleet joined in the bombardment in early May, despite Galvez's original promise not to fire over the town, as the general grew impatient to obtain his goal.

Plan of Fort George (Library of Congress)

The intensity of the barrage only increased in the first week of May, consisting of "a routine fire with cannon, bombs, and howitzers" according to one member of the shell-shocked garrison. Galvez, frustrated at the slow pace, alarmed at diminishing supplies, and concerned that his weary French allies, who had volunteered to come to Pensacola only for a short stint, sped up his work. The aerial barrage reached a crescendo on May 7 in a deafening, earth-rattling fusillade which seemed to portend imminent doom for the British. The withering fire sparked Campbell to report to superiors that he feared the next communication they received from him might be news of the unfortunate surrender of the post. In ominous tones meant to prepare superiors for the inevitable, he reported he found himself "besieged by both land and sea by a powerful combined force of France and Spain," and he seemed to indicate all that could be done to save Pensacola had been attempted.[19]

It all came to a sudden, dramatic end. By chance, a shot from one of the Spanish howitzers about 8:30 in the morning of May 8, 1781, happened to be fired just as the door to the powder magazine of the Queen's Redoubt was opened so that gunpowder could be distributed. The Spanish gunners could not have known the vulnerability they were about to expose, as the small doorway, located in the most protected inner recesses of the fortification, would have been a small and hidden target. Yet the lone shell made a perfect arc for the opening. In the poetic words of General Campbell, this lucky shot "precipitated its (the fort's) destiny and occasioned its falling under the dominion of Spain at least some days sooner than it otherwise would have happened." The spectacular explosion which resulted instantly killed more than seventy-five men and wounded dozens more as the terrific flash of fire and concussive force rendered the redoubt a pile of smoking ruins in the blink of an eye. An eerie pause engulfed the lines of both armies as the smoke and debris cleared. During the brief interlude, a British officer who had somehow collected his wits ordered the remaining guns in the redoubt spiked and had his surviving men make a desperate dash to the nearby Prince of Wales Redoubt. The perhaps equally surprised attackers, after a few moments of astonished observation of the desolation left by the explosion, scrambled to seize the ruined position. Minutes later two columns of infantry were formed to advance on the Prince of Wales Redoubt. Far

Battle of Pensacola (Library of Congress)

from encountering a cowering and disorganized band of troops, though, they walked right into a deadly rain of British fire that mowed down dozens of men and ground the attack to a halt. The Spanish army redoubled its efforts after the setback, sending in more troops along an unexposed route towards the British outpost. As morning wore on into early afternoon, the outnumbered garrison came under a punishing fire while Spanish guns pounded Fort George at point-blank range.[20]

Unable to any longer make an effective defense of his primary fortification, and likely concerned the powerful and accurate Spanish artillery might at any moment render Fort George and the Prince of Wales Redoubt piles of splinters as well, General Campbell had a white flag raised just before three o'clock in the afternoon on May 8, 1781. A quick parley by representatives of the opposing forces followed, with the British agreeing to formal terms of surrender to Galvez the next day. By May 11, the Spanish had taken possession of all of Pensacola's various fortifications. Days later Galvez's jubilant Spanish army, having completed its remarkable conquest of West Florida, together sang "Te Deum" in a warehouse transformed into a Catholic chapel during a ceremony celebrating the conquest. Galvez had the ships in the harbor dressed out and twenty-one gun salutes fired to help mark the occasion.[21]

THE CAMPAIGN FOR PENSACOLA was the largest and longest of the Revolutionary War on the Gulf Coast and remains the greatest battle ever fought in Florida. The contending armies suffered corresponding numbers of casualties that dwarfed those of some of the previous campaigns. The British lost an estimated 100 killed, at least that many wounded, and had an entire army of nearly 1,100 men captured. They also lost more than 150 cannon, in excess of 2,000 muskets and rifles, at least 80,000 pounds of powder, and stockpiles of thousands of rounds of ammunition. The Spanish sustained heavy losses as well, as Galvez had 75 to 100 killed and approximately 200 wounded in the course of the siege. Galvez sent his prisoners to Cuba, from whence most would go on to New York under a promise they would not serve against Spain for the duration of the war. Many would continue to fight for the British against the American army in the closing months of the Revolutionary War.[22]

There remained one last flicker of resistance to the Spanish in West Florida that needed to be put out before Galvez could consider the job finished, and it came from a most unexpected quarter. As the Spanish army had begun its siege of Pensacola, General Campbell had sent blank commissions to Natchez to be distributed to those individuals who would volunteer to raise militia forces to overthrow the Spanish there and, hopefully, open a new front that might relieve the pressure being applied to the capital city. In his communications with the residents of the Natchez area he appealed to their spirit of loyalty to Great Britain as he called on them to resist the "despotism of Spain." Owing to a complex set of motivations—including a genuine desire to reclaim the area from Spain, and, according to some reports, potentially take a first step towards annexation into the United States—a number of disgruntled locals prepared to retake the fort at Natchez from its Spanish captors. Community leaders such as John Blommart, John and Philip Alston, and John Turner, who had been rankled at how the post had been handed over without a shot being fired, became pivotal players in recruiting men for the scheme Campbell had suggested. They gathered a force of as many as 200 men, including an unknown number of Choctaw allies, for the job. While this makeshift militia may have been more mob than army, it far outnumbered the small Spanish garrison of perhaps sixty armed men, a few Indian warriors, and a larger number of civilians in the fort.[23]

On April 22, 1781, Captain Blommart and his volunteers descended on the fort and demanded its surrender. When the commander of the post, Juan de la Villebeuvre, urged the rebels to lay down their arms and disperse, they responded with a volley of musketry. A bizarre, short-lived siege followed as the Spanish closed their gates and the opposing forces stared at each other, neither quite strong enough to go on the offensive nor knowing what exactly to do next. The besiegers employed a number of elaborate and unorthodox tactics to trick the Spanish to capitulate in the coming days. According to one participant, at night they placed the equivalent of scarecrows in the tree line in the distance to give the illusion they had more troops and fashioned facsimiles of artillery out of logs which from far enough away gave the appearance of a battery ready for action. How much of this ruse the Spanish bought is unknown, but they were at last compelled to surrender the post on May 4 when, through the most unusual trickery of all, the besiegers duped Villebeauvre into believing they had dug a tunnel under the fort and rigged enough explosives in it to reduce the garrison to a pile of ashes. It was a near-farcical but only temporary end to Spanish possession of Natchez.[24]

Galvez sent a force to restore order as soon as he learned what had happened and scolded Campbell for what he considered an egregious breach of the terms of surrender of Pensacola. Chided and at Galvez's mercy, Campbell as a prisoner was persuaded to write Captain Blommart ordering him to surrender his post to the Spanish army. If the letter reached Blommart's hands, it would have been about the same time that an army under Esteban Roberto de la Morandiere arrived on the scene in late June. The Spaniards entered the fort unopposed, having sent word ahead on their advance that if the insurgents returned home and offered no resistance they would not

be bothered. It is unlikely the rebels were prepared to offer much of a defense anyway, as division over their course of action going forward had set
into their ranks almost as soon as they had captured the fort. In an affair
which reveals the divided mind of the group, a faction among them had at
first wanted to raise an American flag on the parapet instead of the British
colors which were soon hoisted to the breeze on the banks of the Mississippi. The competing impulses only became more pronounced once word
of the fall of Pensacola reached town. Some insurgents thought it best to
meet whatever Spanish representatives might show up in the region and
return the fort to Spain in good order in hopes of avoiding repercussions,
while others advocated plundering anything worth taking and fleeing the
scene. In the end the militiamen did a little of both. While Blommart sent
a small contingent downriver to meet with the advancing Spanish army,
dozens of others fled in haste. The upshot was that, without a shot being
fired, the Spanish regained control of Natchez. There would continue to be
some small-scale skirmishing between loyalists and the Spanish in the lower
Mississippi region over the coming months, but Spanish authority would
not seriously be challenged there again prior to the Treaty of Paris of 1783.[25]

For the seventy-five or so Natchez area residents who had taken part in
the coup to recapture Fort Panmure and ran upon learning of the surrender
of the provincial capital, a strange saga was just beginning. Hoping to avoid
the wrath of the Spanish army, they embarked as a group on a long and
miserable trek through what are now Mississippi and Alabama in a quest to
reach the supposed safety of British lines somewhere on the Atlantic coast.
They struggled to find water while traveling through the countryside during
a severe spring drought and nearly starved as they wandered through the
Tombigbee and Coosa river valleys into Georgia, convinced Galvez's men
were hot on their heels and prepared to exact brutal vengeance. The group
showed up in Savannah some 130 days after their flight from Natchez, just
prior to the surrender of British forces at Yorktown which would end the
war between the American colonies and Great Britain and result in the
establishment of the United States as an independent nation. Although
they could not have known it at the time, their trek was unnecessary. The
Spanish authorities had no intention of pursuing them and proved lenient

in resolving the matter. They did temporarily hold captive a few of the ringleaders of the short-lived Natchez rebellion, including Blommart, Jacob Winfree, and John Alston and his sons, and confiscated some of their property, but in the end the Spanish were concerned with bigger issues and chose not to attempt to impose any serious punishments on the refugees.[26]

Galvez continued to lead Spanish military forces in actions against the British in the Caribbean until the close of the war in 1783, when he was named Viceroy of New Spain. He died in Mexico during a typhus epidemic in 1786 at age forty. His primary adversary in the Gulf Coast campaign, Brigadier General John Campbell, is today largely forgotten. After his capture at the fall of Pensacola he lived in New York until the end of the Revolutionary War, when he was named Commander in Chief of Great Britain's remaining maritime provinces in North America. He held the post until 1786, at which time he returned to his native Scotland. He died there in 1806. His failure in West Florida haunted him, as he described his service in after-action reports to have been his "great misfortune to have been employed in this ill-fated corner of his Majesty's dominions . . ." His superiors appeared to have not charged the loss against him, for even Lord Germain would later write him that he believed West Florida's fall to have been "unavoidable," and went so far as to praise his effort at "so gallant a defence."[27]

Galvez's campaigns against West Florida achieved every strategic objective the Spanish sought in the Gulf Coast theater of the Revolutionary War. In brilliantly planned and executed actions from the Mississippi River to Pensacola Bay, his forces had overwhelmed British defenses in succession, capturing armies and outposts which resulted in the forcible seizure of the colony of West Florida and led to the negotiated transfer of East Florida in the Treaty of Paris two years later. Galvez won plaudits in the form of advances in rank and honorary titles of nobility for his accomplishments. He is best remembered today, though, for the authorization by King Carlos III to have his family coat of arms emblazoned with a depiction of a warship, above it a banner carrying the phrase "Yo Solo"—"I Alone," in reference to his leading the way into Pensacola Bay during the opening days of the campaign to capture the British capital. It is a fitting tribute to the boldness and audacity which brought West Florida's short eighteen years as a British province to a sudden, dramatic end. The coat of arms is also a poignant reminder that although its time was brief, much of its daily existence dull and monotonous, and our memory of it all somewhat hazy, West Florida's story is in reality one of drama, action, and consequence.[28]

Portrait of Bernardo de Galvez with his coat of arms (The Historic New Orleans Collection, Gift of Mr. Thomas N. Lennox, acc. no. 1991.34.15)

Epilogue

hile Bernardo de Galvez had effectively extinguished British title to West Florida by May of 1781, formal recognition of the reality on the ground would not occur until the 1783 Treaty of Paris ending the Revolutionary War. The compact set the 31st parallel as the boundary between the newly recognized United States and the new Spanish colony and confirmed Spanish possession of the Floridas. The separate treaty between Spain and Great Britain ending hostilities between those nations did not clearly specify the northern border of Spanish West Florida, however. In a secret provision to the compact, British negotiators had attempted to insert a vague stipulation that if in the event they somehow managed to regain West Florida, the border would remain at 32 degrees, 28 minutes latitude, but if it remained in Spanish hands it would be at the 31st parallel as spelled out in the treaty negotiated between Great Britain and the United States. Although it sounds at first blush a far-fetched notion given the way the province had been wrested from their control by Galvez's forces, some British officials held out hope of retaining the colony in the process of the complex treaty parleys which would bring peace and order back to a continent which had been engulfed in war for the better part of a decade. Their hopes were encouraged to some degree by some rather fanciful scheming and plotting by traders and political leaders aiming to force the issue in the unsettled interim between the capture of Pensacola and the signing of the Treaty of Paris. In the end the back-room diplomatic dealing and idle talk of reconquest only led to inevitable confusion over where the border truly lay and how well its location would be respected.[1]

Following the precedent set by the British, Spain determined to assert the

Statue of Bernardo de Galvez in downtown Pensacola (Mike Bunn)

northern border of West Florida at the farthest extent to which its former owners had placed it—a line drawn eastward to the Chattahoochee from where the Yazoo emptied into the Mississippi—and established outposts in the contested region to justify the claim. In addition to shoring up existing outposts in Pensacola, Mobile, Baton Rouge, and Natchez, they also established in the years after the war Fort San Esteban (modern St. Stephens, Alabama), Fort Nogales (modern Vicksburg), and, in an ill-fated effort to lay claim to territory even farther north, established Fort San Fernando de las Barrancas (modern Memphis). They also repaired and rebuilt the long-abandoned Fort Tombecbe along the Tombigbee (in modern Sumter County, Alabama), rechristening it as Fort Confederation. Spanish colonial officials also authorized the construction of a squadron of naval vessels with which to patrol the Mississippi, that being the corridor along which American pressure most visibly manifested itself during their tenure. By the 1790s, as many as 1,500 Spanish troops were on duty in various capacities throughout the region.[2]

Even with the enhanced Spanish military presence in the region, authorities recognized the best chance to maintain any semblance of control of West Florida lay in alliance with Native Americans. The Creeks, Cherokees, Chickasaws, and Choctaws, whose combined populations surpassed by many times that of the Spanish colony, continued to make their homes in the expansive area between Spanish holdings and settled American territory and thus represented a potential buffer to United States expansion which the Spaniards hoped to work to their advantage. Recognizing that trade would be the glue that held any such alliance together, Spanish authorities soon contracted the experienced British firm of Panton and Leslie to carry on their regional trading business. They also aggressively negotiated treaties promising various levels of mutual defense and exclusivity in trading with native groups in compacts signed in Pensacola, Mobile, and along the banks of the Mississippi in the 1780s and 1790s. If nothing else, the Spanish proved adept at leveraging rather limited resources and diplomatic sway to counter United States' expansion into the region for a time.[3]

Yet independence had unleashed among Americans a fever for westward migration and speculation in the trans-Appalachian lands unlike anything with which previous colonial powers in the Gulf had to contend. A host of settlement schemes by Americans on the lands immediately to the north of West Florida threatened to destroy the Native American buffer the Spanish worked so diligently to create. North Carolinians concocted a scheme for settlement of the Chickasaw Bluffs in the 1780s; groups of Tennesseans eyed the Muscle Shoals (now Alabama) region; the state of Georgia asserted its longstanding claim by establishing, on paper, a large county in some of the very land claimed by Spain and then moved to sell territory both in it and beyond. All of these and numerous other efforts, rumored and real, failed in the short run due to a variety of factors, but they only stoked the fires of expansion while Spain's tepid resistance to them highlighted its weak position. Despite its sweeping victory over the British, Spain was declining as a world power at the time of the Revolutionary War, and the postwar years revealed its imposing figurative edifice as a worldwide colonial empire to in fact be a crumbling façade. The more the burgeoning American population challenged the overwhelmed Spaniards, the more the latter revealed their inability to respond to threats both internal and external to the colony.[4]

Spain worked hard to stem the tide of inevitability, however, and tried to leverage its inherently limited government as a lure to win the loyalty of residents. Even though Catholicism was the official religion of the colony, authorities did not enforce a strict loyalty to the Catholic church and in most cases allowed virtual freedom of religion so long as services were conducted in private homes. One prominent resident of Spanish West Florida, William Dunbar, claimed that "the major attraction of Spanish rule was that there was little or no rule at all for honest citizens." It is conservatively estimated that as many as two-thirds of West Florida citizens remained in the province immediately after the Spanish took it over, but the percentage may have been even higher. The response to the change of leadership of course proved different in the colony's varying regions. A substantial portion of those in Pensacola, as thoroughly a British town as any in the province, chose to leave. Similar to the upheaval it experienced at the onset of British rule, the city began life anew as a Spanish town for the second time in its history. Few of the residents of Mobile chose to leave, as most of the population of the city then being run by a third different colonial power in the span of less than twenty years quietly took the required oath of loyalty to Spain rather than endure the disruption and uncertainty of a long and difficult move to another region of the continent or beyond. In settlements along the Mississippi River, bordering the province of Louisiana, there likewise was little out-migration, owing perhaps as much to the hassle of relocation than any referendum on approval of ownership of the land by the Spanish crown. Rugged settlers, drawn by liberal land grants and rich lands, mostly

Epilogue ~ 219

Americans and many former Tories, poured into Spanish West Florida in the years after the Revolution despite its apparent political instability and, in some cases, because of it.[5]

Spain's tenuous hold on the region began to unravel in 1795, when at long last the United States brought the Spanish to the negotiating table over the issue of the northern boundary of the colony. In the 1795 Treaty of San Lorenzo, Spain was forced to acknowledge the 31st parallel as West Florida's northern border. Local authorities took their time in removing from the contested region, however, hoping the decision which had been made in Europe somehow might be overturned or reconsidered. When Spain finally removed its troops from north of the parallel in 1798, the United States immediately set up the Mississippi Territory in the vacated region.[6]

As the Mississippi Territory grew, so did pressure on Spain to maintain its control of what remained of West Florida. Americans flocked to the border communities at Natchez and north of Mobile and instigated new intrigues, agitating and scheming for the ouster of Spanish authority in one way or another, orderly or chaotic, countenanced by law or extralegal. It was no coincidence that America's cotton frontier was beginning to take shape at the same time, fueled by fertile soils, discovery of strains of cotton perfectly suited for the region's environment, and the invention of the cotton gin. Having a decrepit colonial power interfering with their access to world markets via the Gulf was intolerable to the new arrivals. The first serious fissures in Spanish hegemony were revealed internally, as the mostly American population in the Baton Rouge area staged a coup that captured the Spanish fort there in 1810. The brief-lived Republic of West Florida, stretching between the Mississippi and Pearl rivers, within months was annexed into the state of Louisiana. Shortly thereafter, the United States, justifying its actions in a specious claim that the land belonged to it by virtue of the 1803 Louisiana Purchase, pressured Spain to relinquish the remainder of the colony. The section of the province lying between the Pearl River and Mobile was added to the Mississippi Territory without protest in 1812, and the following year American troops forcibly seized the area stretching from Mobile to the Perdido River after arriving in front of Fort Carlota and threatening military action. The remainder of the colony, a sparsely inhabited remnant aside from the city of Pensacola stretching between the Perdido and Apalachicola rivers, was at length ceded to the United States in 1819 following Andrew Jackson's invasion of the region during the First Seminole War. In a dramatic period of less than a decade, regional maps had to be redrawn with dizzying rapidity, and Spain exited the region as a colonial power and a new, distinctly American era of Gulf Coast history began.[7]

Bibliography

MANUSCRIPTS

University of West Florida

British Colonial Office Records (Swain Compilation).

CO 5. Volumes 574–581. Official Correspondence and Documents. The Board of Trade and Plantations.

CO 5. Volumes 582–596. Official Correspondence and Documents. The Secretary of State.

CO 5. Volumes 597–598. Military Correspondence.

CO 5. Volumes 599–617. Entry Books of Letters, Instructions, Warrants, Commissions, Grants, Legal Instruments, etc...

CO 5. Volumes 618–622. Letters From and To the Secretary of State.

Bruce Burgoyne Papers.

Steurnagel Diary.

Alabama Department of Archives and History

West Florida General Assembly Acts, 1767–1771. Government Records Collections.

West Florida General Assembly Commons House Journals, 1767–1778. Government Records Collections .

West Florida Governor Correspondence, 1763–1766. Government Records Collections.

"An Account of the Several Sums of Money Which Have Been Granted by the Parliament of Great Britain, Towards the Establishment and Support of the Civil Government of the Provinces of East and West Florida in America."

Mississippi Department of Archives and History

British West Florida Administrative Papers and Land Records. 1763–1783.

P. K. Yonge Library of Florida History

"Governor Johnstone's Account of West Florida." The Gentleman's Gazette. February, 1765.

Mobile Local History and Genealogy Library

The Haldimand Papers: Correspondence with General Gage. 1758–1777.

PRINTED PRIMARY SOURCES

A Century of Lawmaking for a New Nation: U.S. Congressional Documents and Debates, 1774–1785. https://memory.loc.gov/ammem/amlaw/lawhome.html.

Adair, James. *The History of the North American Indians, Particularly Those Nations Adjoining the Mississippi, East and West Florida, Georgia, South and North Carolina, and Virginia.* London: Edward and Charles Dilly, 1775.

Bartram, William. *Travels Through North and South Carolina, Georgia, East and West Florida, the Cherokee Country, the Extensive Territories of the Muscogulges, or the Creek Confederacy, and the Country of the Chactaws.* Philadelphia: James and Johnson, 1791.

Great Britain Board of Trade. *Journal of the Commissioners for Trade and Plantations.* Preserved in the Public Records Office. 14 Volumes. London: His Majesty's Stationery Office. 1920–1938.

Historical Manuscripts Commission. *Report on American Manuscripts in the Royal Institution of Great Britain.* Dublin: His Majesty's Stationery Office, 1904–1909.

Romans, Bernard. *A Concise Natural History of East and West Florida.* New York: R. Aitken, 1776.

Rowland, Dunbar, ed. *Mississippi Provincial Archives: English Dominion, Letters and Disclosures to the Secretary of State From Major Robert Farmar and Governor George Johnstone.* Nashville: Press of Brandon Printing Company, 1911.

Rowland, Eron O. *Life, Letters, and Papers of William Dunbar, 1749–1810.* Jackson: Mississippi Historical Society, 1930.

Rowland, Eron O. ed. "Peter Chester: Third Governor of the Province of West Florida Under British Dominion, 1770–1781." *Publications of the Mississippi Historical Society.* Centenary Series. Volume 5. (1925): 1–183.

Whitworth, Sir Charles. *State of the Trade of Great Britain in Its Imports and Exports Progressively from the Year 1697.* London, G. Robinson, 1776.

BOOKS

Alden, John Richard. *The South in the Revolution, 1763–1789.* Austin: University of Texas Press, 1957.

_____. *John Stuart and the Southern Colonial Frontier, a Study of Indian Relations, War, Trade and Land Problems in the Southern Wilderness, 1754–1775.* Ann Arbor: University of Michigan Press, 1944.

Alvord, Clarence Walworth. *The Mississippi Valley in British Politics: A Study in the Trade, Land Speculation, and Experiments and Imperialism Culminating in the American Revolution.* Ann Arbor: University of Michigan Library, 1917.

Anderson, Fred. *Crucible of War: The Seven Years' War and the Fate of Empire in British North America, 1754–1766.* New York: Alfred A. Knopf, 2000.

Appleyard, John. *14th Colony: British West Florida, 1763–1781.* Pensacola: Pensacola Home and Savings Association, 1975.

Badger, R. Reid and Lawrence A. Clayton, eds. *Alabama and the Borderlands: From Prehistory To Statehood.* Tuscaloosa: University of Alabama Press, 1985.

Bailyn, Bernard. *Voyagers to the West: A Passage in the Peopling of America on the Eve of the Revolution.* New York: Random House, 1986.

Barnett, Jr., James F. *Mississippi's American Indians.* Jackson: University Press of Mississippi, 2012.

Berlin, Ira. *Many Thousands Gone: The First Two Centuries of Slavery in North America.* Cambridge: Harvard University Press, 2000.

Bolton, Herbert E. and Mary Ross. *The Debateable Land: A Sketch of the Anglo-Spanish Contest For the Georgia Country.* Berkley: University of California Press, 1925.

Born, Jr., John D. *Governor Johnstone and Trade in British West Florida, 1764–1767.* Wichita: Wichita State University, 1968.

Braund, Kathryn E. Holland. *Deerskins and Duffels: Creek Indian Trade with Anglo-America, 1685–1815.* Lincoln: University of Nebraska Press, 1993.

Bridges, Edwin C. *Alabama: The Making of an American State.* Tuscaloosa: University of Alabama Press, 2016.

Brown, Richmond F., ed. *Coastal Encounters: The Transformation of the Gulf South in the Eighteenth Century.* Lincoln: University of Nebraska Press, 2007.

Buchanan, John. *The Road to Guilford Courthouse: The American Revolution in the Carolinas.* New York: Wiley and Sons, 1997.

Bunn, Mike and Clay Williams. *Mississippi: Outpost of Majestic Spain.* Jackson: Mississippi Department of Archives and History, 2001.

Calloway, Colin G. *The American Revolution in Indian Country: Crisis and Diversity in Native American Communities.* New York: Cambridge University Press, 1995.

———. *The Scratch of a Pen: 1763 and the Transformation of North America.* New York: Oxford University Press, 2006.

Cashin, Edward J. *Lachlan McGillivray, Indian Trader: The Shaping of the Southern Colonial Frontier.* Athens: University of Georgia, 1992.

Caughey, John Walton. *Bernardo de Galvez in Louisiana: 1776–1783.* Gretna, LA: Pelican Publishing, 1972.

Chavez, Thomas E. *Spain and the Independence of the United States: An Intrinsic*

Gift. Albuquerque: University of New Mexico Press, 2002.

Claiborne, John Francis Hamtramck. *Mississippi, As a Province, Territory, and State, With Biographical Notices of Eminent Citizens*. Jackson: Power and Barksdale, 1880.

Clark, John Garretson. *New Orleans, 1718–1812: An Economic History*. Baton Rouge: Louisiana State University Press, 1970.

Clavin, Matthew J. *Aiming for Pensacola: Fugitive Slaves on the Atlantic and Southern Frontiers*. Cambridge: Harvard University Press, 2015.

Clune, John J. and Margo S. Stringfield. *Historic Pensacola*. Gainesville: University Press of Florida, 2017.

Coker, William S. *The Siege of Pensacola, 1781, in Maps: With Data on Troop Strength, Military Units, Ships, Casualties, and Related Statistics*. Pensacola: Perdido Bay Press, 1981.

Coker, William S. and Hazel P. *The Siege of Mobile, 1780, in Maps: With Data on TroopStrength, Military Units, Ships, Casualties, and Prisoners of War, Including a Brief History of Fort Charlotte*. Mobile: Perdido Bay Press, 1982.

Coker, William S. and Thomas D. Watson. *Indian Traders of the Southeastern Borderlands: Panton, Leslie and Company and John Forbes*. Gainesville: University Press of Florida,1986.

Coldham, Peter Wilson. *American Migrations, 1765–1799: The Lives, Times, and Families of Colonial Americans Who Remained Loyal to the British Crown Before, During, and After the Revolutionary War, as Related in Their Own Words and Through Their Correspondence*. Baltimore: Genealogical Publishing Company, 2000.

Commager, Henry Steele and Richard B. Morris, eds. *The Spirit of 'Seventy-Six: The Story of the American Revolution as Told by Participants*. Edison, NJ: Castle Books, 2002.

Corkran, David H. *The Creek Frontier, 1540–1783*. Norman: University of Oklahoma Press, 1967.

Crane, Verner Winslow. *The Southern Frontier, 1670–1732*. Ann Arbor: University of Michigan Press, 1964.

Dalrymple, Margaret Fisher, ed. *The Merchant of Manchac: The Letterbooks of John Fitzpatrick, 1768–1790*. Baton Rouge: Louisiana State University Press, 1978.

Davies, Kenneth G., ed. *Documents of the American Revolution, 1770–1783*. 21 Volumes. Shannon: Irish University Press, 1972.

Davis, William C. *Rogue Republic: How Would-Be Patriots Waged the Shortest Revolution in American History*. Boston: Houghton Mifflin Harcourt, 2011.

De Reparaz, Carmen. *Yo Solo: Bernardo de Galvez y la toma de Panzacola en 1781, Una Contribucion Espanaol a la Independencia de los Estados Unidos*. Serbal, Barcelona, 1986.

DeRosier, Jr., Arthur H. *William Dunbar: Scientific Pioneer of the Old Southwest.* Lexington: University Press of Kentucky, 2007.

De Ville, Winston. *British Burials and Births on the Gulf Coast: Records of the Church of England in West Florida, 1768–1770.* Ville Platte, LA: Winston De Ville, 1986.

_____. *English Land Grants in West Florida: A Register for the States of Alabama, Mississippi, and Parts of Florida and Louisiana.* Ville Platte, LA: Winston De Ville, 1986.

Delaney, Caldwell. *The Story of Mobile.* Mobile: Gill Press, 1953.

Dibble, Ernest F. and Earle W. Newton, eds. *In Search of Gulf Coast Colonial History.* Pensacola: Pensacola Preservation Board, 1970.

Din, Gilbert C. *The Canary Islanders of Louisiana.* Baton Rouge: Louisiana State University, 1988.

_____. *War on the Gulf Coast: The Spanish Fight Against William Augustus Bowles.* Gainesville: University Press of Florida, 2012.

Duval, Kathleen. *Independence Lost: Lives on the Edge of the American Revolution.* New York: Random House, 2016.

Eelking, Max Von. *The German Allied Troops in the North American War of Independence, 1776–1783.* Albany: J. Munsell's Sons, 1893.

Elliott, Jr., Jack D. *The Fort of Natchez and the Colonial Origins of Mississippi.* Fort Washington, PA: Eastern National Parks and Monument Association, 1998.

Fabel, Robin. *Bombast and Broadsides: The Lives of George Johnstone.* Tuscaloosa: University of Alabama Press, 1987.

_____. *The Economy of British West Florida, 1763–1783.* Tuscaloosa: University of Alabama Press, 1988.

_____. *Shipwreck and Adventures of Monsieur Pierre Viaud.* Pensacola: University of West Florida Press, 1990.

Ferling, John E. *Almost a Miracle: The American in the War of Independence.* New York: Oxford University Press, 2009.

Ferreiro, Larrie D. *Brothers at Arms: American Independence and the Men of France and Spain Who Saved It.* New York: Knopf, 2016.

Fraser, Walter J. Jr. *Charleston! Charleston! The History of a Southern City.* Columbia: University of South Carolina Press, 1990.

Fretwell, Mark E. *This So Remote Frontier: The Chattahoochee Country of Alabama and Georgia.* Eufaula: Historic Chattahoochee Commission, 1987.

Gannon, Michael. *Florida: A Short History.* Gainesville: University Press of Florida, 2003.

_____. *The New History of Florida.* Gainesville: University Press of Florida, 2012.

Gibson, Arrell M. *The Chickasaws.* Norman: University of Oklahoma Press, 1971.

Gipson, Lawrence Henry. *The British Empire Before the American Revolution, Vol. 10: Triumphant Empire: Thunderclouds Gather in the West, 1763–1766.* New York: Knopf, 1968.

_____. *The British Empire Before the American Revolution Vol, 13. The Triumphant Empire, The Empire Before the Storm.* New York: Alfred A. Knopf, 1974.

Gold, Robert L. *Borderland Empires in Transition: The Triple-Nation Transfer of Florida.* Carbondale, Ill.: Southern Illinois University Press, 1969.

Greene, Jack P. and J.R. Pole. *The Blackwell Encyclopedia of the Revolution.* Hoboken: Wiley-Blackwell, 1992.

Griffith, Lucille. *Alabama: A Documentary History to 1900.* Tuscaloosa: University of Alabama Press, 1968.

Grossman, Mark. *Encyclopedia of the Continental Congress.* Amenia, NY: Grey House Publishing, 2015.

Hamilton, Peter. *Colonial Mobile: An Historical Study of the Alabama-Tombigbee Basin from The Discovery of Mobile Bay in 1519 Until the Demolition of Fort Charlotte in 1821.* Boston: Houghton and Mifflin, 1897.

Haswell, Anthony, ed. *Memoirs and Adventures of Captain Matthew Phelps, Formerly of Harwington in Connecticut, Now Resident of New Haven in Vermont: Particularly in Two Voyages from Connecticut to the River Mississippi, from December 1773 to October 1780.* Bennington: Anthony Haswell, 1802.

Haynes, Joshua S. *Patrolling the Border: Theft and Violence on the Creek-Georgia Frontier, 1770–1796.* Athens: University of Georgia Press, 2018.

Haynes, Robert V. *The Natchez District and the American Revolution.* Jackson: University Press of Mississippi, 1976.

Higginbotham, Jay. *Mobile! City by the Bay.* Mobile: Junior Chamber of Commerce, 1968.

_____. *Pascagoula: Singing River City.* Mobile: Gill Press, 1967.

Hoffman, Ronald, ed. and Peter J. Albert. *Diplomacy and Revolution: The Franco-American Alliance of 1778.* Charlottesville: University of Virginia Press, 1981.

Holmes, Jack D.L. *The 1779 Marcha de Galvez: Louisiana's Giant Step Forward in the American Revolution.* Baton Rouge: Baton Rouge Bicentennial Corporation, 1974.

Howard, Clinton N. *The British Development of West Florida, 1763–1769.* Berkeley: University of California Press, 1947.

Howard, Milo B, Jr., and Robert R. Rea. *The Memoire Justificatif of Chevalier Montault de Monberaut: Indian Diplomacy in British West Florida, 1763–1765.* Tuscaloosa: University of Alabama Press, 1965.

Hudson, Charles M., ed. *Black Drink: A Native American Tea.* Athens: University of Georgia Press, 1979.

Hyde, Samuel C., ed. *A Fierce and Fractious Frontier: The Curious Development of Louisiana's Florida Parishes, 1699–2000*. Baton Rouge: Louisiana State University Press, 2004.

Jackson, Harvey H. *Rivers of History: Life on the Coosa, Tallapoosa, Cahaba, and Alabama*. Tuscaloosa: University of Alabama Press, 1965.

James, James Alton. *Oliver Pollock: The Life and Times of an Unknown Patriot*. Whitefish, MT: Literary Licensing, 2011.

James, D. Clayton. *Antebellum Natchez*. Baton Rouge: Louisiana State University Press, 1993.

Johnson, Cecil. *British West Florida, 1763–1783*. New Haven: Yale University Press, 1943.

Knight, Carolyn Lynn H. *The American Colonial Press and the Townshend Crisis, 1766–1770: A Study in Political Imagery*. Lewiston, NY: Edwin Mellen Press, 1990.

Lakwete, Angela. *Inventing the Cotton Gin: Machine and Myth in Antebellum America*. Baltimore: Johns Hopkins University Press, 2003.

Learned, Marion Dexter, ed. *German American Annals*. Philadelphia: German American Historical Society, 1909.

Libby, David J. *Slavery and Frontier Mississippi, 1720–1835*. Jackson: University Press of Mississippi, 2004.

Livermore, Shaw. *Early American Land Companies: Their Influence on Corporate Development*. New York: Commonwealth Fund, 1939.

Matthews, Hazel C. *British West Florida and the Illinois Country*. Halifax, N.S.: E. Whynot, 1977.

McLemore, Richard A., ed. *A History of Mississippi*. Hattiesburg: University and College Press of Mississippi, 1973.

McLaurin, Melton and Michael Thomason. *Mobile: The Life and Times of a Great Southern City*. Woodland Hills, CA: Windsor Publications, 1981.

McMurtrie, Douglas C. *A Broadside Printed at Mobile in 1763, but Printed on the Island of Jamaica in the Same Year*. Chicago: Chicago School of Printing, 1939.

McDermott, John. *The Spanish in the Mississippi Valley, 1762–1804*. Champaign: University of Illinois Press, 1974.

Meyers, Rose. *A History of Baton Rouge, 1699–1812*. Baton Rouge: Louisiana State University Press, 1999.

Middlekauf, Robert. *The Glorious Cause: The American Revolution, 1763–1789*. New York: Oxford University Press, 1982.

Morgan, Edmund S. and Helen M. Morgan. *The Stamp Act Crisis: Prologue to Revolution*. Chapel Hill: University of North Carolina Press, 1953.

Morrissey, Brendan, and Adam Hook. *Saratoga 1777: Turning Point of a*

Revolution. Oxford: Osprey Publishing, 2000.

Narrett, David. *Adventurism and Empire: The Struggle for Mastery in the Louisiana-Florida Borderlands, 1762–1803*. Chapel Hill: University of North Carolina Press, 2015.

Nester, William R. *The Frontier War for American Independence*. Mechanicsburg, PA: Stackpole Books, 2004.

Nuzum, Kay. *A History of Baldwin County*. Bay Minette: The Baldwin Times, 1971.

O'Brien, Greg. *Choctaws in A Revolutionary Age, 1750–1830*. Lincoln: University of Nebraska Press, 2005.

Odom, Wesley S. *The Longest Siege of the American Revolution: Pensacola*. Pensacola: Wesley S. Odom, 2009.

Owen, Thomas McAdory. *History of Alabama and Dictionary of Alabama Biography*. Chicago: S.J. Clarke Publishing Company, 1921.

Owsley, Frank L., Jr., and Gene A. Smith. *Filibusters and Expansionists: Jeffersonian Manifest Destiny, 1800–1821*. Tuscaloosa: University of Alabama Press, 1997.

Pate, James P., William B. Stuart, and Joe B. Wilkins, Jr. *The Fort Tombecbe Historical Research and Documentation Project*. Livingston: Livingston University, 1980.

Paulett, Robert. *An Empire of Small Places: Mapping the Southeastern Anglo-Indian Trade, 1732–1795*. Athens: University of Georgia Press, 2012.

Pickett, Albert James. *History of Alabama, and Incidentally Georgia and Mississippi, from the Earliest Period*. Charleston: Walker and James, 1851.

Pittman, Philip. *The Present State of the European Settlements on the Mississippi, with a Geographical Description of That River, Illustrated by Plans and Draughts*. London: J. Nourse, 1770.

Proctor, Samuel, ed. *Eighteenth-Century Florida: Life on the Frontier*. Gainesville: University Press of Florida, 1976.

Raab, James W. *Spain, Britain and the American Revolution in Florida, 1763–1783*. Jefferson, NC: McFarland and Company, 2008.

Rakove, Jack N. *The Beginnings of National Politics: An Interpretive History of the Continental Congress*. New York: Knopf, 1979.

Rea, Robert R. *Major Robert Farmar of Mobile*. Tuscaloosa: University of Alabama Press, 1990.

Rea, Robert R., and Milo B. Howard. *The Minutes, Journals and Acts of the General Assembly of British West Florida*. Tuscaloosa: University of Alabama Press, 1979.

Reeves, Carolyn Keller, ed. *The Choctaw Before Removal*. Jackson: University Press of Mississippi, 1985.

Rogers, William Warren, Robert D. Ward, Wayne Flynt, and Leah Rawls Atkins. *Alabama: The History of a Deep South State*. Tuscaloosa: University of Alabama Press, 2010.

Rojas, F. De Borja Medina. *Jose de Ezpeleta, Gobernador de la Mobila 1780–1781*. Seville: Escuela de Estudios Hispano-Americanos, 1980.

Rowland, Dunbar. *Encyclopedia of Mississippi History: Comprising Sketches of Counties, Towns, Events, Institutions and Persons, Volume 1*. Madison: Selwyn A. Brant, 1907.

Rush, N. Orwin *Spain's Final Triumph Over Great Britain in the Gulf of Mexico: The Battle of Pensacola, March 9 to May 8, 1781*. Tallahassee: Florida State University Press, 1966.

Saravia, Gonzalo M. Quintero. *Bernardo de Galvez: Spanish Hero of the American Revolution*. Chapel Hill: University of North Carolina Press, 2018.

Schell, Sidney Henson. *The Continental Navy on the Gulf Coast, 1775–1781: The USS West Florida at the Siege of Mobile, 1780*. CreateSpace, 2014.

Scott, Florence D'Olive and Richard J. Scott. *Montrose: As it Was Recorded, Told About, and Lived*. Montgomery: Parago, 1976.

Servies, James A., ed. *The Log of the H.M.S. Mentor, 1780–1781: A New Account of the British Navy at Pensacola*. Gainesville: University Press of Florida, 1982.

Sledge, John S. *The Mobile River*. Columbia: University of South Carolina Press, 2015.

Smith, F. Todd. *Louisiana and the Gulf South Frontier, 1500–1821*. Baton Rouge: Louisiana State University Press, 2014.

Snider, Billie Ford and Janice B. Palmer, eds. *Spanish Plat Book of Land Records of the District of Pensacola, Province of West Florida: British and Spanish Land Grants, 1763–1821*. Pensacola: Antique Compiling, 1994.

Sosin, Jack M. *The Revolutionary Frontier, 1763–1783*. New York: Holt Rinehart and Winston, 1967.

Swisher, James K. *The Revolutionary War in the Southern Back Country*. Gretna, LA: Pelican Publishing, 2008.

Starr, J. Barton. *Tories, Dons and Rebels: The American Revolution in British West Florida*. Tallahassee: Florida State University Press, 1972.

Sullivan, Charles L. *The Mississippi Gulf Coast: Portrait of a People*. Staunton, VA: American History Press, 1999.

Taylor, Alan. *American Colonies: The Settling of North America*. New York: Penguin Books, 2001.

_____. *American Revolutions: A Continental History 1750–1804*. New York: W.W. Norton, 2016.

Thomason, Michael V. *Mobile: The New History of Alabama's First City*.

Tuscaloosa: University of Alabama Press, 2001.

United States Continental Congress. *Journals of the American Congress: From 1774 to 1788*. Washington: Way and Gideon, 1823.

Usner, Daniel H., Jr. *Indians, Settlers, and Slaves in a Frontier Exchange Economy: The Lower Mississippi Valley Before 1783*. Chapel Hill: University of North Carolina Press, 1992.

Ward, Joseph P., ed. *Britain and the American South: From Colonialism to Rock and Roll*. Jackson: University Press of Mississippi, 2003.

Waselkov, Gregory. *A Conquering Spirit: Fort Mims and the Redstick War of 1813–1814*. Tuscaloosa: University of Alabama Press, 2009.

Waselkov, Gregory, ed. *Powhatan's Mantle: Indians in the Colonial Southeast*. Lincoln: University of Nebraska Press, 1989.

Waselkov, Gregory, and Bonnie L. Gums. *Plantation Archaeology at Rivière aux Chiens, ca. 1725–1848*. Mobile: University of South Alabama, 2000.

Waselkov, Gregory, and Kathryn E. Holland Braund, eds. *William Bartram on the Southeastern Indians*. Lincoln: University of Nebraska Press, 1995.

Weber, David J. *The Spanish Frontier in North America*. New Haven: Yale University Press, 1994.

Weddle, Robert S. *Changing Tides: Twilight and Dawn in the Spanish Sea, 1763–1803*. College Station: Texas A&M Press, 1995.

Whitaker, Arthur P. *The Spanish-American Frontier, 1783–1795*. Boston: Houghton-Mifflin, 1927.

Willie, Leroy E. *West Florida and Its People*. Baton Rouge: Louisiana State University Press, 2000.

Wilson, David K. *The Southern Strategy: Britain's Conquest of South Carolina and Georgia, 1775–1780*. Columbia: University of South Carolina Press, 2008.

Willie, Leroy E. *West Florida and Its People*. Baton Rouge: SAR Books, 2000.

Wright, James Leitch. *Florida in the American Revolution*. Gainesville: University of Florida, 1975.

Wright, Amos J., Jr. *The McGillivray and McIntosh Traders: On the Old Southwest Frontier, 1716–1815*. Montgomery: NewSouth Books, 2007.

Theses and Dissertations

Born, John Dewey, Jr., "British Trade in West Florida, 1763–1783." Doctoral Dissertation, University of New Mexico, 1963.

Brewster, Lawrence F. "The Later History of British West Florida, 1770–1781: Governor Peter Chester and the Hey-Dey of the Province." Master's thesis, Columbia University, 1932.

Conover, Elizabeth May. "British West Florida's Mississippi Frontier During the American Revolution." Master's thesis, Auburn University, 1972.

Gray, Robert Edward. "Elias Durnford, 1739–1794: Engineer, Soldier, Administrator." Master's thesis, Auburn University, 1971.

Ingram, Earl Glynn. "A Critical Study of the British West Florida General Assembly." Master's thesis, Auburn University, 1969.

Simmons, Wilford O'Neal. "The Divergent Colony: British West Florida, 1763–1783." Master's thesis, Southeastern Louisiana University, 2004.

ARTICLES

"A Letter from a Gentleman in Pensacola to His Friend in South Carolina" *Pensacola History Illustrated* 1 (1984): 5–7.

Abbey, Kathryn Trimmer. "Chester's Defense of the Mississippi After the Willing Raid." *The Mississippi Valley Historical Review* 22 (June, 1935): 17–32.

_____. "The Intrigue of a British Refugee Against the Willing Raid, 1778." *The William and Mary Quarterly* 1 (October, 1944): 397–404.

Anderson, John Q. "The Narrative of John Hutchins." *Journal of Mississippi History,* 48 (Spring/Summer, 2016): 43–68.

Baker, Maury and Margaret Bissler Haas. "Bernardo de Galvez's Combat Diary for the Battle of Pensacola, 1781." *The Florida Historical Quarterly* 56 (October, 1977): 176–199.

Bauer, Deborah. "in a strange place...; The Experiences of British Women during the Colonization of East and West Florida." *The Florida Historical Quarterly* 89 (Fall, 2010): 145–185.

Beer, William. "The Surrender of Fort Charlotte, Mobile, 1780." *The American Historical Review* 1 (July, 1896): 696–699.

Beerman, Eric. "Jose de Ezpeleta: Alabama's First Spanish Commandant During the American Revolution." *Alabama Review* 29 (October, 1976): 249–260.

_____. "Yo Solo Not 'Solo': Juan Antonio de Riano." *The Florida Historical Quarterly* 58 (October, 1979): 174–184.

Bitler, James. "Indigo." *New Georgia Encyclopedia,* https://www.georgiaencyclo-pedia.org/articles/history-archaeology/indigo.

Born, John D., Jr. "Charles Strachan in Mobile: The Frontier Mobile of a Scottish Factor, 1764–1768." *Alabama Historical Quarterly* 27 (Spring/Summer, 1965): 23–42.

Bosse, David. "Dartmouth on the Mississippi: Speculators and Surveyors in British North America in the Eighteenth Century." *Imago Mundi* 41 (1989): 2, 9–18.

Boyd, Mark F. and Jose Navarro Latorre. "Spanish Interest in British Florida, and in the Progress of the American Revolution: Relations with the Spanish

Faction of the Creek Indians." *The Florida Historical Quarterly* 32 (October, 1953): 92–130.

Brannon, Peter A. "The Coosa River Crossing of British Refugees, 1781." *Alabama Historical Quarterly* 19 (Spring, 1957): 149–155.

Braund, Kathryn E. Holland. "The Creek Indians, Blacks, and Slavery." *The Journal of Southern History* 57 (November, 1991): 601–636.

Breetzke, David E. "The Sequence of Military Operations on the Barrancas." *Gulf Coast Historical Review* 24 (Fall, 1998): 61–75.

Carpenter, W.M., ed. "The Mississippi River in the Olden Time: A Genuine Account of the Present State of the River Mississippi and of the Land on its Banks to the River Yasous 1776," *De Bow's Review*, III (1847): 115–123.

Carter, Clarence E. "Some Aspects of British Administration in West Florida." *The Mississippi Valley Historical Review* 1 (December, 1914): 364–375.

_____. "The Beginnings of British West Florida." *Mississippi Valley Historical Review*, Vol. 4 (December, 1917): 314–341.

Caughey, John. "Bernardo de Galvez and the English Smugglers on the Mississippi, 1777." *The Hispanic American Historical Review* 12 (February, 1932): 46–58.

_____. "The Panis Mission to Pensacola, 1778." *The Hispanic American Historical Review* 10 (November, 1930): 480–489.

_____. "The Natchez Rebellion of 1781 and Its Aftermath." *Louisiana Historical Quarterly* 16 (1933): 57–83.

_____. "Willing's Expedition Down the Mississippi, 1778." *Louisiana Historical Quarterly* 15 (January, 1932): 5–36.

Coker, William S. "Description and Bibliography of the Map of the British and Spanish Floridas, 1763–1821." *Pensacola History Illustrated* 5 (Summer, 1999): 17–22.

Conover, Bettie Jones. "British West Florida's Frontier Mississippi Posts, 1763–1779." *Alabama Review* 29 (July, 1976): 177–207.

Cubberly, Frederick. "Fort George (St. Michael), Pensacola." *The Florida Historical Society Quarterly* 6 (April, 1928): 220–234.

Cummins, Light Townsend. "Her Weary Pilgrimage: The Remarkable Mississippi River Adventures of Anne McMeans, 1778–1782." *Louisiana History* 47 (Autumn, 2006): 389–415.

Dart, Henry P., ed. "West Florida-The Capture of Baton Rouge By Galvez, September 21, 1779, From Reports of the English Officers." *Louisiana Historical Quarterly* 12 (April, 1929): 255–265.

Dawkins, Mary. "The West Florida Board of Land Commissioners." *Pensacola History Illustrated* 5 (Summer, 1999): 3–6.

DeRosier, Jr., Arthur H. "William Dunbar: A Product of the Eighteenth Century Scottish Renaissance." *Journal of Mississippi History*, 27 (Aug., 1966): 185–227.

Din, Gilbert C. "Protecting the 'Barrera': Spain's Defenses in Louisiana, 1763–1779." *Louisiana History* 19 (Spring, 1978): 183–211.

Drake, W. M. "A Note on the Jersey Settlers of Adams County." *Journal of Mississippi History*, 14 (October, 1953): 274–275.

Dungan, James R. "Sir William Dunbar of Natchez: Planter, Explorer, and Scientist, 1792–1810." *Journal of Mississippi History*, 24 (October, 1961): 211–228.

"Extracts from the Travels of William Bartram." *Alabama Historical Quarterly* 17 (Fall, 1955): 110–124.

Fabel, Robin. "A Letter from Governor George Johnstone." *Pensacola History Illustrated* 3 (Spring/Summer, 1990): 19–24.

_____. "Authenticating Pierre Viaud's *Shipwreck and Adventures*." *Gulf Coast Historical Review* 2(Spring, 1990): 47–55.

_____. "Bernard Lintot: A Connecticut Yankee on the Mississippi, 1775–1805." *Florida Historical Quarterly* 60 (July, 1981): 88–102.

_____. "British West Florida." *Encyclopedia of Alabama*, http://www.encyclopediaofalabama.org/article/h-1085.

_____. "Dauphin Island as the Gateway to Mexico: A Chimera of the 1770s." *Alabama Review* 50 (April, 1997): 83–102.

_____. "Elias Durnford." *Encyclopedia of Alabama*, http://www.encyclopediaofalabama.org/article/h-1090.

_____. "Encounters Up the Mississippi, Yazoo, and Big Black Rivers: The Explorers of the Company of Military Adventurers." *Gulf Coast Historical Review* 8 (Fall 1992): 95– 103.

_____. "George Johnstone and the 'Thoughts Concerning Florida'—A Case of Lobbying?" *Alabama Review* 29 (July, 1976): 164–176.

_____. "George Johnstone of British West Florida." *The Florida Historical Quarterly*, 54 (April, 1976): 497–511.

_____ "Ordeal by Siege: James Bruce in Pensacola, 1780–1781." *The Florida Historical Quarterly*, 63 (January, 1988): 280–297.

_____. "Reflections on Mobile's Loyalism in the American Revolution." *Gulf Coast Historical Review* 19 (2003): 31–45.

Fabel, Robin F. and Robert R. Rea. "Lieutenant Thomas Campbell's Sojourn Among the Creeks." *Alabama Historical Quarterly* 36 (Summer, 1974): 97–111.

Favrot, J. St. Clair. "Baton Rouge: The Historic Capital of Louisiana." *Louisiana Historical Quarterly* 12 (October, 1929): 611–629.

Fisher, Ruth Anna. "The Surrender of Pensacola as Told by the British." *The American Historical Review* 54 (January, 1949): 326–329.

Frederick, John H. "A Question of Authority: Johnstone and Browne, 1766–1767." *Gulf Coast Historical Review* 24 (Spring, 1998): 35–48.

Gold, Robert L. "Politics and Property during the Transfer of Florida from Spanish to English Rule, 1763–1764." *The Florida Historical Quarterly* 42 (July, 1963): 16–34.

Griffith, Lucille. "Peter Chester and the End of the British Empire in West Florida." *Alabama Review* 30 (January, 1977): 14–33.

Groner, Julius, and Robert R. Rea. "John Ellis, King's Agent, and West Florida." *The Florida Historical Quarterly* 66 (April, 1988): 385–398.

Gums, Bonnie L. "Eighteenth-Century Plantations in the Northern Gulf Coast Region." *Gulf Coast Historical Review* 14 (Fall, 1988): 120–142.

Haarman, Albert W. "The Siege of Pensacola: An Order of Battle." *The Florida Historical Quarterly* 44 (January, 1966): 193–199.

_____. "The Spanish Conquest of British West Florida, 1779–1781." *The Florida Historical Quarterly* 39 (October, 1960): 107–134.

Hamer, Philip M. "John Stuart's Indian Policy During the Early Months of the American Revolution." *The Mississippi Valley Historical Review* 17 (December, 1930): 351–366.

Harrell, Laura D.S. "Colonial Medical Practice in British West Florida, 1763–1781." *Bulletin of the History of Medicine* 41 (1967): 539–558.

Haynes, Robert V. "James Willing and the Planters of Natchez: The American Revolution Comes to the Southwest." *Journal of Mississippi History* 37 (February, 1975): 1–42.

Holmes, Jack D.L. "Alabama's Bloodiest Day of the American Revolution: Counterattack at The Village, January 7, 1781." *Alabama Review* 29 (July, 1976): 208–219.

_____. "Alabama's Forgotten Settler: Notes on the Spanish Mobile District, 1780–1813." *Alabama Historical Quarterly* 33 (Summer, 1971): 87–97.

_____. "Charting Mobile Bay and River." *Alabama Historical Quarterly* 44 (Fall/Winter, 1982): 143–170.

_____. "German Troops in Alabama During the American Revolution: The Battle of January 7, 1781." *Alabama Historical Quarterly* 38 (Spring, 1976): 5–9.

_____. "Indigo in Colonial Louisiana and the Floridas." *Louisiana History* 8 (Autumn, 1967): 329–349.

_____. "Jose de Evia and His Activities in Mobile, 1780–1784." *Alabama Historical Quarterly* 34 (Summer, 1972): 105–112.

_____. "Juan de la Villebeuvre: Spain's Commandant of Natchez During the American Revolution." *Journal of Mississippi History* 37 (February, 1975): 97–125.

_____. "The Role of Black Troops in Spanish Alabama: The Mobile District, 1780–1813." *Alabama Historical Quarterly* 38 (Spring, 1975): 5–18.

_____. "Colonial Pensacola: The British Period." *The Florida Historical Quarterly*, (October, 1940): 109–127.

_____. "Colonial Pensacola: The British Period, Part II." *The Florida Historical Quarterly*, 19 (January, 1941): 246–269.

_____. "Colonial Pensacola: The British Period, Part III; The Administration of Governor Chester, 1770–1781." *The Florida Historical Quarterly*, Vol. 19 (April, 1941): 368–401.

_____. "Early Settlers in British West Florida." *The Florida Historical Quarterly* 24 (July, 1945): 45–55.

_____. "Governor Johnstone in West Florida." *The Florida Historical Quarterly* (April, 1939): 281–303.

_____. "The Military Occupation of British West Florida, 1763." *The Florida Historical Quarterly* 17 (January, 1939): 181–199.

Jackson, George B. "John Stuart: Superintendent of Indian Affairs for the Southern District." *Tennessee Historical Magazine* 3 (September, 1917): 165–191.

James, James Alton. "Oliver Pollock, Financier of the Revolution in the West." *The Mississippi Valley Historical Review* 16 (June, 1929): 67–80.

Jarvis, Eric. "His Majesty's Papist Subjects: Roman Catholic Political Rights in British West Florida." *Gulf Coast Historical Review* 16 (Fall, 2000): 6–19.

Jenkins, William H. "Alabama Forts, 1700–1838." *Alabama Review* 12 (July, 1959): 163–179.

Johnson, Cecil. "Expansion in West Florida, 1770–1779." *The Mississippi Valley Historical Review* 20 (March, 1934): 481–496.

_____. "Pensacola in the British Period: Summary and Significance." *The Florida Historical Quarterly* 37 (January - April, 1959): 263–280.

_____. "The Distribution of Land in British West Florida." *Louisiana Historical Quarterly* 16 (October, 1933): 539–553.

_____. "West Florida Revisited." *Journal of Mississippi History* 28 (May, 1966): 121–132.

Kane, Robert B. "Bernardo de Galvez." *Encyclopedia of Alabama.* http://www. encyclopediaofalabama.org/article/h-3763.

Knetsch, Joe. "Early Surveying in West Florida." *Pensacola History Illustrated* 5 (Summer, 1999): 7–16.

Lennon, Rachel Mills. "Loyalist Refugee Petitions in British West Florida,

1776–77." *National Geographic Society Quarterly* 85 (1997): 129–139.

Lewis, Herbert J. "Robert Farmar." *Encyclopedia of Alabama.* http://www.encyclopediaofalabama.org/article/h-2613.

McAlister, Lyle N. "Pensacola During the Second Spanish Period." *The Florida Historical Quarterly* 37 (January-April, 1959): 281–327.

_____. "William Augustus Bowles and the State of Muskogee." *The Florida Historical Quarterly* 40 (April, 1962): 317–328.

McCorvey, Thomas Chalmers. "The Highland Scotch Element in the Early Settlement of Alabama." *Alabama Historical Quarterly* 1 (Spring, 1930): 41–49.

Mielnik, Tara Mitchell. "Alexander Cameron." *Tennessee Encyclopedia.* https://tennesseeencyclopedia.net/entries/alexander-cameron/.

Morgan, Madel Jacobs. "Sarah Truly, Mississippi Tory." *Journal of Mississippi History* 37 (February, 1975): 87–95.

Mowat, Charles L. "The Southern Brigade, 1763–1775." *The Florida Historical Quarterly* 23 (July, 1944): 45–49.

_____. "The Southern Brigade: A Sidelight on the British Military Establishment in America, 1763–1775." *The Journal of Southern History* 10 (February, 1944): 59–77.

Murphy, Kathleen S. "To Make Florida Answer To Its Name: John Ellis, Bernard Romans and the Atlantic Science of British West Florida." *British Journal for the History of Science* 47 (2014): 43–65.

Murphy, W.S. "The Irish Brigade of Spain at the Capture of Pensacola, 1781." *The Florida Historical Quarterly* 38 (January, 1960): 216–225.

Neeley, Mary Ann Oglesby. "Lachlan McGillivray: A Scot on the Alabama Frontier." *Alabama Historical Quarterly* 36 (Spring, 1974): 5–14.

O'Donnell, James H. "Armchair Adventurers and Horseback Botanists: Explorations of Florida's Natural History, 1763–1800." *Gulf Coast Historical Review* 8 (1992): 85–94.

_____. "John Stuart."*NCPedia.* https://www.ncpedia.org/biography/stuart-john.

Osborn, George C. "Major-General John Campbell in British West Florida." *The Florida Historical Quarterly* 27 (April, 1949): 317–339.

_____. "Relations with the Indians in West Florida during the Administration of Governor Peter Chester, 1770–1781." *The Florida Historical Quarterly,* 31 (April 1953): 239–272.

Nunemaker, J. Horace. "Louisiana Anticipates Spain's Recognition of the Independence of the United States." *Louisiana Historical Quarterly* 26 (July, 1943): 755–769.

O'Brien, Greg. "Choctaws in Alabama." *Encyclopedia of Alabama.* http://www. encyclopediaofalabama.org/article/h-1186.

_____. "Southeastern Indians and the American Revolution." *Encyclopedia of Alabama.* http://www.encyclopediaofalabama.org/article/h-1133

Padgett, James A., ed. "Commission, Orders and Instructions Issued to George Johnstone, British Governor of West Florida, 1763–1767." *Louisiana Historical Quarterly* 21 (October, 1938): 1021–1068.

_____. "Governor Peter Chester's Observations on the Boundaries of British West Florida, About 1775." *Louisiana Historical Quarterly* 25 (January, 1943): 5–11.

_____. "The Reply of Peter Chester, Governor of West Florida, To Complaints Made Against His Administration." *Louisiana Historical Quarterly* 22 (January, 1939): 31–47.

Parks, Virginia. "The British Fort at Pensacola." *Pensacola History Illustrated* 3 (Spring/Summer, 1990): 11–18.

Price, Charles L., and Claude C. Sturgill. "The Role of the British Navy in the Landing in West Florida in 1763 as Revealed in the Letters of Captain William Bayne." *Alabama Review* 30 (January, 1977): 51–65.

Rea, Robert R. "1763-The Forgotten Bicentennial: An Historiographic Commentary." *Alabama Historical Quarterly* 25 (Fall/Winter, 1963): 287–293.

_____. "A Naval Visitor in British West Florida." *The Florida Historical Quarterly* 40 (October, 1961): 142–153.

_____. "A New Letter From Mobile, 1763." *Alabama Review* 22 (July, 1969): 230–237.

_____. "A Better Fate! The British West Florida Seal." *Alabama Historical Quarterly* 43 (Winter, 1981): 289–300.

_____. "Assault on the Mississippi—The Loftus Expedition, 1764." *Alabama Review* 26 (July, 1973): 173–193.

_____. "Belles-Lettres in British West Florida." *Alabama Review,* 13 (April, 1960): 145–149.

_____. "Brigadier General Frederick Haldimand: The Florida Years." *The Florida Historical Quarterly* 54 (April, 1976): 512–531.

_____. "British Pensacola." *Pensacola History Illustrated* 3 (Spring/Summer, 1990): 3–10.

_____. "British West Florida Trade and Commerce in the Customs Records." *Alabama Review* 37 (April, 1984): 124–159.

_____. "Elias Durnford: Royal Engineer in British West Florida." *Pensacola History Illustrated* 3 (Spring/Summer, 1990): 25–28.

_____. "Florida and the Royal Navy's Floridas." *The Florida Historical Quarterly*

60 (October, 1981): 186–203.

_____. "Graveyard for Britons, West Florida, 1763–1781." *The Florida Historical Quarterly* 47 (April, 1969): 345–364.

_____. "Henry Hamilton and West Florida." *Indiana Magazine of History* 54 (March, 1958): 49–56.

_____. "John Eliot: Second Governor of British West Florida." *Alabama Review* 30 (October, 1977): 243–265.

_____. "Lieutenant Colonel James Robertson's Mission to the Floridas, 1763." *The Florida Historical Quarterly* 53 (July, 1974): 33–48.

_____. "Lieutenant Hutchins to the Rescue! The Wreck and Recovery of the *Mercury*, 1772." *Gulf Coast Historical Review* 5 (Spring, 1990): 56–61.

_____. "Military Deserters from British West Florida." *Louisiana History* 9 (Spring, 1968): 123–137.

_____. "Outpost of Empire: David Wedderburn at Mobile." *Alabama Review* 7 (July, 1954): 217–232.

_____. "Planters and Plantations in British West Florida." *Alabama Review* 29 (July, 1976): 220–235.

_____. "Problems and Responses in British Pensacola." *Gulf Coast Historical Review* 3 (1987): 43–62.

_____. "Royal Navy 'Remarks' Books and Charles Roberts's 'Observations.'" *Alabama Review* 41 (July, 1988): 163–178.

_____. "Some Notes on Edward Gibbon's Memoire Justicatif." *Studies in Bibliography* 5 (1952/1953): 194–197.

_____. "The Deputed Seal of British West Florida." *Alabama Historical Quarterly* 40 (Fall/Winter, 1978):162–168.

_____. "The Naval Career of John Eliot, Governor of West Florida." *The Florida Historical Quarterly* 57 (April, 1979): 451–467.

_____. "The Royal Navy Base at Pensacola." *Pensacola History Illustrated* 1 (1984): 2–4.

_____. "The Trouble at Tombeckby." *Alabama Review* 21 (January, 1968): 21–39.

Robertson, Henry O. "Tories or Patriots? The Mississippi River Planters During the American Revolution." *Louisiana History* 40 (Autumn, 1999): 445–462.

Robinson, Willard B. "Military Architecture at Mobile Bay." *Journal of the Society of Architectural Historians* 30 (May, 1971): 119–139.

Scramuzza, V.M. "Galveztown: A Spanish Settlement in Colonial Louisiana." *Louisiana Historical Quarterly* 13 (October, 1930): 553–609.

Scott, Kenneth, ed. "Britain Loses Natchez, 1779: An Unpublished Letter." *Journal of Mississippi History*, 26 (February, 1964): 45–46.

Segura, Pearl Mary. "The Capture of the Bluff at Baton Rouge." *Louisiana History* 17 (Spring, 1976): 203–209.

Siebert, Wilbur H. "How the Spaniards Evacuated Pensacola in 1763." *Florida Historical Society Quarterly* 11 (October, 1932): 48–57.

_____. "The Loyalists in West Florida and the Natchez District." *The Mississippi Valley Historical Review* 2 (March, 1916): 465–483.

Smith, Louis R., Jr. "British-Indian Trade in Alabama, 1670–1756." *Alabama Review* 27 (January, 1974): 65–75.

Starr, J. Barton. "Campbell Town: French Huguenots in British West Florida." *The Florida Historical Quarterly*, 54 (April, 1976): 342–357.

_____. "The Case and Petition of His Majesty's Loyal Subjects, Late of West Florida." *The Florida Historical Quarterly* 59 (October, 1980): 199–212.

_____. "The Spirit of What is There Called Liberty: The Stamp Act in British West Florida." *Alabama Review* 29 (October, 1976): 261–272.

Sturdivant, Laura D.S. "One Carbine and a Little Flour and Corn in a Sack: The American Pioneer." *The Journal of Mississippi History* 37 (February 1975): 43–66.

"The British Proclamation of October 7, 1763, Creating the Government of West Florida." *Louisiana Historical Quarterly* 13 (October, 1930): 610–616.

Thomas, Daniel H. "Fort Toulouse—In Tradition and Fact." *Alabama Review* 13 (October, 1960): 243–257.

_____. "Fort Toulouse: The French Outpost at the Alabamas on the Coosa." *Alabama Historical Quarterly* 22 (Fall, 1960): 135–230.

Vickers, Elizabeth D. "Disease: The Unconquerable Foe in British West Florida." *Pensacola History Illustrated* 3 (Spring/Summer, 1990): 29–32.

Wells, Gordon M. "British Land Grants—William Wilton Map, 1774." *Journal of Mississippi History*, 28 (May, 1966): 152–160.

Williams, Harold D. "Bernardo de Galvez and the Western Patriots." *Revista de Historia de America* 65/66 (January-December, 1968): 53–70.

Worcester, Donald E. "Miranda's Diary of the Siege of Pensacola, 1781." *The Florida Historical Quarterly* 29 (January, 1951): 163–196.

Wright, Jr., J. Leitch. "Lord Dunmore's Loyalist Asylum in the Floridas." *The Florida Historical Quarterly* 49 (April, 1971): 370–379.

Notes

CHAPTER ONE

1   For more on the Seven Years' War and how it impacted colonial development in North America, see Fred Anderson, *Crucible of War: The Seven Years' War and the Fate of Empire in British North America, 1754–1766* (New York: Alfred A. Knopf, 2000) and Colin G. Calloway, *The Scratch of a Pen: 1763 and the Transformation of North America* (New York: Oxford University Press, 2006).

2   The history of French Louisiana is chronicled in dozens of excellent books, a number of which are focused on specific regions or communities. For one of the best overviews of the colony's development and the associated rivalry between France and Spain in the Gulf basin in the era see Robert S. Weddle, *The French Thorn: Rival Explorers in the Spanish Sea, 1682–1762* (College Station: Texas A&M University Press), 1991.

3   Milo B. Howard, Milo B, Jr., and Robert R. Rea, *The Memoire Justificatif of Chevalier Montault de Monberaut: Indian Diplomacy in British West Florida, 1763–1765* (Tuscaloosa: University of Alabama Press, 1965), 9.

4   Cecil Johnson, *British West Florida, 1763–1783* (New Haven: Yale University Press, 1943), 2; Daniel H. Usner, Jr. *Indians, Settlers, and Slaves in a Frontier Exchange Economy: The Lower Mississippi Valley Before 1783* (Chapel Hill: University of North Carolina Press, 1992), 105; Michael V. Thomason, *Mobile: The New History of Alabama's First City* (Tuscaloosa: University of Alabama Press, 2001), 41; Robert L. Gold, "Politics and Property during the Transfer of Florida from Spanish to English Rule, 1763–1764," *The Florida Historical Quarterly* 42 (July, 1963): 18; Michael Gannon, *New History of Florida* (Gainesville: University Press of Florida, 2012), 134; John McDermott, *The Spanish in the Mississippi Valley, 1762–1804* (Champaign: University of Illinois Press, 1974), 89.

5   Michel Gannon, *Florida: A Short History* (Gainesville: University Press of Florida, 2003), 17; Robert S. Weddle, *Changing Tides: Twilight and Dawn in the Spanish Sea, 1763–1803* (College Station: Texas A&M Press, 1995), 5–9; John J. Clune and Margo S. Stringfield, *Historic Pensacola* (Gainesville: University Press of Florida, 2017), 71–94.

6   Jack P. Greene, and J.R. Pole, *The Blackwell Encyclopedia of the Revolution* (Hoboken: Wiley-Blackwell, 1992), 107; James Leitch Wright, *Florida in the American Revolution* (Gainesville: University of Florida, 1975), 2; William Warren Rogers, Robert D. Ward, Wayne Flynt, and Leah Rawls Atkins, *Alabama: The History of a Deep South State* (Tuscaloosa: University of Alabama Press, 2010), 32; Robert L. Gold, *Borderland Empires in Transition: The Triple-Nation Transfer of Florida* (Carbondale, Ill.: Southern Illinois University Press, 1969), 118; Clarence E. Carter, "The Beginnings of British West Florida," *Mississippi Valley Historical Review*, 4 (December, 1917): 318–319; David Narrett, *Adventurism and Empire: The Struggle for Mastery in the Louisiana-Florida Borderlands, 1762–1803* (Chapel Hill: University of North Carolina Press, 2015), 24–25; Robert R. Rea, *Major Robert Farmar of Mobile* (Tuscaloosa: University of Alabama Press, 1990),

40; Gannon, *New History of Florida*, 135; Robert R. Rea, "1763-The Forgotten Bicentennial: An Historiographic Commentary," *Alabama Historical Quarterly* 25 (Fall/Winter,
1963), 287.

7   Cecil Johnson, "West Florida Revisited," *Journal of Mississippi History*, 28 (May, 1966),
122; Alan Taylor, *American Revolutions: A Continental History 1750–1804* (New York:
W.W. Norton, 2016), 62; Wilford O'Neal Simmons, "The Divergent Colony: British
West Florida, 1763–1783," (Master's thesis, Southeastern Louisiana University, 2004),
2; Rogers, et al., *Alabama*, 32; Clinton N. Howard, "Early Settlers in British West
Florida," *The Florida Historical Quarterly* 24 (July, 1945), 46–47; Robin Fabel, *Bombast
and Broadsides: The Lives of George Johnstone* (Tuscaloosa: University of Alabama Press,
1987) 39;Gold, *Borderland Empires*, 118, 123–125; Joshua S. Haynes, *Patrolling the Border: Theft and Violence on the Creek-Georgia Frontier, 1770–1796* (Athens: University of
Georgia Press, 2018), 11; Charles L. Mowat, "The Southern Brigade: A Sidelight on the
British Military Establishment in America, 1763–1775," *The Journal of Southern History*,
10 (February, 1944), 59; Johnson, *British West Florida*, 5; Robin Fabel, *The Economy of
British West Florida, 1763–1783* (Tuscaloosa: University of Alabama Press, 1988), 2. The
full text of the proclamation is reproduced in in "The British Proclamation of October
7, 1763, Creating the Government of West Florida," *Louisiana Historical Quarterly* 13
(October, 1930): 610–616. For more on how British borders strategy impacted colonial
North America, see Calloway, *Scratch of a Pen*.

8   David Bosse, "Dartmouth on the Mississippi: Speculators and Surveyors in British North
America in the Eighteenth Century," *Imago Mundi* 41 (1989), 9; James W. Raab, *Spain,
Britain and the American Revolution in Florida, 1763–1783* (Jefferson, NC: McFarland
and Company, 2008), 33; Johnson, *British West Florida*, 6; Clinton N. Howard, *The British Development of West Florida, 1763–1769* (Berkeley: University of California Press,
1947), 7, 47; Clinton N. Howard, "The Military Occupation of British West Florida,
1763," *The Florida Historical Quarterly* 17 (January, 1939), 181; Carter, "The Beginnings
of British West Florida," 314–316, 317, 320.

9   F. Todd Smith, *Louisiana and the Gulf South Frontier, 1500–1821* (Baton Rouge: Louisiana
State University Press, 2014), 131, 164; Fabel, *Bombast and Broadsides*, 28; Robin Fabel,
"British West Florida," *Encyclopedia of Alabama*, http://www.encyclopediaofalabama.
org/article/h-1085; Johnson, *British West Florida*, 6; Clarence E. Carter, "Some Aspects
of British Administration in West Florida," *The Mississippi Valley Historical Review* 1
(December, 1914), 365–367; Howard, "Military Occupation," 181; Carter, "The Begin-
nings of British West Florida," 317–318, 325; Narret, *Adventurism and Empire*, 26; Gold,
Borderland Empires, 130; Howard, *British Development of West Florida*, 7; John Francis
Hamtramck Claiborne, *Mississippi, As a Province, Territory, and State, With Biographical
Notices of Eminent Citizens* (Jackson: Power and Barksdale, 1880), 92; Fabel, *Economy of
British West Florida*, 158; J. Barton Starr, *Tories, Dons and Rebels: The American Revolution
in British West Florida* (Tallahassee: Florida State University Press, 1972), 3; D. Clayton
James, *Antebellum Natchez* (Baton Rouge: Louisiana State University Press, 1993), 13;
Hazel C. Matthews, *British West Florida and the Illinois Country* (Halifax, N.S.: E. Whynot,
1977), 30.

10   Howard, *British Development of West Florida*, 11; Richard A. McLemore, ed. *A History
of Mississippi* (Hattiesburg: University and College Press of Mississippi, 1973), 135;
Howard, "Military Occupation," 183–185; Carter, "The Beginnings of British West

Florida," 314–315; Gold, *Borderland Empires*, 56, 100, 101, 103; Wilbur H. Siebert, "How the Spaniards Evacuated Pensacola in 1763," *Florida Historical Society Quarterly* 11 (October, 1932), 50–51, 52, 54, 56; Raab, *Spain, Britain, and the American Revolution in Florida*, 33; Gold, "Politics and Property," 19; Cecil Johnson, "Pensacola in the British Period: Summary and Significance," *The Florida Historical Quarterly*, 37 (January-April, 1959), 265.

11   Charles L. Mowat, "The Southern Brigade, 1763–1775," *The Florida Historical Quarterly* 23 (July, 1944), 46; Robert R. Rea, "Brigadier Frederick Haldimand: The Florida Years," *The Florida Historical Quarterly* 54 (April, 1976), 513–517, 528; Gannon, *New History of Florida*, 144; David E. Breetzke, "The Sequence of Military Operations on the Barrancas," *Gulf Coast Historical Review* 24 (Fall, 1998), 63–64; Virginia Parks, "The British Fort at Pensacola," *Pensacola History Illustrated* 3 (Spring/Summer, 1990): 11–12; Siebert, "How the Spaniards Evacuated Pensacola," 51; Gold, *Borderland Empires*, 104; Robert R. Rea, "Royal Navy 'Remarks' Books and Charles Roberts's 'Observations," *Alabama Review* 41 (July, 1988), 166; Robert R. Rea, "Lieutenant Colonel James Robertson's Mission to the Floridas, 1763," *The Florida Historical Quarterly* 53 (July, 1974), 43; Dunbar Rowland, ed, *Mississippi Provincial Archives: English Dominion, Letters and Disclosures to the Secretary of State From Major Robert Farmar and Governor George Johnstone* (Nashville: Press of Brandon Printing Company, 1911), Engineer Robertson to Captain Mackinen, October 25, 1764, 123–124; Haldimand to Gage, April, 1767, The Haldimand Papers: Correspondence with General Gage, 1758–1777, Mobile Public Library; Gov. Johnstone's report on the state of the province, February 19, 1765, West Florida Governor Correspondence, 1763–1766, Government Records Collections, Alabama Department of Archives and History.

12   Thomason, *Mobile*, 41; Sledge, *Mobile River*, 48–55; Edwin C. Bridges, *Alabama: The Making of an American State* (Tuscaloosa: University of Alabama Press, 2016), 29; Rea, *Major Robert Farmar*, 35; Rogers, et al., *Alabama*, 32; Johnson, *British West Florida*, 12; Robin Fabel, "Reflections on Mobile's Loyalism in the American Revolution," *Gulf Coast Historical Review* 19 (2003), 32–34; Starr, *Tories, Dons, and Rebels*, 5.

13   Herbert J. Lewis, "Robert Farmar." *Encyclopedia of Alabama*, http://www.encyclopediaofalabama.org/article/h-2613; Caldwell Delaney, *The Story of Mobile* (Mobile: Gill Press, 1953), 38;Howard, *British Development of West Florida*, 11; John S. Sledge, *The Mobile River* (Columbia: University of South Carolina Press, 2015), 53; Howard, "Military Occupation," 187–189; Carter, "The Beginnings of British West Florida," 314–315; Rea, *Major Robert Farmar*, 8, 20, 26–31, 33, 40; Thomas McAdory Owen, *History of Alabama and Dictionary of Alabama Biography* (Chicago: S.J. Clarke Publishing Company, 1921), 154; Fabel, *Bombast and Broadsides*, 28. Fought between Great Britain and Spain over shipping rights and eventually merging with the wider War of Austrian Succession between many of the powers of Europe, the War of Jenkins' Ear received its unusual name from historian Thomas Carlyle, author of *The History of Friedrich II* (1858). In 1731, Spanish soldiers had boarded a merchant ship captained by Robert Jenkins, and in the ensuing altercation actually severed his ear. For more information on how the contest played out in North America between British and Spanish colonial forces, see Herbert E. Bolton and Mary Ross, *The Debatable Land: A Sketch of the Anglo-Spanish Contest for the Georgia Country* (Berkeley: University of California Press, 1925). The War of Austrian Succession was fought 1740–1748 between nearly two dozen European powers over

the issue of the leadership of the Habsburg Monarchy. For more information, see M.S. Anderson, *The War of Austrian Succession, 1740–1748* (London: Routledge Press, 1995).

14 Howard and Rea, *The Memoire Justificatif*, 10; Charles L. Price and Claude C. Sturgill, "The Role of the British Navy in the Landing in West Florida in 1763 as Revealed in the Letters of Captain William Bayne," *Alabama Review* 30 (January, 1977), 55–57; McLemore, ed., *A History of Mississippi*, 135–136; Starr, *Tories, Dons, and Rebels*, 4, 6; Gold, *Borderland Empires*, 107, 111; Johnson, *British West Florida*, 9; Rea, *Major Robert Farmar*, 34–35; Howard, "Military Occupation," 192–193; Thomason, *Mobile*, 41; Rogers, et al., *Alabama*, 32; Rowland, *Mississippi Provincial Archives*, 10, Farmar to Secretary of War, January 24, 1764.

15 Thomason, *Mobile*, 41; Rea, *Major Robert Farmar*, 35; Price and Sturgill, "The Role of the British Navy," 54, 57; Howard, "Military Occupation," 193–194; Rogers, et al., *Alabama*, 32; Rea, "Forgotten Bicentennial," 287; Gold, *Borderland Empires*, 108–109.

16 Rea, *Major Robert Farmar*, 35, 36, 44; Howard, "Military Occupation," 191, 194, 197; Rogers, et al., *Alabama*, 32; Melton McLaurin and Michael Thomason, *Mobile: The Life and Times of a Great Southern City* (Woodland Hills, CA: Windsor Publications, 1981), 17; Robert R. Rea, "Problems and Responses in British Pensacola," *Gulf Coast Historical Review* 3 (1987), 43; Johnson, *British West Florida*, 12; Sledge, *Mobile River*, 54; Willard B. Robinson, "Military Architecture at Mobile Bay," *Journal of the Society of Architectural Historians* 30 (May, 1971), 125; Gold, *Borderland Empires*, 109; Howard and Rea, *The Memoire Justificatif*, 13; Peter Hamilton, *Colonial Mobile: An Historical Study of the Alabama-Tombigbee Basin from the Discovery of Mobile Bay in 1519 Until the Demolition of Fort Charlotte in 1821* (Boston: Houghton and Mifflin, 1897), 252, Gage to Haldimand, July 6, 1770, Haldimand Papers; Rowland, Mississippi Provincial Archives, Farmar to Secretary of War, January April 7, and 1764.

17 Robert R. Rea, "The Trouble at Tombeckby," *Alabama Review* 21 (January, 1968), 21, 23–24, 25, 38; James P. Pate, William B. Stuart, and Joe B. Wilkins, Jr. *The Fort Tombecbe Historical Research and Documentation Project* (Livingston: Livingston University, 1980); Howard, "Military Occupation," 197; Rogers, et al., *Alabama*, 32; F. Todd Smith, *Louisiana and the Gulf South Frontier, 1500–1821* (Baton Rouge: Louisiana State University Press, 2014), 131.

18 Rea, "The Trouble at Tombeckby," 26–27, 28–29, 31–32, 34, 35, 37; Haldimand to Gage, June 17, 1767 and Haldimand to Gage, August 5, 1767, Haldimand Papers; Gold, *Borderland Empires*, 169.

19 James, *Antebellum Natchez*, 14; Jack D. Elliott, Jr., *The Fort of Natchez and the Colonial Origins of Mississippi* (Fort Washington, PA: Eastern National Parks and Monument Association, 1998), 19; Robert R. Rea, "A New Letter From Mobile, 1763," *Alabama Review* 22 (July, 1969), 232; Rea, *Major Robert Farmar*, 38; Philip Pittman, *The Present State of the European Settlements on the Mississippi, with a Geographical Description of That River, Illustrated by Plans and Draughts* (London: J. Nourse, 1770), 38; Elizabeth May Conover, "British West Florida's Mississippi Frontier During the American Revolution," (Master's thesis, Auburn University, 1972), 11; Eron O. Rowland, ed., "Peter Chester: Third Governor of the Province of West Florida Under British Dominion, 1770–1781," *Publications of the Mississippi Historical Society, Centenary Series, Volume 5* (1925), John McIntire to Peter Chester, July 19, 1770.

20 Rogers, et al., *Alabama*, 32; Starr, *Tories, Dons, and Rebels*, 5; Johnson, *British West Florida*,

10; Edward J. Cashin, *Lachlan McGillivray, Indian Trader: The Shaping of the Southern Colonial Frontier*, (Athens: University of Georgia, 1992), 225; Rea, *Major Robert Farmar*, 38.

21 Rea, *Major Robert Farmar*, 38–39, 45, 63–79; Robert R. Rea, "Assault on the Mississippi—The Loftus Expedition, 1764," *Alabama Review* 26 (July, 1973), 173, 175–178, 183–185, 189–190, 192; James F. Barnett, Jr., *Mississippi's American Indians* (Jackson: University Press of Mississippi, 2012), 146–147; Gold, *Borderland Empires*, 115; Arrell M. Gibson, *The Chickasaws* (Norman: University of Oklahoma Press, 1971), 62; Samuel C. Hyde, ed., *A Fierce and Fractious Frontier: The Curious Development of Louisiana's Florida Parishes, 1699–2000* (Baton Rouge: Louisiana State University Press, 2004), 44–59, 45; Conover, "Mississippi Frontier," 6; John McDermott, *The Spanish in the Mississippi Valley, 1762–1804* (Champaign: University of Illinois Press, 1974), 79.

22 Gannon, *New History of Florida*, 137; Matthews, *British West Florida and the Illinois Country*, 26; Rea, *Major Robert Farmar*, 45.

23 Haldimand to Gage, September 6, 1767 and December 6 and 21, 1767, Haldimand Papers; Fabel, *Economy of British West Florida*, 3; Johnson, *British West Florida*, 176; Carter, "The Beginnings of British West Florida," 324.

24 Rea, "Problems and Responses," 43; Robin Fabel, "George Johnstone of British West Florida," *The Florida Historical Quarterly*, 54 (April, 1976), 504; Howard, "Early Settlers in British West Florida," 52; Rea, "New Letter from Mobile," 232; Rea, *Major Robert Farmar*, 33–34; Delaney, *Story of Mobile*, 39; Howard, "Military Occupation," 195–197; Carter, "The Beginnings of British West Florida," 328; Douglas C. McMurtrie, *A Broadside Printed at Mobile in 1763, but Printed on the Island of Jamaica in the Same Year* (Chicago: Chicago School of Printing, 1939); Howard, *British Development of West Florida*, 11–12; Johnson, *British West Florida*, 10, 31; Howard and Rea, *The Memoire Justificatif*, 12.

25 Rogers, et al., *Alabama*, 33; Sledge, *Mobile River*, 56; Rea, *Major Robert Farmar*, 41; Johnson, *British West Florida*, 12, 31; Thomason, *Mobile*, 44; Gold, *Borderland Empires*, 62, 63, 112, 140; Howard, *British Development of West Florida*, 28; Rowland, "Peter Chester," 107, Chester to Hillsborough, Feb. 21, 1772.

26 Robert R. Rea, "British West Florida Trade and Commerce in the Customs Records," *Alabama Review* 37 (April, 1984), 124; Howard and Rea, *The Memoire Justificatif*, 12; Johnson, *British West Florida*, 10; Howard, "Military Occupation," 194; Sledge, *Mobile River*, 55.

27 Thomason, *Mobile*, 47; Sledge, *Mobile River*, 55; Carter, "The Beginnings of British West Florida," 327; Rowland, *Mississippi Provincial Archives*, 11, Farmar to Secretary of War, January 24, 1764; Barnett, *Mississippi's American Indians*, 145; Gold, *Borderland Empires*, 108, 169; Rea, *Major Robert Farmar*, 36–37; Johnson, *British West Florida*, 10; Fabel, *Bombast and Broadsides*, 39.

28 Rea, *Major Robert Farmar*, 36, 38; Owen, *History of Alabama*, 150; Rea, "New Letter from Mobile," 230–231; Rea, "Mission to the Floridas," 43–44; Bernard Romans, *A Concise Natural History of East and West Florida* (New York: R. Aitken, 1776), 72; Sledge, *Mobile River*, 55; Narrett, *Adventurism and Empire*, 33; Jay Higginbotham, *Mobile! City by the Bay* (Mobile: Junior Chamber of Commerce, 1968), 35.

29 Rogers, et al., *Alabama*, 34; Hamilton, *Colonial Mobile*, 228–234; Fabel, *Bombast and Broadsides*, 40; Howard and Rea, *The Memoire Justificatif*, 15, 21–22; Gregory Waselkov

and Bonnie L. Gums, *Plantation Archaeology at Rivière aux Chiens, ca. 1725–1848* (Mobile: University of South Alabama, 2000), 78.

30 Howard and Rea, *The Memoire Justificatif*, 15, 17–18, 23, 25–26, 31; Delaney, *The Story of Mobile*, 40; Rogers, et al., *Alabama*, 34.

31 Howard and Rea, *The Memoire Justificatif*, 30, 32–34. 40–41; Hamilton, *Colonial Mobile*, 230–234; Johnson, *British West Florida*, 11.

32 Howard and Rea, *The Memoire Justificatif*, 47, 50–51, 54–55; Gold, *Borderland Empires*, 64; Gage to Haldimand, September 8, 1767, Haldimand Papers.

CHAPTER TWO

1 Johnson, *British West Florida*, 14–20, 223, 225; Earl Glynn Ingram, "A Critical Study of the British West Florida General Assembly," Master's thesis, (Auburn University, 1969), 27; the full text of the proclamation can be found online at https://avalon.law.yale.edu/18th_century/proc1763.asp; Starr, *Tories, Dons, and Rebels*, 4; Howard, "Military Occupation," 182; Johnson, "Pensacola in the British Period," 264.

2 "An Account of the Several Sums of Money Which Have Been Granted by the Parliament of Great Britain, Towards the Establishment and Support of the Civil Government of the Provinces of East and West Florida in America" Alabama Department of Archives and History; Johnson, *British West Florida*, 21, 225; Johnson, "Pensacola in the British Period," 264–265; Colonial Office's West Florida Papers, Pace Library, University of West Florida: CO 5/Volume 619, Letters from the Secretary of State, 1768–1781, February 14, 1768; CO 5/Volume 619, Copy of Estimate of the Civil Establishment for West Florida from June 24, 1773 to June 24, 1774; CO 5/Volume 619, Estimate for West Florida's Civil Establishment for June 24, 1776 to June 24, 1777.

3 Johnson, *British West Florida*, 97; Robert R. Rea, and Milo B. Howard, *The Minutes, Journals and Acts of the General Assembly of British West Florida* (Tuscaloosa: University of Alabama Press, 1979), 376.

4 Julius Groner and Robert R. Rea, "John Ellis, King's Agent, and West Florida," *The Florida Historical Quarterly* 66 (April, 1988): 385–398; Kathleeen S. Murphy, "To Make Florida Answer To Its Name: John Ellis, Bernard Romans and the Atlantic Science of British West Florida," *British Journal for the History of Science* 47 (2014): 43–65; Wright, *Florida in the American Revolution*, 18.

5 Ingram, "British West Florida General Assembly," 10, 94, 104; Smith, *Louisiana and the Gulf South Frontier*, 133; Clune and Stringfield, *Historic Pensacola*, 101; West Florida General Assembly Acts, 1767–1771, Government Records Collections, Alabama Department of Archives and History; Starr, *Tories, Dons, and Rebels*, 11; McLemore, ed., *A History of Mississippi*, 152; James, *Antebellum Natchez*, 24; Johnson, *British West Florida*, 83–85; Rea and Howard, *The Minutes, Journals, and Acts of the General Assembly*, 275.

6 Johnson, *British West Florida*, 16–17, 86, 89, 91, 95–96, 111; Rea and Howard, *The Minutes, Journals, and Acts of the General Assembly*; Howard, "British Development of West Florida," 46; West Florida General Assembly Commons House Journals, 1767–1778, Government Records Collections, Alabama Department of Archives and History; Matthews, *British West Florida and the Illinois Country*, 25; Clinton N. Howard, "Colonial Pensacola: The British Period," *The Florida Historical Quarterly*, 19 (October, 1940), 117; William Bartram, *Travels Through North and South Carolina, Georgia, East*

and West Florida, the Cherokee Country, the Extensive Territories of the Muscogulges, or the Creek Confederacy, and the Country of the Chactaws (Philadelphia: James and Johnson, 1791), 414; Rowland, "Peter Chester," 30, Chester to Earl of Hillsborough, September 29, 1770; Ingram, "British West Florida General Assembly," 19–20.

7   McLemore, ed., *History of Mississippi*, 142–143, 151; Rea and Howard, *The Minutes, Journals, and Acts of the General Assembly*; West Florida General Assembly Acts; Starr, *Tories, Dons, and Rebels*, 11; Johnson, *British West Florida*, 28–29, 47, 94, 96, 112–114; Lawrence Henry Gipson, *The British Empire Before the American Revolution: The Triumphant Empire: The Empire Beyond the Storm* (New York: Alfred A. Knopf, 1948), 99, 101–102; Howard, "Colonial Pensacola, Part I," 125–127.

8   Rea and Howard, *The Minutes, Journals, and Acts of the General Assembly*; Johnson, *British West Florida*, xii–xiv, 26, 83; McLemore, ed., *History of Mississippi*, 138; Howard, *British Development of West Florida*, 20, 43; Fabel, *Bombast and Broadsides*, 47.

9   Ingram, "British West Florida General Assembly," 25–27, 29; Rea and Howard, *The Minutes, Journals, and Acts of the General Assembly*, 65, 364–366; Carter, "Some Aspects of British Administration," 371.

10 McLemore, ed., *History of Mississippi*, 137; Johnson, *British West Florida*, 24; Carter, "The Beginnings of British West Florida," 328–329; Fabel, *Bombast and Broadsides*, 4–24, 26, 29; Fabel, "George Johnstone of British West Florida," 498, 501–503; Ingram, "British West Florida General Assembly," 5; James A. Padgett, ed., "Commission, Orders and Instructions Issued to George Johnstone, British Governor of West Florida, 1763–1767," *Louisiana Historical Quarterly* 21 (October, 1938), 1021–1022; Robin Fabel, "George Johnstone and the 'Thoughts Concerning Florida'—A Case of Lobbying?" *Alabama Review* 29 (July, 1976), 164, 168, 173.

11 Fabel, "George Johnstone of British West Florida," 203; Rowland, *Mississippi Provincial Archives*, Johnstone to Lord Halifax, June 11, 1765, 256–258.

12 Fabel, *Bombast and Broadsides*, 26–28, 31, 43, 46, 51; Fabel, "Thoughts Concerning Florida," 167, 172; John H. Frederick, "A Question of Authority: Johnstone and Browne, 1766–1767," *Gulf Coast Historical Review* 24 (Spring, 1998), 35; Hamilton, *Colonial Mobile*, 247; Fabel, *Economy of British West Florida*, 77–79, 81; Thomason, *Mobile*, 46; Rogers, et al., *Alabama*, 34; Eric Jarvis, "His Majesty's Papist Subjects: Roman Catholic Political Rights in British West Florida," *Gulf Coast Historical Review* 16 (Fall, 2000): 6–19; Johnson, *British West Florida*, 19; Narrett, *Adventurism and Empire*, 27; John D. Born, Jr., *Governor Johnstone and Trade in British West Florida, 1764–1767* (Wichita: Wichita State University, 1968), 8–9.

13 *Mississippi Department of Archives and History*, British West Florida Administrative Papers and Land Records, 1763–1783, Johnstone to Pownall, October 23, 1766; Clinton N. Howard, "Governor Johnstone in West Florida," *The Florida Historical Quarterly*, (April, 1939), 282; Born, *Johnstone and Trade*, 4–; Alan Taylor, *American Colonies: The Settling of North America* (New York: Penguin Books, 2001), 258–259; Narrett, *Adventurism and Empire*, 36; Rea and Howard, *The Minutes, Journals, and Acts of the General Assembly*, 46; Great Britain Board of Trade, *Journal of the Commissioners for Trade and Plantations Preserved in the Public Records Office*, 14 Volumes (London: His Majesty's Stationery Office, 1920–1938), Volume 12, 61; Simmons, "The Divergent Colony," 35.

14 McLemore, ed., *History of Mississippi*, 138–140; Johnson, "Pensacola in the British Period," 267, 271–272; Thomason, *Mobile*, 41; Johnson, *British West Florida*, 49–56; Rea,

Major Robert Farmar, 40; Rogers, et al., *Alabama,* 33; Howard, "Governor Johnstone," 284–294; Robert R. Rea, "Outpost of Empire: David Wedderburn at Mobile," *Alabama Review* 7 (July, 1954), 222; Padgett, ed., "Commission, Orders, and Instructions," 1021; Robin Fabel, "A Letter from Governor George Johnstone." *Pensacola History Illustrated* 3 (Spring/Summer, 1990), 19–20.

15 Johnson, *British West Florida,* 49, 53–56; Starr, Tories, Dons, and Rebels, 12, 14; Rea, *Major Robert Farmar,* 50–52; Fabel, "A Letter from Governor George Johnstone," 22; Born, *Johnstone and Trade,* 17; Howard, "Governor Johnstone," 295–296; Robert Edward Gray, "Elias Durnford, 1739–1794: Engineer, Soldier, Administrator," Master's thesis (Auburn University, 1971), 39; *Mississippi Department of Archives and History,*
British West Florida Administrative Papers and Land Records, 1763–1783, Johnstone to Tayler, April 27, 1766, Johnstone to Tayler, July 4, 1766, Johnstone to Boddington, July 5, 1766; Rowland, *Mississippi Provincial Archives,* Letter from Montfort Browne, 297–303; Matthews, *British West Florida and the Illinois Country,* 36.

16 Fabel, *Bombast and Broadsides,* 33–36; Rea, *Major Robert Farmar,* 48–59; 81–111; Howard, *British Development of West Florida,* 23; McLemore, ed., *History of Mississippi,* 140; Johnson, *British West Florida,* 50–51; Carter, "Beginnings of British West Florida," 330–334; Haldimand to Gage, November 28, 1767, Haldimand Papers; *Mississippi Department of Archives and History,* British West Florida Administrative Papers and Land Records, 1763–1783, Johnstone to Tayler, May 26, 1766..

17 Fabel, *Bombast and Broadsides,* 38; Frederick, "A Question of Authority," 39–40; *Mississippi Department of Archives and History,* British West Florida Administrative Papers and Land Records, 1763–1783, Johnstone to Pownall, October 29, 1766; Rowland, *Mississippi Provincial Archives,* 293–296, Governor Johnstone to Secretary Conway, January 28, 1766; Johnson, *British West Florida,* 26–27, 53–57, 95; McLemore, ed., *A History of Mississippi,* 142; Starr, Tories, Dons, and Rebels, 11–12; Great Britain Board of Trade, *Journal of the Commissioners for Trade and Plantations, Volume 12,* 343.

18 Fabel, *Bombast and Broadsides,* 54; Rowland, *Mississippi Provincial Archives,* 303–306, Memorial to John Pownall, April, 1766; Born, *Governor Johnstone and Trade,* 16–17; Frederick, "A Question of Authority, 43; Starr, Tories, Dons, and Rebels, 40; Johnson, "Pensacola in the British Period," 272; Fabel, "A Letter from George Johnstone," 22.

19 Fabel, *Bombast and Broadsides,* 53, 55–57; Johnson, *British West Florida,* 58–59; McLemore, ed., *History of Mississippi,* 143; Narrett, *Adventurism and Empire,* 43–44; Howard, "Governor Johnstone," 300–303; Starr, Tories, Dons, and Rebels, 16.

20 Colonial Office's West Florida Papers, Pace Library, University of West Florida: CO 5/ Volume 618, Letters from the Secretary of State, 1766–1767, Shelbourne to Johnstone, February 19, 1767; McLemore, ed., *History of Mississippi,* 144; Starr, Tories, Dons, and Rebels, 15, 17; Rogers, et al., *Alabama,* 34; Frederick, "A Question of Authority," 45; Fabel, *Bombast and Broadsides,* 53, 57; Matthews, *British West Florida and the Illinois Country,* 40; Johnson, *British West Florida,* 60.

21 Johnson, "Pensacola in the British Period," 273; Colonial Office's West Florida Papers, Pace Library, University of West Florida: CO 5 Volume 618, Letters from the Secretary of State, 1766–1767, Shelbourne to Browne, February 19, 1767; Fabel, "George Johnstone," 511; Frederick, "A Question of Authority," 35, 45; McLemore, ed., *A History of Mississippi,* 144; Hamilton, *Colonial Mobile,* 269; Owen, *History of Alabama,* 155; Johnson, *British of West Florida,* 62; Haldimand to Gage, September 1, 1767, Haldimand Papers; Lucille

Griffith, *Alabama: A Documentary History to 1900* (Tuscaloosa: University of Alabama Press, 1968), 39.

22 Starr, *Tories, Dons, and Rebels*, 17–19; McLemore, ed., *History of Mississippi*, 144–145; Conover, "Mississippi Frontier," 14; Johnson, *British West Florida*, 64–68; Ingram, "British West Florida General Assembly," 62–63; Clinton N. Howard, "Colonial Pensacola: The British Period, Part II," *The Florida Historical Quarterly* 19 (January, 1941), 258; Mowat, "The Southern Brigade," 66–67, 69; "A Letter from a Gentleman in Pensacola to His Friend in South Carolina" *Pensacola History Illustrated* 1 (1984): 5–7.

23 Ingram, "British West Florida General Assembly," 36–37, 51; Rea and Howard, *The Minutes, Journals, and Acts of the General Assembly*, 71–73, 107–108.

24 Robert R. Rea, "John Eliot: Second Governor of British West Florida," *Alabama Review* 30 (October, 1977), 245, 246–250, 254–255; Starr, *Tories, Dons, and Rebels*, 18; Rogers, et al., *Alabama*, 34; Johnson, *British West Florida*, 69; McLemore, *History of Mississippi*, 146; Ingram, "British West Florida General Assembly," 80.

25 Rea, "John Eliot," 244, 250, 257, 263–264; Ingram, "British West Florida General Assembly," 80; Starr, *Tories, Dons, and Rebels*, 18; Johnson, *British West Florida*, 69; Matthews, *British West Florida and the Illinois Country*, 43; Johnson, "Pensacola in the British Period," 273–274.

26 McLemore, ed., *History of Mississippi*, 146–147; Griffith, *Documentary History*, 39; Starr, *Tories, Dons, and Rebels*, 20, 22; Johnson, *British West Florida*, 70–72; Matthews, *British West Florida and the Illinois Country*, 47; Gray, "Elias Durnford," 45–47.

27 Johnson, *British West Florida*, 72; McLemore, ed., *History of Mississippi*, 147; Gray, "Elias Durnford," 47; Starr, *Tories, Dons, and Rebels*, 23; Haldimand to Gage, June 22, 1770, Haldimand Papers. Browne would go on to serve as governor of the Bahamas and see action at the head of a loyalist regiment during the Revolutionary War.

28 McLemore, ed., *History of Mississippi*, 146–147; Johnson, "Pensacola in the British Period," 273–274; Robert R. Rea, "Elias Durnford: Royal Engineer in British West Florida," *Pensacola History Illustrated* 3 (Spring/Summer, 1990): 25–28; Gray, "Elias Durnford," 5, 19–20; Owen, *History of Alabama*, 155.

29 Gray, "Elias Durnford," 22, 24–25, 58; Robin Fabel, "Elias Durnford." *Encyclopedia of Alabama*, http://www.encyclopediaofalabama.org/article/h-1090; Howard, *British Development of West Florida*, 32–33; Matthews, *British West Florida and the Illinois Country*, 47; Johnson, *British West Florida*, 29; McLemore, ed., *History of Mississippi*, 39; Rea, "Problems and Responses," 45; Robert R. Rea, "Planters and Plantations in British West Florida," *Alabama Review* 29 (July, 1976), 231; Rea, "Elias Durnford," 26.

30 McLemore, ed., *History of Mississippi*, 147; Griffith, *Documentary History*, 39; Fabel, "Elias Durnford"; Rea, "Elias Durnford." Durnford died in 1793 in Tobago.

31 Starr, *Tories, Dons, and Rebels*, 27; Owen, *History of Alabama*, 156; McLemore, ed., *History of Mississippi*, 153, 156; Rowland, "Peter Chester," 1–2; Clinton N. Howard, "Colonial Pensacola: The British Period, Part III; The Administration of Governor Chester, 1770–1781," *The Florida Historical Quarterly*, Vol. 19 (April, 1941), 369–370, 374–375, 380–381; Lucille Griffith, "Peter Chester and the End of the British Empire in West Florida," *Alabama Review* 30 (January, 1977), 18–20, 30; Fabel, *Economy of British West Florida*, 132; James A. Padgett, ed., "The Reply of Peter Chester, Governor of West Florida, To Complaints Made Against His Administration." *Louisiana*

Historical Quarterly 22 (January, 1939): 31–47; Griffith, *Documentary History*, 40.

32 Ingram, "British West Florida General Assembly," 93, 98–99; Rowland, "Peter Chester," 160–161.

CHAPTER THREE

1 Mark E. Fretwell, *This So Remote Frontier: The Chattahoochee Country of Alabama and Georgia* (Eufaula: Historic Chattahoochee Commission, 1987), 124.

2 Kathryn E. Holland Braund, *Deerskins and Duffels: Creek Indian Trade with Anglo-America, 1685–1815* (Lincoln: University of Nebraska Press, 1993), 9, 26; David H. Corkran, *The Creek Frontier, 1540–1783* (Norman: University of Oklahoma Press, 1967), 7, 15; James Adair, *The History of the North American Indians, Particularly Those Nations Adjoining the Mississippi, East and West Florida, Georgia, South and North Carolina, and Virginia.* (London: Edward and Charles Dilly, 1775), 6; Narrett, *Adventurism and Empire*, 47; Daniel H., Usner, Jr., *Indians, Settlers, and Slaves in a Frontier Exchange Economy: The Lower Mississippi Valley Before 1783* (Chapel Hill: University of North Carolina Press, 1992), 113; McLemore, ed., *History of Mississippi*, 154; Thomas Chalmers McCorvey, "The Highland Scotch Element in the Early Settlement of Alabama," *Alabama Historical Quarterly* 1 (Spring, 1930), 46; Fabel, *Economy of British West Florida*, 19; Colin G. Calloway, *The American Revolution in Indian Country: Crisis and Diversity in Native American Communities* (New York: Cambridge University Press, 1995), 44, 214; Greg O'Brien, *Choctaws in Revolutionary Age, 1750–1830* (Lincoln: University of Nebraska Press, 2005), 121; Richmond F. Brown, ed., *Coastal Encounters: The Transformation of the Gulf South in the Eighteenth Century* (Lincoln: University of Nebraska Press, 2007), 61; Hamilton, *Colonial Mobile*, 240.

3 West Florida Governor Correspondence, 1763–1766, Government Records Collections, Alabama Department of Archives and History, Receipt and Certificate of Stephenson and Satterwaite for Goods Delivered to Indians April 1, 1766; Fretwell, *This Remote Frontier*, 90; Braund, *Deerskins and Duffels*, 126; Brown, ed., *Coastal Encounters*, 85; Joshua S. Haynes, *Patrolling the Border: Theft and Violence on the Creek-Georgia Frontier, 1770–1796* (Athens: University of Georgia Press, 2018), 31.

4 Braund, *Deerskins and Duffels*, 121–125, 130; Harvey H. Jackson, *Rivers of History: Life on the Coosa, Tallapoosa, Cahaba, and Alabama* (Tuscaloosa: University of Alabama Press, 1965), 13; O'Brien, *Choctaws in a Revolutionary Age*, 74–75, 80.

5 From its founding in 1670 until after the Revolutionary War, Charleston, South Carolina was known first as Charles Town, and later, as Charlestown. I have chosen to use "Charlestown" in this book, as that was the most common spelling during the period under discussion. For more on the city during this era, see Walter J. Fraser, Jr., *Charleston! Charleston! The History of a Southern City* (Columbia: University of South Carolina Press, 1990); Fretwell, *This Remote Frontier*, 88, 91–92; Verner Winslow Crane, *The Southern Frontier, 1670–1732* (Ann Arbor: University of Michigan Press, 1964), 34; Louis R. Smith, Jr., "British-Indian Trade in Alabama, 1670–1756," *Alabama Review* 27 (January, 1974): 65–75; Braund, *Deerskins and Duffels*, 28–29; Corkran, *The Creek Frontier*, 50–51; Simmons, "The Divergent Colony," 42–43; John Richard Alden, *John Stuart and the Southern Colonial Frontier, a Study of Indian Relations, War, Trade and Land Problems in the Southern Wilderness, 1754–1775* (Ann Arbor: University of Michigan Press, 1944), 14.

6　Alden, *John Stuart and the Southern Colonial Frontier*, 15; Bridges, *Alabama*, 29; O'Brien, *Choctaws in a Revolutionary Age*, 47, 81; Usner, *Indians, Settlers, and Slaves*, 123–125; Haynes, *Patrolling the Border*, 23; Brown, ed., *Coastal Encounters*, 66; Fabel, *Economy of British West Florida*, 51, 54.

7　Braund, *Deerskins and Duffels*, 58, 64–65, 68; Jackson, *Rivers of History*, 13; Fabel, *Economy of British West Florida*, 57–58, 237.

8　Braund, *Deerskins and Duffels*, 29, 70–71, 97–98, 136; O'Brien, *Choctaws in a Revolutionary Age*, 82; Smith, Jr., "British-Indian Trade," 70; Fabel, *Economy of British West Florida*, 54; McLaurin and Thomason, *Mobile*, 18; Amos J. Wright, Jr., *The McGillivray and McIntosh Traders:On the Old Southwest Frontier, 1716–1815* (Montgomery: NewSouth Books, 2007), 113–145.

9　Braund, *Deerskins and Duffels*, 30, 57, 96; Haynes, *Patrolling the Border*, 22; Gregory Waselkov, ed., *Powhatan's Mantle: Indians in the Colonial Southeast* (Lincoln: University of Nebraska Press, 1989), 11; Crane, *Southern Frontier*, 39, 127–128; Owen, *History of Alabama*, 152.

10　"Extracts from the Travels of William Bartram," *Alabama Historical Quarterly* 17 (Fall, 1955), 110–114, 117; Braund, *Deerskins and Duffels*, 53; Gregory Waselkov and Kathryn E. Holland Braund, eds., *William Bartram on the Southeastern Indians* (Lincoln: University of Nebraska Press, 1995), 97, 99, 100, 120; Robert Paulett, *An Empire of Small Places: Mapping the Southeastern Anglo-Indian Trade, 1732–1795* (Athens: University of Georgia Press, 2012), 123.

11　Kathryn E. Holland Braund, "The Creek Indians, Blacks, and Slavery," *The Journal of Southern History* 57 (November, 1991), 602, 605, 607–609; Braund, *Deerskins and Duffels*, 31; Waselkov and Gums, *Plantation Archaeology*, 68.

12　McLemore, ed., *History of Mississippi*, 138, 148; Braund, *Deerskins and Duffels*, 110–111, 117; Fabel, *Economy of British West Florida*, 60–61; Thomason, *Mobile*, 60; James H. O'Donnell, "John Stuart," *NCPedia*, https://www.ncpedia.org/biography/stuart-john; Robert V. Haynes, *The Natchez District and the American Revolution* (Jackson: University Press of Mississippi, 1976), 109; George C. Osborn, "Relations with the Indians in West Florida during the Administration of Governor Peter Chester, 1770–178," *The Florida Historical Quarterly*, Vol. 31 (April 1953), 266; Tara Mitchell Mielnik, "Alexander Cameron." *Tennessee Encyclopedia*, https://tennesseeencyclopedia.net/entries/alexander-cameron/; Philip M. Hamer, "John Stuart's Indian Policy During the Early Months of the American Revolution," *The Mississippi Valley Historical Review* 17 (December, 1930), 351; Rea, *Major Robert Farmar*, 47; George B. Jackson, "John Stuart: Superintendent of Indian Affairs for the Southern District," *Tennessee Historical Magazine* 3 (Sept., 1917): 165–191; Simmons, "The Divergent Colony," 46–47.

13　Paulett, *An Empire of Small Places*, 142; Howard and Rea, *The Memoire Justificatif*, 14, 28; Sledge, *Mobile River*, 55; Rea, "A New Letter from Mobile," 234; Calloway, *American Revolution in Indian Country*, 136.

14　Johnson, *British West Florida*, 74–75; Braund, *Deerskins and Duffels*, 112, 116; Alden, *John Stuart*, 210; McLemore, ed., *History of Mississippi*, 148–150; Rea and Howard, *The Minutes, Journals, and Acts of the General Assembly*, 379; Brown, ed., *Coastal Encounters*, 70; Simmons, "The Divergent Colony," 51; Gibson, *The Chickasaws*, 68; Gold, *Borderland Empires*, 172; Born, *Governor Johnstone and Trade*, 15.

15 Rowland, *Mississippi Provincial Archives*, 92–94, Major Farmar's Instructions to Officers, October 24, 1763.

16 McLemore, ed., *History of Mississippi*, 141, 150–151; Rea, *Major Robert Farmar*, 59; Fabel, *Bombast and Broadsides*, 40–41; Johnson, *British West Florida*, 38–41, 78–82; Carter, "The Beginnings of British West Florida," 337–338; Gold, *Borderland Empires*, 174–177; Fabel, *Economy of British West Florida*, 60; Osborn, "Relations with Indians," 240, 246; Rowland, *Mississippi Provincial Archives*, 211–214, Text of the Treaty; Brown, ed., *Coastal Encounters*, 59; Alden, *John Stuart*, 321; Rowland, "Peter Chester," 44–45, Chester to Earl of Hillsborough, April 13, 1771, 46–49, Charles Stuart to Chester, April 15, 1771; Haynes, *Patrolling the Border*, 28; Rea, "Outpost of Empire," 223–224.

17 Rowland, "Peter Chester," 113, "Report of Congress with the Creek Indians"; Haynes, *Patrolling the Border*, 25; Gibson, *The Chickasaws*, 66–67; Rowland, *Mississippi Provincial Archives*, 236.

18 O'Brien, *Choctaws In A Revolutionary Age*, 72; Brown, ed. *Coastal Encounters*, 77; Alden, *John Stuart*, 201, 204; Johnson, *British West Florida*, 40; Corkran, *The Creek Frontier*, 249; Joseph P. Ward, *Britain and the American South: From Colonialism to Rock and Roll* (Jackson: University Press of Mississippi, 2003), 66–68.

19 Usner, *Indians, Settlers, and Slaves*, 124; Corkran, *The Creek Frontier*, 247–248; Barnett, *Mississippi's American Indians*, 148; Haynes, *Patrolling the Border*, 29; Johnson, *British West Florida*, 42; Hamilton, *Colonial Mobile*, 238, 242–245, 251; Gold, *Borderland Empires*, 176–177; Alden, *John Stuart*, 202, 207, 322; Thomason, *Mobile*, 47, Howard and Rea, *The Memoire Justificatif*, 11; Cashin, *Lachlan McGillivray*, 229; Rowland, *Mississippi Provincial Archives*, 238, 251; Ward, ed., *Britain and the American South*, 71–74; Sledge, *Mobile River*, 55; Owen, *History of Alabama*, 150; Rowland, "Peter Chester," 132, Stuart to Peter Chester, November 2, 1771; Haynes, *Patrolling the Border*, 31.

20 Rowland, "Peter Chester," 101, 105–106, Chester to John Stuart, September 10, 1771; Braund, *Deerskins and Duffels*, 153, Haynes, *Patrolling the Border*, 30.

21 Howard, "Colonial Pensacola, Part III," 375; Smith, *Louisiana and the Gulf South Frontier*, 139; Wright, Jr., *The McGillivray and McIntosh Traders*, 113–132; Smith, "British-Indian Trade," 71; Braund, *Deerskins and Duffels*, 103–104; Rea, *Major Robert Farmar*, 42; Paulett, *An Empire of Small Places*, 42.

22 Alden, *John Stuart*, 194, 213; Johnson, *British West Florida*, 74–75; Braund, *Deerskins and Duffels*, 104–105, 107, 109, 113; Haynes, *Patrolling the Border*, 31; O'Brien, *Choctaws in a Revolutionary Age*, 83; Brown, ed., *Coastal Encounters*, 60, 67, 72; Usner, *Indians, Settlers, and Slaves*, 125; Fabel, *Economy of British West Florida*, 50, 59.

23 Smith, *Louisiana and the Gulf South Frontier*, 136–137; McLemore, ed., *History of Mississippi*, 150; Johnson, *British West Florida*, 81; Brown, ed., *Coastal Encounters*, 58, 68–69; Fabel, *Economy of British West Florida*, 52, 60; Usner, *Indians, Settlers, and Slaves*, 127; O'Brien, *Choctaws in a Revolutionary Age*, 81; Braund, *Deerskins and Duffels*, 105, 113; Gibson, *The Chickasaws*, 68, 70; Haynes, *Patrolling the Border*, 31; Osborn, "Relations with Indians," 249; Samuel Proctor, ed., *Eighteenth-Century Florida: Life on the Frontier* (Gainesville:University Press of Florida, 1976), 65.

24 Howard, "Colonial Pensacola, Part III," 375–378; Rea and Howard, *The Minutes, Journals, and Acts of the General Assembly*, 216, 280; Simmons, "The Divergent Colony," 44–45; Rowland, "Peter Chester," 8–9, 38–40, 46–49 Chester to Earl of Hillsborough, March

9, 1771 and Stuart to Chester, April 15, 1771; Barnett, *Mississippi's American Indians*, 148–149; Brown, ed., *Coastal Encounters*, 71.

25 Alden, *John Stuart*, 224–225; Smith, *Louisiana and the Gulf South Frontier*, 138; Barnett, *Mississippi's American Indians*, 153; Brown, ed., *Coastal Encounters*, 60–61; Rowland, "Governor Peter Chester," 103.

26 Braund, *Deerskins and Duffels*, 108; McLemore, ed., *History of Mississippi*, 148; Alden, *John Stuart*, 226, 234, 315; Brown, ed., *Coastal Encounters*, 60, 67; Haynes, *Patrolling the Border*, 23, 27.

CHAPTER FOUR

1   Starr, *Tories, Dons, and Rebels*, 29; Clarence Walford Alvord, *The Mississippi Valley in British Politics: A Study in the Trade, Land Speculation, and Experiments and Imperialism Culminating in the American Revolution* (Ann Arbor: University of Michigan Library, 1917), 213; Gannon, *New History of Florida*, 136; Fabel, *Economy of British West Florida*, 7, 10, 110; Johnson, *British West Florida*, 117–119, 122–123, 125; Howard, "Early Settlers in British West Florida," 33, 45, 54; Howard, "Colonial Pensacola, Part I," 122; Owen, *History of Alabama*, 152; Rogers, et al,. *Alabama*, 34; Smith, *Louisiana and the Gulf South Frontier*, 133; Howard, *British Development of West Florida*, 7; Margaret Fisher Dalrymple, ed., *The Merchant of Manchac: The Letterbooks of John Fitzpatrick, 1768–1790* (Baton Rouge: Louisiana State University Press), 1978, 18; Raab, *Spain, Britain, and the American Revolution in Florida*, 34; Waselkov and Gums, *Plantation Archaeology*, 72; Narrett, *Adventurism and Empire*, 66–67; Cecil Johnson, "The Distribution of Land in British West Florida," Louisiana Historical Quarterly 16 (October, 1933), 544.

2   Johnson, *British West Florida*, 125–126; Fabel, *Economy of British West Florida*, 7; Gray, "Elias Durnford," 22; Great Britain Board of Trade, *Journal of the Commissioners for Trade and Plantations, Volume 13*, 18; Johnson, "The Distribution of Land," 548.

3   Johnson, *British West Florida*, 116, 121, 127, 129; Howard, *British Development of West Florida*, 7; Alvord, *Mississippi Valley in British Politics*, 283; Gold, *Borderland Empires*, 120–121; Johnson, "The Distribution of Land in British West Florida," 545; Fabel, *Economy of British West Florida*, 8.

4   Howard, "Early Settlers in British West Florida," 49–51; Fabel, *Economy of British West Florida*, 124; Howard, *British Development of West Florida*, 38; Gold, "Politics and Property," 24; Gold, *Borderland Empires*, 57; Johnson, *British West Florida*, 118–119, 130–131; Conover, "British West Florida's Mississippi Frontier," 22.

5   Wright, *Florida in the American Revolution*, 103; Johnson, *British West Florida*, 119, 131; Claiborne, *Mississippi, As a Province, Territory, and State*, 107; Fabel, *Economy of British West Florida*, 6, 12; Fabel, *Bombast and Broadsides*, 47; Howard, *British Development of West Florida*, 37; Howard, "Early Settlers in British West Florida," 49; Haynes, *The Natchez District and the American Revolution*, 12; Thomason, *Mobile*, 44; Rea, *Major Robert Farmar*, 114–120; Robin Fabel, "Dauphin Island as the Gateway to Mexico: A Chimera of the 1770s," *Alabama Review* 50 (April, 1997), 92–93; Waselkov and Gums, *Plantation Archaeology*, 63.

6   Winston De Ville, *English Land Grants in West Florida: A Register for the States of Alabama, Mississippi, and Parts of Florida and Louisiana* (Ville Platte, LA: Winston De Ville, 1986); Gordon M. Wells, "British Land Grants—William Wilton Map, 1774," *Journal of Mississippi History*, 28 (May, 1966): 152–160.

7   Narrett, *Adventurism and Empire*, 47; "Governor Johnstone's Account of West Florida," in *The Gentleman's Gazette*, February, 1765, P.K. Yonge Library of Florida History; Rowland, "Governor Peter Chester," 173, An Attempt Towards a Short Description of West Florida.

8   Alvord, *The Mississippi Valley in British Politics*, 168; Haynes, *The Natchez District and the American Revolution*, 8; Wright, *Florida in the American Revolution*, 3; Charles L. Sullivan, *The Mississippi Gulf Coast: Portrait of a People* (Staunton, VA: American History Press, 1999), 23; Haldimand to Gage, June 16, 1767, and June 18, 1767, Haldimand Papers; Robert R Rea, "British Pensacola," *Pensacola History Illustrated* 3 (Spring/Summer, 1990): 3–10; Rea, "British Pensacola," 3.

9   McCorvey, "The Highland Scotch Element," 47; Taylor, *American Revolutions*, 65; Fabel, *Economy of British West Florida*, 20, 68–69; Johnson, *British West Florida*, 152–154; Howard, "Early Settlers of British West Florida," 50, 52; John D. Born, Jr., "Charles Strachan in Mobile: The Frontier Mobile of a Scottish Factor, 1764–1768," *Alabama Historical Quarterly* 27 (Spring/Summer, 1965), 25; Bernard Bailyn, *Voyagers to the West: A Passage in the Peopling of America on the Eve of the Revolution* (New York: Random House, 1986), 478; Gannon, *New History of Florida*, 141.

10 Fabel, *Economy of British West Florida*, 12–13; Johnson, *British West Florida*, 151; McLemore, ed., *History of Mississippi*, 154; Howard, "Early Settlers of British West Florida," 51; Clune and Stringfield, *Historic Pensacola*, 108; Howard, *British Development of West Florida*, 29; Bailyn, *Voyagers to the West*, 478–479; Proctor, ed., *Eighteenth-Century Florida*, 53–54, 56–57; Wright, *Florida in the American Revolution*, 15; West Florida General Assembly Acts, 1767–1771, Government Records Collections, Alabama Department of Archives and History, An Act to Encourage Foreigners to Come Into and Settle in This Province, December 23, 1766 and January 3, 1767; Colonial Office's West Florida Papers, Pace Library, University of West Florida: CO 5 Volume 620, List of Emigrants Shipped to West Florida 1768.

11 Barnett, *Mississippi's American Indians*, 149–151; Usner, *Indians, Settlers, and Slaves*, 130.

12 Laura D.S. Sturdivant, "One Carbine and a Little Flour and Corn in a Sack: The American Pioneer," *The Journal of Mississippi History* 37 (February 1975), 49; Rogers, et al., *Alabama*, 33; Fabel, *Bombast and Broadsides*, 33; Fabel, *The Economy of British West Florida*, 11.

13 Dalrymple, ed., *The Merchant of Manchac*, 19; Smith, *Louisiana and the Gulf South Frontier*, 134; Starr, *Tories, Dons, and Rebels*, 32; Howard, *British Development of West Florida*, 13, 33–36; Delaney, *The Story of Mobile*, 41, 43; Gregory A. Waselkov, *A Conquering Spirit: Fort Mims and the Redstick War of 1813–1814* (Tuscaloosa: University of Alabama Press, 2009), 17.

14 Howard, *British Development of West Florida*, 33; Sturdivant, "The American Pioneer," 48; Conover, "British West Florida's Mississippi Frontier," 35.

15 Smith, *Louisiana and the Gulf South Frontier*, 134; Fabel, *Economy of British West Florida*, 6, 15; Johnson, *British West Florida*, 133, 136; Dalrymple, ed., *The Merchant of Manchac*, 19; Gipson, *The British Empire Before the American Revolution*, 105–106; James, *Antebellum Natchez*, 15–17; McLemore, ed. *History of Mississippi*, 154; Carter, "Some Aspects of British Administration," 372–373; Cecil Johnson, "Expansion in West Florida, 1770–1779," *The Mississippi Valley Historical Review* 20 (March, 1934), 482–486; Wright, *Florida in the American Revolution*, 4; Haynes, *The Natchez District and the American Revolution*, 11–18.

16 Matthews, *British West Florida and the Illinois Country*, 64; McLemore, ed., *History of Mississippi*, 145; Haynes, *The Natchez District and the American Revolution*, 7; Narrett, *Adventurism and Empire*, 7, 55–57; Johnson, *British West Florida*, 64–65, 138; Bailyn, *Voyagers to the West*, 480–481; Haldimand to Gage, February 19, 1772, Haldimand Papers; Hyde, ed. *A Fierce and Fractious Frontier*, 49; Bosse, "Dartmouth on the Mississippi," 12; Rowland, "Peter Chester," 20, Chester to Earl of Hillsborough, September 26, 1770 and 62, Narrative of Edward Mease.

17 Jackson, *Rivers of History*, 25; Rowland, "Peter Chester," 20–24, Chester to Earl of Hillsborough, September 26, 1770, and 94, Chester to Hillsborough September 28, 1771, and 65, 69, "Narrative of Edward Mease" and 173, An Attempt Towards a Short Description of West Florida; Sturdivant, "The American Pioneer," 43, 46; Anthony Haswell, ed., *Memoirs and Adventures of Captain Matthew Phelps, Formerly of Harwington in Connecticut, Now Resident of New Haven in Vermont: Particularly in Two Voyages from Connecticut to the River Mississippi, from December 1773 to October 1780* (Bennington: Anthony Haswell, 1802), 55–56; Bailyn, *Voyagers to the West*, 480.

The Carolina parakeet is an extinct species of bird once found throughout much of eastern North America. Its colorful plumage and tendency to move in large noisy flocks made it one of the most easily recognized avian species of the era and figures into numerous accounts of the southeast in the colonial era. Its numbers declined dramatically in the first half of the nineteenth century due to a combination of factors including deforestation and hunting for its feathers. For more on the bird, see Joseph M. Forshaw, *Vanished and Vanishing Parrots: Profiling Extinct and Endangered Species* (Ithaca, NY: Comstock Publishing, 2017).

18 Bailyn, *Voyagers to the West*, 480, 182–483; Johnson, *British West Florida*, 138; Pittman, *The Present State of the European Settlements on the Mississippi*, 37; W. M. Carpenter, ed., "The Mississippi River in the Olden Time: A Genuine Account of the Present State of the River Mississippi and of the Land on its Banks to the River Yasous 1776," *De Bow's Review*, III (1847), 123; Narrett, *Adventurism and Empire*, 62; Conover, "British West Florida's Mississippi Frontier," 30; Lawrence F. Brewster "The Later History of British West Florida, 1770–1781: Governor Peter Chester and the Hey-Dey of the Province," Master's thesis, (Columbia University, 1932), 45; Haynes, *The Natchez District and the American Revolution*, 11; Claiborne, *Mississippi As a Province, Territory, and State*, 113; Johnson, "Expansion in West Florida," 488–489; Rowland, "Peter Chester," 11–12.

19 Rowland, "Peter Chester," 72, Narrative of Edwar Mease and 19, Chester to Earl of Hillsborough, September 26, 1770 and 25, John McIntire to Peter Chester, July 19, 1770; Matthews, *British West Florida and the Illinois Country*, 104, 113–114; Haynes, *The Natchez District and the American Revolution*, 13; Bailyn, *Voyagers to the West*, 482–483.

20 Madel Jacobs Morgan, "Sarah Truly, Mississippi Tory," *Journal of Mississippi History* 37 (February, 1975), 87–88; Johnson, *British West Florida*, 136; Fabel, *Economy of British West Florida*, 164; W. M. Drake, "A Note on the Jersey Settlers of Adams County," *Journal of Mississippi History*, 14 (October, 1953): 274–275; Haynes, *The Natchez District and the American Revolution*, 12–15; McLemore, ed., *History of Mississippi*, 155; Johnson, *British West Florida*, 139; Narrett, *Adventurism and Empire*, 66.

21 Johnson, *British West Florida*, 140; Dunbar Rowland, *Encyclopedia of Mississippi History: Comprising Sketches of Counties, Towns, Events, Institutions and Persons, Volume 1* (Madison:

Selwyn A. Brant, 1907), 307–310; John Q. Anderson, "The Narrative of John Hutchins," *Journal of Mississippi History* 48 (Spring/Summer, 2016), 44.

22 Anderson, "The Narrative of John Hutchins," 45–46.

23 Howard, "Early Settlers in British West Florida," 49; Johnson, *British West Florida,* 139; Fabel, *Economy of British West Florida,* 153–197; Bailyn, *Voyagers to the West,* 485; Robin Fabel, "Encounters Up the Mississippi, Yazoo, and Big Black Rivers: The Explorers of the Company of Military Adventurers," *Gulf Coast Historical Review* 8 (Fall 1992), 95–97; Haynes, *The Natchez District and the American Revolution,* 14–17; Great Britain Board of Trade, *Journal of the Commissioners for Trade and Plantations, Volume 13,* 174; Alvord, *The Mississippi Valley in British Politics,* 173–176; Albert James Pickett, *History of Alabama, and Incidentally Georgia and Mississippi, from the Earliest Period* (Charleston: Walker and James, 1851), 331–333.

24 Fabel, *Economy of British West Florida,* 165–170, 174, 176–178; Matthews, *British West Florida and the Illinois Country,* 111–112; Fabel, "Encounters Up the Mississippi," 100–101; Bailyn, *Voyagers to the West,* 486.

25 Robin Fabel, "Bernard Lintot: A Connecticut Yankee on the Mississippi, 1775–1805," *Florida Historical Quarterly,* 60 (July 1981 88–102), 89; Narrett, *Adventurism and Empire,* 65–66; Johnson, "Expansion in West Florida," 490–491; Fabel, "Encounters Up the Mississippi," 95; Shaw Livermore, *Early American Land Companies: Their Influence on Corporate Development* (New York: Commonwealth Fund, 1939), 97–102; Fabel, *Economy of British West Florida,* 183; Jack M. Sosin, *The Revolutionary Frontier, 1763–1783* (New York: Holt Rinehart and Winston, 1967), 62–64; William R. Nester, *The Frontier War for American Independence* (Mechanicsburg, PA: Stackpole Books, 2004), 46; Claiborne, *Mississippi As a Province, Territory, and State,* 109.

26 Matthews, *British West Florida and the Illinois Country,* 115; Pickett, *History of Alabama,* 333–337; Haswell, ed., *Memoirs and Adventures of Captain Matthew Phelps,* 12–13; 29, 34; James, *Antebellum Natchez,* 20–21; Fabel, *Economy of British West Florida,* 187.

27 Haswell, ed., *Memoirs and Adventures of Captain Matthew Phelps,* 50, 70, 74–75, 77–78.

28 Ibid., 31, 87, 89, 102, 105, 110–209.

29 Fabel, *Economy of British West Florida,* 23, 30–37; Hyde, ed., *A Fierce and Fractious Frontier,* 62; David J. Libby, *Slavery and Frontier Mississippi, 1720–1835* (Jackson: University Press of Mississippi, 2004), 22; Kathleen Duval, *Independence Lost: Lives on the Edge of the American Revolution* (New York: Random House, 2016), 60; Johnson, *British West Florida,* 176; Sledge, *Mobile River,* 56.

30 Howard, "Early Settlers in British West Florida," 52, 54; Fabel, *Bombast and Broadsides,* 51; Howard, *The British Development of West Florida,* 44; Wright, *Florida in the American Revolution,* 19; Alvord, *The Mississippi Valley in British Politics,* 166; Fabel, *Economy of British West Florida,* 18, 20; Starr, *Tories, Dons, and Rebels,* 231; Johnson, *British West Florida,* 149, 155; Haynes, *The Natchez District and the American Revolution,* 12, 18; Thomason, *Mobile,* 44; Gipson, *The British Empire Before the American Revolution, Volume 13,* 106; Sledge, *Mobile River,* 56; McLemore, ed. *History of Mississippi,* 154; Fabel, "British West Florida," Dalrymple, ed., *The Merchant of Manchac,* 31; Gannon, *New History of Florida,* 136.

Chapter Five

1 "Governor Johnstone's Account of West Florida," in *The Gentleman's Gazette*, February, 1765, P. K. Yonge Library of Florida History, University of Florida; Sledge, *Mobile River*, 57; Kathleen S. Murphy, "To Make Florida Answer To Its Name: John Ellis, Bernard Romans and the Atlantic Science of British West Florida," *British Journal for the History of Science* 47 (2014), 59; Romans, *A Concise Natural History*, 95; Smith, *Louisiana and the Gulf South Frontier*, 135.

2 Fabel, *Bombast and Broadsides*, 49; Rea, *Major Robert Farmar*, 3.

3 Starr, *Tories, Dons, and Rebels*, 6–7; Fabel, *Bombast and Broadsides*, 30, 49; Rogers, et al., *Alabama*, 33; Rea, *Major Robert Farmar*, 45; Johnson, *British West Florida*, 13; Matthews, *British West Florida and the Illinois Country*, 33, 99; Elizabeth D. Vickers, "Disease: The Unconquerable Foe in British West Florida," *Pensacola History Illustrated* 3 (Spring/ Summer, 1990), 30; Fabel, *Economy of British West Florida*, 13; Thomason, *Mobile*, 44; Sledge, *Mobile River*, 57; Alvord, *The Mississippi Valley in British Politics*, 285; Born, Jr., "Charles Strachan," 40; Hamilton, *Colonial Mobile*, 264–268; Robert R. Rea, "Graveyard for Britons, West Florida, 1763–1781," *The Florida Historical Quarterly* 47 (April, 1969), 345–364.

4 Winston De Ville, *British Burials and Births on the Gulf Coast: Records of the Church of England in West Florida, 1768–1770* (Ville Platte, LA: Winston De Ville, 1986), 28–29; Laura D.S. Harrell, "Colonial Medical Practice in British West Florida, 1763–1781," *Bulletin of the History of Medicine* 41 (1967), 543–548; Rowland, "Peter Chester," 42, "Register of Births and Burials, June 24-December 24, 1770"; Deborah Bauer, "in a strange place...; The Experiences of British Women during the Colonization of East and West Florida," *The Florida Historical Quarterly* 89 (Fall, 2010), 181; West Florida Governor Correspondence, 1763–1766, Government Records Collections, Alabama Department of Archives and History, "Maintenance of Prisoners in Public Gaols."

5 Howard, *British Development of West Florida*, 13; Romans, *Concise Natural History*, 94.

6 Fabel, *Bombast and Broadsides*, 49; Starr, *Tories, Dons, and Rebels*, 7; Johnson, *British West Florida*, 13; Vickers, "Disease," 29–30; Rea, "Graveyard for Britons," 347, 352–355; Rea, "Outpost of Empire," 225; Haldimand to Gage, April 31, 1767, January 16, 1768, October 2, 1768, and November 28, 1769, Haldimand Papers.

7 Robert R. Rea, "Military Deserters from British West Florida," *Louisiana History* 9 (Spring, 1968), 124; Matthews, *British West Florida and the Illinois Country*, 37; Vickers, "Disease," 30; Haldimand to Gage, June 6, 1767, June 13, 1767, June 16, 1767, and August 5, 1767, Haldimand Papers; Rea, "British Pensacola," 9.

8 Harrell, "Colonial Medical Practice," 541, 545, 550, 552; Vickers, "Disease," 30–31; Colonial Office's West Florida Papers, Pace Library, University of West Florida: CO 5 Volume 597, Campbell to Germain, May 10, 1779, and The Memorial of John Lorimer, M.D., Surgeon to the Hospitals for His Majesty's Forces at Pensacola, March 22, 1779.

9 Matthews, *British West Florida and the Illinois Country*, 100; Rowland, "Peter Chester," 36, "Return of His Majesty's Troops Quartered in West Florida," March 10, 1771 and "Narrative of Edward Mease," 59; Harrell, "Colonial Medical Practice," 346–347; Hamilton, *Colonial Mobile*, 260–261, 266–272; Rea, "Graveyard for Britons," 362; Rea and Howard, *The Minutes, Journals, and Acts of the General Assembly*, 47; Haldimand to Gage, May 14, 1772, Haldimand Papers.

10 Rea, "Military Deserters," Haldimand to Gage, May 26, 1768, Haldimand Papers.

11 McLemore, ed., *History of Mississippi*, 154; Fabel, *Bombast and Broadsides*, 30, 48; Rea, "Problems and Responses," 46; Smith, *Louisiana and the Gulf South Frontier*, 133; Rea, "Royal Navy," 174; Thomason, *Mobile*, 43, 45; Howard, *British Development in West Florida*, 12; Rea, *Major Robert Farmar*, 46; Sledge, *Mobile River*, 54; Gregory Waselkov and Kathryn E. Holland Braund, eds., *William Bartram on the Southeastern Indians* (Lincoln: University of Nebraska Press, 1995), 94; West Florida Governor Correspondence, 1763–1766, Government Records Collections, Alabama Department of Archives and History, Johnstone's Report on the State of the Province, February 19, 1765; Howard, "Early Settlers in British West Florida," 52; Howard, *British Development in West Florida*, 13; Matthews, *British West Florida and the Illinois Country*, 27; Pittman, *The Present State of the European Settlements on the Mississippi*, vii-viii; Holmes, Jack D.L. "Charting Mobile Bay and River." *Alabama Historical Quarterly* 44 (Fall/Winter, 1982), 144; Johnson, *British West Florida*, 67.

12 Howard, "Military Occupation," 187; Hamilton, *Colonial Mobile*, 223; Rea, "Royal Navy," 166–167, 174; Holmes, "Charting Mobile Bay," 149; Rea, "British West Florida Trade and Commerce," 138; Matthews, *British West Florida and the Illinois Country*, 38; Thomason, *Mobile*, 44; Fabel, *Economy of British West Florida*, 18; McLaurin and Thomason, *Mobile*, 18; Howard, "Early Settlers in British West Florida," 51; Fabel, *Bombast and Broadsides*, 52.

13 Howard, "Colonial Pensacola, Part I," 112–114, 116; Fabel, *Bombast and Broadsides*, 30, 47; Billie Ford Snider and Janice B. Palmer, eds., *Spanish Plat Book of Land Records of the District of Pensacola, Province of West Florida: British and Spanish Land Grants, 1763–1821* (Pensacola: Antique Compiling, 1994), 530; West Florida Governor Correspondence, 1763–1766, Government Records Collections, Alabama Department of Archives and History, "Johnstone's Report on the State of the Province," February 19, 1765; Matthews, *British West Florida and the Illinois Country*, 23; Wright, *Florida in the American Revolution*, 9; Rogers, et al., *Alabama*, 33; Howard, *British Development in West Florida*, 12; "A Letter From a Gentleman in Pensacola," *The Gentleman's Gazette*, February, 1765, P. K. Yonge Library of Florida History, University of Florida; Johnson, British West Florida, 9; McLemore, ed. *History of Mississippi*, 136; Howard, "Military Occupation," 184; Johnson, "Pensacola in the British Period," 265; Haldimand to Gage, May 1, 1767, May 22, 1767, June 16, 1767, and November 17, 1767, Haldimand Papers, Rea, "British Pensacola," 7.

14 Matthews, *British West Florida and the Illinois Country*, 25; Johnson, *British West Florida*, 155; "Governor Johnstone's Account of West Florida," in *The Gentleman's Gazette*, February, 1765, P. K, Yonge Library of Florida History; Robert R. Rea, "The Royal Navy Base at Pensacola," *Pensacola History Illustrated* 1 (1984), 2–4.

15 Fabel, *Bombast and Broadsides*, 47; Johnson, *British West Florida*, 30; Howard, "Colonial Pensacola, Part I," 112, 123; Fabel, *Economy of British West Florida*, 14; Rea, "British Pensacola," 3–4.

16 Rowland, "Peter Chester," 29–30, Chester to Earl of Hillsborough, September 29, 1770; Gray, "Elias Durnford," 33–35; Rea, "Problems and Responses," 51; Bartram, *Travels*, 412, 414.

17 Rea, "British Pensacola," 4, 9; Snider and Palmer, eds., *Spanish Plat Book*, 531; West Florida General Assembly Acts, 1767–1771, Government Records Collections, Alabama

Department of Archives and History; Rea, "Problems and Responses," 51, 54–55; Rea and Howard, *The Minutes, Journals, and Acts of the General Assembly*, 12, 221, 228, 320, 376–377, 389–391, An Act to Restrain Drunkenness and Promote Industry, Jan. 3, 1767, and An Act for the Better Regulation of Taverns and Public Houses and For Repealing an Act of the General Assmebly of this Province Entitled An Act for Granting of Licenses to Retailers of Spiritous Liquores, Imposing a Duty on Said Licenses, and for Regulating of Taverns or Public Houses, July 30, 1771.

18 Johnson, *British West Florida*, 123; Simmons, "The Divergent Colony," 12–13; J. Barton Starr, "Campbell Town: French Huguenots in British West Florida," *The Florida Historical Quarterly*, 54 (April, 1976), 342–357.

19 *Mississippi Department of Archives and History*, British West Florida Administrative Papers and Land Records, 1763–1783, Minutes of Council, March 7, 1767; Starr, "Campbell Town," 545–546.

20 Dalrymple, ed., *Merchant of Manchac*, 12; Matthews, *British West Florida and the Illinois Country*, 39; John G. Clark, *New Orleans 1718–1812: An Economic History* (Baton Rouge: Louisiana State University Press, 1970), 163; Pittman, *State of the European Settlements on the Mississippi*, 28–32; Haynes, *The Natchez District and the American Revolution*, 9; Born, Jr., *Governor Johnstone and Trade*, 12–13; Fabel, *Bombast and Broadsides*, 42; Smith, *Louisiana and the Gulf South Frontier*, 131.

21 Gray, "Elias Durnford," 27–28; Narrett, *Adventurism and Empire*, 36–39, 58; Dalrymple, ed., *The Merchant of Manchac*, 12; Gipson, *The British Empire Before the American Revolution, Volume 13*, 104–105; Alvord, *The Mississippi Valley in British Politics*, 171; Fabel, *Bombast and Broadsides*, 43–45; Robert R. Rea, "A Naval Visitor in British West Florida," *The Florida Historical Quarterly* 40 (October, 1961), 144–145, 152–153: 142–153; Conover, "British West Florida's Mississippi Frontier," 9; Rowland, "Peter Chester," 88, "Estimate of the Expence Which Will Attend Making the Proposed Cut from the River Mississippi to the River Iberville"; Haldimand to Gage, November 25, 1769, February 11, 1770, and June 6, 1770, Haldimand Papers; Bosse, "Dartmouth on the Mississippi, 10–11; Colonial Office's West Florida Papers, Pace Library, University of West Florida: CO 5 Volume 597, Germain to Whitehall, June 24, 1779.

22 Rea, *Major Robert Farmar*, 54; Fabel, *Bombast and Broadsides*, 43; Johnson, *British West Florida*, 32–36, 138, 146; Haynes, *The Natchez District and the American Revolution*, 11, 21–22; Dalrymple, ed., *The Merchant of Manchac*, 12, 16; Rose Meyers, *A History of Baton Rouge, 1699–1812* (Baton Rouge: Louisiana State University Press, 1999), 22–24; West Florida Governor Correspondence, 1763–1766, Government Records Collections, Alabama Department of Archives and History; Fabel, "Bernard Lintot," 94–95; Hyde, ed., *A Fierce and Fractious Frontier*, 48–53; Johnson, "Expansion in British West Florida," 49. Harwich and Dartmouth were both named for secretaries of state for American colonies.

23 Rowland, "Peter Chester," 60; Kay Nuzum, *A History of Baldwin County* (Bay Minette: The Baldwin Times, 1971), 39; Florence D'Olive Scott and Richard J. Scott, *Montrose: As it Was Recorded, Told About, and Lived* (Montgomery: Parago, 1976), 4–8; Holmes, "Charting Mobile Bay," 49; Sullivan, *The Mississippi Gulf Coast*, 21–22; Jay Higginbotham, *Pascagoula: Singing River City* (Mobile: Gill Press, 1967), 10–11; Johnson, *British West Florida*, 157–158; Haldimand to Gage, February 19, 1772 and August 25, 1770, Gov.

Chester to Lord Hillsborough, September 26, 1770, Haldimand Papers; Dalrymple, ed., *Merchant of Manchac*, 19.

24 Dalrymple, ed., *Merchant of Manchac*, 20; Johnson, *British West Florida*, 157; Hyde, ed., *A Fierce and Fractious Frontier*, 45, 56–57; Haynes, *The Natchez District and the American Revolution*, 19; Robert V. Haynes, "James Willing and the Planters of Natchez: The American Revolution Comes to the Southwest," *Journal of Mississippi History* 37 (February, 1975), 3; Rowland, "Peter Chester," 18–19; Elliott, Jr., *The Fort at Natchez*, 23; Starr, *Tories, Dons, and Rebels*, 34; James, *Antebellum Natchez*, 15–19; Wright, *Florida in the American Revolution*, 10.

25 Jackson, *Rivers of History*, 21; Waselkov and Braund, eds., *William Bartram on the Southeastern Indians*, 25–26.

26 Waselkov and Braund, *William Bartram on the Southeastern Indians*, 15, 90, 93; Bartram, *Travels*, 324.

27 Waselkov and Braund, *William Bartram on the Southeastern Indians*, 90–91, 93, 127.

28 Waselkov and Braund, *William Bartram on the Southeastern Indians*, 101, 102, 104; "Extracts from the Travels of William Bartram," 115–117; Rowland, "Peter Chester," 86. For more information on the "black drink" and its symbolic importance in Creek culture, see Charles M. Hudson, ed., *Black Drink: A Native American Tea* (Athens: University of Georgia Press, 1979).

29 Waselkov and Braund, *William Bartram on the Southeastern Indians*, 102, 113, 115–116.

30 Ibid., 100; Bartram, *Travels*, 328–329, 331, 360, 402, 405; Rea, *Major Robert Farmar*, 3; Corkran, *The Creek Frontier*, 278.

31 Romans, *Concise Natural History*, 112; Johnson, *British West Florida*, 154, 159.

32 Johnson, *British West Florida*, 112, 185; Howard, *British Development of West Florida*, 36–37; Howard, "Colonial Pensacola, Part I," 120; West Florida General Assembly Commons House Journals, 1767–1778, May 18, 1767, Government Records Collections, Alabama Department of Archives and History; Owen, *History of Alabama*, 152; Matthews, *British West Florida and the Illinois Country*, 37; Wright, *Florida in the American Revolution*, 8; Rowland, "Peter Chester," 57, Chester to Earl of Hillsborough, August 28, 1771.

33 Johnson, *British West Florida*, 134, 186; Fabel, *Economy of British West Florida*, 128–131, 134–135; Haynes, *The Natchez District and the American Revolution*, 9–10; James, *Antebellum Natchez*, 14; Rea, *Major Robert Farmar*, 3; Rowland, "Peter Chester," 28–29, Thomas Gallimore to Peter Chester, August 28, 1770; *Mississippi Department of Archives and History*, British West Florida Administrative Papers and Land Records, 1763–1783, Browne to Shelburne, June 29, 1767.

34 Fabel, *Economy of British West Florida*, 42; Rea, "Problems and Responses," 57–58, 60; McLemore, ed., *History of Mississippi*, 154–155; Delaney, *Story of Mobile*, 43; Johnson, *British West Florida*, 163–166; Gold, *Borderland Empires*, 143, 145; Howard, "Colonial Pensacola, Part I," 124; Rowland, "Peter Chester," 31, Chester to Earl of Hillsborough, September 29, 1770, 43, "Register of Births and Burials June 24-December 24, 1770"; McLaurin and Thomason, *Mobile*, 19; Wright, *Florida in the American Revolution*, 15; Rea and Howard, *The Minutes, Journals, and Acts of the General Assembly*, 361–362 An Act for Appointing Vestries and Parish Officers For the Towns of Pensacola and Mobile, June 28, 1769.

35 Johnson, *British West Florida*, 19; McLaurin and Thomason, *Mobile*, 18; Jarvis, "His Majesty's Papist Subjects"; Owen, *History of Alabama*, 153.

36 Johnson, *British West Florida*, 168–169; McLemore, ed., *History of Mississippi*, 155; Great Britain Board of Trade, *Journal of the Commissioners for Trade and Plantations, Volume 12*, 163, 166; Fabel, *Economy of British West Florida*, 158.

37 Arthur H. DeRosier, Jr., *William Dunbar: Scientific Pioneer of the Old Southwest* (Lexington: University Press of Kentucky, 2007), 25–38; Arthur H. DeRosier, Jr., "William Dunbar: A Product of the Eighteenth Century Scottish Renaissance," *Journal of Mississippi History*, 27 (Aug., 1966), 185; Smith, *Louisiana and the Gulf South Frontier*, 136.

38 Romans, *Concise Natural History*, 4–8, 11–12, 17, 18, 30, 32, 41, 51–53; Murphy, "To Make Florida Answer To Its Name," 63.

39 Robert R. Rea, "Belles-Letters in British West Florida." *Alabama Review*, 13 (April, 1960): 145–149; Rea, "British Pensacola," 8; Robin Fabel, *Shipwreck and Adventures of Monsieur Pierre Viaud*. Pensacola: University of West Florida Press, 1990, 1–32.

Chapter Six

1 Fabel, *Economy of British West Florida*, 112–116; Howard, *British Development in West Florida*, 17; Hamilton, *Colonial Mobile*, 290; Haynes, *The Natchez District and the American Revolution*, 20; Matthews, *British West Florida and the Illinois Country*, 59.

2 Robert R. Rea, "Planters and Plantations in British West Florida," *Alabama Review* 29 (July, 1976), 228; Rowland, "Peter Chester," 60; Haldimand to Gage, November 29, 1767, Haldimand Papers; Rowland, *Mississippi Provincial Archives*, 31, "The Produce of the Country"; Matthews, *British West Florida and the Illinois Country*, 52–53, 100–101; Johnson, *British West Florida*, 169–170; Fabel, *Economy of British West Florida*, 116–117; Hamilton, *Colonial Mobile*, 290, 300; Fabel, *Bombast and Broadsides*, 48; Howard, *British Development in West Florida*, 40.

3 Johnson, *British West Florida*, 169–171; Rea, "Planters and Plantations," 227; Fabel, *Economy of British West Florida*, 118–119.

4 Jack D.L. Holmes, "Indigo in Colonial Louisiana and the Floridas." *Louisiana History* 8 (Autumn, 1967), 341–342; James Bitler, "Indigo." *New Georgia Encyclopedia*, https://www.georgiaencyclopedia.org/articles/history-archaeology/indigo; Fabel, *Economy of British West Florida*, 113; Johnson, *British West Florida*, 158; Rea, "British West Florida Trade and Commerce," 155–156; Matthews, *British West Florida and the Illinois Country*, 56; Padgett, ed., "Commission, Orders, and Instructions," 1063; Usner, *Indians, Settlers, and Slaves*, 119; Waselkov and Gums, *Plantation Archaeology*, 66.

5 Sir Charles Whitworth, *State of the Trade of Great Britain in Its Imports and Exports Progressively from the Year 1697* (London, G. Robinson, 1776), 85; Holmes, "Indigo," 338–339; Fabel, *Economy of British West Florida*, 119, 121; Bridges, *Alabama*, 29; Howard, *British Development in West Florida*, 40, Fabel, "British West Florida."

6 Rea, "British West Florida Trade and Commerce," 157; Wright, *Florida in the American Revolution*, 14; Fabel, *Economy of British West Florida*, 123; Matthews, *British West Florida and the Illinois Country*, 54–55; Marion Dexter Learned, ed., *German American Annals* (Philadelphia: German American Historical Society, 1909), 58–59; Angela Lakwete, *Inventing the Cotton Gin: Machine and Myth in Antebellum America* (Baltimore: Johns Hopkins University Press, 2003), 38; Proctor, ed., *Eighteenth-Century Florida*, 78; Johnson,

British West Florida, 182–183; Hamilton, *Colonial Mobile*, 291; Romans, *Concise Natural History*, 139–142.

7 Howard, *British Development in West Florida*, 39; "An Attempt Towards a Short Description of West Florida, in Rowland, Chester p. 176; Johnson, *British West Florida*, 158, 183–184; Rea, "British West Florida Trade and Commerce," 153–154; Fabel, *Economy of British West Florida*, 119–121; McLaurin and Thomason, *Mobile*, 18; Thomason, *Mobile*, 47; Matthews, *British West Florida and the Illinois Country*, 53–54; Fabel, "British West Florida"; Simmons, "The Divergent Colony," 39–40; Waselkov and Gums, *Plantation Archaeology*, 67–68.

8 Johnson, *British West Florida*, 7, 129, 158; Fabel, *Bombast and Broadsides*, 52; Mathews, *British West Florida and the Illinois Country*, 60; Rowland, "Peter Chester," 125, "Report of Congress with the Creek Indians" and 173, "An Attempt Towards a Short Description of West Florida"; Fabel, *Economy of British West Florida*, 110–112; Thomason, *Mobile*, 47; Howard, *Development in British West Florida*, 14; Haswell, ed., *Memoirs and Adventures of Captain Matthew Phelps*, 55, appendix.

9 Fabel, *Economy of British West Florida*, 57–58; Rea, "British West Florida Trade and Commerce," 147, 149; Thomason, *Mobile*, 47; Johnson, *British West Florida*, 187; Sullivan, *Mississippi Gulf Coast*, 23; Gray, "Elias Durnford," 41: Fabel, *Bombast and Broadsides*, 51; Haldimand to Gage, February 12, 1770, Haldimand Papers; Wright, *Florida in the American Revolution*, 103.

10 Rea, "British West Florida Trade and Commerce," 126 129, 137–138, 140, 142–47; Fabel, *Economy of British West Florida*, 127, 145.

11 Rea, "British West Florida Trade and Commerce," 125, 141, 125; Thomason, *Mobile*, 46; John Dewey Born, Jr., "British Trade in West Florida, 1763–1783." PhD diss., (University of New Mexico, 1963), 150; McLemore, ed., *History of Mississippi*, 153; Rowland, *Mississippi Provincial Archives*, 456–468.

12 Born, Jr., "Charles Strachan," 25, 27, 29, 30, 32, 39, 41.

13 Dalrymple, ed. *Merchant if Manchac*, 3–33; Smith, *Louisiana and Gulf South Frontier*, 135.

14 Rea, "British West Florida Trade and Commerce," 132; Howard, *British Development in West Florida*, 18; Mathews, *British West Florida and the Illinois Country*, 28; Johnson, *British West Florida*, 184, 198; West Florida Governor Correspondence, 1763–1766, Johnstone to Secretary of the Board of Trade, December 29, 1765; Government Records Collections, Alabama Department of Archives and History; Fabel, *Economy of British West Florida*, 77, 83–87, 109, 146–147; Dalrymple, ed., *Merchant of Manchac*, 8; Thomas E. Chavez, *Spain and the Independence of the United States: An Intrinsic Gift* (Albuquerque: University of New Mexico Press, 2002), 108; Usner, *Indians, Settlers, and Slaves*, 122; James A. Padgett, ed., "Governor Peter Chester's Observations on the Boundaries of British West Florida, About 1775," Louisiana Historical Quarterly 25 (January, 1943), 9–10; Conover, "British West Florida's Mississippi Frontier," 36; Haynes, *The Natchez District and the American Revolution*, 41; Hyde, ed., *A Fierce and Fractious Frontier*, 48. For more on the failed efforts to develop trade with Spanish Louisiana, see John Dewey Born, Jr. "British Trade in West Florida, 1763–1783" Dissertation, (University of New Mexico, 1963).

15 Fabel, *Economy of British West Florida*, 78, 81, 85; Fabel, "Dauphin Island as the Gateway to Mexico," 84, 85, 88, 91–92; Johnson, *British West Florida*, 43–45; West Florida

Governor Correspondence, 1763–1766, Johnstone to Secretary of the Board of Trade, December 29, 1765, Government Records Collections, Alabama Department of Archives and History.

16 Thomason, *Mobile*, 47; Waselkov and Gums, *Plantation Archaeology*, 63; Hyde, ed., *A Fierce and Fractious Frontier*, 53; Rea, "Planters and Plantations," 229, 233–234; Fabel, *Economy of British West Florida*, 110–111.

17 Peter Wilson Coldham, *American Migrations, 1765–1799: The Lives, Times, and Families of Colonial Americans Who Remained Loyal to the British Crown Before, During, and After the Revolutionary War, as Related in Their Own Words and Through Their Correspondence* (Baltimore: Genealogical Publishing Company, 2000), 800–804.

18 Rea, *Major Robert Farmar*, 114, 131–135; Rea, "Planters and Plantations,"231, 233–234; Lewis, "Robert Famar," Waselkov and Gums, *Plantation Archaeology*, 83–84; Fabel, *Economy of British West Florida*, 47; Bonnie L. Gums, "Eighteenth-Century Plantations in the Northern Gulf Coast Region." *Gulf Coast Historical Review* 14 (Fall, 1988), 127–128.

19 Rea, "Planters and Plantations,"232–233; Waselkov and Gums, *Plantation Archaeology*, 63; Thomason, *Mobile*, 47; Fabel, *Economy of British West Florida*, 23, 47; Duval, *Independence Lost*, 60; Usner, *Indians, Settlers, and Slaves*, 112; Johnson, *British West Florida*, 175–177; Proctor, ed., *Eighteenth-Century Florida*, 77; Dalyrmple, ed., *Merchant of Manchac*, 21.

20 Fabel, *Economy of British West Florida*, 29–36, 45; Johnson, *British West Florida*, 159.

21 Rea and Howard, *The Minutes, Journals, and Acts of the General Assembly*, 331–336, An Act for the Regulation and Government of Negroes and Slaves, 342–347, An Act for the Order and Government of Slaves; Fabel, *Economy of British West Florida*, 23–25; West Florida General Assembly Acts, 1767–1771, Government Records Collections, Alabama Department of Archives and History; Smith, *Louisiana and Gulf South Frontier*, 133; Johnson, *British West Florida*, 172, 175; Proctor, ed., *Eighteenth-Century Florida*, 76; Sledge, *Mobile River*, 56.

22 Waselkov and Gums, *Plantation Archaeology*, 69; McLaurin and Thomason, *Mobile*, 19; Johnson, *British West Florida*, 177.

23 Johnson, *British West Florida*, 172–175; Rea and Howard, *The Minutes, Journals, and Acts of the General Assembly*, 331–336, An Act for the Regulation and Government of Negroes and Slaves and 342–347, An Act for the Order and Government of Slaves; Fabel, *Economy of British West Florida*, 25–26; Thomason, *Mobile*, 45; Sledge, *Mobile River*, 56; Proctor, ed., *Eighteenth-Century Florida*, 76; West Florida General Assembly Acts, 1767–1771, "Government of Slaves," January 15, 1772, Government Records Collections, Alabama Department of Archives and History.

24 Johnson, *British West Florida*, 172–173; Matthew J. Clavin, *Aiming for Pensacola: Fugitive Slaves on the Atlantic and Southern Frontiers*, (Cambridge: Harvard University Press, 2015; 12–25); Braund, "The Creek Indians, Blacks, and Slavery," 611–613; Narrett, *Adventurism and Empire*, 99; Braund, *Deerskins and Duffels*, 74; Usner, *Indians, Settlers, and Slaves*, 139; Ira Berlin, *Many Thousands Gone: The First Two Centuries of Slavery in North America* (Cambridge: Harvard University Press, 2000), 327–328; Fabel, *Economy of British West Florida*, 28; Duval, *Independence Lost*, 61–62; Rowland, *Mississippi Provincial Archives*, 315, M. Aubry to Gov. Johnstone, June 3, 1766; Evan Jones to Haldimand, October 9, 1768, Haldimand Papers.

25 James R. Dungan, "Sir William Dunbar of Natchez: Planter, Explorer, and Scientist,

1792–1810," *Journal of Mississippi History*, 24 (October, 1961), 212; DeRosier, Jr. *William Dunbar*, 38–47; Johnson, *British West Florida*, 172–173; Fabel, *Economy of British West Florida*, 40–41.

26 Fabel, *Economy of British West Florida*, 42–43; Thomason, *Mobile*, 44–45; Johnson, *British West Florida*, 177–181; Gannon, *New History of Florida*, 136; Wright, *Florida in the American Revolution*, 108–109; Rea and Howard, *The Minutes, Journals, and Acts of the General Assembly*, 317–318, An Act for the Regulation of Servants.

CHAPTER SEVEN

1   Johnson, *British West Florida*, 231; Griffith, "Peter Chester and the End of the British Empire," 32–33; Starr, *Tories, Dons, and Rebels*, 36; Dalrymple, ed., *Merchant of Manchac*, 23; Wright, *Florida in the American Revolution*, 18; Taylor, *American Revolutions*, 145.

2   Wright, *Florida in the American Revolution*, 21; Johnson, *British West Florida*, 233–234; Duval, *Independence Lost*, 55; Dalrymple, ed., *Merchant of Manchac*, 23; Starr, *Tories, Dons, and Rebels*, 225, 228; Henry O. Robertson, "Tories or Patriots? The Mississippi River Planters During the American Revolution," *Louisiana History* 40 (Autumn, 1999), 449; Taylor, *American Revolutions*, 145; Conover, "British West Florida's Mississippi Frontier, 33; Wright, *Florida in the American Revolution*, xiv.

3   Fabel, "Reflections on Mobile's Loyalism"; Campbell to Germain, September 14, 1779, Starr, *Tories, Dons and Rebels*, 226; Haldimand to Gage, August 28, 1768, Haldimand Papers; Gray, "Elias Durnford," 63.

4   Robert, Middlekauf, *The Glorious Cause: The American Revolution, 1763–1789* (New York: Oxford University Press, 1982), 60–63, 150–151; Starr, *Tories, Dons, and Rebels*, 45–46; Johnson, *British West Florida*, 124; Griffith, "Peter Chester and the End of the British Empire," 32. For more on how this helped foment rebellion in the northeast, see Carolyn Lynn H. Knight, *The American Colonial Press and the Townshend Crisis, 1766–1770: A Study in Political Imagery*, (Lewiston, Edwin Mellen, 1990).

5   J. Barton Starr, "The Spirit of What is There Called Liberty: The Stamp Act in British West Florida," *Alabama Review* 29 (October, 1976), 261, 263–265, 272; Starr, *Tories, Dons, and Rebels*, 37; Simmons, "Divergent Colony," 29–31; Rowland, *Mississippi Provincial Archives*, 417–419, Johnstone to Board of Trade, February 26, 1766; Howard, *British Development in West Florida*, 39; West Florida Governor Correspondence, 1763–1766, July , 1766, Government Records Collections, Alabama Department of Archives and History; Colonial Office's West Florida Papers, Pace Library, University of West Florida: CO 5 Volume 574, Johnston to Pownal, April 1, 1766.

6   West Florida Governor Correspondence, 1763–1766, July 1, 1766, Government Records Collections, Alabama Department of Archives and History; Starr, "The Spirit of What is There Called Liberty," 265, 268, 271; Starr, *Tories, Dons, and Rebels*, 37, 39, 40, 42; 271.

7   Fabel, "Reflections on Mobile's Loyalism; Starr, "The Spirit of What is There Called Liberty," 264–265, 267; Starr, *Tories, Dons, and Rebels*, 38; Rowland, *Mississippi Provincial Archives*, 417; Howard, "Early Settlers in British West Florida," 53–54; Mathews, *British West Florida and the Illinois Country*, 28; Gipson, *The British Empire Before the American Revolution*, 324.

8   Gipson, *The British Empire Before the American Revolution*, 294.

9   Haldimand to Mr. Maar, November 14, 1768, Haldimand Papers; Rea, "Brigadier

General Frederick Haldimand," 530; "A Letter from a Gentleman in Pensacola"; 5–8' Howard, "Colonial Pensacola, Part III, 384.

10 Starr, *Tories, Dons, and Rebels*, 46; United States Continental Congress, *Journals of he American Congress: From 1774 to 1788* (Washington: Way and Gideon, 1823), 38, October 22, 1774; Johnson, *British West Florida*, 205; Dalrymple, ed., *Merchant of Manchac*, 23; Rea and Howard, *The Minutes, Journals, and Acts of the General Assembly*, 274.

11 *Journal of the Proceedings of the American Congress*, 50, May 17, 1775; Middlekauf, *The Glorious Cause*, 234–252, 327–332; Haynes, *The Natchez District and the American Revolution*, 27; Rowland, *Mississippi Provincial Archives*, 461–462, Chester to Dartmouth, December 10, 1775. For the most in-depth study of the Contintenal Congress's origins and functioning, see Mark Grossman, *Encyclopedia of the Continental Congress* (Amenia, NY: Grey House Publishing, 2015).

12 Starr, *Tories, Dons, and Rebels*, 47–49; Johnson, *British West Florida*, 144–145; Rogers, et al., *Alabama*, 35; Haynes, *The Natchez District and the American Revolution*, 29–31; Griffith, *Documentary History*, 40; Smith, *Louisiana and the Gulf South Frontier*, 159; Thomason, *Mobile*, 45; Fabel, *Economy of British West Florida*, 7–8; (Johnson, "Expansion in West Florida," 492; Mathews, *British West Florida and the Illinois Country*, 115; West Florida Governor's Council Minutes, 1764–1780, Government Records Collections, Alabama Department of Archives and History; Rachel Mills Lennon, "Loyalist Refugee Petitions in British West Florida, 1776–77," *National Geographic Society Quarterly* 85 (1997), 130–135.

13 Lennon, "Loyalist Refugee Petitions," 131–132, 135 136; Haynes, *The Natchez District and the American Revolution*, 31–32; Leroy E. Willie, *West Florida and Its People* (Baton Rouge: Louisiana State University Press, 2000), 24; Robertson, "Tories or Patriots?," 451.

14 Johnson, *British West Florida*, 145–148; Rogers, et al., *Alabama*, 36; Starr, *Tories, Dons, and Rebels*, 48–49, 230; Mathews, *British West Florida and the Illinois Country*, 115–116; Gipson, *The British Empire Before the American Revolution*, Vol. 13, 109; Fabel, "British West Florida"; Smith, *Louisiana and the Gulf South Frontier*, 159; Hamilton, *Colonial Mobile*, 308; Howard, "Colonial Pensacola, Part 3," 386; Griffith, *Documentary History*, 41; Thomason, *Mobile*, 45; Haynes, *The Natchez District and the American Revolution*, 30, 32; Wright, *Florida in the American Revolution*, 22; Jack D.L. Holmes, "Juan de la Villebeuvre: Spain's Commandant of Natchez During the American Revolution," *Journal of Mississippi History* 37 (February, 1975), 105; Proctor, *Eighteenth-Century Florida*, 8. Willie, *West Florida and Its People*, 24; Fabel, *Economy of British West Florida*, 69–70; Johnson, "Expansion in British West Florida," 495; McLemore, ed., *History of Mississippi*, 153; Wright, *Florida in the American Revolution*, 23; Conover, "British West Florida's Mississippi Frontier," 34.

15 Narrett, *Adventurism and Empire*, 88; Hamer, "John Stuart's Indian Policy, 358; Calloway, *American Revolution in Indian Country*, 44, 226; Gray, "Elias Durnford," 62; Starr, *Tories, Dons, and Rebels*, 137–138; Raab, *Spain, Britain, and the American Revolution in Florida*, 131; Corkran, *The Creek Frontier*, 293, 312; John Richard Alden, *The South in the Revolution, 1763–1789* (Austin: University of Texas Press, 1957), 275; Osborn, "Relations With Indians," 260.

16 Corkran, *The Creek Frontier*, 295, 308–309; Greg O'Brien, "Choctaws in Alabama," *Encyclopedia of Alabama*, http://www.encyclopediaofalabama.org/article/h-1186;

Fabel, *Economy of British West Florida*, 61; Osborn, "Relations With Indians," 256, 259; Wright, *Florida in the American Revolution*, 35; Calloway, *American Revolution in Indian Country*, 223, 226; Barnett, *Mississippi's American Indians*, 158; Gibson, *The Chickasaws*, 71; O'Brien, *Choctaws in a Revolutionary Age*, 72; Greg O'Brien, "Southeastern Indians and the American Revolution. *Encyclopedia of Alabama*, http://www.encyclopediaofalabama.org/article/h-1133; Narrett, *Adventurism and Empire*, 96–97; Duval, *Independence Lost*, 121; Conover, "British West Florida's Mississippi Frontier," 133; Simmons, "The Divergent Colony," 56–57.

17 Starr, *Tories, Dons, and Rebels*, 50–58; Thomason, *Mobile*, 49; Colonial Office's West Florida Papers, Pace Library, University of West Florida: CO 5/Volume 619, Letters from the Secretary of State, to Governor Peter Chester, Feburary 7, 1777; Haldimand to Gage, February 13, 1771, Haldimand Papers.

18 Narrett, *Adventurism and Empire*, 47; John Walton Caughey, *Bernardo de Galvez in Louisiana: 1776–1783* (Gretna, LA: Pelican Publishing, 1972), 78; Haynes, *The Natchez District and the American Revolution*, 33, 35, 37–38; Starr, *Tories, Dons, and Rebels*, 69; James, *Antebellum Natchez*, 21–22; Simmons, "The Divergent Colony," 63–64; Abbey, "The Intrigue of a British Refugee Against the Willing Raid, 1778," *The William and Mary Quarterly* 1 (October, 1944), 397; Chavez, Spain and the Independence of the United States, 29–31; Kathryn Trimmer Abbey, "Chester's Defense of the Mississippi After the Willing Raid," *The Mississippi Valley Historical Review* 22 (June, 1935), 18–19; Conover, "British West Florida's Mississippi Frontier," 41.

19 Johnson, *British West Florida*, 206; Haynes, *The Natchez District and the American Revolution*, 39, 47; Starr, *Tories, Dons, and Rebels*, 59; Clark, *New Orleans*, 203; Fabel, *Economy of British West Florida*, 97; Conover, "British West Florida's Mississippi Frontier, 52; Caughey, *Bernardo de Galvez*, 158l Raab, *Spain, Britain, and the American Revolution in Florida*, 130–131, 134; Colonial Office's West Florida Papers, Pace Library, University of West Florida: CO 5/Volume 619, Letters from the Secretary of State, to Governor Chester, January 25, 1776.

20 Harold D. Williams, "Bernardo de Galvez and the Western Patriots," *Revista de Historia de America* 65/66 (January-December, 1968), 57; Haynes, *The Natchez District and the American Revolution*, 33–35; James Alton James, *Oliver Pollock: The Life and Times of an Unknown Patriot* (Whitefish, MT: Literary Licensing, 2011), 68; Smith, *Louisiana and the Gulf South Frontier*, 135; Duval, *Independence Lost*, 35–39.

21 Haynes, *The Natchez District and the American Revolution*, 34; Caughey, *Bernardo de Galvez*, 86–87, 94–99; James, *Oliver Pollock*, 71–73, 76; Duval, *Independence Lost*, 41, 142–145; Narret, *Adventurism and Empire*, 72; Jack D.L. Holmes, *The 1779 "Marcha de Galvez": Louisiana's Giant Step Forward in the American Revolution* (Baton Rouge: Baton Rouge Bicentennial Corporation, 1974), 9; Clark, *New Orleans*, 203–204; Williams, "Bernardo de Galvez and the Western Patriots,"; Chavez, *Spain and the Independence of the United States*, 216–217; Albert W. Haarman, "The Spanish Conquest of British West Florida, 1779–1781," *The Florida Historical Quarterly* 39 (October, 1960), 107; Dalrymple, ed., *Merchant of Manchac*, 24–25. Pollock was eventually bankrupted in large part owing to non-payment on the loans he made to the American government and sent to prison at the end of Revolutionary War. Galvez worked to obtain his release. He at length got some of his money back from Congress and the state of Virginia.

22 Robert B. Kane, "Bernardo de Galvez." *Encyclopedia of Alabama*, http://www.

encyclopediaofalabama.org/article/h-3763; Caughey, *Bernardo de Galvez*, 62–68; Haarman, "The Spanish Conquest of British West Florida," 108; Raab, *Spain, Britain, and the American Revolution in Florida*, 134; Williams, "Bernardo de Galvez and the Western Patriots," 56; McDermott, *The Spanish in the Mississippi Valley*, 91; Chavez, *Spain and the Independence of the United States*, 12–14, 29–30; Starr, *Tories, Dons, and Rebels*, 65; Clark, *New Orleans*, 204; see Gonzalo M. Quintero Saravia, *Bernardo de Galvez: Spanish Hero of the American Revolution* (Chapel Hill: University of North Carolina Press, 2018).

23 Fabel, *Economy of British West Florida*, 90–96, 105–107; John Caughey, "Bernardo de Galvez and the English Smugglers on the Mississippi, 1777," *The Hispanic American Historical Review* 12 (February, 1932), 46–48, 50; Narrett, *Adventurism and Empire*, 64) David J. Weber, *The Spanish Frontier in North America* (New Haven: Yale University Press, 1994), 266; Clark, *New Orleans*, 180, 204–205; Wright, *Florida in the American Revolution*, 64; Conover, "British West Florida's Mississippi Frontier," 47; Dalyrmple, ed., *Merchant of Manchac*, 24; Johnson, *British West Florida*, 196; Caughey, *Bernardo de Galvez*, 71; Gilbert Din, "Protecting the 'Barrera': Spain's Defenses in Louisiana, 1763–1779," *Louisiana History* 19 (Spring, 1978), 203; McDermott, *The Spanish in the Mississippi Valley*, 96; Chavez, *Spain and the Independence of the United States*, 95; Mark F. Boyd and Jose Navarro Latorre, "Spanish Interest in British Florida, and in the Progress of the American Revolution: Relations with the Spanish Faction of the Creek Indians," *The Florida Historical Quarterly* 32 (October, 1953), 98; Robert R. Rea, "Florida and the Royal Navy's Floridas," *The Florida Historical Quarterly* 60 (October, 1981), 199; Fabel, *Economy of British West Florida*, 97; Haynes, *The Natchez District and the American Revolution*, 41–42; Starr, *Tories, Dons, and Rebels*, 66, 99.

24 Fabel, *Economy of British West Florida*, 64, 95, 98; Johnson, *British West Florida*, 200, 203; Haynes, *The Natchez District and the American Revolution*, 43–46; Chavez, *Spain and the Independence of the United States*, 95–98; Caughey, "Bernardo de Galvez and the English Smugglers," 57; Starr, *Tories, Dons, and Rebels*, 68; Caughey, *Bernardo de Galvez*, 139; Conover, "British West Florida's Mississippi Frontier," 48–49.

25 Din, "Protecting the 'Barrera'," 202–203; Chavez, *Spain and the Independence of the United States*, 90, 93–94; McDermott, *The Spanish in the Mississippi Valley*, 91–98; Haarman, "The Spanish Conquest of British West Florida," 109; Starr, *Tories, Dons, and Rebels*, 60, 78; Holmes, *The Marcha de Galvez*, 9; Caughey, *Bernardo de Galvez*, 140–145; Haynes, *The Natchez District and the American Revolution*, 110; Light Townsend Cummins, *Spanish Observers and the American Revolution, 1775–1783* (Baton Rouge: Louisiana State University Press, 1991), 62–63, 90–91; Narrett, *Adventurism and Empire*, 85; Wright, *Florida in the American Revolution*, 20; Kathryn Trimmer Abbey, "Chester's Defense of the Mississippi," 26.

Chapter Eight

1 The Continental Congress, which met from 1774 to 1789, was the first official governing body for the United States. For more information on that body, see Jack N. Rakove, *The Beginnings of National Politics: An Interpretive History of the Continental Congress* (New York: Knopf, 1979); Haynes, *The Natchez District and the American Revolution*, 52–55; Johnson, *British West Florida*, 207; James, *Antebellum Natchez*, 21; Williams, "Bernardo de Galvez and the Western Patriots," 67; Narrett, *Adventurism and Empire*, 76–80; Wright, *Florida in the American Revolution*, 65–66; Starr, *Tories, Dons, and Rebels*, 70–71,

81; Caughey, *Bernardo de Galvez*, 90–93, 103; Robertson, "Tories or Patriots?," 453–454.

2 Duval, *Independence Lost*, 93; Robertson, "Tories or Patriots?," 447.

3 Eron O. Rowland, *Life, Letters, and Papers of William Dunbar, 1749–1810* (Jackson: Mississippi Historical Society, 1930), 60–61; Haynes, *The Natchez District and the American Revolution*, 56–57; Caughey, *Bernardo de Galvez*, 103; Starr, *Tories, Dons and Rebels*, 82; Claiborne, *Mississippi as a Province, Territory, and State*, 117; James, *Antebellum Natchez*, 19; Caughey, "James Willing and the Planters of Natchez," 6; Taylor, *American Revolutions*, 264.

4 Haynes, "James Willing and the Planters of Natchez," 5–7; Caughey, *Bernardo de Galvez*, 102–104; Haynes, *The Natchez District and the American Revolution*, 56, 58; Robertson, "Tories or Patriots?, 454–456; Narrett, *Adventurism and Empire*, 80; Wright, *Florida in the American Revolution*, 47; Light Townsend Cummins, *Spanish Observers and the American Revolution, 1775–1783* (Baton Rouge: Louisiana State University Press, 1991), 84; Johnson, *British West Florida*, 208; Starr, *Tories, Dons, and Rebels*, 83.

5 West Florida General Assembly Acts, 1767–1771, March 17, 1778, Government Records Collections, Alabama Department of Archives and History; John Caughey, "Willing's Expedition Down the Mississippi, 1778," *Louisiana Historical Quarterly* 15 (January, 1932), 5, 8; Johnson, *British West Florida*, 208; Haynes, *The Natchez District and the American Revolution*, 58–61; Cummins, *Spanish Observers and the American Revolution*, 85; Starr, *Tories, Dons, and Rebels*, 84; Robertson, "Tories or Patriots?," 457; Abbey, "Chester's Defense of the Mississippi," 21; West Florida Governor's Council Minutes, 1764–1780, Government Records Collections, March 5, 1778, Alabama Department of Archives and History.

6 Abbey, "Chester's Defense of the Mississippi," 21; Haynes, "James Willing and the Planters of Natchez," 6–7, 11; Starr, *Tories, Dons, and Rebels*, 85–86; Claiborne, *Mississippi as a Province, Territory, and State*, 118; Caughey, *Bernardo de Galvez*, 106–107; James, *Antebellum Natchez*, 22–23; Haynes, *The Natchez District and the American Revolution*, 64–65; Conover, "British West Florida's Mississippi Frontier," 62; Wright, *Florida in the American Revolution*, 48.

7 Elliott, Jr., "The Fort at Natchez," 23; John Richard Alden, *The South in the Revolution, 1763–1789* (Austin: University of Texas Press, 1957), 276; Johnson, *British West Florida*, 208–209; Cummins, *Spanish Observers and the American Revolution*, 87; Abbey, "Chester's Defense of the Mississippi, 21; Haynes, *The Natchez District and the American Revolution*, 63–67; Dalrymple, ed., *Merchant of Manchac*, 25; Robertson, "Tories or Patriots," 462; Conover, "British West Florida's Mississippi Frontier," 66; Caughey, *Bernardo de Galvez*, 108; Kathryn Trimmer Abbey, "The Intrigue of a British Refugee," 399; Haynes, "James Willing and the Planters of Natchez," 6; Claiborne, *Mississippi as a Province, Territory, and State*, 118; Caughey, "Willing's Expedition Down the Mississippi, 1778," 9.

8 Haynes, *The Natchez District and the American Revolution*, 70–71; Narrett, *Adventurism and Empire*, 81; Abbey, "Chester's Defense of the Mississippi," 30; Haswell, ed., *Memoirs and Adventures of Captain Matthew Phelps*, 110–112; Caughey, "Willing's Expedition Down the Mississippi, 1778," 13; West Florida Governor's Council Minutes, 1764–1780, March 18, 1778, Government Records Collections, Alabama Department of Archives and History.

9 Johnson, *British West Florida*, 208; Starr, *Tories, Dons, and Rebels*, 87; Dalrymple, ed., *Merchant of Manchac*, 26; James, *Antebellum Natchez*, 23; Smith, *Louisiana and the Gulf*

South Frontier, 159; Haynes, *The Natchez District and the American Revolution*, 9, 67–69, Rowland, *Life, Letters, and Papers of William Dunbar*, 60–62; Robertson, "Tories or Patriots?," 457; Dungan, "Sir William Dunbar of Natchez," 213; Caughey, *Bernardo de Galvez*, 108, 109.

10 Saravia, *Bernardo de Galvez*, 122–125; V. M. Scramuzza, "Galveztown: A Spanish Settlement in Colonial Louisiana," *Louisiana Historical Quarterly* 13 (October, 1930), 566. 569–570-571, 581, 583, 592; Duval, *Independence Lost*, 135; Gilbert C. Din, *The Canary Islanders of Louisiana* (Baton Rouge: LSU, 1988), 28–37.

11 West Florida Governor's Council Minutes, 1764–1780, March 2, 1778, Government Records Collections, Alabama Department of Archives and History; Haynes, *The Natchez District and the American Revolution*, 61–62, 67; Haynes, "James Willing and the Planters of Natchez," 7–8, 13; Caughey, *Bernardo de Galvez*, 108, 115; Abbey, "Chester's Defense of the Mississippi, 23–24; Starr, *Tories, Dons, and Rebels*, 89; Fabel, *Economy of British West Florida*, 63, 149; Chavez, *Spain and the Independence of the United States*, 104; Griffith, *Documentary History*, 39.

12 Sidney Henson Schell, *The Continental Navy on the Gulf Coast, 1775–1781: The USS West Florida at the Siege of Mobile, 1780* (CreateSpace, 2014); Delaney, *Story of Mobile*, 45; Caughey, "Willing's Expedition Down the Mississippi, 1778," 12; Haynes, "James Willing and the Natchez Planters," 10.

13 Taylor, *American Revolutions*, 265; Conover, "British West Florida's Mississippi Frontier," 72; Rea, "Planters and Plantations," 226; Wright, *Florida in the American Revolution*, 108; Coldham, *American Migrations*, 801; Johnson, *British West Florida*, 99, 209; Caughey, *Bernardo de Galvez*, 125; Dalrymple, ed., *Merchant of Manchac*, 26; Haynes, *The Natchez District and the American Revolution*, 84; Starr, *Tories, Dons, and Rebels*, 104; Abbey, "Chester's Defense of the Mississippi," 30.

14 James A. Servies, ed., *The Log of H.M.S. Mentor, 1780–1781: A New Account of the British Navy at Pensacola* (Gainesville: University Press of Florida, 1982), 3; Haynes, "James Willing and the Planters of Natchez," 15, 17, 20–21; Abbey, "Chester's Defense of the Mississippi," 17, 24–25; McLemore, ed., *History of Mississippi*, 156; Haynes, *The Natchez District and the American Revolution*, 78, 83; Conover, "British West Florida's Mississippi Frontier," 71; Narrett, *Adventurism and Empire*, 86.

15 Haswell, ed., *Memoirs and Adventures of Captain Matthew Phelps*, 114–115, 117–118, 119; Haynes, "James Willing and the Natchez Planters," 22, 24; Abbey, "The Intrigue of a British Refugee," 403.

16 Haynes, *The Natchez District and the American Revolution*, 84–88, 91; Abbey, "The Intrigue of a British Refugee," 399–404; Abbey, "Chester's Defense of the Mississippi," 29–30; Conover, "British West Florida's Mississippi Frontier," 85, 88; Haynes, "James Willing and the Natchez Planters," 24, 29; Starr, *Tories, Dons, and Rebels*, 111; James, *Antebellum Natchez*, 26; Caughey, *Bernardo de Galvez*, 125–126; Wilbur H. Siebert, "The Loyalists in West Florida and the Natchez District," *The Mississippi Valley Historical Review* 2 (March, 1916), 471; Wright, *Florida in the American Revolution*, 52.

17 Haswell, ed., *Memoirs and Adventures of Captain Matthew Phelps*, 155–156; Conover, "British West Florida's Mississippi Frontier," 102.

18 Starr, *Tories, Dons, and Rebels*, 89–90; Williams, "Bernardo de Galvez and the Western Patriots, 65–66; Din, "Protecting the Barrera," 206; Chavez, *Spain and the Independence*

of the United States, 106; Caughey, "Willing's Expedition Down the Mississippi, 1778," 16; Haynes, *The Natchez District and the American Revolution*, 73; Cummins, *Spanish Observers and the American Revolution*, 88–89; Haynes, "James Willing and the Natchez Planters," 12, 20.

19 Caughey, "Willing's Expedition Down the Mississippi, 1778," 31; Caughey, *Bernardo de Galvez*, 127–130; Williams, "Bernardo de Galvez and the Western Patriots," 67; Haynes, *The Natchez District and the American Revolution*, 92–93, 95–96, 98; Conover, "British West Florida's Mississippi Frontier," 92–93, 96; United States Continental Congress. *Journals of the American Congress*, August 11, 1778; Haynes, "James Willing and the Natchez Planters," 34–37.

20 Haynes, *The Natchez District and the American Revolution*, 98–99; Caughey, *Bernardo de Galvez*, 132; Starr, *Tories, Dons, and Rebels*, 117; Duval, *Independence Lost*, 123; Caughey, "Willing's Expedition Down the Mississippi," 34, 38.

21 Cummins, *Spanish Observers and the American Revolution*, 91; Colonial Office's West Florida Papers, Pace Library, University of West Florida: CO 5 Volume 597, Campbell to Galvez, no date, and March 22, 1779, Galvez to Campbell, February 20, 1779; Haynes, *The Natchez District and the American Revolution*, 89; Starr, *Tories, Dons, and Rebels*, 101.

CHAPTER NINE

1 Conover, "British West Florida's Mississippi Frontier," 105; Caughey, *Bernardo de Galvez*, 129; Starr, *Tories, Dons, and Rebels*, 106; Thomason, *Mobile*, 49; Johnson, *British West Florida*, 209.

2 Johnson, *British West Florida*, 210; Din, "Protecting the Barrera," 207; Caughey, "Willing's Expedition Down the Mississippi," 35; Colonial Office's West Florida Papers, Pace Library, University of West Florida: CO 5/Volume 619, Letters from the Secretary of State, to Governor Chester, July 1, 1778 and July 4, 1778; Rea and Howard, *The Minutes, Journals, and Acts of the General Assembly*, 279; Howard, "Colonial Pensacola, Part III," 391; Smith, *Louisiana and the Gulf South Frontier*, 160–161.

3 Colonial Office's West Florida Papers, Pace Library, University of West Florida: CO 5/Volume 619, Letters from the Secretary of State, to Governor Chester, May 27, 1776; Starr, *Tories, Dons, and Rebels*, 57, 129–130; Raab, *Spain, Britain, and the American Revolution in Florida*, 133; Johnson, *British West Florida*, 207–211; Robert R. Rea, "Henry Hamilton and West Florida," *Indiana Magazine of History* 54 (March, 1958), 49; Wright, Florida in American Revolution, 50; Elliott, Jr., "The Fort at Natchez," 24; McLemore, ed., *History of Mississippi*, 156; Bettie Jones Convoer, "British West Florida's Frontier Mississippi Posts, 1763–1779," *Alabama Review* 29 (July, 1976), 190; Haynes, *The Natchez District and the American Revolution*, 105; Conover, "British West Florida's Mississippi Frontier," 106–107, 112; Wesley S. Odom, *The Longest Siege of the American Revolution: Pensacola* (Pensacola: Wesley S. Odom, 2009), 39.

4 Kenneth G. Davies, ed., *Documents of the American Revolution, 1770–1783* 21 Volumes (Shannon: Irish University Press, 1972), 63, 57, George C. Osborn, "Major-General John Campbell in British West Florida," *The Florida Historical Quarterly* 27 (April, 1949), 317–318; Haynes, *The Natchez District and the American Revolution*, 105–107, 110; Abbey, "Chester's Defense of the Mississippi, 31; Starr, *Tories, Dons, and Rebels*, 133, 137; Thomason, *Mobile*, 50; Conover, "British West Florida's Mississippi Frontier," 116, 118; Johnson, *British West Florida*, 212.

5   Thomason, *Mobile*, 50; Starr, *Tories, Dons, and Rebels*, 135, 138–140; Haynes, *The Natchez District and the American Revolution*, 106, 108; Osborn, "Major-General John Campbell," 324; Colonial Office's West Florida Papers, Pace Library, University of West Florida: CO 5/Volume 597, Military Correspondence and Documents, 1778–1781, List of Public Works to be Carried on at the Several Places Under Mentioned, February 20, 1779.

6   Max Von Eelking, *The German Allied Troops in the North American War of Independence, 1776–1783* (Albany: J. Munsell's Sons, 1893), 220; Haynes, *The Natchez District and the American Revolution*, 107; Starr, *Tories, Dons, and Rebels*, 132; Pace Library, University of West Florida, Steuernagel Diary, 40; Osborn, "Major-General John Campbell," 321; Conover, "British West Florida's Mississippi Frontier, 122; Wright, *Florida in the American Revolution*, 74.

7   Colonial Office's West Florida Papers, Pace Library, University of West Florida: CO 5/ Volume 597, Military Correspondence and Documents, 1778–1781.

8   Rea and Howard, *The Minutes, Journals, and Acts of the General Assembly*, 324. When the General Assembly created Charlotte County in "An Act to Erect Mobile Into a County and to Establish A Court of Common Pleas Therein," it specified it included lands "five miles eastward of the Bay of Mobile, together with all the lands westward of the said Bay of Mobile as far as the River and Bay of Pascagoula and the settlements thereon and to the northward of the said Bay of Mobile as far as Tombigby, including Dauphin Island and all other islands westward thereof." Johnson, *British West Florida*, 20, 107, 109; Hamilton, *Colonial Mobile*, 105; Robin Fabel, "Reflections on Mobile's Loyalism in the American Revolution," *Gulf Coast Historical Review* 19 (2003): 31–45; Padgett, "Reply of Peter Chester," 39–41.

9   Starr, *Tories, Dons, and Rebels*, 123–128; Haynes, *The Natchez District and the American Revolution*, 104; Johnson, *British West Florida*, 108–110, 211; Ingram, "British West Florida's General Assembly, 109–116; Hamilton, *Colonial Mobile*, 306; Howard, "Colonial Pensacola, Part III," 394–395; Fabel, "Reflections on Mobile's Loyalism"; McLemore, ed., *History of Mississippi*, 152; Griffith, "Peter Chester and the End of the British Empire," 26.

10 Colonial Office's West Florida Papers, Pace Library, University of West Florida: CO 5/ Volume 598, Minutes of West Florida Council, September 11 and 14, 1779; Conover, "British West Florida's Frontier Mississippi Posts," 184–185; Wright, Jr., *The McGillivray and McIntosh Traders*, 150; Fabel, "Reflections on Mobile's Loyalism; Osborn, "Relations with Indians," 263–264; Wright, *Florida in the American Revolution*, 50.

11 For information on the course of the Revolutionary War at the time, see Alden, *The South in the Revolution*; John Buchanan, *The Road to Guilford Courthouse: The American Revolution in the Carolinas* (New York: Wiley and Sons, 1997); David K. Wilson, *The Southern Strategy: Britain's Conquest of South Carolina and Georgia, 1775–1780* (Columbia: University of South Carolina Press, 2008); James K. Swisher, *The Revolutionary War in the Southern Back Country* (Gretna, LA: Pelican Publishing, 2008); John E. Ferling, *Almost a Miracle: The American in the War of Independence* (New York: Oxford University Press, 2009).

12 Cummins, *Spanish Observers and the American Revolution*, 92–93. The Saratoga Campaign involved two battles, fought on September 19 and October 7, 1777 and is the subject of numerous books. For a concise summary of the fighting and its importance in the outcome of the Revolutionary War, see Brendan Morrissey and Adam Hook, *Saratoga*

1777: Turning Point of a Revolution (Oxford: Osprey Publishing, 2000). Chavez, *Spain and the Independence of the United States*, 79; Weber, *The Spanish Frontier*, 266; Ferling, *Almost a Miracle*, 90, 262–263; J. Horace Nunemaker, "Louisiana Anticipates Spain's Recognition of the Independence of the United States," *Louisiana Historical Quarterly* 26 (July, 1943), 756. For more on the decision by the French to enter the war, see Ronald Hoffman and Peter J. Albert, eds., *Diplomacy and Revolution: The Franco-American Alliance of 1778* (Charlottesville: University of Virginia Press, 1981).

13 Ferling, *Almost a Miracle*, 321; Haarman, "The Spanish Conquest of British West Florida," 107–108; Nunemaker, "Louisiana Anticipates Spain's Recognition," 759–761; Wright, *Florida in the American Revolution*, 75; Din, "Protecting the Barrera," 209; Johnson, *British West Florida*, 212; Caughey, *Bernardo de Galvez*, 149; Haynes, *The Natchez District and the American Revolution*, 111.

14 Chavez, *Spain and the Independence of the United States* contains among the best summaries of the backstories behind Spain's entrance into the war. Starr, *Tories, Dons, and Rebels*, 142; Raab, *Spain, Britain, and the American Revolution in Florida*, 133; Johnson, *British West Florida*, 204; McLaurin and Thomason, *Mobile*, 20; Haarman, "The Spanish Conquest of British West Florida," 108; Haynes, *The Natchez District of the American Revolution*, 111; Williams, "Bernardo de Galvez and the Western Patriots," 55, 57; Weber, *The Spanish Frontier*, 176.

15 Starr, *Tories, Dons, and Rebels*, 149–150; Caughey, *Bernardo de Galvez*, 137–138, 149–151; Nunemaker, "Louisiana Anticipates Spain's Recognition," 762; Holmes, *The Marcha de Galvez*, 7; Smith, *Louisiana and the Gulf South Frontier*, 160; Haarman, "The Spanish Conquest of British West Florida," 109; Haynes, *The Natchez District and the American Revolution*, 112–113; Din, "Protecting the Barrera," 210.

16 Smith, *Louisiana and the Gulf South Frontier*, 160; Weber, *The Spanish Frontier*, 267; Johnson, *British West Florida*, 144, 212–213; Williams, "Bernardo de Galvez and the Western Patriots," 66; Osborn, "Major-General John Campbell," 325–326; Starr, *Tories, Dons, and Rebels*, 64, 142; Wright, *Florida in the American Revolution*, 73; Robertson, "Tories or Patriots?," 461 Colonial Office's West Florida Papers, Pace Library, University of West Florida: CO 5/Volume 598, Minutes of West Florida Council, James Campbell to Le Montrais, Captain of the *Stork*, September 10, 1779.

17 John Caughey, "The Panis Mission to Pensacola, 1778." *The Hispanic American Historical Review* 10 (November, 1930), 480–489; Caughey, *Bernardo de Galvez*, 145–147, 150; Haarman, "The Spanish Conquest of British West Florida, 110; Starr, *Tories, Dons, and Rebels*, 144-; Holmes, *The Marcha de Galvez*, 9; Raab, *Spain, Britain, and the American Revolution in Florida*, 129; Clark, *New Orleans*, 205; Duval, *Independence Lost*, 154; Kane, "Bernardo de Galvez" Colonial Office's West Florida Papers, Pace Library, University of West Florida: CO 5/Volume 597, Military Correspondence and Documents, 1778–1781, Germain to Campbell, June 25, 1779.

18 Caughey, *Bernardo de Galvez*, 151–153; Holmes, *The Marcha de Galvez*, 9–11; Conover, "British West Florida's Frontier Mississippi Posts," 200; Starr, *Tories, Dons, and Rebels*, 150–151; Chavez, *Spain and the Independence of the United States*, 170; Duval, *Independence Lost*, 138; Historical Manuscripts Commission, *Report on American Manuscripts in the Royal Institution of Great Britain* (Dublin: His Majesty's Stationery Office, 1904–1909), 31, Campbell to Clinton, September 14, 1779; Nunemaker, "Louisiana Anticipates Spain's Recognition," 763–764; Haynes, *The Natchez District and the American Revolution*,

113; Davies, ed., *Documents of the American Revolution*, 216, Campbell to Germain, September 14, 1779; Osborn, "Major-General John Campbell," 326; Conover, "British West Florida's Mississippi Frontier," 135.

19 Haynes, *The Natchez District and the American Revolution*, 113–114; Conover, "British West Florida's Frontier Mississippi Posts," 200; Caughey, *Bernardo de Galvez*, 152; Duval, *Independence Lost*, 136–137; Starr, *Tories, Dons, and Rebels*, 151; Haarman, "The Spanish Conquest of British West Florida"; Dalrymple, ed., *Merchant of Manchac*, 28.

20 Conover, "British West Florida's Frontier Mississippi Posts," 201–202; Dalrymple, ed. *Merchant of Manchac*, 27–29; Davies, ed., *Documents of the American Revolution*, 216, Campbell to Germain, September 14, 1779; Haynes, *The Natchez District and the American Revolution*, 117, 119; Conover, "British West Florida's Mississippi Frontier," 132, 139–140; Raab, *Spain, Britain, and the American Revolution in Florida*, 134; Starr, *Tories, Dons, and Rebels*, 153–154; Smith, *Louisiana and the Gulf South Frontier*, 160; Haarman, "The Spanish Conquest of British West Florida, 111; Mathews, *British West Florida and the Illinois Country*, 127; Holmes, *The Marcha de Galvez*, 15; Caughey, *Bernardo de Galvez*, 155; Chavez, *Spain and the Independence of the United States*, 171; Wright, *Florida in the American Revolution*, 77.

21 Conover, "British West Florida's Mississippi Frontier," 142–143; Holmes, *The Marcha de Galvez*, 16; Schell, *The Continental Navy on the Gulf Coast*; Chavez, *Spain and the Independence of the United States*, 108–109; Starr, *Tories, Dons, and Rebels*, 152; Haynes, *The Natchez District and the American Revolution*, 123; Caughey, *Bernardo de Galvez*, 159; Narrett, *Adventurism and Empire*, 93–94; Rea, "Florida and the Royal Navy's Floridas," 199–200; Conover, "British West Florida's Frontier Mississippi Posts," 203; Duval, *Independence Lost*, 147; Larrie D. Ferreiro, *Brothers at Arms: American Independence and the Men of France and Spain Who Saved It* (New York: Knopf, 2016), 161.

22 Jay Higginbotham, *Pascagoula: Singing River City* (Gill Press, Mobile, 1967), 10–11; Holmes, *The Marcha de Galvez*, 16; Caughey, *Bernardo de Galvez*, 161; Haarman, "The Spanish Conquest of British West Florida," 113; Conover, "British West Florida's Mississippi Frontier," 141; Chavez, *Spain and the Independence of the United States*, 171.

23 Osborn, "Major-General John Campbell," 327; Starr, *Tories, Dons, and Rebels*, 156–158; Haarman, "The Spanish Conquest of British West Florida," 114; Alden, *The South in the Revolution*, 277.

24 Holmes, *The Marcha de Galvez*, 12–17; Starr, *Tories, Dons, and Rebels*, 154–155; Conover, "British West Florida's Mississippi Posts," 204; Haynes, *The Natchez District and the American Revolution*, 117–120; Colonial Office's West Florida Papers, Pace Library, University of West Florida: CO 5/Volume 597, Military Correspondence and Documents, 1778–1781, Germain to Campbell, April 14, 1780; Caughey, *Bernardo de Galvez*, 155–156; Haarman, "The Spanish Conquest of British West Florida," 111–112; Conover, "British West Florida's Mississippi Frontier," 121, 143; Wright, *Florida in the American Revolution*, 78.

25 Holmes, *The Marcha de Galvez*, 17; Duval, *Independence Lost*, 149–150; Caughey, *Bernardo de Galvez*, 156–157; Haynes, *The Natchez District and the American Revolution*, 121–124; Conover, "British West Florida's Mississippi Frontier," 143–146; "J. St. Clair Favrot, "Baton Rouge, the Historic Captial of Louisiana," *Louisiana Historical Quarterly* 12 (October, 1929), 615; Conover, "British West Florida's Mississippi Posts," 204; Raab, *Spain, Britain, and the American Revolution in Florida*, 135; Chavez, *Spain and the Independence of the*

United States, 171; Wright, *Florida in the American Revolution*, 78; Haarman, "The Spanish Conquest of British West Florida," 112–113; Starr, *Tories, Dons, and Rebels*, 155–156.

26 James, *Antebellum Natchez*, 25; Smith, *Louisiana and the Gulf South Frontier*, 160; "Articles of Captiulation agreed upon and granted between his Excellency Don Bernardo de Galvez, his Catholick Majesty's Governor and Commander in Chief of the Province and Forces of Louisiana, and Alexander Dickson, Esq., Lieutentant-Colonal of the 16th Regiment of Infantry, and Commander of Troops of His Britannick Majesty upon the Mississippi, &c. for the garrison and district of Baton Rouge in West Florida," in Henry P. Dart, ed., "West Florida-The Capture of Baton Rouge By Galvez, September 21, 1779, From Reports of the English Officers," *Louisiana Historical Quarterly* 12 (April, 1929), 259–262; Holmes, *The Marcha de Galvez*, 17; Starr, *Tories, Dons, and Rebels*, 158.

27 Conover, "British West Florida's Mississippi Posts," 205; Caughey, *Bernardo de Galvez*, 157; Haynes, *The Natchez District and the American Revolution*, 24; Haarman, "The Spanish Conquest of British West Florida," 113; Starr, *Tories, Dons, and Rebels*, 157; James, *Antebellum Natchez*, 25; 125; Colonial Office's West Florida Papers, Pace Library, University of West Florida: CO 5/Volume 597, Military Correspondence and Documents, 1778–1781, Letter to Dickson, October 4, 1779; Kenneth Scott, ed., "Britain Loses Natchez, 1779: An Unpublished Letter," *Journal of Mississippi History*, 26 (February, 1964): 45–46.

28 Holmes, *The Marcha de Galvez*, 17, 20; Haynes, *The Natchez District and the American Revolution*, 126; Haarman, "The Spanish Conquest of British West Florida," 114; Ferreiro, *Brothers at Arms*, 248; Caughey, *Bernardo de Galvez*, 158; Pearl Mary Segura, "The Capture of the Bluff at Baton Rouge," *Louisiana History* 17 (Spring, 1976): 203–209.

29 Conover, "British West Florida's Mississippi Frontier," 155; Colonial Office's West Florida Papers, Pace Library, University of West Florida: CO 5/Volume 597, Military Correspondence and Documents, 1778–1781, Campbell to Germain, December 15, 1779; Segura, "The Capture of Baton Rouge by Galvez," 256–257; Starr, *Tories, Dons, and Rebels*, 43; Davies, *Documents of the American Revolution*, 75, Germain to Chester, April 5, 1780.

30 Starr, *Tories, Dons, and Rebels*, 147, 161, 164; Haynes, *The Natchez District and the American Revolution*, 116; Fabel, "Reflections on Mobile's Loyalism; Haldimand to Gage, March 21, 1770 and Gage to Haldimand, March 23, 1770, Haldimand Papers; Servies, ed., *The Log of H.M.S. Mentor*, 12, 19.

31 Servies, ed., *The Log of H.M.S. Mentor*, 4–16, 40, 42, 44.

CHAPTER 10

1 William S. and Hazel P. Coker, *The Siege of Mobile, 1780, in Maps: With Data on Troop Strength, Military Units, Ships, Casualties, and Prisoners of War, Including a Brief History of Fort Charlotte* (Mobile: Perdido Bay Press, 1982), 1, 7, 11; Caughey, *Bernardo de Galvez*, 173; Haynes, *The Natchez District and the American Revolution*, 127; Starr, *Tories, Dons, and Rebels*, 164–165; Duval, *Independence Lost*, 168.

2 Caughey, *Bernardo de Galvez*, 174; Starr, *Tories, Dons, and Rebels*, 164–167; Narrett, *Adventurism and Empire*, 92; Haarman, "The Spanish Conquest of British West Florida," 115; Haynes, *The Natchez District and the American Revolution*, 127.

3 Jack D.L. Holmes, "Alabama's Bloodiest Day of the American Revolution: Counterattack at The Village, January 7, 1781," *Alabama Review* 29 (July, 1976), 210; Starr, *Tories, Dons,*

and Rebels, 168; Din, "Protecting the Barrera, 83; Haynes, *The Natchez District and the American Revolution*, 127; Haarman, "The Spanish Conquest of British West Florida, 116; Duval, *Independence Lost*, 172; Wright, *Florida in the American Revolution*, 79; Ferreiro, *Brothers at Arms*, 163; Coker and Coker, *The Siege of Mobile*, 13, 21; Caughey, *Bernardo de Galvez*, 173–175; Alden, *The South in the Revolution*, 277; Smith, *Louisiana and the Gulf South Frontier*, 161; Johnson, *British West Florida*, 215.

4   Coker and Coker, *The Siege of Mobile*, 27–43; Haynes, *The Natchez District and the American Revolution*, 128; Starr, *Tories, Dons, and Rebels*, 168; Caughey, *Bernardo de Galvez*, 175–176; Hamilton, *Colonial Mobile*, 253; Sledge, *Mobile River*, 60; Holmes, "Jose de Evia," 108; Haarman, "The Spanish Conquest of British West Florida," 116.

5   Holmes, "Jose de Evia," 108–109; Haynes, *The Natchez District and the American Revolution*, 128; Coker and Coker, *The Siege of Mobile*, 49; Starr, *Tories, Dons, and Rebels*, 168; William Beer, "The Surrender of Fort Charlotte, Mobile, 1780," *The American Historical Review* 1 (July, 1896), 696. Jose de Evia was a skilled naval chart producer whose soundings of regional waters became the standard such materials in Spanish naval academies for years after the war.

6   Starr, *Tories, Dons, and Rebels*, 169; Haynes, *The Natchez District and the American Revolution*, 128; Coker and Coker, *The Siege of Mobile*, 51, 55, 57, 59; Smith, *Louisiana and the Gulf South Frontier*, 161; Caughey, *Bernardo de Galvez*, 177; Haarman, "The Spanish Conquest of British West Florida, 117–118; Sledge, *Mobile River*, 60; Gray, "Elias Durnford," 66–67.

7   Coker and Coker, *The Siege of Mobile*, 51, 61, 101; Rea, "Elias Durnford," 27; Starr, *Tories, Dons, and Rebels*, 170, 173; Alden, *The South in the Revolution*, 277; Hamilton, *Colonial Mobile*, 312; Caughey, *Bernardo de Galvez*, 182; Raab, *Spain, Britain, and the American Revolution in Florida*, 135; Haarman, "The Spanish Conquest of British West Florida," 116; Gray, "Elias Durnford," 64, 69; Haynes, *The Natchez District and the American Revolution*, 128.

8   Coker and Coker, *The Siege of Mobile*, 51, 61; Fabel, "Reflections on Mobile's Loyalism"; Starr, *Tories, Dons, and Rebels*, 169–170; Haarman, "The Spanish Conquest of British West Florida," 117; Sledge, *Mobile River*, 61; Colonial Office's West Florida Papers, Pace Library, University of West Florida: CO 5/Volume 597, Military Correspondence and Documents, 1778–1781, Durnford to Galvez, March 1, 1780 and Durnford to Campbell, March 2, 1780; Beer, "The Surrender of Fort Charlotte," 697–698; Thomason, *Mobile*, 51; Gray, "Elias Durnford," 68.

9   Beer, "The Surrender of Fort Charlotte," 698; Starr, *Tories, Dons, and Rebels*, 170–171; Coker and Coker, *The Siege of Mobile*, 61, 69; Sledge, *Mobile River*, 61; Gray, "Elias Durnford," 68; Caughey, *Bernardo de Galvez*, 178; Hamilton, *Colonial Mobile*, 315; Haarman, "The Spanish Conquest of British West Florida," 117; Von Eelking, *The German Allied Troops in the North American War of Independence*, 222.

10 Starr, *Tories, Dons, and Rebels*, 170; Coker and Coker, *The Siege of Mobile*, 62–63; Haynes, *The Natchez District and the American Revolution*, 128; Caughey, *Bernardo de Galvez*, 180; Schell, *The Continental Navy on the Gulf Coast*; Hamilton, *Colonial Mobile*, 313; Davies, *Documents of the American Revolution*, 124, Cameron to Germain, July 18, 1780; Wright, *Florida in the American Revolution*, 87; Beer, "The Surrender of Fort Charlotte," 698.

11 Haynes, *The Natchez District and the American Revolution*, 128–129; Sledge, *Mobile River*, 61; Hamilton, *Colonial Mobile*, 314; Starr, *Tories, Dons, and Rebels*, 170–172; Caughey,

Bernardo de Galvez, 178–180; Coker and Coker, *The Siege of Mobile*, 65–73, 89; Thomason, *Mobile*, 51; McLaurin and Thomason, *Mobile*, 20; Haarman, "The Spanish Conquest of British West Florida," 117–118; Beer, "The Surrender of Fort Charlotte"; Raab, *Spain, Britain, and the American Revolution in Florida*, 135.

12 Caughey, *Bernardo de Galvez*, 179–180; Sledge, *Mobile River*, 61; Coker and Coker, *The Siege of Mobile*, 79, 81; Starr, *Tories, Dons, and Rebels*, 172; Din, "Protecting the Barrera," 84; Haarman, "The Spanish Conquest of British West Florida," 118.

13 Caughey, *Bernardo de Galvez*, 181; Haarman, "The Spanish Conquest of British West Florida, 118–119; Haynes, *The Natchez District and the American Revolution*, 129–130; Starr, *Tories, Dons, and Rebels*, 172–173; Coker and Coker, *The Siege of Mobile*, 87; Mathews, *British West Florida and the Illinois Country*, 128; Johnson, *British West Florida*, 216; Smith, *Louisiana and the Gulf South Frontier*, 161; Beer, "The Surrender of Fort Charlotte," 697.

14 Starr, *Tories, Dons, and Rebels*, 172; Wright, *Florida in American Revolution*, 80; Pace Library, University of West Florida, Steuernagel Diary, 42; Caughey, *Bernardo de Galvez*, 180; Colonial Office's West Florida Papers, Pace Library, University of West Florida: CO 5/Volume 597, Military Correspondence and Documents, 1778–1781, Campbell to Germain, March 24, 1780; Gray, "Elias Durnford," 72; Mathews, *British West Florida and the Illinois Country*, 129; Coker and Coker, *The Siege of Mobile*, 75.

15 Haynes, *The Natchez District and the American Revolution*, 129; McLaurin and Thomason, *Mobile*, 20; Starr, *Tories, Dons, and Rebels*, 173; Caughey, *Bernardo de Galvez*, 181; Raab, *Spain, Britain and the American Revolution in Florida*, 135; Fabel, "British West Florida"; Sledge, *Mobile River*, 62; Chavez, *Spain and the Independence of the United States*, 176; Gray, "Elias Durnford," 74; Coker and Coker, *The Siege of Mobile*, 87, 89, 91–93; Haarman, "The Spanish Conquest of British West Florida," 119; Hamilton, *Colonial Mobile*, 315; Beer, "The Surrender of Fort Charlotte," 699.

16 Haarman, "The Spanish Conquest of British West Florida," 119; Sledge, *Mobile River*, 61; Starr, *Tories, Dons, and Rebels*, 173–174; Caughey, *Bernardo de Galvez*, 182–184; Raab, *Spain, Britain, and the American Revolution*, 135; Jack D.L. Holmes, "Jose de Evia and His Activities in Mobile, 1780–1784," *Alabama Historical Quarterly* 34 (Summer, 1972), 109; Haynes, *The Natchez District and the American Revolution*, 130; Coker and Coker, *The Siege of Mobile*, 95; Osborn, "Major-General John Campbell, 331; Hamilton, *Colonial Mobile*, 316.

17 Caughey, *Bernardo de Galvez*, 186; Haarman, "The Spanish Conquest of British West Florida," 120; Chavez, *Spain and the Independence of the United States*, 178; Starr, *Tories, Dons, and Rebels*, 175–176; Rogers, et al., *Alabama*, 37; Thomason, *Mobile*, 51; Eric Beerman, "Jose de Ezpeleta: Alabama's First Spanish Commandant During the American Revolution," *Alabama Review* 29 (October, 1976), 249, 251–252; Smith, *Louisiana and the Gulf South Frontier*, 161; Coker and Coker, *The Siege of Mobile*, 97; McLemore, ed., *History of Mississippi*, 159; F. De Borja Medina Rojas, *Jose de Ezpeleta, Gobernador de la Mobila 1780–1781* (Seville: Escuela de Estudios Hispano-Americanos, 1980), 29, 215; Odom, *The Longest Siege of the American Revolution*, 65; Duval, *Independence Lost*, 173–174.

18 Rojas, *Jose de Ezpeleta*, 52–191, 264–277; Duval, *Independence Lost*, 180–182; Fabel, "Reflections on Mobile's Loyalism"; Caughey, *Bernardo de Galvez*, 183; Sledge, *Mobile River*, 62.

19 The site of "The Village" is located in modern Daphne, Alabama. Raab, *Spain, Britain,*

and the American Revolution in Florida, 135; Starr, Tories, Dons, and Rebels, 183; Rojas, Jose de Ezpeleta, 295; Haynes, The Natchez District and the American Revolution, 132; Holmes, "Alabama's Bloodiest Day of the American Revolution," 208–210.

20 Starr, Tories, Dons, and Rebels, 182; Rojas, Jose de Ezpeleta, 296, 377–380; Wright, Florida in American Revolution, 85; Davies, Documents of the American Revolution, 220, Cameron to Lord Germain, October 31, 1780; Howard, "Colonial Pensacola, Part 3," 398.

21 The siege of Charles Town (Charleston) took place between March 29 and May 12, 1780. The city's fall was one of the most devastating losses of the war for American forces, and marked a high point in British efforts in the South. For more information, see Carl P. Borick, A Gallant Defense: The Siege of Charleston, 1780 (Columbia: University of South Carolina Press, 2003; Colonial Office's West Florida Papers, Pace Library, University of West Florida: CO 5/Volume 597, Military Correspondence and Documents, 1778–1781, Germain to Campbell, July 4, 1780 and Germain to Campbell, November 1, 1780; Osborn, "Major-General John Campbell," 336; Davies, Documents of the American Revolution, 58, Cameron to Germain, February 10, 1781; William S. Coker and Hazel P. Coker, The Siege of Pensacola, 1781, in Maps: With Data on Troop Strength, Military Units, Ships, Casualties, and Related Statistics (Pensacola: Perdido Bay Press, 1981), 16; Pace Library, University of West Florida, Steuernagel Diary, 43; Holmes, "Alabama's Bloodiest Day of the American Revolution," 209.

22 Rojas, Jose de Ezpeleta, 529–538; Starr, Tories, Dons, and Rebels, 183; Haynes, The Natchez District and the American Revolution, 131–132; Holmes, "Alabama's Bloodiest Day of the American Revolution," 210–213; Haarman, "The Spanish Conquest of British West Florida," 120; Jack D.L. Holmes, "German Troops in Alabama During the American Revolution: The Battle of January 7, 1781," Alabama Historical Quarterly 38 (Spring, 1976), 5, 7–8; Von Eelking, The German Allied Troops in the North American War of Independence, 257; Davies, Documents of the American Revolution, 59, Cameron to Germain, February 10, 1781.

23 Holmes, "Alabama's Bloodiest Day of the American Revolution," 212–213; Caughey, Bernardo de Galvez, 194; Rea, "Royal Navy 'Remarks' Books," 175; Servies, ed., The Log of H.M.S. Mentor, 18–19; Beerman, "Jose de Ezpeleta," 253; Starr, Tories, Dons, and Rebels, 183; Haarman, "The Spanish Conquest of British West Florida," 120; Thomason, Mobile, 51.

24 Holmes, "Alabama's Bloodiest Day of the American Revolution," 208, 214; Starr, Tories, Dons, and Rebels, 183; Haarman, "The Spanish Conquest of British West Florida," 120; Coker and Coker, The Siege of Pensacola, 16; Caughey, Bernardo de Galvez, 195; N. Orwin Rush, Spain's Final Triumph Over Great Britain in the Gulf of Mexico: The Battle of Pensacola, March 9 to May 8, 1781 (Tallahassee, Florida State University Press, 1966), 24; Pace Library, University of West Florida, Steuernagel Diary, 43; Holmes, "German Troops in Alabama During the American Revolution," 8. One report of the battle would claim the attack occurred "during a tempestuous night."

25 Rojas, Jose de Ezpeleta, 534, 536; Von Eelking, The German Allied Troops in the North American War of Independence, 223; Holmes, "Alabama's Bloodiest Day of the American Revolution," 214, 216; Holmes, "German Troops in Alabama During the American Revolution," 8; Wright, Florida in American Revolution, 85; Davies, Documents of the American Revolution, 59, Cameron to Germain, February 10, 1781; Hamilton, Colonial

Mobile, 316; Chavez, *Spain and the Independence of the United States*, 182; Beerman, "Jose de Ezpeleta," 253.

26 Holmes, "Alabama's Bloodiest Day of the American Revolution," 214, 217; Caughey, *Bernardo de Galvez*, 195; Chavez, *Spain and the Independence of the United States*, 182; Davies, *Documents of the American Revolution*, 59, Cameron to Germain, February 10, 1781; Rush, *Spain's Final Triumph Over Britain in the Gulf of Mexico*, 24; Colonial Office's West Florida Papers, Pace Library, University of West Florida: CO 5/Volume 597, Military Correspondence and Documents, 1778–1781, Campbell to Germain, January 7, 1781; Starr, *Tories, Dons, and Rebels*, 183; Rojas, *Jose de Ezpeleta*, 534, 536; Haynes, *The Natchez District and the American Revolution*, 132; Wright, *Florida in American Revolution*, 85.

27 Haarman, "The Spanish Conquest of British West Florida," 121; Rojas, *Jose de Ezpeleta*, 535; Holmes, "Alabama's Bloodiest Day of the American Revolution," 214–215; Caughey, *Bernardo de Galvez*, 195; Starr, *Tories, Dons, and Rebels*, 183; Pace Library, University of West Florida, Steuernagel Diary, 43; Holmes, "German Troops in Alabama During the American Revolution," 8; Gilbert C. Din, *War on the Gulf Coast: The Spanish Fight Against William Augustus Bowles* (Gainesville: University Press of Florida, 2012), 21–23; Lyle N. McAlister, "Pensacola During the Second Spanish Period," *The Florida Historical Quarterly* 37 (January-April, 1959): 281–32; Haynes, *The Natchez District and the American Revolution*, 132; Osborn, "Major-General John Campbell," 336.

28 Holmes, "Alabama's Bloodiest Day of the American Revolution," 214–216; Caughey, *Bernardo de Galvez*, 195; Servies, ed., *The Log of H.M.S. Mentor*, 19; Hamilton, *Colonial Mobile*, 317. Pace Library, University of West Florida, Steuernagel Diary, 44. According to Hamilton, a fence was later placed around the gravesite. Its location is unknown today.

29 Holmes, "Alabama's Bloodiest Day of the American Revolution," 216–218; Colonial Office's West Florida Papers, Pace Library, University of West Florida: CO 5/Volume 597, Military Correspondence and Documents, 1778–1781, Campbell to Germain, "Return of the Killed and Wounded at the Village Opposite of Mobile," January 11, 1781; Holmes, "German Troops in Alabama During the American Revolution," 9; Coker and Coker, *The Siege of Pensacola*, 101–102; Starr, *Tories, Dons, and Rebels*, 184; Haarman, "The Spanish Conquest of British West Florida," 120; Pace Library, University of West Florida, Steuernagel Diary, 44.

30 Holmes, "Alabama's Bloodiest Day of the American Revolution," 219; Rush, *Spain's Final Triumph Over Britain in the Gulf of Mexico*, 42.

CHAPTER ELEVEN

1 Caughey, *Bernardo de Galvez*, 186, 192–193, 198, 200; Starr, *Tories, Dons, and Rebels*, 175, 195; Haarman, "The Spanish Conquest of British West Florida," 121; Raab, *Spain, Britain, and the American Revolution in Florida*, 136; Haynes, *The Natchez District and the American Revolution*, 131; Coker and Coker, *The Siege of Pensacola*, 10; Johnson, *British West Florida*, 216–218.

2 Frederick Cubberly, "Fort George (St. Michael), Pensacola," *The Florida Historical Society Quarterly* 6 (April, 1928), 221–222; Odom, *The Longest Siege of the American Revolution*, 56; Rush, *Spain's Final Triumph Over Britain in the Gulf of Mexico*, 30; 58–59; Starr, *Tories, Dons, and Rebels*, 187; Wright, *Florida in American Revolution*, 86.

3   Haarman, "The Spanish Conquest of British West Florida, 122; Odom, *The Longest Siege of the American Revolution*, 23–26, 54; Starr, *Tories, Dons, and Rebels*, 188, 191, 204; Servies, ed., *The Log of H.M.S. Mentor*, 23; Rush, *Spain's Final Triumph Over Britain in the Gulf of Mexico*, 31.

4   Albert W. Haarman, "The Siege of Pensacola: An Order of Battle," *The Florida Historical Quarterly* 44 (January, 1966), 193, 197; Caughey, *Bernardo de Galvez*, 191; Starr, *Tories, Dons, and Rebels*, 184–187, 190–192; Odom, *The Longest Siege of the American Revolution*, 46, 53, 197; Holmes, "Alabama's Bloodiest Day of the American Revolution," 209, Haarman, "The Spanish Conquest of British West Florida," 122–123; Fabel, *Economy of British West Florida*, 39; Baker and Haas, "Bernardo de Galvez's Combat Diary," 196.

5   Haynes, *The Natchez District and the American Revolution*, 132; Haarman, "The Spanish Conquest of British West Florida," 123–124; Caughey, *Bernardo de Galvez*, 200; Servies, ed., *The Log of H.M.S. Mentor*, 21; Odom, *The Longest Siege of the American Revolution*, 20–23, Davies, *Documents of the American Revolution*, 136, Campbell to Germain, May 7, 1781.

6   Starr, *Tories, Dons, and Rebels*, 196; Eric Beerman, "Yo Solo Not 'Solo': Juan Antonio de Riano," *The Florida Historical Quarterly* 58 (October, 1979), 178–179; Rush, *Spain's Final Triumph Over Britain in the Gulf of Mexico*, 28, 44–45; Duval, *Independence Lost*, 189; Servies, ed., *The Log of H.M.S. Mentor*, 21–23; Odom, *The Longest Siege of the American Revolution*, 23–25.

7   Odom, *The Longest Siege of the American Revolution*, 26–30, 128; Starr, *Tories, Dons, and Rebels*, 176; Caughey, *Bernardo de Galvez*, 201–206; Chavez, *Spain and the Independence of the United States*, 189.

8   Haarman, "The Spanish Conquest of British West Florida, 124–125; Rush, *Spain's Final Triumph Over Britain in the Gulf of Mexico*, 28, 54–57; Starr, *Tories, Dons, and Rebels*, 198–199; Caughey, *Bernardo de Galvez*, 202–203; Coker and Coker, *The Siege of Pensacola*, 32, 36; Beerman, "Yo Solo Not Solo," 180; Odom, *The Longest Siege of the American Revolution*, 31; Maury Baker and Margaret Bissler Haas, "Bernardo de Galvez's Combat Diary for the Battle of Pensacola, 1781," *The Florida Historical Quarterly* 56 (October, 1977), 180; Chavez, *Spain and the Independence of the United States*, 190–191; Carmen de Reparaz, *Yo Solo: Bernardo de Galvez y la toma de Panzacola en 1781, Una contribucion espanaol a la independencia de los Estados Unidos* (Serbal, Barcelona, 1986), 86–93.

9   Caughey, *Bernardo de Galvez*, 214; Ferreiro, *Brothers at Arms*, 254.

10   Odom, *The Longest Siege of the American Revolution*, 33; Beerman, "Yo Solo Not Solo," 180; Starr, *Tories, Dons, and Rebels*, 199; Caughey, *Bernardo de Galvez*, 204; Coker and Coker, *The Siege of Pensacola*, 38; Baker and Haas, "Bernardo de Galvez's Combat Diary," 180.

11   Haarman, "The Spanish Conquest of British West Florida," 121, 124; Chavez, *Spain and the Independence of the United States*, 190; Coker and Coker, *The Siege of Pensacola*, 20, 34, 42, 66; Odom, *The Longest Siege of the American Revolution*, 17, 64; Starr, *Tories, Dons, and Rebels*, 193.

12   Rush, *Spain's Final Triumph Over Britain in the Gulf of Mexico*, 67, 70–82; Wright, *Florida in the American Revolution*, 89–90; Starr, *Tories, Dons, and Rebels*, 202, 205; Baker and Haas, "Bernardo de Galvez's Combat Diary," 181–193; Coker and Coker, *The Siege of Pensacola*, 42–84; Haarmann, "The Spanish Conquest of British West Florida," 126–130;

Davies, *Documents of the American Revolution*, 136, Campbell to Germain, May 7, 1781; Donald E. Worcester, "Miranda's Diary of the Siege of Pensacola, 1781," *The Florida Historical Quarterly* 29 (January, 1951), 177–191; Beerman, "Jose de Ezpeleta," 254; Caughey, *Bernardo de Galvez*, 208; Chavez, *Spain and the Independence of the United States*, 192, Rush, *Spain's Final Triumph Over Britain in the Gulf of Mexico*, 71; Odom, *The Longest Siege of the American Revolution*, 77.

13 Rush, *Spain's Final Triumph Over Britain in the Gulf of Mexico*, 57–63; Caughey, *Bernardo de Galvez*, 205; Baker and Haas, "Bernardo de Galvez's Combat Diary," 181; Chavez, *Spain and the Independence of the United States*, 191; Starr, *Tories, Dons, and Rebels*, 200; Coker and Coker, *The Siege of Pensacola*, 40, 72; Robin Fabel, "Ordeal by Siege: James Bruce in Pensacola, 1780–1781," *The Florida Historical Quarterly*, 63 (January, 1988), 290.

14 Fabel, "Ordeal by Siege," 287, 289, 297.

15 Wright, *Florida in the American Revolution*, 87–88; Sosin, *The Revolutionary Frontier*, 125; O'Brien, *Choctaws in a Revolutionary Age Revolutionary Age*, 78; Haarmann, "The Spanish Conquest of British West Florida," 125; Osborn, "Major-General John Campbell," 338; Colonial Office's West Florida Papers, Pace Library, University of West Florida: CO 5/Volume 597, Military Correspondence and Documents, 1778–1781, Galvez to Campbell, April 9, 1780 and Campbell to Galvez, April 20, 1780; Caughey, *Bernardo de Galvez*, 189, 207; Starr, *Tories, Dons, and Rebels*, 177; Alden, *The South in the Revolution*, 278; Baker and Haas, "Bernardo de Galvez's Combat Diary," 181–186; Rush, *Spain's Final Triumph Over Britain in the Gulf of Mexico*, 74–75.

16 Odom, *The Longest Siege of the American Revolution*, 69, 70, 78; Rush, *Spain's Final Triumph Over Britain in the Gulf of Mexico*, 94.

17 Rush, *Spain's Final Triumph Over Britain in the Gulf of Mexico*, 65, 68, 71, 72, 75, 76, 77, 95, 99; Baker and Haas, "Bernardo de Galvez's Combat Diary," 185–189; Odom, *The Longest Siege of the American Revolution*, 66; Coker and Coker, *The Siege of Pensacola*, 74, 80; W. S. Murphy, "The Irish Brigade of Spain at the Capture of Pensacola, 1781," *The Florida Historical Quarterly* 38 (January, 1960), 220; Colonial Office's West Florida Papers, Pace Library, University of West Florida: CO 5/Volume 597, Military Correspondence and Documents, 1778–1781, Campbell to Germain, May 7, 1781.

18 Caughey, *Bernardo de Galvez*, 206, 208–209; Baker and Haas, "Bernardo de Galvez's Combat Diary," 188; Starr, *Tories, Dons, and Rebels*, 206; Odom, *The Longest Siege of the American Revolution*, 80–82; Haarmann, "The Spanish Conquest of British West Florida," 125–130; Raab, *Spain, Britain, and the American Revolution in Florida*, 136; Johnson, *British West Florida*, 217; Beerman, "Yo Solo Not Solo," 181, 211; Worcester, "Miranda's Diary of the Siege of Pensacola, 1781," 176; Chavez, *Spain and the Independence of the United States*, 193; Haarman, "The Siege of Pensacola: An Order of Battle," 193–195; Murphy, "The Irish Brigade of Spain," 219.

19 Rush, *Spain's Final Triumph Over Britain in the Gulf of Mexico*, 31, 98, 100; Odom, *The Longest Siege of the American Revolution*, 95, 101–103; Cubberly, "Fort George," 228; Pace Library, University of West Florida, Steuernagel Diary, 48; Starr, *Tories, Dons, and Rebels*, 207, 209; Baker and Haas, "Bernardo de Galvez's Combat Diary, 193; Colonial Office's West Florida Papers, Pace Library, University of West Florida: CO 5/Volume 597, Military Correspondence and Documents, 1778–1781, Campbell to Germain, May 7, 1781.

20 Johnson, *British West Florida*, 217–218; Smith, *Louisiana and the Gulf South Frontier*, 162; Beerman, "Yo Solo Not Solo," 182; Caughey, *Bernardo de Galvez*, 209–210; Baker and Haas, "Bernardo de Galvez's Combat Diary," 193–194; Coker and Coker, *The Siege of Pensacola*, 86; Haarman, "The Spanish Conquest of British West Florida," 131–132; Chavez, *Spain and the Independence of the United States*," 194; Rush, *Spain's Final Triumph Over Britain in the Gulf of Mexico*, 31, 82; Cubberly, "Fort George," 229; Duval, *Independence Lost*, 212–217; Odom, *The Longest Siege of the American Revolution*, 105–108; Wright, *Florida in the American Revolution*, 90; Starr, *Tories, Dons, and Rebels*, 209–210; Davies, *Documents of the American Revolution*, 138, Campbell to Germain, May 12, 1781; Servies, ed., *The Log of H.M.S. Mentor*, 24; Haynes, *The Natchez District and the American Revolution*, 133; Raab, *Spain, Britain and the American Revolution in Florida*, 137; Von Eelking, *The German Allied Troops in the North American War of Independence*, 224; Pace Library, University of West Florida, Steuernagel Diary, 48.

21 Davies, *Documents of the American Revolution*, 139, Campbell to Germain, May 12, 1781; Mathews, *British West Florida and the Illinois Country*, 130; Worcester, "Miranda's Diary of the Siege of Pensacola, 1781," 191–192; Rush, *Spain's Final Triumph Over Britain in the Gulf of Mexico*, 82; Alden, *The South in the Revolution*, 278; Haarmann, "The Spanish Conquest of British West Florida," 132; Starr, *Tories, Dons, and Rebels*, 211; Caughey, *Bernardo de Galvez*, 210–211; Odom, *The Longest Siege of the American Revolution*, 110–111; Coker and Coker, *The Siege of Pensacola*, 86, 88.

22 Odom, *The Longest Siege of the American Revolution*, 20; Haarmann, "The Spanish Conquest of British West Florida, 133; Murphy, "The Irish Brigade of Spain," 221; Caughey, *Bernardo de Galvez*, 212; Baker and Haas, "Bernardo de Galvez's Combat Diary," 196; Chavez, *Spain and the Independence of the United States*, 194; Starr, *Tories, Dons, and Rebels*, 211–213; Rush, *Spain's Final Triumph Over Britain in the Gulf of Mexico*, 83; Wright, *Florida in American Revolution*, 115.

23 Haynes, *The Natchez District and the American Revolution*, 134–135; Peter A. Brannon, "The Coosa River Crossing of British Refugees, 1781," *Alabama Historical Quarterly* 19 (Spring, 1957), 151–152; Holmes, "Juan de la Villebeuvre," 106–110; James, *Antebellum Natchez*, 26; Narrett, *Adventurism and Empire*, 100–101; Caughey, *Bernardo de Galvez*, 216; Wright, *Florida in the American Revolution*, 91–92.

24 Holmes, "Juan de la Villebeuvre," 97, 108; John Caughey, "The Natchez Rebellion of 1781 and Its Aftermath," *Louisiana Historical Quarterly* 16 (1933), 59, 64; Haswell, ed., *Memoirs and Adventures of Captain Matthew Phelps*, 48–49; Starr, *Tories, Dons, and Rebels*, 80, 217; McLemore, ed., *History of Mississippi*, 158; Caughey, *Bernardo de Galvez*, 217; Chavez, *Spain and the Independence of the United States*, 197; Haynes, *The Natchez District and the American Revolution*, 136.

25 Caughey, "The Natchez Rebellion," 60–63; Colonial Office's West Florida Papers, Pace Library, University of West Florida: CO 5/Volume 597, Military Correspondence and Documents, 1778–1781, Campbell to Blommart, June 4, 1781; Caughey, *Bernardo de Galvez*, 218, 220–222; Narrett, *Adventurism and Empire*, 104–107; Holmes, "Juan de la Villebeuvre," 109–110; Starr, *Tories, Dons, and Rebels*, 217; Haynes, *The Natchez District and the American Revolution*, 135–138, 142, 146–152; James, *Antebellum Natchez*, 26–27; Siebert, "The Loyalists in West Florida," 477–479.

26 Haynes, *The Natchez District and the American Revolution*, 142–143; Caughey, "The Natchez Rebellion," 65–68; Brannon, "The Coosa River Crossing," 151–152, 155; Caughey,

Bernardo de Galvez, 223, 224–242. Some of the British citizens who had fled Natchez eventually petitioned Parliament for claims of losses during the war. They were at first denied, as they had suffered not at the hands of the American army. A small group printed a pamphlet in 1787 titled *The Case and Petition of His Majesty's Loyal Subjects, Late of West Florida* in which they claimed to have been "incurring every danger, difficulty, and expence incident to first settlers, cultivated plantations, and formed commercial arrangements" in West Florida. They cited the Willing Raid and the campaign of Galvez, and recounted how they volunteered time and money for defense of the colony. Some claimed to have "had their plantations plundered and burnt by the rebels when they invaded the province in the year 1778; others had their properties laid waste, and large stocks of cattle destroyed by rebel Indians and Spaniards; and some of the petitioners had their houses burnt by order of the officers commanding in forts, to prevent their being used by the enemy as covers for erecting batteries; and others had their property taken in the forts, and condemned by the Spaniards..." It appears only three individuals ever received compensation for claims. For more information, see J. Barton Starr, "The Case and Petition of His Majesty's Loyal Subjects, Late of West Florida," *The Florida Historical Quarterly* 59 (October, 1980): 199–212.

27 Rush, *Spain's Final Triumph Over Britain in the Gulf of Mexico*, 15–18, 106; Haarmann, "The Spanish Conquest of British West Florida," 133; Weber, *The Spanish Frontier in North America*, 268; Caughey, *Bernardo de Galvez*, 256; Osborn, "Major-General John Campbell," 339; Colonial Office's West Florida Papers, Pace Library, University of West Florida: CO 5/Volume 597, Military Correspondence and Documents, 1778–1781, Campbell to Germain, August 17, 1781 and Germain to Campbell, September 15, 1781.

28 Haarmann, "The Spanish Conquest of British West Florida," 134; Rush, *Spain's Final Triumph Over Britain in the Gulf of Mexico*, 10, 25; Chavez, *Spain and the Independence of the United States*, 196; Odom, *The Longest Siege of the American Revolution*, 118–119; Starr, "The Case and Petition of His Majesty's Loyal Subjects," 208; Caughey, *Bernardo de Galvez*, 214.

EPILOGUE

1 *A Century of Lawmaking for a New Nation: U.S. Congressional Documents and Debates, 1774–1785*, "Definitive Treaty of Peace Between the United States and his Britannic Majesty," 80–83, https://memory.loc.gov/cgi-bin/ampage?collId=llsl&fileName=008/llsl008.db&recNum=93; Henry Steele Commager and Richard B. Morris, eds., *The Spirit of 'Seventy-Six: The Story of the American Revolution as Told by Participants*, (Edison, NJ: Castle Books, 2002), 1270; Griffith, *Documentary History*, 43; Thomason, *Mobile*, 52; Duval, *Independence Lost*, 231, 234; Starr, *Tories, Dons and Rebels*, 219–220, 223–224; Johnson, *British West Florida*, 219) Arthur P. Whitaker, *The Spanish-American Frontier, 1783–1795* (Boston: Houghton-Mifflin, 1927), 65–68; Cecil Johnson, "West Florida Revisited," *Journal of Mississippi History* 28 (May, 1966), 129; Wright, *Florida in the American Revolution*, 130.

2 Haynes, *The Natchez District and the American Revolution*, 136; Narrett, *Adventurism and Empire*, 110; Whitaker, *The Spanish-American Frontier*, 10; Pate, et al., *The Fort Tombecbe Historical Research and Documentation Project*, 172; McLaurin and Thomason, *Mobile*, 21; McLemore, ed., *History of Mississippi*, 162–163.

3 Pate, et al., *The Fort Tombecbe Historical Research and Documentation Project*, 171–173;

Whitaker, *The Spanish-American Frontier*, 24, 42, 45; Rogers, et al., *Alabama*, 37; McLaurin and Thomason, *Mobile*, 20; Raab, *Spain, Britain, and the American Revolution in Florida*, 138; Thomason, *Mobile*, 52–53; For more on trade with Native Americans during Spanish administration of West Florida, see William S. Coker and Thomas D. Watson, *Indian Traders of the Southeastern Borderlands: Panton, Leslie and Company and John Forbes* (Gainesville: University Press of Florida, 1986).

4   Whitaker, *The Spanish-American Frontier*, 53–58; Pickett, *History of Alabama*, 361; Abernathy, *The South in the Revolution*, 75.

5   McDermott, *The Spanish in the Mississippi Valley*, 70; McLaurin and Thomason, *Mobile*, 21; McLemore, ed., *History of Mississippi*, 159, 168, 171; Thomason, *Mobile*, 52–54; Duval, *Independence Lost*, 227; Starr, *Tories, Dons, and Rebels*, 232; Wright, *Florida in the Amercian Revolution*, 92–93, 127, 142; Haynes, *The Natchez District and the American Revolution*, 6; Abernathy, *The South in the Revolution*, 45. Frank L. Owsley, Jr. and Gene A. Smith, *Filibusters and Expansionists: Jeffersonian Manifest Destiny, 1800–1821* (Tuscaloosa: University of Alabama Press, 1997), 81.

6   Rogers, et al., *Alabama*, 41. For more on the development of the Mississippi Territory and surrounding region, see Robert V. Haynes, *The Mississippi Territory and the Southwest Frontier, 1795–1817* (Lexington: University Press of Kentucky, 2010).

7   McLemore, ed. *History of Mississippi*, 167; Whitaker, *The Spanish-American Frontier*, 16.

Index